THE ANCIENT GRUDGE

THE
ANCIENT GRUDGE

By

Arthur Stanwood Pier

"I will feed fat the ancient grudge I bear him."
Merchant of Venice.

WILDSIDE PRESS

COPYRIGHT 1905 BY ARTHUR STANWOOD PIER
ALL RIGHTS RESERVED

Published September 1905

CONTENTS

I.	"A Hero — Always".	1
II.	Stewart confers a Favor	13
III.	The Parting	29
IV.	Halket and Company	46
V.	Floyd begins at the Bottom	66
VI.	Investigating the Depths	86
VII.	Diversions of a Workingman	96
VIII.	Lydia	114
IX.	A Holiday	129
X.	The End of an Apprenticeship	142
XI.	Mrs. Halket	156
XII.	A Client for Stewart	173
XIII.	Called Home	189
XIV.	A Failure and a Success	197
XV.	The Autobiographer	215
XVI.	Stewart acquires Some New Interests	231
XVII.	Large Idea of a Philanthropist	248
XVIII.	Two Amateurs	273
XIX.	Colonel Halket addresses an Audience	298
XX.	Last Words	316
XXI.	The Great Opportunity	328
XXII.	Difficulties of a Man of Taste	344
XXIII.	Forcing the Issue	365
XXIV.	A Letter to a Newspaper	378
XXV.	Interlude	396
XXVI.	Widening the Breach	407
XXVII.	New Rome and Avalon	427
XXVIII.	In Loyalty and Love	443
XXIX.	Stewart takes the Field	454
XXX.	The Night Attack	467
XXXI.	The Two Women	473

THE ANCIENT GRUDGE

I

"A HERO — ALWAYS"

A WIDE, white beach ran for a quarter of a mile from a rocky promontory to a point covered with trees. Here and there, through the fringe of pine woods, houses, white and red, thrust their gables; the windows of these caught the blaze of the afternoon sun that was now withdrawing inland. But the beach was so wide that the shadows from the woods had not yet reached and dulled the bright crowd assembled on the sand. People had gathered from all along this part of the Massachusetts shore to see the Chester Water Carnival.

Out upon the raft, fifty yards from shore, a diving-tower was built, tall and slender. The boy who was the first to climb it knelt for a moment when he reached the top. Then, having steadied himself, he rose and stood erect. The sun glistened kindly on his yellow hair, on his wet arms raised above his head; as he stood straight and still, he formed the last mark against sea and sky, and he had a gracefully heroic quality, which appealed to the women and girls. The other boys upon the raft looked up at him; everybody looked at him.

With a spring so light that no one quite recognized the movement with which it was made, he shot out through the air, arching with a perfect curve the space from tower to sea. Slim as a greyhound in the leap, he cut the water gently and then rose to the surface in time to hear the pattering applause.

He had drawn himself up again on the sunny raft when another of the swimmers climbed the tower to dive. This was a black-haired, thick-set boy; standing on the top, he presented a sturdy but not a gracefully heroic figure. And he did not start vibrating the sympathetic nerve in the women and girls.

Suddenly he gathered himself and leaped with clumsy but impetuous power. At the height in mid-air, giving a frog-like kick, he straightened out and descended into the water with arrowy calmness. There was applause for that, too, but diving deep, he did not arise to hear it; and the clapping was of a careless kind and dwindled before his head emerged.

The boy with the yellow hair took a low, shooting dive from the raft and came up close to the judge's rowboat, which was moored near by. He addressed not the judge but the girl sitting in the stern.

"May I come in, Lydia?"

"You will be so messy," she objected.

Without regarding this protest, he paddled round to the bow and climbed aboard. The girl's face showed an ingenuous satisfaction; the judge, a young man in white flannels, said, without taking his eyes from the raft, —

"I could n't give you a prize now if I wanted to, Stewart. It would n't look right."

"I 'm letting this event go by default," Stewart answered.

"Why?" asked the girl.

"I did my best first thing."

"Floyd Halket beat you by six feet."

"Yes, that 's why I 'm stopping."

"Lydia," said the judge patiently, "would you just as soon ask your young friend to come over into the stern with you? He is very distracting."

Stewart changed his position with alacrity, and sitting in the bottom of the boat at the girl's feet, he embraced his bare knees with his bare arms.

"You ought to be ashamed to sit there," she said, "when all the others are going on!"

"Yes, they're turning somersaults and things, are n't they?" he answered placidly. "I don't do those stunts."

"Floyd Halket does them beautifully."

"Yes. It seems — well, don't you think — not quite refined?"

He spoke with a twinkle in his eyes, and so she forgave him and laughed. She was of about the same age as the boy, seventeen or eighteen, perhaps, a brown, out-of-door-looking girl, with a ripened autumnal color and with dark hair that was now being blown forward about her temples. There was a merry, reckless light in her gray eyes, and pleasure-loving laughter seemed always perching on her lips.

"Of course," she said, "it's much more dignified to dive only once and be the most perfect, graceful thing that ever was."

"Well," Stewart answered comfortably, "so long as you thought I was that."

"And yet," she continued, "I hate to see anybody give a thing up because he's beaten."

"I have n't given up," he answered. "I'm only saving myself for the swim under water."

"Good gracious, you stand no chance at all in that! Why, Floyd Halket simply lives under water."

"Oh, Floyd Halket!" He spoke wearily. "Who is he, anyway? Does n't he come from your town?"

"Yes, of course; you must have heard of the Halket Steel Mills. Where have you lived all your life?"

"Funny how he learned to swim so well in that inland place!"

"As if all the good swimmers lived on the Massachusetts coast!"

"It does n't seem right for a fellow to turn up here for just a part of a summer, go into the water sports, and beat everybody that's been coming to Chester for years."

"You Bostonians"— she liked to tease him with the term—"make me wonder sometimes why I'm allowed here. And yet you are really very nice.— Oh, Bob, what *is* that crazy boy going to do?"

She appealed to her cousin, the judge. Floyd Halket had climbed up for his last performance; the other contestants had all dropped out; and now he stood, nearly thirty feet in air, balancing, glancing over his shoulder at the spot where he meant to make his plunge. He was evidently preparing for a backward dive, and that, from such a height, was a bolder thing than any that the others had dared to try.

On the beach the little fluttering movements in the crowd were stilled, and the light sound of talk and laughter was hushed. Backward the boy went with a whirl, and as before he seemed to straighten out in mid-air and drop slenderly. Applause volleyed for a perfect dive.

"He wins," said Bob Dunbar, the judge, to Stewart. "Now, then, it's time for you fellows to get ready for the swim under water." He picked up his megaphone and spoke through it, ordering those who had entered for this contest out to the raft. Stewart stood up to jump overboard.

"Do you think you will win?" asked Lydia.

"Do you want me to win?" he answered.

"Suppose I said yes?"

"Then I'll do it or stay down till I bust."

She laughed in mild derision.

"Oh, I'll show you," he cried indignantly, and leaped far out so that he might not splash her.

"Do you think he has the least chance of winning, Bob?" she asked her cousin.

"Not the least."

She sighed twice, but her cousin had an uncomforting habit of silence.

There were only six to start in the race. When they stood in a row along the edge of the raft, ready for the dive,

Bob Dunbar called out the final instructions. "Are you ready?" he cried, and he raised his pistol and fired. The six figures flashed and splashed into the smooth water; the crowd on the beach gave a surge of interest; Bob Dunbar and his cousin leaned over the edge of their boat, peering along the surface.

"Will any of them get out as far as this, Bob?" asked Lydia.

"One or two, maybe; it's about the limit. Hello! There's Halket."

He pointed to the figure gliding smoothly a foot below the surface. Lydia gazed with fascination. "He moves like an automaton, — almost as if he weren't alive," she murmured. "Oh, look at Jack Folsom!" and she laughed as a red face popped above the surface and settled, gasping, to its chin.

"There!" cried Lydia. "There! It's Stewart! See, Bob, it's Stewart!" She leaned out over the gunwale; her cousin, on the watch for other emerging heads, paid little attention and did not see that Stewart was beginning to turn round under water with a slow, lifeless stroke. If he had seen, he would have known that something was wrong, that the boy was in a daze, and was staying down with a confused and obstinate effort of will. Lydia, not understanding, was amused. "Why, the idiot boy! He's swimming in circles! I'm going to jab him!" And she caught up an oar and poked the blade into the water. Instantly the lips on which a laugh seemed always perching were transfixed with terror; the oar slashed down below the surface in her limp grasp.

"Bob!" she cried. "He's gone down! He's gone — I don't see him — oh, quick, Bob, quick!"

"Where?" Her cousin stared at her blanched face.

"There — right there." She put her strength frantically to the oar and raised it till only the tip of the blade touched the surface.

Bob Dunbar was unfastening his shoes. From the shore came the patter of applause, and he glanced up, hoping for one wild moment that it might be for Stewart's appearance. But it was Floyd Halket's head emerging a half-dozen yards beyond the other swimmers that had drawn the applause. Bob Dunbar stood up in the stern and dove overboard. And at that there was another cheer from the crowd and a ripple of laughter; they appreciated the judge's dive, in his white trousers and pink shirt, as a clownish jest, the climax to the afternoon's entertainment, and they were amused.

"Mr. Halket!" The cry came sharp and imploring from the girl's lips.

Just then her cousin emerged gasping; he caught his breath. "Halket! Jack! Stewart Lee's gone down!"

He seized the gunwale of the boat; Floyd Halket was swimming up with powerful overhand strokes; Jack Folsom was already clambering in over the stern.

"There — right where the oar touches," said Lydia; she had taken her cousin's seat and was holding the oars.

Her voice quivered and hurried upon the last words, and there was no longer any light or color in her face; the strands of hair blown about it by the breeze made it seem all the more stark and desolate. But she was trying to keep the boat steady, even while her eyes marked the spot where Stewart had gone down.

Jack Folsom sprang from the thwart, drenching her with the splash; instantly Floyd Halket crawled aboard and stood up ready to follow. And now there was a confused outcry from the people on shore, who after the first laughter had stood in puzzled silence. From some one came a loud shout, "What's happened?" Then fell the stillness of suspense; and when there was no answer, the cry broke from many voices, imperious and insistent. Another rowboat was drawing near. Bob Dunbar crawled in beside Lydia and caught up the megaphone. Jack Folsom came up, shaking his head, and Floyd Halket dove.

"It's Stewart," Bob Dunbar called through the megaphone to the approaching boat. "Row ashore, Steve; tell them we'll get him."

The boat turned; another, in which were two boys, was approaching. There came from the shore a woman's piercing cry, "Where's Stewart? I don't see Stewart!" After that there was silence.

Lydia could not bear the anguish of that cry; she turned her face imploringly toward the shore. And then she saw a woman in a white dress start from the crowd and run forward wildly. Two men sprang out and stopped her, and began leading her away.

"Don't look," Floyd Halket said to Lydia. "Just keep the boat steady. You other fellows get into that boat." He pointed to the one which had drawn near. "We can't all do this; Folsom and Blair and I will take turns."

Then, as Blair's head reappeared above the surface, he jumped, and Lydia braced with her oars while the boat rocked.

"If I were only of some use!" groaned Dunbar. "These clothes!"

"It's all eel-grass," Jack Folsom said. "If a fellow goes down into that — to the bottom — "

Floyd emerged and swam up with great lunging strokes.

"Could you see him?" Blair asked, and Floyd shook his head. Then Folsom jumped.

"We'll have to go into the eel-grass to get him," Blair said.

"I think so," Floyd answered. He pulled himself up and into the boat. "The stuff's thick; the only chance is to go in."

Lydia hardly heard the words; they were subdued to the endless, hopeless reiteration of her unspoken thought, "He is drowned by now — he is drowned by now." She was dizzy and faint, but with a sense of her dreadful responsibility she clung to the oars and did not move her steadfast eyes from the small circle of water beneath which she knew that Stewart lay.

Folsom came up from a dive. "I don't dare," he panted. "The eel-grass — the slimy stuff against my face — it choked me. If Stewart were alive — but — but now I don't dare."

Floyd spoke to Lydia.

"Will you tell me exactly where he went down?"

"The boat's moored," Lydia answered. "I've tried not to let it swing. He must be there — just there. He went down — straight."

She had not moved her eyes; they were resting on the small circle of water that she defined with her oar; and her voice was light and quivering.

Floyd filled his lungs, fixed with his eyes the place where he must strike, and made his dive. Swimming headlong down, he crushed with all speed into the mass of slimy plants. They brushed across his face, forcing him to close his eyes; they wrapped themselves about his arms, his body, his legs with cold, leisurely cruelty; but he kept crowding on his way. Then his hands touched bottom and gripped the tough stalks, and he opened his eyes.

The light was dim among the waving grasses; he could see only for a few inches, and then the mat grew tight and held its secret. His breath was leaving him fast; he turned his head, and there at his hand, face down as he had sunk, lay Stewart.

Floyd seized him under the arms and tried to raise him, but in his death grip he was clutching the tough fibres of the grass. Going upon his knees, Floyd tried to loosen the grip, but his fingers, working in a frenzy, were powerless. In desperation he raised the body, thrust a shoulder under it, and heaved. The strands of eel-grass were uprooted; Floyd clutched a fold of Stewart's bathing-suit, and with breath struggling in his throat tried to force a way up through the weeds. Once off the bottom, he thought he had won the fight; but the mass clung and tripped his legs, and the muscles in them ached as he struggled to mount upward. If a cramp should seize him now! But his head and shoulders were free at last; he tightened his grip on Stewart's shirt, for his breath was going and his brain was reeling; he swam frantically up and up and up, with the light growing and bursting before his face, yet with water always covering him; his breath was gone, and he opened his mouth on what had been a groan if the water had not rushed in to strangle it. And then, coughing, gulping, he was on the surface, within reach of Lydia's oar; he caught it and dragged Stewart's face to the air, and there he hung, gasping, and seeing only the blurred outlines of the faces in the boat. Folsom and Blair jumped overboard and took Stewart from him; the other rowboat darted up, and the boys lifted in the lifeless body and then made for shore.

Floyd crawled into the boat with Bob Dunbar and Lydia, and curled himself up in the stern, dripping and silent; his chest heaved painfully and his arms and legs were trembling.

"Let go the mooring, Bob," Lydia said; "I'll row;" and she bent to the oars. Floyd struggled up to a sitting posture and gazed over her shoulder; they were carrying Stewart up the beach.

"Oh, if you could only have got him the moment he went down!"

The girl's passionate exclamation echoed Floyd's own passionate wish. But he answered, —

"Perhaps — sometimes — they bring drowned people to life."

He glanced at her face, but it admitted no comfort or hope; tragic, desolate, cold with grief, it seemed denied even the relief of tears. Floyd dropped his eyes and watched her slender brown wrists as she pulled resolutely on the oars, and was aware of the little feet set sturdily against the braces.

Bob Dunbar said, —

"You did a mighty fine thing, Halket, to get him at all!"

"Oh, you did!" Lydia cried. "I did n't mean —" She choked for a moment, and turned her head away, still pulling on the oars. When she looked again at Floyd, there were tears on her cheeks, and her face, though utterly sad, seemed softened in its grief. "I did it — I pushed him down," she said. "That was why I spoke so — one reason why —"

She could not finish; she looked away again; and in another moment the boat ran on the sand. Lydia stepped ashore and then stood undecided.

"Come home, Lydia," said her cousin.

"Yes," she answered, "but — please find out first, Bob."

Here and there along the beach, little detached groups of women and girls stood, waiting, withdrawn some distance from a larger gathering of men. Toward this Bob Dunbar and Floyd Halket started running; one of the men was turning away, and seeing them shook his head.

"No hope?" asked Bob. And again the man, whose face was very grave, shook his head. Bob turned back, and Floyd saw him lead Lydia away.

He himself drew near the intent gathering. He noticed that several of the men were in their shirt-sleeves, and vaguely he wondered why. Then he found himself in the circle, gazing at Stewart, who lay stripped to the waist, stretched on his back; a man stood over him, chafing him with a rough towel; a young doctor, with his coat off, knelt at the boy's head and was moving his arms up and down, up and down, making his chest heave almost as if he were alive. A roll of coats was under the boy's shoulders, so that his chest should be elevated and his lungs expanded. But stark and staring-eyed he lay; and it seemed to Floyd almost gruesome that this lifeless body should be put through such exercise and caused to assume such mockery of life. And then, gazing at the handsome face and slim, straight form, he felt a thickening in his throat and turned away. Some one was rolling a barrel along the sand toward the crowd.

Floyd had seen enough; chilled and shivering, he ran to his bath-house, a hundred yards up the beach, rubbed himself down, and dressed. When he had put on his shoes, he sat down on the narrow bench of the bath-house. "Why could n't I have got him sooner!" he murmured; "why could n't I!" He added, after a moment, "And to think of his mother — and that girl — how that girl must feel!"

There came a knock on his door. "You there, Halket?"

He recognized the voice as Folsom's, and let the boy in. "Have they given up yet?" he asked.

"No, but pretty nearly," Folsom answered. He leaned against the wall. "You have n't got a comb, have you?" And then, without waiting for a reply, he said, "Is n't it awful! Halket, he was the best fellow I knew."

"Yes," said Floyd. "I liked him."

They went out upon the beach in silence, and stood for a moment looking toward the ominous circle of men. Suddenly it broke, a hat was flung into the air, and there was a cheer. The two boys ran breathlessly forward. A man, hurrying away, rushed up to them with his face all aglow; he seized Floyd's hand.

"He's alive!" he cried. "You've done the most splendid thing!"

Floyd, with his heart pounding, hurried on. As he approached, men rushed to meet him, crowded around him, grasping his hand, congratulating him, with emotion in their voices; he pressed on through them and looked for Stewart, but saw only the shining face of the young doctor, bending over a roll of blankets.

"He's unconscious yet, but breathing," some one whispered to him. "He'll pull through."

Floyd stood dazed with happiness, hearing nothing of the fine things that his clustering admirers were saying. Suddenly he broke away from them and ran, with but one thought, "I must tell Lydia Dunbar; she will be so glad." But the news had been spreading and was still spreading before him, faster than he could run; boys and men were speeding up the beach, and off through the woods. Floyd plunged into the woods path toward the Dunbar cottage, and came face to face with Lydia; she was hurrying back to learn if the word that some one had cried out to her was true. She looked at Floyd; her lips began to tremble, and there was the radiance of happy tears in her eyes. The hand that she gave Floyd was as cold as the sea.

"You will be a hero — always," she said.

She had pronounced Floyd's doom.

II

STEWART CONFERS A FAVOR

For three days Stewart lay threatened with pneumonia; then slowly he began to regain his strength. Within a week he was sitting on the piazza of his house, looking out across the tennis-court and over the rocky knoll, beyond which he could see the ocean. Sometimes when he had been dozing, he awoke with a strangling cry, with both arms raised to ward off the blind, dripping monster that knelt on his chest and crazily choked him. But wide awake, he did not dwell on the sensation of drowning; he hardly recalled it; he lay in a contented, ethereal, purifying languor.

Floyd Halket came once and sat with him, rather shy and conscious at first, for he had been dodging tributes for four days; but he responded soon to Stewart's eager and quite objective interest in the details of the rescue. " Just five minutes before it happened, I was telling Lydia Dunbar you had no business here, taking our prizes," Stewart said. " What a lucky thing for me that you *were* here ! "

" That was a good doctor," said Floyd. " He stuck to his job."

" Like you," Stewart laughed.

The boys were both to enter Harvard that fall; in the enthusiasm roused by this mutual discovery, they exchanged certain confidences and expectations. Floyd had studied at home with a tutor and was afraid his freshman year would be lonely unless he could do something in athletics. " Oh, I 'll see that you are n't lonely," Stewart assured him. " I know lots of fellows."

Followed by her little girl of six or seven, Mrs. Lee came out on the piazza. She had the same light, waving hair as Stewart, the same slender grace; her kind gray eyes and sensitive lips made her seem as charming to the boy as when, a week before, she had come to him and thanked him in gentle, broken words. She now held out both hands, and said, "You see he is quite well, Floyd;" and Floyd shyly gave her his right hand and was pleased because she had called him by his Christian name. The little girl, hiding behind her mother's skirt, peered out at Floyd with a grave and silent curiosity.

"Come here, Goldilocks," he besought her; and then, as she only shrank from sight, he tried coaxing. "I want to show you something."

Mrs. Lee stooped and brought the child round to him.

"When your hair is all gold, I don't see why you want to mix silver with it," Floyd said gravely; and he reached out his hand, stroked the child's head, and then displayed to her astonished eyes a silver quarter.

"Oh, you had it in your hand all the time!" she cried accusingly, while her mother and brother laughed.

Floyd was hurt by the suspicion. He passed his right hand over the left and showed her his empty palm. "Why, I do believe I see more money!" he exclaimed. She turned up her eyes, trying to follow the movement of his hand; she felt it snuggle for a moment under her little pigtail, and then — he was holding another silver quarter before her face!

She laughed a little, but she was awed.

"Are there any more on me?" she asked, turning slowly round.

"No — wait a moment — no," Floyd said. "I thought I saw a ten-cent piece, but it wasn't, after all." He held out his hand to Stewart. "Good-by," he said. "I'm awfully glad that you're all right again. Good-by, Mrs. Lee; good-by, Goldie."

STEWART CONFERS A FAVOR

But the little girl, who had been twisting her hands and swaying in agitation, piped, —

"Are n't those *my* quarters?"

Floyd stared for a moment; then they all broke into a laugh. Mrs. Lee bent down to explain, but Floyd, fishing in his pocket, cried, —

"Why, of course; as long as I took them out of your hair, they certainly do belong to you, Goldie." And then he turned with a comical face to Stewart, who lay giggling. "I've got only one; did n't I give one of them to you?"

The little girl watched her brother with hopefulness while he felt in his pockets. "Yes, this must be it," said Stewart, bringing out a quarter and handing it to Floyd.

"There," said Floyd, as he transferred the two pieces to the child; "I did n't mean to forget. And you 'd better be careful not to let them get into your hair again, or somebody will steal them." He patted the bright head, and then he turned and went down the steps.

Mrs. Lee seated herself beside Stewart.

"What a nice boy he is!" she said.

"Yes, and I did n't suppose he was so amusing."

"I was thinking," Mrs. Lee suggested after a pause, "that you and he might room together at college, Stewart. It would be a fine thing if, after the way your acquaintance has begun, it could grow into something close and permanent."

"Why," said Stewart, "I'll think about it. I don't know that I have any objections, if he has n't."

"We must do everything we can for him," Mrs. Lee said fervently. She leaned over and kissed her son, and then exclaimed, laughing, yet with an earnestness which he fully appreciated and accepted, "I'm sure that to room with my Stewart would be a privilege for any boy."

The first morning that Stewart walked down to the bathing beach a warm sea breeze was blowing, the sun, pouring through the birches and maples that arched over the woodland path, distilled the hot dampness from the soil, the little insects of the wood hummed in busy clouds, now over a greenish-golden pool, now about a rotting stump. There were no notes of birds, only the murmuring quiver of the leaves, yet to Stewart the freshness and gladness in the air was that of spring. Before he emerged from the woods he heard the cries of those on the beach; it was a warm August morning such as sends bathers shouting into the water, sure of its welcome.

When Stewart came out on the sand, walking slowly, a cry went up, and boys and girls ran to meet him. They were delighted to see him out once more. How good and lovable people are, he thought; he was glad to be among them and alive; and he felt that until now he had never understood the sympathy and kindness in every human heart; he recalled and regretted uncharitable opinions that he had expressed about some of those who were now walking by his side.

They sat down with him on the smooth sand in front of the bath-houses; one of the girls changed her position in order that she might not keep the sunlight from him, — her hat had cast a shadow on his legs, — and another girl offered him candy. Three boys who had been swimming came ashore, ran up, and pranced around the group, waving their hands at him. "We can't shake hands, we'd get you all wet," one of them shouted; and another said, "The water's great to-day; wish you could come in, Stewart." With a juvenile impulse to amuse him, they played leap-frog, and then raced into the water, yelling and diving with the greatest possible splash.

Stewart laughed aloud. "Oh, I must n't keep you here," he said, looking round. "You ought to be doing that."

"Oh, we're in no hurry," said Lydia, who was sitting beside him.

She was the prettiest girl, and to Stewart's eyes the most attractive, even in the fact that little things about her were always awry. He noticed with a sort of affection that her broad white hat was crazily tilted, that a strand of brown hair hung down over one ear, that the blue bow which should have been at her throat was twisted round to one side of her neck, and, with most amusement of all, that she had repaired one of her shoestrings, tying the broken ends together in a clumsy knot. When he looked away, her figure tripped through his vision with an airy, dancing grace to which even carelessness contributed, — a flying wisp of hair, a ribbon half untied.

The door of one of the bath-houses was flung open, and Floyd Halket, in his bathing-suit, came running out. Stewart's satellites called to him and he joined them. With naked arms and legs tanned to the hue of polished oak, he seemed a being suddenly strong and elemental by contrast with so many carefully dressed figures. And for his own part he stood before the two persons, boy and girl, who to his hotly grasping and tenacious nature were endowed with charm beyond all others that he had ever known.

"Will you give me fifteen yards start and race me to the raft, Mr. Halket?" asked Lydia.

"Yes — just as you are," Floyd answered, with a laugh.

"Oh, you'd like a subject for another rescue," she exclaimed. "But wait till I get ready and I believe I can beat you. Come along; are n't you all going in?"

So she drew the others away, leaving Floyd and Stewart alone.

Stewart thought of his mother's suggestion; in the expansive, sympathetic mood induced by the kindly companionship of his friends it appealed more than ever to his sentiment; it would be appropriate and beautiful to found a great, lasting friendship on Floyd's heroism.

"What do you say, Floyd," he asked, "to our rooming together at Harvard?"

"Oh!" said Floyd, in a tone that seemed to Stewart delightfully startled. His face had lighted in an instant smile. "I'd like it better than anything else."

"I guess we can hit it off," Stewart answered. "Let's try."

He could not have helped showing a certain gracious condescension had he been making the proposal to a prince. This graciousness and poise of manner Floyd, even in the short time he had known Stewart, had come extravagantly to admire; it was part of the boy's personal charm, which had enslaved Floyd from the first. For Floyd had a humble reverence — and a morbid dread of showing it — for beauty and grace and wit, qualities which he believed Stewart possessed more than any other masculine creature. Floyd liked to watch him, observing with an equal fascination the shape of his head, the wave of his striking yellow hair, his decisive, perhaps a little arrogant nose and chin, his slim hands, and long, narrow fingers.

Turning over, Floyd lay with his elbows in the sand and his hands supporting his chin. He lifted his bare feet and dropped them gently at measured intervals, each time digging his toes into the warm sand; it was a pleasant little sensation to accompany his happiness. His biceps, big and loose as he lay resting thus, quivered at each trifling jolt when his feet struck the sand. He gazed off with a dreamy unconsciousness of his own strength, of his smoothly undulating muscles, which to Stewart in his convalescent state seemed a theme for agreeable contemplation.

"What are you thinking of?" Stewart asked.

Floyd turned his dark eyes and smiled.

"Oh, nothing. Just feeling — feeling good. I want to celebrate; I'm just busting!" Rolling over on his back, he snapped himself to his feet and then stood looking toward the water; half a dozen heads were bobbing near the raft. "Folsom thinks he can swim; watch me duck him."

STEWART CONFERS A FAVOR

He raced into the water, shouting and splashing, dove under and reappeared, and plunged out toward Jack Folsom, shouting threats as he came. Jack retorted and scuttled for the raft; on shore Stewart watched the chase, delighted as Jack's efforts to increase his speed grew more and more frantic. Suddenly Floyd disappeared beneath the surface; there was a furious splashing then of Jack's feet; an instant later he was drawn under quietly. Then the two heads emerged again; the boys dragged themselves up on the raft and sat amicably side by side, wringing the water out of their hair.

Stewart thought Floyd a queer fellow, to lie for a while in such comatose contentment and then to jump suddenly out of his skin and run like a wild Indian for joy. He liked him for it, at the same time feeling a slight mental superiority. Why should the mere prospect of rooming with a certain fellow arouse such intense exultation? Stewart watched Floyd and the others diving and disporting themselves, and in the warm noonlight his tolerance became more comprehensive. After all, occasional demonstrativeness in persons who were ordinarily self-contained was a rather attractive trait.

On further acquaintance Stewart confessed a slight disappointment in his new friend. Floyd was amiable and could be amusing when one was alone with him, but in a crowd, and especially among girls, he was silent and showed none of the promising gay spirit with which he had first surprised and gratified Stewart. When Mrs. Lee had dinner parties for Stewart's friends, Floyd showed an odd clumsiness; ideas, words, sentences failed him or became so involved that even while he was making the mental struggle for utterance, the moment for them passed. Once Stewart induced him to show his sleight of hand; with this he won a good deal of admiration and applause, but he would never again display his skill. Stewart urged him, " Some of them have never seen it; anyway, none of them are tired of it." There was a wistful, humorous appeal in Floyd's answer, "But don't you see, Stewart, when a fellow has only one parlor trick, he's got to look out that *he* does n't get tired of it?"

Little by little Stewart was able to depose Floyd from the mental eminence on which he had at first joyously placed him; he was never willing to let any one occupy such a position long. He became able to view him with the complacency which a clever person extends to a friend who is pleasant but indisputably dull.

The opening of the college term approached. Stewart and Floyd went one day to Cambridge to engage rooms. Floyd was of little importance in the search; he was easily satisfied. If Stewart pointed out to him that here there would be no morning sun, or that the wall-paper was cold and cheerless, or that the bedrooms were too small, or that steam heat was an abomination and they *must* have an open fire, Floyd assented, but he did not care. With his simple tastes, he was indifferent to luxuries; with plenty of money at his command, he could spend as much or as little as the persons about him and be happy if only he liked them. So the choice of the room and afterwards the furnishing of it were dictated by Stewart. It was in a private house; this was before the era of the great new dormitories, with their marble corridors, oak wainscoting and ceilings, porcelain bath-tubs, swimming-tanks, and tennis-courts; when these institutions came to pass, Stewart sighed and felt that he had been born too soon. But considering the time in which he lived, the room of his choice was highly desirable. There was a bay window, with a maple-tree just outside; there were two bedrooms (Floyd insisted that Stewart should take the one with the sun), and there was a bath-room up only one flight.

The doors and mantel were painted an execrable light brown,—so Stewart said,—and their color was transformed to a dark green. "I should scream if I had to live with that wall-paper," said Stewart; and he spent a day, leading Floyd from one shop to another, Floyd

STEWART CONFERS A FAVOR 21

approving vaguely — until Stewart condemned — every sample that was held up for inspection. Finally Stewart chose a paper with a background of dark red and an involved pattern of large fruits in gold and green; it was absurdly expensive, but, as Stewart pointed out, rich and distinguished. Floyd tentatively ventured to contribute but one picture, a double-page drawing from "Harper's Weekly" of an Indian fight; the thing had taken his eye, and he had cut it out and had it put in a frame that he realized tardily was of the same execrable color as the late mantel and doors. But he liked the picture so much that he showed it to Stewart, who tactfully said he thought it would hardly "go" with the paper. So Floyd hung it on the wall of his bedroom, and then under Stewart's guidance bought some carbon prints of Michael Angelo, Velasquez, and Rembrandt; also a set of Holbein's drawings. Floyd was amazed at his room-mate's taste in carpets and curtains. Hitherto it had never occurred to him as possible that a boy of his own age could have a knowledge of such things.

As for college life — at the phrase Stewart conjured up a world of polite adventure, in which there would be whimsical plots, gay exploits, a merry warfare waged without malice against all representatives of law and discipline, a life by night at hotels and theatres in Boston and at clubs in Cambridge, and for himself eventually the leadership of all the joyous, reveling company that give to college life its irresponsible, humorous, lovable name. For Floyd, the phrase held a different meaning, other possibilities. It included the most ultimate athletic prowess; high above all men loomed for him the glorious figure of the captain of the team. It meant, too, that at last he could give up Latin and Greek and spend his working time in laboratories, with blow-pipes and test-tubes and inexhaustible experiments at his command. Beyond these two facts the world was a mystery that would be unfolding for four delightful years. All Floyd was sure of was that Harvard was the best college, his class the best class, his room-mate the one boy in all the world that he would have chosen; and some day he would do something — he hoped in athletics — to make his college and his class and his room-mate glad he belonged to them.

The night that the freshmen gave their first demonstration of class spirit, assembling in the Yard, cheering themselves, and charging the sophomores who gathered in opposition, Floyd felt that he was tasting college life. He thrust himself into the front rank for every scrimmage, and in the groaning, rib-displacing press he exulted that he was one of those who bore the brunt for the class. When the tight jam swung slowly upon an axis until it burst apart into two reeling, fighting bodies, Floyd helped to rally the host and incite it to a fresh onset. The freshmen were driven against the walls of brick buildings, tripped over low wire fences that lurked for their unfamiliar feet; but they rose to rush more lustily, shouting with delirious affection the numerals of their class. In the brief intervals of rest, Floyd looked for Stewart, but there was no finding any one in such a crowd.

Late in the evening the sophomores began to disperse. Then the freshmen, gathering close for the last time, crowed over their victory. Their cheer brought derisive outcries from the groups of upper classmen skulking away through the Yard, outcries that merited chastisement. By instinct the freshman body resolved itself into a number of small vigilance committees. In a short time the Yard, instead of being one great battle-ground, was the scene of multitudinous small affrays. Occasionally a window was flung open and a pitcher of water emptied on a scuffling group below. Jeering cries, shrill whistles, and a song as half a dozen fellows in lock-step went scouring by, were the noises of the night. Floyd and a few others roamed about, coming to close quarters with whoever offered. When at last all visible opposition was subdued, they bade one another good-night and separated.

STEWART CONFERS A FAVOR

It was nearly twelve o'clock. Floyd walked down the street to his room. His necktie had been torn off, and his bruised feet and ankles caused him to limp gingerly. He raised an examining hand to his nose; from there it strayed to the bruise swelling under his right eye. He was very happy; he had had a good time, and he felt that he had done something now for his class — in a way, even for Harvard University. He was eager to see Stewart and talk the exciting evening over with him.

As he ascended the stairs, he wondered at the noise; then, when he opened the door, he stood bewildered. Stewart was in the middle of the room, ladling punch from a wash-bowl that was placed on his new mahogany desk; eight or ten fellows were grouped round him, pledging him with their glasses.

"Hello!" he cried. "Hello, Floyd!" He waved him forward from the doorway, and with an unsteady hand held out to him the glass he had filled. "Just in time. Cæsar's ghost! you're a mess!"

Floyd took the glass, embarrassed at becoming on the instant an object for many bright, young, intoxicated eyes.

"He's the fellow I was telling you about," Stewart continued. "I say we all drink to him — bumpers. Bumpers to a hero — and the fellow that saved my life! A-ay!"

"A-ay!" shouted his friends obediently. And they drank.

Stewart came up and threw his arm across Floyd's shoulders. The dripping ladle waved in his hand.

"Foolish old thing!" he said. "Fighting when you might have been drinking! Foolish old thing!"

"Why, but were n't you all out rushing with the class?" asked Floyd.

"No — been having a nice quiet noisy evening right at home. You," Stewart giggled, — "you 've been out making enemies, and I 've been home making friends. 'For he's a jolly good fellow' — "

The others took the song up and carried it on while

Stewart gazed at them solemnly. Then he turned again to Floyd and confided in his ear, "They sing *rotten*. Cæsar's ghost! they're rotten!"

"Where did you get the punch?" asked Floyd, still bewildered.

"Jim Hobart had the fizz. But he rooms over a proctor, so we had to have it here — we *had* to have it here," Stewart repeated with sober emphasis. "And when we looked for you, you'd gone off no one knew where. — Oh, they're *rotten!*" He turned to the others. "'For he's a jolly good fellow!'" — and he sang, leading them extravagantly, solemnly, with the ladle.

While Floyd was looking on with a broadening smile, one of the guests detached himself from the group of singers and came up to him. He was a tall, narrow-faced boy, with black eyebrows that met thickly across his nose, sallow cheeks, and the concentrated, single-minded expression common to extremely narrow faces. "You're Floyd Halket," he said. "I'm Hobart — Jim Hobart." And promptly he grasped the lapels of Floyd's coat, and penning him into a corner, talked to him, with a mild, wavering gaze directed at the spot where his necktie should have been. Was it true that Stewart Lee had been under water half an hour? And dead when he came out? And how had Floyd saved him, anyway? "Don't mind their singing," Jim said imperiously, when Floyd tried to evade the close, redundant questioning. "You caught him under the arms? Go on, go on, go on, g'on, g'on, g'on, g'on —"

Floyd stemmed the torrent with a precipitant explanation; the others raised their glasses aloft, straining for a high note. "For he's a jolly good fel-lo-o-o-ow" — they came down panting — "which nobody can deny." Stewart called for a repetition.

"I didn't believe you were a real hero when Stewart Lee told us," said Jim Hobart, still browsing at Floyd's lapels. "You don't look it. Hero, hero, hero, hero —"

STEWART CONFERS A FAVOR

"Oh, shut up!" said Floyd, choking him by the back of the neck playfully.

Stewart cut the song off with an ornate sweep of the ladle.

"Hero, hero," muttered Jim Hobart, squirming in Floyd's grip.

"He is a hero!" Stewart proclaimed contentiously. "I was under water thirty-five minutes. Some say an hour. I was dead."

"How did it feel to be dead?" asked one boy. He swayed a little as he asked the question, but he was serious and pop-eyed.

"Why, just dead, that's all. The way you'll be feeling to-night."

"I'm not tight; I've never been tight in my life. I—"

The indignant protest was suddenly reduced to a gurgle. Stewart had spied the boy's collar-button, and with a whimsical impulse had darted at it and was pressing it into his windpipe.

"Press his button!" shrieked Stewart in delight, releasing him. "Get him talking! Press his button!"

The youth talked in resentment; Stewart sprang again, sure-fingered, and held him writhing and gasping. The others admired the trick; one after another tested it on the impotently raging victim.

Suddenly Stewart turned to Floyd. "Here, you dirty old thing, why don't you get tight? Here's another glass for you. You've got to get tight — can't always be a hero."

"Oh, sure," said Floyd good-humoredly, taking the glass. But he drank only a little of the punch, and after that made a pretense of drinking.

They sang two more songs; then Jim Hobart came up, and after inspecting Floyd again for a while, suggested that they should all dress like heroes. This proposal met with an instant response; neckties were carefully taken off and pocketed, and the left side of each collar unbuttoned, to correspond to Floyd's, which had been torn loose and was sticking up about his ear. Then they went round, scuffing and stepping on one another's shoes, to give them the battered appearance possessed by Floyd's. Highly amused by all this, Floyd suggested that they still lacked something to complete the likeness, — a swollen eye. This was admitted, and there was some discussion as to how a swollen eye could be best obtained, but no one wished to make the first experiment. The boy whose button had been pressed achieved a discovery. "Why, it's getting the swollen eye that would make us heroes!" And then Jim Hobart struck out a solution of the difficulty, declaring haughtily, "After all, we are gentlemen, not heroes." For some time after that they took turns in stalking up to Floyd, snapping their fingers at him, and saying in a lordly voice, "After all, *we* are gentlemen, not heroes."

At two o'clock Floyd felt that so far as he was concerned, this diverting evening must close. He announced, "I must turn in. Football practice begins to-morrow. Good-night, fellows." He stepped into his bedroom and closed the door.

As he undressed, he heard a murmur of discussion that his withdrawal had provoked. Suddenly Stewart's voice, high-pitched and silencing, rang out.

"No, you don't either! I wouldn't care if it was anybody but a hero. But I owe him my life — and you'll let him alone."

Floyd smiled, touched by the maudlin loyalty that was protecting him from annoyance. He crawled into bed; the scuffling, singing, and laughter went on in the next room, but Floyd in his healthy weariness soon fell asleep.

The next morning when he went to rouse Stewart, he found an empty room and an untouched bed. He dressed himself, surveying the disorder of the night before; his own desk was encumbered with all the books and papers that Stewart had removed from his to make room for the

STEWART CONFERS A FAVOR

punch-bowl; the rug was pulled up into a heap in the centre of the room, the red cushion with the large white "H" on it was propped above a picture near the ceiling, an elaborate jest; sticky glasses stood or lay upset on a sticky mantel.

Floyd went to breakfast and then to lectures; at noon, when he returned to his room, there was Stewart, as fresh and blooming as in the midst of revelry.

"It was a wild wet night on the Swedish coast," Stewart informed him. "We organized the Aurora Club; there was some talk of making you join it. We strayed from one room to another, and then at dawn we saw the milk wagons. I got a perfectly crazy idea; we took a bottle of whiskey from Jim Hobart's room and followed a wagon for — oh, I don't know, miles — and wherever it stopped we stopped, too, and turned the can of milk into a milk punch. Everybody in Cambridge had milk punch for breakfast this morning."

Floyd laughed. "Pretty hard on the babies."

"Well, yes," Stewart admitted. "But you don't think much about them when you 're perfectly pie-eyed."

"What happened then?" asked Floyd.

"We were chased by a policeman, but I guess he was n't very sincere about catching us. Anyway we 'd emptied the bottle by that time. I went back to Jim Hobart's room and had a few hours of innocent slumber on his window-seat. Look here, Floyd; did I say anything nasty and cheap to you last night?"

"No. Why?"

"I was afraid I might have. And I 'd rather be anything than cheap when I 'm tight. A fellow who gets cheap ought never to get tight. — You took hardly anything; why not?"

"I don't like it," said Floyd.

"You 're so confounded hygienic," Stewart complained. "What 's the use? We 've got only one life to live. Jim Hobart's a gay bird."

He collected his note-books, knocking to the floor a tablet that he did not stoop to pick up, and left the room singing cheerfully.

Floyd tried to overthrow his own instinctive conviction that in Jim Hobart Stewart had recognized his kindred spirit and companion. Failing in this, he tried to suppress or at least dismiss from mind a smarting little jealousy of Jim. As the days passed, that became the task to which he schooled himself; he could not escape from a hurt, surprised feeling that an important element in college life which he had taken for granted was denied him. The paths of the two room-mates had already diverged; they drew no nearer together as the year passed.

III

THE PARTING

At the beginning of the sophomore year it came to Floyd's understanding that Stewart and Jim Hobart had been elected into a club; there they ate and sat, and did what studying seemed to them necessary. For the time being they seemed to Floyd, who was in training for football, to have withdrawn entirely from the rest of the college world. On Sundays he usually took luncheon with the Lees in Boston, and these were almost the only occasions when he saw his room-mate. Sometimes Stewart did not appear for this Sunday meal, having been at a club dinner in Cambridge the night before, and finding it necessary to send Floyd in to his mother with the most plausible invention he could command. So Floyd would sit alone with Mrs. Lee and Anna, and afterwards the little girl would call on him to perform tricks with a silver quarter; she no longer believed in them as she had done at first, but she never gave up trying to detect how he did them. They became very good friends, Mrs. Lee and Anna and the boy.

One afternoon in December, when Floyd was walking from the laboratory to his room, he heard his name called behind him, and turning saw Stewart.

"I haven't seen you for a dog's age," said Stewart, coming up and linking his arm in Floyd's, "and I can't stay but a moment with you now; I'm in an awful rush. What I want to know is, have you any engagement for next Friday night?"

"No," Floyd answered; "none."

"That's good; you wouldn't have been allowed to keep it if you had. We're arranging to get you good and sewed up that night — down at the club."

Floyd looked at him blankly. "What! You mean — I'm — I'm elected?"

"Of course, that's just what I mean, you old fool!" cried Stewart, laughing and giving Floyd a good-natured slap on the back. "I've got to run; I have a date, and I'm late as usual. But I'm awfully glad you're elected, Floyd." And then, before he ran away, he gave his room-mate not a good-natured thump, but a gentle, affectionate little tap.

It was a raw, cloudy afternoon, the moisture in the air clung like a net to one's face, and the streets along which Floyd took his unheeding way were bare and dreary; but he would not have been happier if it had been an afternoon in spring, with the birds calling from trees and hedges. He was indifferent to social honors, but this election revived his hope of coming again into close relations with Stewart; more than that, it pleased him as a sign that Stewart cared for him. He laughed to himself now at the way in which the boy had notified him of the event; it seemed to him the most genial, merry, affectionate way. When at last from a hilltop he turned his face homeward, a few scattered lights of Cambridge were appearing in the dusk; he watched for new flashes, the thickening glow on the bosom of the town. "That's the way it happens," he murmured to himself. "First one little light inside you, and then another, and then you warm up all of a sudden."

He learned afterwards that Stewart had made a personal issue of his election, battering down the opposition of members who did not know him or thought he would not be quite "genial;" Stewart had gone about, cajoling, demanding, proclaiming, "He's my room-mate, he's the best fellow that ever lived, he's a hero too, and saved my life and almost lost his own." And nobody had thought it worth while to oppose such a headstrong, determined canvass.

Stewart did his best to make Floyd at home in the club;

THE PARTING

he sat with him at dinners, he would call Floyd from another room to join the group gathered about the piano to sing, and then he would stand leaning on Floyd's shoulder. Yet there was always a faint politeness in his manner toward his room-mate, a veiled deferential constraint which had suffered few lapses since the day he had beaten him on the back and called him an old fool. And he was conscious that, in spite of all his devotion, he was failing to make Floyd "go;" Floyd did not show quite the right side to the other fellows, and they did not show quite the right side to him.

"It's damned fine the way you stand by a friend," Jim Hobart said to Stewart. Jim had an antipathy to Floyd and created a little sentiment against him, saying that he didn't take an interest and would never get tight with the crowd. "He has a revolving stomach," Stewart pleaded in defense. Everybody agreed that in that case Stewart's devotion was all the more noble.

Suddenly criticism became more impatient. "Oh, what's the use of pushing Floyd Halket everywhere you go!" Jim Hobart exclaimed to Stewart one evening in irritation. "Drop it, for heaven's sake. If you want to come to the theatre with us, come ahead, but we don't want him."

Stewart abhorred the idea of presenting a ridiculous figure; if his championship of Floyd no longer seemed fine, perhaps it was beginning to appear grotesque. Thenceforth Stewart ceased to pay Floyd the obvious little friendly attentions at the club. Floyd, working hard in the laboratory, exercising with the crew candidates in the gymnasium, visiting the club only occasionally, was not aware of any change.

Through Stewart and Mrs. Lee, Floyd received invitations to dances in Boston. "You'd better go to the Vanes'," Stewart advised. "A friend of yours from Avalon will be there, and she'll be disappointed if you don't come — Lydia Dunbar."

"Is she in town?" asked Floyd.

"Not yet, but she will be; she'll be at the Vanes'," Stewart repeated.

Floyd looked forward to the event with less reluctance than before. He was an awkward dancer and bashfully apprehensive of strange girls, but the prospect of seeing Lydia Dunbar again altered the forbidding aspect of the evening. When he entered the ballroom, hers was the first figure that he spied, and he made for her at once. She was just rising to dance, but she waited to give him her hand.

"You'll come up for the next, won't you?" she said. "Don't forget, please."

She floated away, nodding and smiling at him over her partner's shoulder.

He followed her with his eyes. When she disappeared in a swirl of dancers, he watched intently for glimpses of her blue dress, of her slender, leaning figure, and of her brown head with the white plume in her hair. How well she danced, he thought; the boy, too, he had to include the boy.

When his own turn came, he discovered his inappropriateness. Trying to talk into her ear, he blundered with his feet, he seemed always out of step and jigging instead of gliding, he bumped her knees, he tore some one's gown. At last she said to him, "I don't know what is the matter with me; I don't seem able to dance that nice way you do. Let's sit down."

"Yes, let's," said Floyd, with a frank laugh. "Or — don't you want to teach me to dance the nice way you do?"

"All right," she agreed. "We can go into the little room off here."

She taught him seriously in spite of her laughter; boys kept interrupting to ask her to dance, but she sent them all away, Stewart among them. Floyd at last protested. "I'm spoiling your evening; I wish you'd dance."

THE PARTING 33

"Oh," she said, looking up at him with a smile, and the sincerity of her voice made this one of the shining moments of his life, "I love to do this for you. And it's such a little thing!"

But Floyd insisted that the lesson should end; he led her out and danced with her, and she told him he was a credit to his teacher. Then some one came and took her away from him, and Floyd was introduced to other girls. He tried to dance with them, but they gave a scooping sort of motion to their bodies as they glided; it was a new thing in Boston that winter, and the girls were emulating one another in the practice of it. Lydia had not attempted it, and it introduced into the waltz a problem with which Floyd could not cope. He adopted Lydia's gentle, apologetic phrase, "I'm sorry; I don't seem able to dance that nice way you do;" and then, having drawn a good-natured laugh from his partner, he felt a humorous shame at the success of his second-hand utterance. Most of the time he stood in the doorway among the superfluous boys. Lydia had become immensely popular; in the intermissions boys swarmed about her; as she danced, she slanted laughs right and left, her cheeks glowed with a richer color, a tendril of hair, shaken down, hung at her temple, curling round into her face; at a sudden turn of her head it fluttered across her laugh caressingly. Floyd would have liked to dance with her again, but he felt it would be hardly fair; already she had given him a good part of her evening, and now to ask her to bump round with him when she was finding so many better partners — no, he wouldn't ask her. But finally she sent for him, pretended to be aggrieved because he had not come of his own accord, and said that she wasn't engaged for the next waltz. With all his blundering, that dance made a happy climax to his evening.

The next morning he came into his room after a ten o'clock lecture and found Stewart bending over his drawing-board.

"Something for the 'Lampoon'?" asked Floyd, knowing that Stewart had made one or two sketches for the paper.

"No — that is," Stewart said, jumping up and snatching the picture close to his breast, "it's not finished yet."

He tucked it away behind his desk, and Floyd sat down at the other side of the room to study. By and by he was conscious that Stewart had gently taken out his drawing-board again and resumed work on it. Once Floyd looked up from his book and saw his room-mate's face intent and illuminated by an amused smile. Floyd smiled in sympathy and wished that he, too, had a gift for drawing.

At noon Floyd rose.

"Got it done yet?" he asked, putting on his hat.

"No, not yet," Stewart answered, and he again shielded the picture from inspection.

Some time after luncheon Floyd dropped into the club. As he closed the door, he heard loud laughter in the sitting-room, and entering saw half a dozen fellows with their backs turned toward him examining something on the opposite wall.

"Just like him!" one of the fellows said; and then Stewart turned, caught sight of Floyd, and tore the sketch from the wall. He stood with it under his arm, undecided and flushed.

"Oh, go on, let Halket see it!" cried Jim Hobart, grabbing an edge of the drawing. "Here, Halket, look here!"

Stewart, seeing that concealment was impossible, relinquished his hold on the picture and allowed Hobart and the others to exhibit it. Floyd saw a series of caricatures representing himself in a ballroom — a square, stiff-legged figure with a wooden block of a head, an unmistakable if extravagant likeness. The first sketch showed him dancing, with a thick splay hand spread upon his partner's back, a wide flat smile directed foolishly over her head, and one foot ripping a flounce from the bottom of another girl's dress. Underneath was written, "Could n't you just die waltzing!" In the second picture he presented the same fatuous figure of abstracted enjoyment, except that his head was tilted a little farther back, and his eyes were half closed. By this time the torn flounce had wound round and round his leg, and the girl, beginning to suffer from exposure, stood helplessly staring at the trailing yards; others were gazing with amusement or disgust at the rapt dancer. The picture was labeled, "Do you like to talk while you 're waltzing?" The third and last exhibited the hero with head thrown far back, his wide flat smile fixed on the ceiling, his eyes closed in final ecstasy; the flounce had now wound his leg from the ankle to the thigh, a spiral bandage; the victim was reduced to a mere ballet skirt, and stood covering her face in shame. The title was, "What a heavenly dance!"

Floyd laughed as he studied the pictures. "That 's just the way I felt," he said, turning to Stewart. "Why did n't you tell me what you were doing? I 'd have posed for you."

"Oh, I don't know," Stewart answered in some confusion. "You were busy, you know." He picked up the drawings and started toward the fire with them.

"Here! what are you going to do?" cried Floyd, running after him. "Don't burn them. Post 'em up on the wall here; give the other fellows a laugh. They 're too good to burn."

He took them from Stewart and tacked them up in the place where they had been exhibited when he entered. Then he stood off and, surveying them again, said a little ruefully, "They do look like me, don't they?"

"Oh, not really, — not very much," one of the boys assured him.

Stewart detached himself from the group, and sitting apart in a corner began to read a magazine. After a while the others left the club, all except Floyd, who had stretched himself prone on the big window-seat and was working out a problem in mathematics. Then Stewart came over to him.

"Floyd," he said, "I want to beg your pardon. It was a low-down thing for me to do."

Floyd raised his eyes slowly; his face looked dull in its effort to comprehend.

"What are you talking about?" he asked.

"The picture," Stewart answered. "I'm ashamed of having made fun of you that way."

"Why," cried Floyd, "it was —" And then he stopped short. Looking up at Stewart's downcast face and evasive eyes, he began to understand. He sat up, and then reaching out dragged Stewart down to the seat beside him.

"See here," he said, "why do you treat me differently from your other friends? If you'd made that drawing of Jim Hobart, you'd have rushed right off to show it to him. You'd never have apologized. What's the matter, Stewart?"

"There's a difference," Stewart replied uneasily. "I can do things to other fellows that I ought n't to you. I owe you too much — and I can't forget it — or if I do forget it, then I'm ashamed and ungrateful. You see, when you owe a fellow your life —"

He stopped with a helpless wave of the hand. Floyd was silent. Stewart sat with one foot cocked up over his knee, plucking nervously at his shoe-strings.

"You see," he went on, "you have an advantage over me, a perfectly hopeless advantage; nothing I can ever do, nothing I can ever say, can even things up between us. And I hate this knowing inside me that I'm always at a disadvantage."

"Well," said Floyd, after a moment, "I hate to hear you talk of 'evening things up' and 'being at a disadvantage.' It sounds almost as if you had a grudge to square off." He laughed uncomfortably, while Stewart's fingers worked at the shoe-string, untying it, retying it.

THE PARTING

"Oh, Stewart," — and he pinched the firm muscles of the boy's leg gently with his big hand, — " I don't want you to act toward me in any way that is n't natural to you; but if you do have a joke on me, for heaven's sake spring it, and don't think about hurting my feelings. And if ever I get the same chance, I'll lay it on to you just as hard as I can."

He gave the leg a final squeeze and then slid down from the window-seat and got his hat.

"Going along?" he asked.

If Stewart had gone with him that time and the two had talked the matter out and then turned to ordinary things, it might all have been different. But for no particular reason Stewart was prompted to say, "No, I think I'll stay here awhile and read;" and Floyd departed, not realizing that he had separated himself from his roommate. The magnanimity with which Floyd had treated him rankled in Stewart's jealous disposition; the episode that Floyd promptly forgot left in Stewart a sting. He had spoken truly in saying that he could not endure to be at a disadvantage. In the days that followed he glanced back frequently on this interview with a sense that Floyd had pressed his advantage. Gradually to his mind Floyd's magnanimity became remote and shaded into an exaction.

"Why should he expect me to slap him on the back and lean on his neck if I don't feel like it?" became the discontented question that Stewart asked himself, perverting the lesson of the episode. He drew no more caricatures of his room-mate and he had no jokes to "spring."

They rubbed along together for the rest of the year, during which time their intimacy diminished. Floyd became involved in athletics and was in training the year round; his chemistry engrossed him morning and afternoon on most days; one evening a week he taught mathematics at the University Settlement House; he had little leisure to give to the clubs and societies into which Stewart and his other friends drew him. For Stewart was still loyal in doing all he could for his room-mate, even while disapproving of his pursuits. Athletics, chemistry, "philanthropic work among the laboring classes" — even if one had a keen interest in them and expected, as Floyd sometimes declared he did, to pass one's life in intimate relations with them — seemed to Stewart a lamentable perversion of a college career. He had no remorse whatever for his own, diversified as it was by adventurous experiences with the Faculty and, once or twice, with the Cambridge police.

The break came one afternoon in the fall of their junior year. The Harvard football eleven was playing a game with an Indian college team; Floyd had arrived early and taken a seat in the middle section of the stand. The first half had hardly begun when the spectators near the gate rose and cheered something that was evidently not a feature of the game; the others stood up in curiosity, and finally Floyd saw three odd figures dancing along at the foot of the bank of seats. Clad in red and blue blankets ornamented with beads, wearing feather head-dresses and yellow moccasins, and with their faces hideously painted, they came capering and yelling. Floyd stared. Then he saw that they were closely followed by Stewart and Jim Hobart. They stopped in front of the centre section; Stewart and Jim led them up to seats beside Floyd, who now recognized the three as sophomores recently elected into a society of which he was a member. Stewart and Jim had evidently taken them in hand and devised this performance as part of their initiation.

Stewart, having seated himself, turned to Floyd with a gleam of enthusiastic amusement.

"Pretty good Indians, are n't they?" he said. "Look at their tom-toms." He pointed to the tin pails slung at their waists, on which they had been beating with drumsticks. "Between the halves we're going to send them out on the field to do a war-dance."

THE PARTING

"What! right before the Indian team?" asked Floyd.

"Yes; why not?" Stewart answered sharply.

He turned and talked in an undertone to Jim Hobart, and Floyd gave his attention to the game. At the end of the half, when the Indian team came over to the substitutes' bench to wrap themselves in blankets, Stewart turned to the neophytes.

"Go down into the middle of the field and do a war-dance," he commanded.

They rose obediently and started to pass out into the aisle.

"Sit down!" cried Floyd.

They hesitated; they knew that he was a member of the society, and that they were as much subject to his orders as to Stewart's. But Stewart turned upon him with his eyes flashing.

"Mind your own business," he said.

Floyd caught him by the arm.

"Stewart," he said, "don't make a fool of yourself. Cool off. You neophytes, sit down."

Stewart, red with anger and with his lips trembling, looked at Floyd. Then he leaned back in his seat and nodded to the neophytes.

"Sit down," he said curtly.

After the game he let Jim Hobart conduct his Indians from the field; he himself fell back and walked silently with Floyd. Together they turned aside from the crowd into an unfrequented street.

"That ends it," Stewart said suddenly, stopping and facing Floyd. "You seem to think that what you once did for me gives you the right to rule me. You think you have only to turn on the screws. Well, you've done it, you've humiliated me, you can have that satisfaction. You've made me know that having once saved my life you look on me as somehow your property—"

"Stewart!" cried Floyd in reproach.

"Oh, it had to come," Stewart swept on; "the sooner

the better, I suppose. There can be no real friendship between us."

Floyd looked at him in silence.

"Good Lord, Stewart!" he cried at last, stretching out his hand. Then he saw it was in vain, and for a moment his attitude changed and his face hardened. "I have never done or said anything to you that I regret," he stated proudly.

"I will say this much," Stewart conceded. "I don't blame you more than myself. It was my mistake. After you pulled me out of the water, I ought never to have seen you again — except once, to thank you. You had too great an advantage over me; it was something I could never forget."

"It was something of which I was never conscious," answered Floyd. "Well, I am sorry, Stewart."

Jim Hobart had a spare bedroom, and Stewart arranged to go in with him. That year Stewart spent a few days of his Christmas vacation visiting the Dunbars in Avalon, and did not let Floyd know of his presence in the town; and Floyd, learning of it afterwards, felt a little contemptuous of his former friend.

Yet as time passed and the senior year ran its course, they lost the sense of bitterness. Stewart, who had an ability for political management, helped to secure Floyd's election to an important Class Day office, and said to him lightly, "No matter how we act, we know who are the best people." And one Sunday in May, when Floyd entered the club, which for a couple of years he had visited but little, he found Stewart there alone.

"Let's go for a walk in the country and see the apple blossoms," suggested Stewart after a while.

They took a car to Lexington, and then walked all the way to Concord along the Great Road that the British troops had traversed in distress more than a century before. Now and then they paused to read a sign over a cottage door, commemorating some rustic patriot of that

THE PARTING

day, who with flint-lock and powder-horn had joined the neighbors behind the stone wall of the pasture, had lain there with musket primed, awaiting the first flutter of scarlet down the long road against the green of the spring, waiting until the first flutter spread and split into the broken ranks of soldiery, and then —

"What are you thinking of?" asked Stewart, as Floyd stood looking up at one of the memorial signs.

"Just of how the British went by here — running, with their tongues hanging out of their mouths," answered Floyd. "That's the gloating sentence I remember in my boys' history. And I was wondering about this Jonathan Hawkins that lived here — and probably squatted behind that wall. I was sort of hoping that as the poor devils jogged by he and the others did n't fire."

"If he did," said Stewart, "with a name like that I'll bet he could shoot straight. That's one thing you notice about these names along here; somehow they call up men with a steady gray eye and no smile."

A little farther on they climbed over a fence and came out on a warm, sunny hillside. The Concord River flowed below, glimmering through the vivid green spray of the arching willows; here and there along it a swamp-maple showed pink, and across the stream on the crest of the opposing hillside an apple orchard in full bloom sunned itself, lying there like a tinted cloud against the sky. The boys sat down to rest; the spot was quiet; a canoe slipped by on the stream, and the flashing of the paddle, the voices of the man and the girl came faintly up to them through the foliage; then at the bend in the river the sound and the sight faded away.

"What will you do when you graduate?" Stewart asked after an interval of silence.

"I'm going abroad for a year; then I'm going into my grandfather's mills," Floyd answered.

"I was in a steel mill once," Stewart remarked. "It's my idea of hell — at least it gave me an idea of hell. But of course you won't have to bother with that; you'll be in the offices."

"No," said Floyd. "I'm going through the whole thing."

"Stripped to the waist and broiling at a furnace!" exclaimed Stewart. "Well, it seems like martyrdom to me."

"It won't be that, for it will be interesting," Floyd answered. "If you'd gone in for athletics more, Stewart, you'd know what fun it is, when you're stripped for it, to get tired and blown and knocked around. And here you add to that the fun of making something."

Stewart shook his head.

"You wait," he said. "Your hands will be black and greasy from one year's end to another; you *can't* get them clean; you'll have to go to meals with dirty hands; it seems a trifle, but I should go nutty like Lady Macbeth if all the scrubbing in the world couldn't make my hands clean. What's the use anyway of working! How much better just to keep moving round and round the world, following the spring!"

"Is that what you mean to do?" asked Floyd.

"Oh, I have a streak of New England conscience. I'm going to study architecture. I don't know where I shall settle down." After a pause he added, "I think Avalon might be a good place."

"You were out there a year ago."

"Yes." Stewart plucked a bunch of grasses and wound them round his finger. "I — I thought of letting you know — of looking you up. And then I felt it might be awkward for you — as well as for me — considering everything. Lydia thought it was queer; she wanted to have you at a dinner party — I was staying at her house — and when she asked me about you, I had to tell her — well, that it was all off and my fault. 'Then we'll have him round and you can make it up,' she said. But I said no, it was just one of those things that couldn't be helped,

THE PARTING

but might come round all right in time. I — I told her it was all my fault, Floyd."

"Oh, it was n't!" Floyd cried, his reserve quite broken down. "If I 'd known how to do things tactfully — Stewart, I 've always liked you better than any fellow I ever knew!"

He poured out this declaration with an uncontrolled haste unlike his usual deliberateness and with an impulsive yet gentle outward gesture of his hand. Stewart seized it.

"I 'm sorry," he said.

Indeed, he had a facile, amiable impulse to show a feeling that would please his old room-mate. And while he continued winding and unwinding the grass stems about his finger, he said, —

"You 're the first person we 've told, Floyd, outside of our families; Lydia as well as I wanted you to know it long before any one else should. She and I are engaged."

Floyd's dark eyes flashed a question and then a message of delight, even before his lips could frame it. He took Stewart's hand again in his slow, warm grip, murmuring, "Good work, Stewart! good work!" Then, feeling that this was inadequate, he patted him on the back, yet a little awkwardly, saying, "It 's fine; it 's the finest thing I 've heard. I 'm awfully glad."

"It 's the best thing that ever happened to me — or that ever will happen," said Stewart.

"Yes, and to her, too," Floyd insisted, as sincerely as if his own alliance with Stewart had been the happiest arrangement in the world. "I want to write to her — and tell her what I think of you — what I 've always thought. How does it feel, Stewart, to be so happy — so fixed — so —" Ideas even for questions failed him.

"Like this hillside and the sun and the river down there — warm all the time," said Stewart, with a laugh. "Of course," he went on, "it does make a difference in a fellow; it 's got to. I 've led a pretty wild life here at college and done things I'm ashamed of; and I guess I've turned over a new leaf. Why, I'd sort of taken it for granted, you know, that when I got to Paris and began studying architecture, I'd be as gay as any of them; but I'm glad, I honestly am, that I have somebody that whether she's there or here will keep me straight."

"Well, it's wonderful," Floyd said after a pause. "Being so — complete. Finding you love a girl — and she loves you. How anybody ever dares to — to think she might — to touch her — " The conception was too vast for him to formulate it; he relapsed into silence.

"You'll be finding out some day," Stewart assured him. "It will hit you all of a heap."

Floyd shook his head. "You know, when I think about it — a fellow gets foolish and does sometimes," he interjected deprecatingly — " it seems as if I'd never grow up to it. Why, I remember, just as if it were yesterday — " He stopped suddenly.

"What?" said Stewart.

"Oh, nothing. It was the day you stayed under water too long. I hadn't meant to speak of it."

"Go on," urged Stewart, with a laugh. "I don't mind hearing about it."

"Why, I was just remembering the way Lydia — Miss Dunbar — rowed me ashore — after they'd taken you," Floyd said, sitting up and clasping his hands about his knees. "The way she sat, not crying at all, but with her eyes sort of wet and yet minding what she was about, and pulling just as smooth and coming up just as straight — I remember looking at her wrists as she gripped the oars, and seeing how tanned they were by the sun — and small. I wanted to touch them, I remember; I don't know why, except somehow to let her know I was sorry and would like to help her if I could. It seems foolish, but I guess that was it; anyway, I've always remembered how I wanted to touch those little brown wrists. And then I realized I didn't dare — and I wondered if I'd ever dare — do that sort of thing. I've often wondered since. But how it must feel — to have done it all — even before you've graduated — to — to be so complete!"

"Oh, you'll go and do it some day," Stewart laughed, "just as soon as you've seen the girl. That's the trouble; you've never yet seen the girl."

"I suppose that's it," Floyd said; but even as he spoke, he was thinking of Lydia, and the thought brought her before him with a poignant vividness, — as she had been that day in the boat, as she had appeared to him later among the trees, radiant yet in tears, and said to him, "You will be a hero, always;" as she had stood one evening innocently in his arms, teaching him to dance. He had not many memories of her, for since coming to college he had spent his summers in Canada or abroad and most of his short winter vacations elsewhere than in Avalon; but now he realized with a vague sadness that no other memories of his life had the charm of these. He tried not to show any trace of sadness.

"To be so complete!" he reiterated, and Stewart caught the reverent feeling hidden in the wondering jocoseness of his tone. "It doesn't seem right at your age, Stewart, to be so complete."

IV

HALKET AND COMPANY

FLOYD climbed to a point on the hillside above the last row of houses, and then turned to look down on what was to be the scene of his labors.

It was a hot July day, and as the climb had started the perspiration, he took off his hat and wiped his forehead, not reluctant to defer for a moment the view. Behind him rose a bare slope, with only a few weeds growing out of the gullied and stony soil; below him, its streets slanting up and along the hillside, was the town of New Rome. From the height Floyd looked over the tops of the houses, down upon his grandfather's mills, the steel works of Halket and Company, the enterprise that had built and made New Rome.

"What a huge great smirch it is!" he murmured.

The "works" filled the arc of a mile curve made by the Yolin River, of which Floyd could see only a narrow yellow strip. The mills, mostly corrugated iron sheds, with red sides and black, sloping roofs, and the machine-shops and mill offices, buildings of yellow fire-brick, were pitched together, lengthwise, sidewise; railroad tracks, congested with freight cars, subtended the river arc and formed the inner boundary; other tracks wove in among the mills. In the centre of all was the greatest of the open-hearth furnaces — a huge shed, bearing twenty-two high black chimneys, from each of which a purulent yellow smoke was issuing. Hundreds of chimneys, varying in height and size, broke and confused the vision; some of them stood silent and breathless, but from many smoke was pouring, smoke of all colors as it took the rays of the sun, smoke of but one dull gray as it spread and merged above the chimney line. At the farther end towered the stacks of the blast furnaces, dull red monsters with bloated bodies tapering up to sloping shoulders and narrow throats; even while Floyd looked towards them a car ascended spider-like the webby strands of the incline, pitched forward, and vomited its load of ore into the funnel. Then it slid down again deftly, complacently, scuttling with an apparent human intelligence for another load. Here and there through openings in the sheds appeared the dull cruel glow of red-hot iron; and from a tower that capped the sloping roof of one of the mills blazed an intermittent flame. The clash of great hammers, the shriek of the blast, the throb of mighty engines, the rattle of huge chains, the trundling and jarring of locomotives and cars mingled in discordant, varying, but always continuous clamor.

Under the canopy of smoke that spread high above the mills, the opposite shore of the river revealed itself — hilly as this, but thinly settled and descending almost bare to the water's edge. On the ridge there were a few scattering trees; and an occasional frame house enjoyed a prominence to which neither its size nor its architecture would have entitled it. These houses were the outlying edge of the city of Avalon, eight miles down the river, a city of workshops and forges, indicated by the smoky blur that limited the view in that direction. Below the works a bridge crossed the river, and Floyd saw a trolley car passing slowly over it.

For all that was squalid and grimy in the aspect of the place, there was little that was human; and this fact commanded in Floyd a kind of awe. The reverberating noises of the mills, the scream of steam, the slow, perpetual unfurling of smoke, the trundling cars of stone and ore without visible hand to guide or control, the swinging of huge cranes and beams, — and then in comparison the tininess, the unimportance of the scattering human forms passing in the mill-yards, made it seem as if mighty forces had been put in operation and then abandoned to their fate.

No less dehumanized was the town. Lying on the hillside, it was empty and lifeless. A few children played in the streets, a few women toiled here and there up the hill; but apathy, as if initiative had been crushed by the nearness to elemental and tremendous forces, lay over New Rome.

Yet even as this singular desolation was impressing itself on Floyd, something happened close at hand suggesting that there was life here, and that it was not always in shadow. From the door of the green frame house just below him — the last house up the hill — a girl issued singing; her head was uncovered, and Floyd's attention was fixed by her gorgeous hair. It was brilliantly, radiantly red; in the whole panorama of the view there had been before not one beautiful detail to emerge from the overpowering black ugliness; yet now, suddenly, there had appeared this, which caught at once Floyd's admiring eyes.

He stood quite near, but the girl, coming out with definite purpose, did not see him; she stopped beside the blackened young peach-tree in the front yard and looked up. Floyd, following her eyes, observed that they rested on one large peach — the only one that the tree bore. Her face showed a childish desire and an equally childish hesitation; she put up her hand and rose on tip-toe, but though she stretched her arm and stood for a moment quivering, the peach was just beyond her grasp. She dropped back with an air of petulance; then bending over, she hunted on the ground for a stick, and finding one, took aim and hurled it, with an awkward push-motion, at which Floyd was amused. The branch shook and the peach jumped, but that was all. She looked round in despair, and saw Floyd; then, with a very stiff show of indifference, she began to saunter about the tree, as if she expected to find something lying on the ground, but had no particular interest in the search.

Floyd came near and leaned upon the fence. " Would you like to have that peach?" he asked. "I think I could get it."

She turned and looked at him with disconcerting composure. She had a good white complexion, a little freckled, large blue eyes, and a perfectly able mouth.

"Oh, thank you, I don't really care about it," she said.

Then, as if to show that she was not quite lacking in appreciation, she smiled. And with the smile her expression of self-sufficiency disappeared, and was succeeded by one of shyness and dependence. Floyd raised his hat and started away.

" Do you suppose," she called after him, in a hesitating voice, "you could tell me if it was really ripe?"

He turned and she was smiling at him, with a more open friendliness. He entered the yard and stretched his hand up for the peach, but with the tips of his fingers he could barely touch it. " Usually a ripe peach drops when you shake the branch," he said. " This is so black you can't tell by looking at it."

"Yes," she answered, " things get awfully smoky up here."

He caught the branch and drew it down.

" I should call it pretty ripe," he said. " It might be better in a day or two. It's a fine big one."

She seemed in doubt, while he waited for the word to pluck it or to let go.

"I wanted it for my mother," she explained. " This is her birthday. It's the only peach there's been on the tree this year, — it's been a bad peach year, you know, — and then anyway things don't grow very well here. I'd been watching it and thinking it might be just about right for her birthday."

"Here," said Floyd, " feel it for yourself."

He dragged the branch down a little more, and standing on tip-toe she made her investigations.

"Oh," she said; "it's pretty soft. And I think mother would like it just because it's her birthday."

She broke the stem. "It will look better when it's washed. I wish I could give you half of it for helping me, — but —"

"Indeed I wouldn't spoil a birthday present," he answered.

"Thank you," she said; and with a nod and another demure little smile she went into the house.

Floyd loitered a moment by the fence; the sign in an upper window, "Room to Let," had caught his attention. He glanced, too, about the trim yard; the peach-tree was in the corner; in front of the door was a bed of petunias, sweetwilliams, and verbenas; at the side of the house was a small trellis covered with grapevines, and more grape-vines screened the porch. He detected now a feminine touch in the aspect of the place that gave him a pang of compassion and sympathy. What discouragement must have met all their painstaking little efforts to give it some prettiness and charm! He glanced at his hand; grasping the branch of the peach-tree had blackened it.

In the large office building at the foot of the hill and directly opposite the bridge which led over the railroad tracks into the works, Floyd found the superintendent, Mr. Gregg, a grave, deliberate man, big of body, with a massive head and an iron-gray beard, parted in the middle and combed out into two prongs. His face lighted up when he greeted Floyd, but afterwards relapsed into its usual serious gravity; the cares of his position were evidently never far from his mind. Something of Gregg's record Floyd knew; it was that of one who had entered the works as a boy, and by faithfulness, industry, and ability attained this important place.

"You're coming in with us, your grandfather tells me," he said to Floyd. "Have you any ideas about where you would like to begin?"

"None," said Floyd. "My grandfather feels that I ought to start about where he did."

"Yes," said Gregg slowly. "Yes. That's a maxim that is much esteemed in Avalon." His hesitating tone showed that personally he questioned its wisdom; and Floyd, in spite of his respect for his grandfather's opinion, warmed toward the superintendent at this indication of an enlightened point of view. "I think," Gregg proceeded, "you might spare yourself the blast furnaces. We can put you in one of the open-hearth mills — say, Number Two."

"I should rather not be given any special advantages," Floyd said.

"Oh," Gregg answered, with a smile, tipping back in his chair and stroking first one prong of his beard and then the other, "a man that goes into this business had better not reject any good thing that's offered him. You'll find it hard enough — and different enough from college and abroad. I suppose you would like to go through the works? You'll find they have grown a little since you last went through, two years ago."

He wrote out a pass and handed it to Floyd. "Come in and see me before you go home," he said.

Then he turned seriously to his work, — a man of mild nature harassed by having to be often stern and hard.

In the little house at the entrance to the bridge, the company policeman took Floyd's pass, and reading his name upon it, touched his hat. "Keep a sharp lookout on the tracks, sir," he said. He spoke with reason; an empty sleeve was pinned across his breast.

There was a roadway from the bridge almost to the bank of the river; there it stopped at a tangle of tracks which spread and branched out on either side, running round and through the mills. Floyd walked up the tracks along the river-bank. He passed idle trains of freight cars, he looked up at the donkey engines that trundled back and forth dragging the ladles to and from the blast furnaces; brakemen, switchmen, engineers, laborers among the heaps of scrap iron and limestone threw him a curious glance as he went by. Each shed had its own fierce noise, a rumble, a thud, a clang, or a shriek, repeated and repeated and repeated, here rapidly, here at measured and deliberate intervals. The mingling of sound and the increasing maze of tracks bewildered Floyd, and he kept looking behind him with a sense that he might at any moment be borne down by some ungovernable mass.

Two blast furnaces towered before him, connected with each other by half a dozen high red stacks, in which the blast was heated and reheated. Between them and the river were the heaps of ore and limestone and coke, which the indefatigable little climbing cars fed into the furnace. A steamboat and two barges were moored at the bank, discharging a cargo of coke; a crane lifted up a great scoop that had been filled, and two of the laborers on the barges, released for a moment from toil, fell to at good-natured fisticuffs. Floyd stopped to watch them; they ducked and dodged about on the loose footing of coke; one got the other's head under his arm and began knuckling it. But by that time the crane had dumped its scoop-load, and with inflexible insistence had swung back demanding more; the laborers stumbled again to their task, and Floyd moved on to Open-Hearth Mill Number Two, where his apprenticeship was to begin.

This was a long shed with a row of twelve yellow fire-brick ovens along each side and a chaotic space between — containing excavations, cranes, sunken iron bowls, sand heaps, and narrow-gauge tracks. Floyd walked down the broad steel-plate pavement in front of one row of furnaces. Each had its iron door with round open eyehole, through which glared a light so blinding that the man looking in to examine the condition of the "heat" had to wear black glasses. Now and then he would catch up a long-handled spoon, draw out a little of the "heat," and spill it on the pavement, testing it. This man was the melter; and he

HALKET AND COMPANY 53

had charge of six furnaces. Under him at each furnace were three helpers, who fired and fed and stirred and tapped the "heats." One of them, having closed the iron door after the last scoop of steel had been emptied, seated himself on a bench near where Floyd was standing and lighted a pipe. He looked like a communicative soul, — the first of the workmen who had seemed to have that character, — and after two or three puffs on his pipe, he said to Floyd, —

"The fire in that furnace ain't been out in fourteen months."

"Pretty steady going," Floyd said. "I suppose it's better, though, for the furnaces to be kept burning than to lie idle."

"Better for the furnaces, better for the men." He seemed a sententious as well as cheerful person; there was a good-humored twinkle in his eyes that Floyd liked. He wore a blue cloth cap; he was a man of thirty-five, perhaps, short, thick-set, with a flat nose and a square, cleanshaven jaw; his undershirt, thrown open at the breast, showed a skin whiter than that of most of the other men.

"We use natural gas in the furnaces," he said to Floyd. "No coal, no coke — except over at the blast furnace."

Floyd caught the man winking to another, who drew near, and he suspected that this urbane volunteering of information was prompted by a desire to have amusement with an uneducated visitor. He was not unwilling to furnish this, and he displayed interest at the idea of natural gas.

"I suppose you have frightful explosions sometimes," he said.

"Yes; fierce. You see them masons down there — working on that eighth furnace? Well, that was because the gas got turned on when nobody was looking, blowed the front off the furnace, and took off a Dago's head. But worse than the explosions is the fumes."

"The fumes?" Floyd asked wonderingly.

"Yep. Danger of their overpowerin' a man. And a man never knows when he's goin' to be overpowered — not till it drops him. Ain't that so, Bill? Why, look here —"

He rose impressively and led Floyd out behind the furnace. The one next below was being tapped; that is, the liquid steel, or "heat," was being drawn off into the huge bowl set in the cavity just behind. As it flowed in, hissing and leaping up in flame, a man standing a little back from the brink tossed in at intervals fragments of steel and chunks of limestone. Each lump sent up a lashing burst of flame.

"There!" said Floyd's informant. "There was a fellow doing just what that man is. He was a rash sort of fool — always showing off and showing how nothing ever troubled his nerve. He'd stand on the edge of a thing like that — stand on one foot and then wave the other one out over the heat — just to let us know he wasn't afraid. If a place was too hot for a man to stand in, he'd go and stand there and let on he liked it. Always lookin' for trouble — that was him. Well, one day he was pitchin' scrap into the heat as it was being drawed off, and nothing would do but he must stand right up on the very brink — step up and take a look."

"It doesn't seem possible a man could stand so close as that," said Floyd with due innocence.

"That's because you ain't used to it. I was off just about there, making ready to tap my furnace; I happened to look up and it struck me he was kind of queer. There was a kind of blankness on his face, and he was standing holding a chunk of stone like this, — just hanging in his fingers, — and next thing it slipped right out of 'em, glanced off the edge, and plunked in. And then all of a sudden he slumped together and pitched forward, head first. He never made no sound."

"How awful!" said Floyd.

"Well, if he was overcome by the fumes, as we all thought, he probably did n't suffer none. Of course, we never strained out so much as a toe-nail. And there was a funny thing about that heat, — it qualified as first-class steel. Likely he's now helping to hold up some skyscraper in New York."

Floyd expressed his horror and his hope that the men were generally more cautious.

"Oh, we take care. But the fumes is something you can't exactly guard against." He was evidently on the verge of another story, when the melter spied round the corner of the furnace and summoned him.

Floyd strolled the length of the mill and passed out at the farther end. The afternoon was waning; the sun stood above the hill across the river, red through the smoke; except for a few open patches here and there, the mill-yards were in shadow. But within the works there was no slackening of energy, and for the first time it struck Floyd with a sense of awfulness that night might fall and that still the hammers would ring and the forges glow and the blast shriek — that here was a town which might never be all at rest.

Through an opening in one of the buildings he noticed a red, weaving thread; he entered and found himself in the rod-mill. Here, instead of the ingots, billets of steel, a little larger than an ordinary brick, were rolled. A man took the white-hot billet out of the furnace in tongs hung by a chain, and pushed it, suspended in the air, to the first roller. He in turn received it in his tongs, thrust it through the rolls to his partner, who caught it and returned it; back and forth they passed it, drawing it out each time; then it was put through a second set of rolls, and then through a third, each time a different pair of men handling it with tongs in the manner required by its constantly increasing length. At last the little white-hot block came out a squirming red serpent twenty feet long, and lay curved and still.

56 THE ANCIENT GRUDGE

The work of the rollers was dexterous and pretty. The white-hot billet came hissing and menacing through the press. The roller stood close, caught it with his tongs just in front of his right leg, drew back a step, and then shot it forward and through. A misstep, a slip of the hand on the tongs, a sudden failure of the eye, and the white-hot metal would drop on the bungler's foot and sear it to the ankle. The men worked rapidly, each one seeming to hurry the next, harassed by anxiety or by eagerness to turn out a larger and yet larger number of rods, for by tonnage were they paid.

Only one did Floyd notice who seemed not only unworried, but even nonchalant and gay in the performance of his work. This was the younger of the two men at the first set of rolls, the one who received the billet from the furnace-man. The others stood tense or nervous to grapple with the steel; he displayed an easy grace, he did not crouch with tongs already open, but waited quietly erect, caught and stepped back with the same motion, passed the steel forward with a lithe swing, and fell into position, resting but ready. He was heavy and strong, and at the same time cleanly built; his weight, as Floyd could see from the outline of chest and hips and thighs, was more of muscle than of bone. Blackened as was his face, it had a cheerful look; it seemed the face of a boy to whom this work was still, in spite of his expertness, a novelty, and who found somewhat the same sport in catching hot blocks of steel as he might have found in catching a ball. He came over to the tank of greenish, scum-covered water near which Floyd was standing, and plunged his tongs into it. Floyd glanced at his bare arms; the sweat was streaming down them, the muscles seemed oiled and glistening. He looked at Floyd with a genial smile and addressed him with a particularly outrageous oath. That it was hot was the burden of his remark. Then he hastened back to his place and caught the next billet on the run.

It was growing late. Floyd turned and made his way out of the yards across the bridge. The one-armed policeman at the wicket saluted him again as he passed. He went to the office of the superintendent, who looked up with a smile and said, " Well ? "

" I 'll be ready to start at the beginning of the week," Floyd answered.

" All right; report to the foreman of Number Two on Monday morning. You 'll live out here, I suppose ? "

" Yes; I wondered if you could suggest a boarding-house — "

" We keep a list," said the superintendent, and from one of the drawers in his desk he produced some typewritten pages. " Any of these places is all right."

" There 's a house at the top of this street — the last house," Floyd said. " I liked its looks; is that here? I made a note of the number. Yes, this is it; I think I 'll go there. Good-night, Mr. Gregg."

The superintendent rose and held out his hand.

" Good-night and good luck," he answered.

It was nearly six o'clock, and low as the sun was, the heat seemed not to have abated. The intermittent breeze of the day had ceased and a heavy sultriness prevailed; the western sky was brassy, and the smoke hung low over the river — cupped as it were between the hills. Down the sloping streets of the town men were going to their work, carrying their wicker lunch-baskets or tin pails — most of them in their undershirts, with their coats upon their arms. New Rome had now a more busy aspect than earlier in the afternoon, when Floyd had surveyed it from the hill. He strolled up one street and along another and another, but there was no need of much travel to acquaint oneself with New Rome. It lay spread out upon the hillside, open for any one to read.

It was a feudal town. The central block on the hillside was occupied by the house and grounds of the superintendent of the works. The house was very large, of yellow brick, of a Moorish type of architecture; the grounds were terraced, in green, well-kept lawns that seemed to thrive in spite of smoke and dirt. In the block below were six smaller yellow brick houses, also of a Moorish type of architecture — smaller, and yet large, and each having its own spacious grass plot. In these dwelt the superintendents of the largest mills. One block lower down there were ten yellow brick houses of very respectable size, occupied by the lesser superintendents. Then, above and below, came houses of wood, for the foremen and rollers and melters, more numerous, all pretty much of a pattern, all prosperous looking. Beyond these were smaller houses still, dwindling down to the wretched two-room hovels, painted red or whitewashed, which clung just outside the high board fence that marked the mill inclosure.

The town was full of monuments to Colonel Halket's beneficence. Above the general superintendent's house rose the Halket Free Public Library, again of yellow brick, though of a subdued Moorishness. In one wing of it was an auditorium, in another, club-rooms and a gymnasium. The Halket Hotel stood at the bottom of the hill, opposite the company's office. Halket Park was a large inclosed field adjoining the mill inclosure; a baseball ground was laid out here, and it held two stands for spectators.

New Rome was a model town. And now, walking along its streets, confronting it and the problem it presented to him, Floyd felt depressed, for the first time since he had been brought up to meet this problem.

His grandfather had created the place and the industry; his was the honor and his had been the joy of creation. And for the grandson, what was left? Nothing except to stand ready with a hand to guide or restrain, and let the great machine run itself. The whole organization was complete and efficient, and merely to be occupied with maintaining it seemed a tame and languid task.

There was nothing for Floyd to build. Worst of all, he had a discouraged feeling that this was not the kind of thing that he would have most cared to build.

The six o'clock whistle blew while Floyd was still walking the homogeneous streets and indulging in these meditations. The "day turn" was at an end, the "night turn" was beginning. Floyd had a thought of the diversity of workmen he had seen that afternoon, of the men who were giving up their lives to the performance of some trifling task, — spooning along hot metal in a trough, kicking hot steel rods to one side, measuring steel plates, pulling levers. Floyd thought of them all compassionately. He did not pity himself for having to work with them; indeed, he still looked forward to that experience as to an adventure in which the interesting would counterbalance the unpleasant. But the years afterwards — when he had ceased to work with his hands and these men were growing old in his service, and other men, young and with life to face, were entering it — these years loomed suddenly before Floyd, and their image seemed sombre and reproachful to his mind.

It was growing late; Floyd betook himself to the house where he had seen the girl with the red hair. When he rang the bell, she came to the door.

"I am looking for a room," he said. "I remembered the sign in your window and thought I would come here."

She had recognized him, and as he spoke he thought that the expression of her face became unfriendly.

"If you will step inside," she said in a tone which held out no welcome, "I will speak to my mother."

He entered a cramped and dark hallway and followed her into the parlor. There she left him and ran upstairs. The folding-doors between the parlor and the dining-room were open; through them Floyd saw the table set for three, and on it in the centre a white frosted cake, surrounded with a palisade of pink candles. He hoped very much that the girl was not going to be unfriendly, for already he liked the family; he wondered who the third member was.

He seated himself in a rocking-chair on a patchwork cushion. There was an oak bookcase with glass doors in one corner, in which a set of Scott and another of Dickens were conspicuous. It also held a small "handy volume" set of Shakespeare. On the marble-topped centre table beside the large Bible was a copy of "Ben-Hur," bound in alligator skin. On the mantel was a clutter of shells, little china figures, matchsafes, deep-sea crustacea, vases, and above it hung an engraving of the Madonna of the Chair. On the wall opposite was a still-life watercolor in a stout gilt frame, the subject, strawberries pouring out of a tin pail that lay on its side. There was an upright piano, and in the corner beside it a bass viol in a green baize cover. All the length of the top of the piano, propped against the wall, ran a line of photographs. The carpet was a faded gray, the wall-paper a cheerless yellow, the window-curtains were of lace, white and clean and with thick-looking mended places. Floyd had leisure enough to examine all that the room contained.

By and by he heard footsteps tripping down the stairs; then the girl entered.

"Don't rise," she said haughtily. "My mother will be down in a moment."

She passed into the dining-room, where she busied herself about the table. Floyd glanced at her from time to time; her movements were quick and decisive. He was beginning to suspect the cause of her abruptness with him; no doubt she thought he was trying to force an acquaintance. He sat, therefore, meek and patient, and only now and then threw furtive glances at her. She had changed her dress of the afternoon, and wore something now that was light and airy-looking and sprinkled over with red crescents. The sleeves, fringed with lace, reached only to her elbows; there was a blue sash round her waist; and her hair, instead of being piled loosely on her head, was coiled low down against the nape of her neck. She was, Floyd thought, a very handsome and imperial looking girl.

Her mother came down the stairs, a plain and insignificant old woman, dressed in black, grayhaired, with gold-rimmed spectacles and an upward, short-sighted perk of her faded face. Her fingers were rheumatic and twisted, and coarsened by hard work; Floyd noticed this as he took her timidly offered hand. But like her daughter, she had an indefinably festive air, imparted, perhaps, by the white cuffs on the black sleeves, and the bit of lace at her throat, fastened with a gold pin.

"I came," said Floyd, "to look at rooms."

"Yes," she answered hesitatingly. "I have a room to let. I don't know, though, as I want to let it just for a few days; I'd like to get somebody who'd take it by the month or year."

"If I find it satisfactory," said Floyd, "I should want to take it for a year."

"Oh," said the woman, confused by this unexpected reply. Well—" Her daughter spoke up.

"The room does n't look very well, mother, but perhaps," and she turned to Floyd, "you'll be able to tell if it would suit."

She led the way upstairs. Somewhat bewildered by her sudden change of manner, he followed at her heels. Behind them the older woman toiled slowly. The room was under the roof and had two gable windows, neither of which, to judge by the hot, close air of the place, had been open all summer.

"My!" said the girl, and she raised one and then the other.

The furniture was meagre, an iron bedstead, a brown chest of drawers and a washstand, a small pine table and one chair. There was a fireplace with an asbestos lining for natural gas.

"There is n't a window in town that gives a better view," said the girl, "if you care for the view." The grimness of her humor indicated that she had not quite shaken off distrust.

"There is always the sky," Floyd said.

"Generally," she answered.

He said he would like to sign a lease for a year. The older woman appeared embarrassed, the younger indifferent.

"I generally ask for references," the girl's mother said at last. "I suppose you're in the company's office?"

"No," Floyd admitted. "I'm just going to begin in one of the mills. I think, though, the superintendent, Mr. Gregg, would vouch for me."

"Oh." The woman seemed reassured. "Some relation of his, I presume?" — for shrinking though she was, she had, as Floyd afterwards found out, her full measure of inquisitiveness.

"No, no relation," he replied. "But he found a place for me in one of the open-hearth mills."

"Well, if Mr. Gregg says it's all right;" she added in apology, "You see, two women living alone, we have to be careful."

The daughter interjected, —

"You forgot to say, mother, that payment is always a month in advance."

"Of course," Floyd said. "That is what I expected. I came prepared." He took out a roll of bills.

There was still an awkward pause; then the girl spoke frankly.

"You don't somehow look as if you belonged at the mills."

"Don't I?" Floyd laughed. "Well, you wait till you see me next Monday."

She looked at him steadily, and surrendered before the open honesty and amusement of his laugh. "All right," she said. "I'll wait and see how you look then." And as they descended the stairs, she remarked to him, "That peach *was* ripe."

"Yes," her mother said, turning round, "Letty told me you were the young man that got it for her. And it was a nice peach; I enjoyed it."

"That peach-tree and the grapevines and the garden were why I came here," Floyd said. "Not because I hope to eat up your fruit — but your place looked so much prettier than the others."

At this the girl gave him a most friendly smile. "Mother does most of the tending to it," she said.

"Now, Letty!" her mother cried protestingly. And then she broke off into a startling and independent speech. "She's giving me a birthday supper — I guess maybe you saw the cake. We'd be happy, so long as you're soon to be one of the family, so to speak, if you'd stay to it."

Letty failed to second the invitation, and Floyd suspected from her expression that she did not approve of it. He regretted that he had to go to Avalon, and then he said that he would just sign the lease and be off, Mrs. — Mrs. — ?

"Bell — Mrs. Edward Bell. Oh, we won't bother with no lease. Just so long as you say you'll take it for a year and you've paid a month in advance, why, that's all right. Just you leave your name, and I'll see the room is read up for you."

A few minutes before, Floyd was wandering the streets, melancholy and oppressed by the responsibilities to which he was heir; now he delivered up the card bearing his name with a secret pleasure and pride. Had he not at such a moment enjoyed these sensations, he would surely have had none of his grandfather in him.

Mrs. Bell's demonstration at reading the name was gratifyingly melodramatic. She fell back against the wall of the cramped hallway. "Mr. Floyd Halket!" she exclaimed. "Read it, Letty! Oh, my goodness!

To think of Colonel Halket's grandson coming here to live!"

"But," asked Floyd, with some curiosity, "what makes you think I'm his grandson?"

"Why, would n't I know the name?" cried the widow. "And all about the family? Who in New Rome would not? The idea of me asking you to sit down to the supper-table!"

"Indeed," said Miss Bell, quite haughtily, "I did n't approve of it at the time, mother; but I see nothing wrong about it now."

"I hope you'll be asking me just about every night," Floyd said gallantly. "You know I want board here as well as a room."

"And there's no joke about your coming?" cried Mrs. Bell.

"Not the least."

"Well," Mrs. Bell said, "if you can put up with it here — "

There was a sudden rattling tattoo played with stout fingers on the glass of the front door. The girl stepped forward and opened it, and with the greeting, "Hello, Let," a young man entered. As he took off his hat and showed his light straight hair and red face, Floyd recognized, in spite of the white collar and blue coat which now adorned him, the young roller in the rod-mill.

"What is it, Mrs. Bell? — your thirty-fifth?" the newcomer asked cheerfully. "Many happy returns."

While he spoke he ran his eyes over Floyd with a glance of recognition.

Floyd turned and held out his hand to Mrs. Bell. "I won't keep you any longer from lighting those candles in the dining-room," he said. "I'll send my things Saturday and come out here Sunday night to sleep, if that's convenient. Good-by."

"I suppose," interrupted Miss Bell, "you might as well meet now as later. Mr. Farrell, this is Mr. Halket.

Mr. Farrell's a neighbor, and Mr. Halket's the new boarder, and going to work next week at the Open Hearth," she explained to each of them in turn.

"I mind seeing you this afternoon," said Mr. Farrell, "and it seems like I had heard your name before, Mr. Halket."

"I shouldn't wonder; it seems a common one out here," Floyd answered.

"Well, there's no shame in being a poor relation of such folks, if that's what you are," Farrell assured him consolingly.

"*Hugh!*" cried Mrs. Bell, agonized, and Letty, clapping her handkerchief to her mouth, choked back her laughter.

"Made a break, have I?" asked Farrell; and as he looked round, his face lighted up intelligently. "Well, I suppose, then, you ain't a *poor* relation. And that's better yet, and it makes no difference with me."

"Then I'm glad to meet you," said Floyd, as they shook hands.

"You won't mind my talk," Farrell promised him. "The only thing that puts a brake on it is the presence of ladies."

"A sort of hot-air brake," suggested Floyd in the slang of the period.

"One on me," Farrell cried. "One on me — eh, Let?"

He was still chuckling and Mrs. Bell was still aghast at his daring and at the use of slang by Colonel Halket's grandson when Floyd passed out of the house.

V

FLOYD BEGINS AT THE BOTTOM

In Avalon the very rich and the miserably poor lived upon the same street. It entered the town at the western end low down by the river, skirting the foundries and mills; it emerged at the eastern end upon a hilltop, which was covered with great houses and wide gardens and lawns. Floyd, looking out of the trolley car, saw an almost precipitous slope ascending on one side, descending on the other, with houses flattening themselves against the wall, seeming to hang on one another's shoulders, boosting, clinging hard for toe-hold, — some with only the top story peering above the sidewalk, others mounting for two stories in front and dropping down for four behind. They all seemed temporary, as if a gust of wind would sweep them down in an avalanche of rotten wood and broken brick. Below them were the abysmal iron mills, in a continuous, three-mile line. At this hour the families, having finished supper, were strewn along the sidewalks or crowded together upon the doorsteps; the children playing hopscotch or dancing to the tune of a hand-organ, the women resting and gossiping, the men smoking their pipes, reading newspapers, sitting most of them coatless and collarless. They had brought chairs out upon the sidewalk and were tipped back against the house walls, or against their picket fences, for there were some who had reserved and fenced in a few feet of slanting, weedy green. The young men loafed in front of the saloons. Along this street of squalid, swarming life the car traveled with incessantly clanging gong; then it climbed a hill and drew away from the river and the iron works, and entered a neighborhood of patient, dingy, retiring poverty. And at last, at the summit of another hill, the closely built-up city ceased; shrillness and smoke did not reach here; and along the shaded street and off over the wide gardens and lawns that stretched away from it were the cool silence and smell of the benignant summer. The hydrangea bushes were in bloom; the gardeners were sprinkling lawns and flowers, and the spraying water trickled pleasantly upon the quiet of the evening; the shade-trees, maple and oak and poplar, were still and dark against the lingering yellow rim of the sky.

"Halket's Road," called the conductor; the car stopped and Floyd alighted in front of a great arched gateway of yellow brick. The two iron wings were wide open, in hospitable contrast to the fence of eight-foot iron spears which ran for several hundred yards along the pavement, and to which the lawn descended in an open, gradual slope. Except for one great clump of willows, every tree and shrub had been uprooted in this sweep of acres; it was now all one clean, clear lawn, with just the horse-shoe of maples fringing the driveway, which ascended on one side and descended on the other. This double row of trees curving up over the distant hill concealed the house, but even in the dusk one could see from the street the terrace of the garden — a yellow brick wall against which grew grapevines, and above that the dim masses of the shrubs and flowers and low trees, and the great fountain playing in the centre.

Floyd walked up the smooth driveway between the rows of maples. He was tired and hungry and thinking of nothing but how good it would be to get into a bath and then in clean clothes sit down to dinner. He looked at his watch and quickened his steps; the family dined at half-past seven, and it was a quarter past seven now. Where the driveway turned toward the house, the hill that he had been ascending fell away slowly on the other side, and he looked down its slope upon the park that his grandfather had given to the city. Avalon as well as New Rome had its Halket Park. The electric lamps here had been lighted and shone at intervals among the trees. In the near foreground the Casino was illuminated and the strains of band music came faintly from it up the hill. Floyd, hurrying toward the house, had a moment's thought of the families he had passed who spent their summer evenings in the street. The city park was at the doors of the rich, and remote from the poor. "Downtown," where the poor lived, there was no place for parks — not a green square or public grass-plot; land could not be wasted upon such purposes. There was not much gayety in Avalon.

The Halket house had not been built; it had been contrived from time to time. Its one homogeneous feature was the yellow brick, for which in all his constructive undertakings its owner had so marked a liking. Originally a square building with a mansard roof and conventional tower, it now bristled with additions; on each side a new wing had been built, and these wings had in turn received accessions, — on the right, a great dome-like music-room, on the left a long, flat-topped bowling-alley. Jutting out in front from one end of the piazza was the conservatory, and projecting from the upper part of the house were afterthoughts in the way of bath-rooms and canopied galleries.

Floyd crossed the loggia of red tiles that had the year before replaced the old wooden piazza, pushed open the iron gateway and then the ponderous iron-bound and barred door, and entered the house. The hall had recently been done over into what Colonel Halket termed "early baronial;" its dark panels were hung with tapestries and armor, under which were heavy carved stalls; at the back rose the winding staircase; great candelabra of twisted iron stood on the newel-posts, every antler tipped with an incandescent light. Over the stairway was a stained-glass window, representing the combat of Saint

George and the Dragon, and under this was the Halket coat-of-arms, for the Colonel, whose knowledge of his family went back but two generations to his blacksmith grandfather, had engaged a professional genealogist to make researches. These had resulted in the gratifying discovery that the Colonel was a lineal descendant of Sir John Hakluyt, the Elizabethan voyager. "Why the devil did this Samuel Halket back in 1720 want to change a distinguished name!" exclaimed the Colonel, poring over the records; and he set about making a collection of all the early editions of Sir John's Travels, and of contemporary books in which there was reference to his ancestor. Eventually he came to have the most extensive library of Hakluytiana in America; and being a thorough person he made himself familiar with Sir John's career.

Floyd ran up the red-carpeted stairs to his room, which was not early baronial at all, but had matting on the floor and a small writing-desk in one corner, half a dozen sporting prints and a couple of photographs upon the walls; he shed his dusty clothes hastily and stepped into his bathroom under the shower, where on the marble slabs he soaped and scrubbed himself and whistled "Fair Harvard" — his one tune, which he had acquired with great difficulty and patriotism, and which was his invariable companion in the bath. Then he dressed by leaps and bounds, and just as he was slipping into his dinner-coat the electric bell in his room rang, and he opened the door while the chimes downstairs were still sounding. He congratulated himself on not being late; it annoyed Colonel Halket exceedingly if one of the family was tardy to a meal.

Floyd entered the library, kissed his grandmother and made a quick playful military salute to his grandfather, who gravely returned it. A stately pair they were, carrying off their years with youthful grace; Mrs. Halket, with a tiny cap on her gray head, very tall and slender in her black dress — indeed, with the same figure that she had had thirty years before, — with a light Indian shawl thrown over her bare shoulders, with her head held as proudly as ever on her slim, unwrinkled neck, yet with her gray eyes and pale face showing a kindly soul; her husband, big, deep-chested, with white hair carefully parted on one side and then allowed to wave plume-like and unbrushed, with a face lean, and of a hard, sunburned brown, with lines across the brow and about the mouth that gave him an expression of thoughtfulness as well as of decision, with white mustache and imperial, and dark, deep-set eyes, of a singular piercing luminousness, but always piercing, never softening into a merry and twinkling light, never really accompanying his smile — and he smiled now at Floyd. He was striking, impressive, very handsome; he could hardly have been put into a gathering of men where he would not have been one of the two or three most commanding. Avalon was preëminently a town in which the richest must have been the leading citizen; it was extraordinary that this man should in all respects have the natural outward gifts to carry such distinction. It is quite probable that the professional genealogist was an inventive diplomat, but no one who ever saw Colonel Halket could doubt that blood as noble as Sir John Hakluyt's flowed in his veins.

In the dining-room, the butler was standing behind Mrs. Halket's chair; behind each of the other chairs waited a footman. The family entered to their places; with a concerted movement, the three servants thrust the three chairs forward; the family sat down. They bowed their heads; behind them the servants stood erect, staring; Colonel Halket said in his deep, musical voice, "Bless, O Lord, this food to Thy use, for Jesus Christ's sake. Amen."

Then, after this moment of stillness, there was brisk activity, — a shaking of napkins, a scurrying back of the servants, and a scurrying forward again with three plates of soup. Floyd fell to hungrily; his grandfather, more deliberate, asked in a complacent way, "And how did you find things, Floyd?"

"First-rate — booming," Floyd answered. "I've fixed it all up — had a good talk with Mr. Gregg — went into the works and watched the job that I'm to begin on next Monday — engaged a room — "

"Oh, Floyd!" His grandmother leaned back in her chair; she seemed distressed. "You're going to start in so soon?"

"Oh, we must n't coddle ourselves and spoil the boy," her husband said in his cheerful, authoritative voice. "The sooner he begins his apprenticeship, the sooner he'll be through with it. Open-Hearth Number Two, Gregg thought; was that it? — Hendricks, take away this soup; say to the cook that I'm surprised at his sending up soup that's burnt. Floyd, don't take any more of it; see, your grandmother can't touch it."

"I don't mind it," Floyd said. "I'm too hungry." Inwardly a whimsical question occurred to him, — whether after saying grace, one should reject in disfavor food that had possibly been blessed in answer to the prayer. He knew that it would be unwise to suggest this to his grandfather, but he thought he might amuse his grandmother with the query when they should be alone.

"There's one thing I can do," Mrs. Halket said, speaking in a resigned voice, "and that is, come out and see that you are comfortable in your rooms, Floyd. I do hope they are pleasant. I will help you to fix them up. I shall feel so much better if I know you're comfortable."

Floyd's eyes twinkled, and he reached out and stroked his grandmother's hand.

"I have the cosiest quarters in New Rome," he said, "and I won't allow you to do a thing to them. When I get tired, I'll move somewhere else. You see, Grandmother, when you're a mill-hand, you've got to live like one; — is n't that so, Grandfather?"

"That's the way I started," said the Colonel, nodding his head with vast approval. "And it's a good thing for a young fellow to know what plain and simple living is."

"Indeed, Robert, if you really think so, wouldn't it have been better to bring him up to have some experience of it before now?" cried Mrs. Halket.

"Am I such a tender little plant?" asked Floyd reproachfully. "I feel as if I had had some knocking round in my life."

"Oh, I know; boys will be boys, of course, and at school and college it was all well enough; I suppose you did knock round," said his grandmother with spirit. "And it was good for you. And though, as you and your grandfather know, I don't want you to go into the mills, I do not stand in the way, since your grandfather says it is necessary. But it isn't necessary for you to live — to live — oh, I don't know how — "

"And just because you don't know how, you think it's sure to be horrible," Floyd laughed.

"No, but in squalor and bareness and on poor food and with rough, coarse people; it's all wrong, Floyd; you don't know what you're doing."

"Now, listen," said Floyd, "and while you're listening sit up to the table like a good girl and pretend you like our food. I picked out my room because it was in the most attractive looking house in all New Rome, with a nice little lawn and garden and peach-tree in front, the best kept-up little place that I saw. It's a small room, of course, but I'll be comfortable enough in it. As for the rough, coarse people, — there are just two people in the house, — mother and daughter, — and I broke in on them while the girl was giving her mother a birthday supper and entertaining her young man. And he was a good fellow, too."

"That sounds better," conceded Mrs. Halket. "I'm glad you were so sensible. But anyway I shall go out and see what I can do to make the room attractive. We can drive out to-morrow."

"All right," said Floyd. "It will only make you unhappy, but if you insist. — You'll think the girl is quite a wonder, anyway — splendid red hair."

"Did you let them know who you were?" the Colonel asked.

"Yes, they found out."

"And how did they take it? A little surprised, were they — and agitated?"

Colonel Halket leaned forward, with an eager smile to hear the gratifying details. Floyd rehearsed them all; Colonel Halket was greatly amused upon hearing how overcome Mrs. Bell had been. He was less pleased to learn of the daughter's indifference and self-possession, and shook his head over it, though Mrs. Halket thought she must be a girl of some character — rather bright, too. "The young women of the present day," pronounced Colonel Halket, "are too independent — they have a tendency to fortify themselves against the proprieties — not to be deferential. In all classes."

"I should imagine," Floyd said, "from the way she looks and carries herself, that she's more used to getting deference than to giving it. She's handsome enough, too."

"When I was young," continued Colonel Halket, "the girl who was pert and had an air and all that was n't much courted; it was the quiet, gentle girl who was always pleased with any little attention and acted as if she never expected it and was n't used to having it, that was attractive to men."

"Robert," cried Mrs. Halket, with some asperity, "was I that kind of girl?"

Colonel Halket paused, somewhat confused, and then his face cleared in a smile. Only with his wife did he seem to have a simple humor, untainted by vanity or self-consciousness, always courtly in expression. "Now that you remind me of it, my dear," he said, "I do recollect some infirmities of spirit — I will not say of temper — on your part, which I should otherwise have forgotten. But just the same, Floyd," — and he spoke loudly behind his hand, — "your grandmother was quite a nice, attractive girl. What did you say is the landlady's name?"

"Bell," said Floyd. "Mrs. Edward Bell."

"We will look it up in the card-catalogue after dinner," his grandfather promised.

This card-catalogue was perhaps the crowning achievement of Colonel Halket's genius — or insanity — for organization. It required a room for itself. The name of every man who had ever worked in any capacity in the Halket Mills was registered; also his record — his time of entering employment, his promotions if any, his time of leaving the mills if he had left them, the cause, and, when it was known, his occupation since. When a man died his card was not removed; it remained to record the history of his family. The catalogue contained more than fifteen thousand names — all the past and present employees of the works. Once a month the registrar of the company came to Colonel Halket's house to go over the list, make such additions or corrections as he could, and bring it up to date.

After dinner, Floyd accompanied his grandparents into the long, high-raftered library. Books lined one side from floor to top, and their bright bindings and the leather chairs of cardinal red that were set about the great mahogany table gave the room a tone of warmth and cheerfulness. Here Colonel Halket read his evening newspaper, his wife took up a magazine, and Floyd, having mounted the little movable ladder, found on the top book-shelf "Richard Feverel," — the novel that he had already been through three times. With the book in his hand he stopped by his grandmother's chair to whisper in her ear the humorous query that had occurred to him during dinner; she laughed a little, but with an apprehensive glance towards her husband. Then Floyd lighted one of his grandfather's cigars and settled himself by an open window. Deep in the story, he did not notice that his grandfather had left the room; he looked up with some surprise when Colonel Halket stood before him holding a card in his hand and saying, —

"Here it is, Floyd; here's the record. Edward Bell was a machinist in the company's employ; drew twenty-five dollars a week; he died two years ago. Good workman; thrifty; left wife and daughter comfortably off. They still live in the same house. The daughter a year ago obtained a position in the Halket Library, and has made a satisfactory record there. Now we know what sort of people they are; it seems all right, Rebecca."

"Yes, that part of it," answered his wife; and Colonel Halket turned and walked into the next room to restore the card to its place.

Floyd's thoughts lapsed for a few moments from his book. What an untiring assiduity his grandfather had in tracking down details! what a memory for trivialities, as well as for real matters! what a wonderful devotion, even in the pettiest affairs, to the idea of organization! It had oppressed Floyd to find since his return from college how complicated life in the household must be — not so far as family relations were concerned, for they had remained singularly natural and simple, but in the mere ordering of one's day. His grandfather seemed to have introduced an elaborate formality into the most ordinary performances, and to take pleasure in its observance; Mrs. Halket supported him in it, Floyd suspected, glancing at her pale face, loyally, but a little wearily. Colonel Halket, as Floyd began to understand, caused to be observed towards himself, even in his most secluded and private moments, the ceremonious deference that he deemed due to the first citizen of Avalon. What pleased his vanity had also honestly become to his mind a duty. Floyd had an uncomfortable sense at times that there was something in this grotesque even to the verge of mania. Yet now, when he thought of the establishment which he had seen that afternoon, created, mills and town, out of nothing by this one man, carrying with it the hopes and fears and destinies of ten thousand souls, dominated still as it had been developed by one man, who had in his grasp every detail of its workings, every detail of its life, down even to the condition of its pensioners, it seemed then fitting, if it pleased him, that Colonel Halket should bear himself imperially and conduct his household on as stately principles as if it were a royal court. And Floyd had a glimmering perception that just as his grandfather had turned with more and more favor to this mode of life, by so much the more might Avalon feel that he was honoring it and be glad to exhibit him as its first citizen.

So the boy returned to the book that records the disaster of an attempt to build and guide a life by a system.

At half-past ten o'clock, chimes sounded remotely from the dining-room. Floyd laid aside his book; Colonel Halket took up the Bible and sat waiting. Presently the servants, men and women, fifteen or twenty in number, entered the room and stood in line across one end of it. Colonel Halket put on his glasses and read a chapter from Job; then, closing the Bible, he took the Prayer-Book and rose. Floyd and Mrs. Halket rose with him; they and the servants stood with bowed heads while he read the prayer. After the general mumbled Amen, the servants marched out in single file.

Usually Mrs. Halket went to her room after prayers, leaving her husband to sit reading or writing till midnight; these late evening hours he gave with a methodical regularity to what he had not yet advanced beyond terming "self-culture." Since his attainment of eminence, he found himself called upon frequently and often unexpectedly to preside at meetings, to introduce speakers, to present prizes, to address assemblages of all kinds. With his natural dignity of speech and his retentive memory, which supplied him on occasions with happy passages from Shakespeare or Milton, he had acquired a facility in this on which he plumed himself; but he was ambitious, wishing in everything that he undertook to excel on each new occasion his past accomplishments. Therefore he read widely, made notes, and memorized, devoting at least one hour every evening to this employment. He liked to have the library to himself, that he might walk up and down repeating aloud what he had learned, and accordingly Mrs. Halket had submitted to withdrawing after prayers. But this evening Floyd said, before she could leave the room, —

"Grandfather, when are you and Grandmother going to open the Ridgewood house?"

"Oh, Floyd," Mrs. Halket cried, before her husband had time to answer, "I don't want to go to Ridgewood this year; I want to stay right at home and be near you. I can't bear to think of leaving you all forlorn at New Rome, with no home to go to on Sundays —"

"There," said Floyd to his grandfather, "I suspected that was what would come next when she insisted on staying here till after I had started in to work. It's perfectly senseless, when you own a whole Canadian lake, not to use it; and you know, Grandmother, you'd rather be there than here; you hate the summer here. And I'll make a bargain with you; I'll let you come out to-morrow and fix up my room if you and Grandfather will promise to start for Ridgewood next Monday."

"Good enough," said Colonel Halket. "Throw yourself entirely on your own resources; burn your bridges behind you; that's right. I'm ready for Ridgewood whenever your grandmother is; what do you say, Rebecca?"

"Floyd," — she addressed her grandson entreatingly, — "do say you want me to stay. I don't care about going to Ridgewood now — truly, I don't."

"If you stayed, I should be so angry that I would never come to see you," he answered firmly. "Next Monday for Ridgewood, Grandfather."

"Next Monday, I think," Colonel Halket agreed. He was quite impatient to have them both leave the room and to resume his digging of feasible remarks out of Boswell. "Good-night, my dear; good-night, Floyd."

But neither of them went immediately to bed. Mrs. Halket took Floyd into her sitting-room and talked to him for nearly an hour; he came away feeling a little sad and more than ever touched by her affection. For she had made him see how much indeed he was to her; she had told him of his father, her only child, who for his thirty years of life had been the growing light and happiness of Colonel Halket and of herself. After his untimely death, the young widow had not long survived him; and then the grandparents had taken the baby, and, said Mrs. Halket to Floyd, "It was as if we were beginning life all over, and with the knowledge that the best of it could never be ours again. Oh, it was worse than that, Floyd; I can't tell you what it was at first when we had to feel that we had you, poor little baby indeed, but not, not our dear boy. Yet now you're ours, just as much as your father ever was; we began life all over again, your grandfather and I; we've toiled through it again, watching you grow and develop; we love you as if you were your father, and now you're about to continue and fill out his career. Can you see how much you mean? You've been away from me much the last few years; it was necessary; I don't lament it; you must be away from me now; that is hard, too, and still I won't complain. But oh, Floyd, if anything should happen to you — do I seem very silly and absurd, my dear? Yet it wakes me in the night, to think of — and it is, you know, dangerous there in the mills — it's a dangerous employment, Floyd, and I say a prayer every night of my life for the safety of the poor men who work there for your grandfather. And if anything should happen to you, and I were away — not that it would be any less awful if I were here, but the idea of being away somehow makes it seem more possible that something might happen — my not being here to warn you to be careful and to be silly about you — ah, Floyd, you're laughing, but you *will* be careful, won't you? — for you see, you must see, how much you mean."

Floyd kissed her and laughed and said that she must not worry about him. He knew why she was nervous; she wanted to get away into the country where she could rest. She admitted that perhaps she was tired. "At Ridgewood you won't have so many complications," Floyd said, and she smiled a little. "No, it's simple — comparatively — there," she answered. "Good-night, Floyd; we'll drive out to New Rome to-morrow."

The next morning Mrs. Halket and Floyd alighted at Mrs. Bell's gate from the victoria that had been the amazement of all the women who lived upon the street and happened to be looking out of their windows at that hour. Mrs. Bell was one of these and was filled with consternation and pride. "How ever shall I go to the door!" she exclaimed, bursting into the dining-room where her daughter sat sewing. And at that moment the bell rang. "It's Mr. Halket and the old lady herself — in their carriage — and me looking as I am. Go, for goodness gracious, child, and hold them in the parlor till I can change my dress."

"I don't look any too well myself," observed Letty, with feminine dissatisfaction, but her mother was already on the stairs. "Well, *somebody's* got to answer the bell," and she rose, and with her capable hands pushed and puffed her mass of brilliant hair up above her ears. Then, smoothing out her dress, she went to the door.

"This is my grandmother, Miss Bell," Floyd said to her. "She thought she would like to see the room; she's going away next week and wants to give me some pictures and things for it."

"I'll tell my mother you've come," said Letty ingenuously. "She's just gone upstairs. Won't you walk into the parlor?"

She left them and escaped to her mother, who was struggling into her best dress. "Letty!" cried Mrs. Bell reproachfully, "you didn't leave them alone down there! Run right back and entertain them till I come."

"Here," said Letty, putting aside her mother's ineffectual, trembling fingers and buttoning her dress for her.

"What *do* they want?" cried Mrs. Bell.

"To make his room more like what he's used to," Letty replied, baldly, but without bitterness.

"It's aired out and read up anyway. To think of having Mrs. Robert Halket in my house! Letty, do go down and talk to her till I can come."

"I guess they can sit alone together for a few minutes without fighting," rejoined Letty.

"To think of having Mrs. Robert Halket in my house!" repeated Mrs. Bell, in lamentation and ecstasy. "Was she awful, Letty?"

"She's a human being," said Letty.

"There, there, that'll do — where's my handkerchief? Shall I help you fix yourself up — your hair?"

"No, I'm not going down, mother."

"Letty, you must." Mrs. Bell was in despair. "I can't face her alone — my goodness, child."

Letty was obdurate. "She's just come on business; she's not making a call on us; I'm not going to tag round and look at her."

"Oh, if you ain't the unmanageable!" cried Mrs. Bell, on the verge of tears.

Letty opened the door and gently pushed her out into the hall; then closed the door definitely upon her.

Mrs. Halket was not inclined to be severe. The timorousness of the little woman touched her kindly heart; she was never the grand lady in the homes of the poor. She complimented Mrs. Bell on her garden, climbed the two flights of stairs to the attic room, and refrained from discouraging comment. "I think you will be quite snug here, Floyd," she said. She poked the mattress and approved of it, was surprised at the roominess of the closet, and said that with the pictures she would send and a little bookcase he would be as comfortable as possible.

"I suppose that was your daughter, Mrs. Bell, that I saw at the door," she said casually.

"Yes, ma'am, my daughter Letty; she does the cataloguing at the library; but she's having her vacation now."

"She's a very handsome girl," Mrs. Halket observed.

"And as good as she is beautiful, I think," Mrs. Bell replied.

At the door Mrs. Halket shook hands with the landlady, who immediately became agitated and began to murmur unintelligible hopes and fears.

"Oh," laughed Mrs. Halket, "I know you'll take good care of him; I see that he's in good hands."

Then Mrs. Bell had one blissful moment, standing at her gate, while Mrs. Halket, from her seat in her open carriage, in full view of all the neighborhood, smiled and nodded to her as she was rolled away.

Floyd went to work at Open-Hearth Mill Number Two the next Monday morning. He was assigned to the squad at the furnace where a few days before he had watched operations; he found himself working with the man from whom he had derived the story of the unfortunate victim of fumes. This man looked hard at him several times, but said nothing. Floyd was kept busy obeying directions to stir the heat, to take a crowbar and turn a valve, to pitch in steel scrap or limestone, to give a hand at a hoist; he did not have much time to rest and talk; the mills were running full, and every man was eager to make his tonnage.

By noon, Floyd's hands, that he had believed were well toughened, were blistered, and his muscles, that he thought compared not unfavorably with those of the other men, ached. He took his tin dinner-pail in which Mrs. Bell had put up his luncheon of cold beef sandwiches, apple pie, and cold coffee, and seated himself on a bench beside the workman who had entertained him a few days before.

"Ain't used to this kind of thing?" said the workman, not unfriendly, glancing at Floyd's hands.

"No," Floyd said soberly. "But I find that the worst of it is the fumes."

The man stopped with his pie poised in air. "Say," he said, "I thought your face was familiar. Was that you I was joshing the other day?"

"It was," said Floyd.

"And you knowed it all the time and didn't let on. Say, that was a good one. What's your name?"

"Floyd Halket."

"Come off."

"That's right."

"Ah, you're tryin' to get even with me for my jolly."

"I'll get even with you all right. But that's my name."

The man was silent for some time. At last he remarked, mainly to himself, "Well, if that ain't the hell of a note."

"What's your name?" said Floyd.

"Shelton — Joe Shelton."

Floyd drew out his pipe and tobacco-pouch.

"Have some?" And he opened the pouch for his friend.

"Thanks, don't mind if I do," and Shelton dug down with his grimy fingers and wadded a capacious pipe. He turned to Floyd with a twinkle in his eyes. "This what the old man smokes?"

"My grandfather?"

"Yep."

"Once in a while. But he doesn't care much for a pipe,"

"To think," Shelton observed, again mainly to himself, "of me using some of his mixture! Boardin' out here, are you? The Widow Bell's? Good folks they are, too. — Here, Bill! here, Tom!" and he called to two of the workmen who, having finished their lunch, were going outside to pitch quoits; "let me make you acquainted with the new helper, Mr. Floyd Halket. Grandson of the old man."

They shook hands with Floyd silently, staring at him with steady, prejudiced eyes. They were heavy and surly looking young men, with none of Shelton's geniality. "I'll bet you and me could lick 'em at that game," Shelton said to Floyd. "Come along." As they passed out, Floyd heard Tom say to Bill, "Let's lick the hell out of 'em," and he gathered that the impression he had made had not been favorable.

Tom and Bill and Shelton were experts at pitching quoits; Floyd, with his blistered and sore fingers, was by no means their equal. When they saw after a few minutes that his hand was bleeding and that he continued to pitch without paying attention to his hurt, they showed less indifference, and unbent so far as to utter an objurgation when one of their throws went wild. Once Tom stooped to pick up his quoits and claim the point, and Floyd stopped him peremptorily and demanded that the distance be measured. The measurement showed Tom's claim to have been good, and Floyd said good-naturedly, "Your eye is better than mine." A few moments later Tom suggested to him that he might tie a rag round his hand; the suggestion was made grudgingly, with embarrassment. Floyd replied that he could pitch better just as he was. By the end of the game Tom and Bill, whose surliness had principally been shyness, were not unfriendly to the new helper.

In the course of ten days Floyd had accustomed himself to the work; his hands had toughened, and his muscles did not ache when he went home at night or when he awoke in the morning. He went to bed at half-past eight

and was roused at five by Letty or her mother knocking
at his door. He began to receive letters from his grandmother at Ridgewood; the lake was beautiful, the country
lovely after the smoke and grime of Avalon, his grandfather was like a boy again; if only they could have Floyd
with them! She hoped he was not having too hard a
time; she could hardly wait to hear, and he must write
frankly. The letters that he sent in reply were cheerful;
it was hard work, but he was learning how to make steel;
his studies in chemistry had helped him and he thought
he should graduate from the open-hearth furnaces in a
few months. Three nights a week he sat with Mrs. Bell
and Letty after supper and talked or read Dickens aloud
— taking turns in this with Letty; the other three nights
he went up to his room and read by himself or wrote
letters, "for on Mondays, Wednesdays, and Fridays," he
explained, "the young roller, Hugh Farrell, comes to see
Letty. They pretend they're not engaged, but you ought
to see me get Letty rattled whenever I want to. She's
a pretty good girl, too, and does n't get rattled about other
things. I'm quite one of the family now." And he wrote
in an equally cheerful vein about his work. "Plenty of
time for breathing-spells when you once get on to your
job," he assured his grandmother. "And you soon get
used to being a salamander. At noon we gobble our
lunch; then Joe Shelton and I pitch quoits with Tom and
Bill the rest of the hour. We're pretty even now; they
used to beat us. Joe and I can pretty near lick any team
in the works. They say there are a couple of coons over
at Open-Hearth One that are the champions; when we get
a little better, we'll challenge them. Mr. Gregg is very
nice; he had me round at his house to dinner last Sunday.
It made me a little uncomfortable, though, because Mrs.
G. had so evidently laid herself out on my account; she
was worried all through lest things should n't be done just
right, and it was n't half as natural as it is at the Bells'.
It's kind of hard luck on Mrs. Gregg; I guess she's

a relic of the Superintendent's early days and has never had an opportunity to learn anything else — been stuck here in New Rome all her life; stepped from doing all her own work into command of an establishment; her husband never takes her away for more than a month at a time, and then they go to some big summer hotel. The two young Greggs are purse-proud little brats, that ought to be sent to boarding-school and have the snobbishness knocked out of them; then I'd like to have them put under me in the works. They are quite too good for anybody else in New Rome. I'm comfortable; the bath-room is always mine between six and half-past. On the odd nights, Letty plays the piano and Hugh Farrell the bass viol; Letty is pretty good, but Farrell is better with the tongs. He is making a thundering noise just now, and all the windows are wide open, for it's a hot night, so I will close."

If in his letters to his family Floyd put his best foot foremost, it was no more than many another forlorn and lonely soul has done.

VI

INVESTIGATING THE DEPTHS

ONE hot Saturday night in August Floyd had gone to his room and stretched himself out on the bed by the open window. It was too hot to light the lamp and read, and besides he was feeling out of sorts. Another Sunday was at hand, and nothing that he cared to do; the freshness had gone from his work; and the mood, rare with him, was on him which made him ask, "What is the use?" He had taken out his little telescope, and lying on the bed adjusted it lazily, tracing with it the outline of the constellations that were within its range. While he was thus amusing himself, he was aware that Mrs. Bell was in the yard below him, sprinkling her lawn, and occasionally exchanging a word with the neighboring housewife, who was engaged in similar employment. Floyd's arm grew weary of holding up the glass, and having laid it down he listened without shame to the fragments of conversation that reached him.

"Did Hugh come to see Letty to-night?" asked the neighbor.

"No; Saturday nights he goes off with his friends; he does enjoy skylarking round."

"Well, I presume it's all right; I presume it's innocent. Does Letty approve that he should?"

"She encourages him. 'There ain't much fun here,' she says to him. 'I want you should have a good time when you can. I guess two folks like us can trust each other.' That's the way she takes it."

"Maybe"—and the suggestion was delayed a moment by sly and smothered laughter—"Hugh will be getting jealous first—about her and the new boarder."

INVESTIGATING THE DEPTHS 87

"Now, don't you go to putting any such nonsense into her mind," said Mrs. Bell sharply. "Not that she'd be weak-headed enough to believe it."

"Stranger things have happened," insisted the neighbor, while Floyd, lying in the dark, scowled and muttered about the foolishness of women. "'T ain't every girl neither that has Letty's chance. And if she's the smart one I take her to be, she's making the best of her opportunities."

Floyd lost Mrs. Bell's answer, but that it was emphatic he judged from the way in which she spattered the plank walk. Then as she eased the stream off upon the grass, he heard the other woman say in a conciliatory voice, "Oh, well, I was just suggestin' it as a pleasant possibility. And as for Hugh Farrell, I was just thinking that Saturday night is a bad time for him to be staying away from her he's keeping company with. But of course if *she* don't mind —"

"The cat!" thought Floyd.

Mrs. Bell preserved silence.

"I wonder," said the neighbor's voice, with a wheedling accent, "if I'm ever to get to meet Mr. Halket? It does seem as though living next door — Do tell me, Mrs. Bell; what like is he?"

"Why, he's a real nice fellow," said Mrs. Bell. "And my, how fond he is of all kinds of preserves! I never seen anybody with such a taking for 'em."

"Ain't that interestin'!" exclaimed the neighbor. "But then your put-up things is always so good, Mrs. Bell; 't ain't really a wonder."

"Well, he certainly does enjoy them. And he ain't stuck up neither; my goodness, it does seem hard sometimes to realize that he ain't just one of us."

"He ain't actually different, then, from other boarders?"

"Why, no; don't seem as if he was now. He has some habits, of course — must always take a bath when he comes back from work. It makes supper a little late, and he does slop up the bathroom terrible, but Letty and me we agree we don't mind. And how he does whistle when he's warshin' himself! Always one tune. Letty does laugh and laugh to hear him! She says he can't whistle no more than a cow."

Floyd shook with laughter; he was surely meeting the fate of the eavesdropper. "I must try to be more quiet and gentlemanly in my bathing," he thought.

"As for breakfast I never knowed a boarder that was so little trouble," continued Mrs. Bell. "Always wants just his cup of coffee and three eggs boiled three minutes. Nothing else ever. Most boarders is everlastingly wanting variety, now a steak, now a piece of pie."

"Ain't there a difference in the way he eats?"

"He lays his napkin acrost his knees instead of tucking it in at his chin. But I guess that's because he's wearing his old clothes here and don't care if they get spotted or not. I don't know as other ways he's any different."

"I suppose he ain't used to doin' his own reachin'."

"He don't seem to mind."

"Well, it does seem like a fairy tale. Mrs. Bell, ain't I ever again to hear Letty perform on the piano? She does perform so well."

"She and I was talking of having in a few friends for a little music some evening," Mrs. Bell answered. "Her, and Hugh to play on the bass viol. When we set an evening, I'll let you know."

"Oh, that will be grand. I do just love to hear Letty perform. I suppose, not being musical, Mr. Halket won't attend?"

"We meant to ask him," Mrs. Bell said.

"Did you ever find out how he came to stay with you?"

"Through Mr. Gregg's recommend, I believe. And he said, too, he liked the looks of the place."

INVESTIGATING THE DEPTHS

"You certainly are a wonder at getting things to grow. Though I must say I do think my hydrangey has come out better this year than yours, Mrs. Bell. Ain't you afraid of warshin' those flowers up by the roots? Well, we do have different methods."

Mrs. Bell made no reply. At last Floyd heard her say, "There, I guess that's sprinkling enough for my plants."

"Going in, are you? I think I'll stay and water a while longer. Now don't forget, Mrs. Bell; you're going to tell me when Letty's going to give that musical; I do love to see her when she performs, as well as hear."

"Yes," said Mrs. Bell, "I expect she'll let you know."

"And" — there was another insinuating ripple of laughter — "if anything *should* come of having Mr. Halket in the house — well, you never can tell, but I guess you could trust her to let Hugh Farrell down as easy as possible."

Floyd bounced up from his bed; he had at first been amused, now he was disgusted by the vulgarity of the conversation. Putting on his coat, he went out of doors to stroll about the town. The streets were lighted by streamers of natural gas from the tops of lamp-posts, flaring loose and unconfined against the dark. There was an additional weird illumination from the mills, which sent up gusts of fire and showed red, searing, squirming lines that were never visible by day. Down in the main street at the bottom of the hill these were shut from view, though glancing up the slope Floyd noticed how great waves of light suddenly overflowed and obliterated the wavering shadows flung by the gas-lamps.

The shops and stores were all open, gay, doing a brisk business; hucksters of fruit had their handcarts crowded up against the curbstone, and were trying by shouting and by placarding cheap prices to dispose of berries, peaches, and pears while there was yet time; they waved paper bags and held up grimy fingers, soliciting custom. Bare-headed women with baskets on their arms scuttled about doing their marketing; fathers of families, a week's pay in their pockets, stood by in the stores while wives or children tried on new hats or new shoes. But mainly the street was given over to those of both sexes who were in pursuit of pleasure, — young men and girls idling along together, laughing loudly; no need for any one to lack for a companion.

Hot and thirsty, Floyd stepped into one of the numerous saloons. At the rear was a partition with an opening partly screened by a stained drab curtain, and the sign "Wine Room" over it. From within this sanctuary issued much hilarious laughter; Floyd crossed over to the doorway. The place was not for men alone; at the tables there was a sprinkling of gaudy women, and others were coming in through the "Ladies' Entrance" on the farther side. Noisy with unrestrained voices and the thump and rattle of glasses, stale with the smell of spilled liquor and old pipes and low-hanging tobacco smoke, filthy with moist sawdust and cast-away stogies, the room was a scene of squalid gayety.

"Hello!" cried a voice from one of the nearer tables, and Floyd saw Hugh Farrell rise and beckon to him. He smiled and waved a hand in reply, and was turning away when Farrell sprang forward and seized his arm.

"Come and have a drink," said Farrell. With tipsy insistence he clutched Floyd's arm and drew him to the table, at which four men were seated. "Billings, Ryan, Pulaski, Schmidt — here's Mr. Halket — six beers!" He hailed a waiter, and kicked a chair from a neighboring table to Floyd.

Billings, hardly more than a boy, had a weak, silly face; Ryan was a good-natured, freckled young Irishman with a sandy beard; Pulaski had black, scowling brows and a surly mouth, and was plainly the most brutal of the company. Schmidt was stolid, serene, and smiling. The beer was brought. "How!" said Farrell, raising his glass toward Floyd, who bowed and waved to the other four, but they were already drinking. It was etiquette to drain the glass, ambition to finish first. Floyd lost prestige because he was the last; he regained it by rapping on the table and crying to the waiter, "Six beers."

At the table close beside Floyd sat three men, two of whom were quietly listening while the third talked glibly, passionately. He was an angular, narrow-chested man, with long black hair, a drooping mustache, wild flashing eyes; he wore dirty white cuffs much too long for his coat-sleeves; they slid down upon his knuckles when he gesticulated, as he did often.

"Organize," Floyd heard him imploring, "organize! The hope of labor, the dread of capital; the day of the workingman is marching on."

"He's an anarchist," Farrell said to Floyd. "He'll give you an earache quicker than any man in New Rome."

Floyd listened; Pulaski was already listening. The speaker, feeling with the acuteness of his kind that his audience was enlarged, raised his voice.

"You say you've got no grievance; I say there never yet was a laboring man without a grievance. And what if you ain't a grievance? In time of peace prepare for war. I make no doubt Mr. — or Colonel — Halket is a very fine gentleman indeed; you've got a library and a baseball park and a few other things to show for it; but let me ask you a question: Does either of you own the house you live in? No!" — and the speaker pounded his fist on the table — "no! and never will."

Billings spoke from across the table with an accent of defiance, — but spoke so that his words reached no farther than Floyd. "Ah, hell! I ain't got no use for no labor union."

The manner of the speech was that of a weak boy seizing an opportunity to curry favor. Floyd looked at him pityingly, and then with more consideration at Pulaski, who sat with his arms on the table, leaning forward and listening with close attention to the "anarchist's" words.

"Understand me," — the speaker shook his forefinger impressively, — "I'm saying nothing against Mr. — *or* Colonel — Halket. Maybe he's better than most capitalists; maybe he ain't. But, one thing's sure; he's got you men sewed up here in New Rome, that's what he has; and it ain't as if you was in a city where you could keep your home and change your employment; here there's just one thing you can do, and you've got to do it as he says for what he says, or you're uprooted, you and your families, and you've got no place to go. It's the duty of you men to band together for the protection of the individual. Within three months there won't be a mill in all Avalon that ain't organized, and there ain't half the reason for it there that there is here. Labor there is naturally more independent, capital has to make concessions."

"Oh, you make me tired," Farrell interrupted hotly. "You talk like an anarchist, — you work with your mouth. I've got no kick coming; I get good wages — better than any of your union men in Avalon. You run your union in here, — and you limit my output, and you make me pay so much a week to the union, and you call me out when I don't want to go — and then you or some bum like you fixes up the deal for a hundred or two, and I go back to work, and I'm out maybe a month's and maybe two months' pay. To hell with the unions!"

The walking delegate heard him with a bland and scornful sneer. "My young friend," he said, "I ain't going to condescend to resent your remarks. That ain't the part of a missionary — and I am tryin' to do as Christian missionary work as was ever carried to the heathen in Africa. *I* don't descend to personalities. *I* don't seek to obscure the issue. I say nothing against you or them that holds views similar to yours, I say nothing against Mr. — *or* Colonel — Halket. He may be wanting to do more for labor than labor wants to do for itself. But some day he may be no longer with us. There may be a change of policy, and there may be somebody come in who won't want to do for labor more than it wants to do for itself, but who will want to get out of labor all that it can give for as little as he can give. And it's against that time that I'm calling on the men of New Rome to arise and organize and protect themselves and their families."

"Oh, say," cried Farrell. "I know something more interesting than this; come along." He rose, turning his back on the walking delegate. Floyd and Billings and Ryan followed him; Pulaski and Schmidt remained behind to listen. Floyd looked back as he was passing out between the stained drab curtains; Pulaski was pointing towards him, and the walking delegate was screwed round over the back of his chair, staring in amazement.

"Now I'll take you where there's some fun," said Farrell, when they were once again out upon the pavement. "We've got a slick dance-hall this year, and there's always a smooth line of girls on hand on a Saturday night. You can pick up anything."

Ryan made a tolerably broad observation.

"Hold on," Floyd said to Farrell. "This is not in my line, and I don't believe it's in yours."

"Oh, come along," Farrell urged him. "All the fellows'll be there. Just watch 'em dancing and take a turn; no harm in that."

Thus Floyd suffered himself to be persuaded. The dance-hall was up two flights, hot, stuffy, and crowded. At one end a man in his shirt-sleeves played on a tinny piano, and beside him on a box stood another man in his shirt-sleeves, scraping a violin. To this thin music two hundred people revolved. Others sauntered or stood round the walls; the notes of violin and piano were faint, and sometimes almost drowned in the chatter. Ryan and Billings had partners and were spinning away before Floyd was aware that they had separated themselves from him.

"See anybody you'd like to meet?" asked Farrell. "I'll introduce you. Or just step up and speak. That's the way it's done."

"Thank you," said Floyd. "I'm not much of a dancer. I'll look on."

"You don't mind if I go off and take a turn?"

"No; go ahead."

Farrell picked out a girl with black hair and cherry-colored ribbons, and somewhat more cherry color on lips and cheeks than Floyd thought attractive. But as they danced they matched each other in their utter nonchalance of movement; the girl let her left arm hang limply, and indeed from her hips up seemed paralyzed, except for the continuous action of her jaw, for she was chewing gum. Farrell waltzed with that superb, blasé air of one who is too languid to take the steps, but glides and walks through them nevertheless with marvelous accuracy in time. For all the talk that passed between the two, or animation on their faces, or interest in their surroundings, they might have been dancing in their sleep; and Floyd thought they avoided collisions and disasters with the traditional dexterity of the somnambulist.

Most of the girls were chewing gum without cessation, and danced with the same absolute silence. As for the men, those who had been long active had discarded coats and vests; the red or cerulean dye from their brilliant suspenders was spreading out upon their shirts, and the habit of perspiration seemed not to be one that they left behind them in the mills.

When the music ceased, Floyd waited, curious to see what sort of girl his friend would lead out for the next dance. Somewhat to his surprise, Farrell continued with the same partner. They had gone round the room three or four times when they stopped near Floyd, and Farrell, leaving the girl to chew her gum unconcernedly, came over to him.

"I'm going to leave before long," he said. "Don't

you want to meet some lady? I won't give away your name."

"No, thank you," said Floyd, looking him in the eyes; "I'm ready to leave whenever you are."

Farrell returned the look stolidly, then turned again to his partner. They waltzed round the room twice more; then they stopped again, and the girl tucked her hand in Farrell's arm. They approached the doorway near which Floyd was standing.

"Better get a lady and come along," Farrell said to him as they passed.

Floyd looked straight ahead as if he had not heard; and Farrell, passing out with his partner, flushed angrily, but said nothing.

A few moments later Floyd descended the stairs alone.

"Why the devil should I care!" he muttered to himself fiercely, as he walked along the street. But he did care, — that a man whom he liked, who was engaged to a nice girl, who had kissed her the night before and would kiss her again to-morrow, could be so base. Billings or Ryan might have done this thing, but Farrell — Floyd swore to himself in pessimism, "By God, it makes me ashamed myself to look at Letty."

Up on the hill the Halket Free Public Library glowed with all its lighted windows, the music-hall wing and the club-room and gymnasium wing alike showed beacons of welcome. Floyd looked up at these beneficent works of his grandfather, scornful and cynical.

"And how many of our mill-hands are amusing themselves there to-night?" he thought.

VII

DIVERSIONS OF A WORKINGMAN

COLONEL HALKET had proposed Floyd's name at the Avalon Club soon after his birth, in fact, the day after his christening, and as a consequence of this wise forethought Floyd had found himself, after graduating from college, on the active list of membership. His grandfather had taken him to lunch at the club once or twice in the early summer, and had introduced him to one after another of the lawyers and business men, all of whom had a friendly enough greeting for young Halket. But Floyd had been too much oppressed by the dignity of the place and the age of its members to venture there very often alone, even had he had the opportunity. One Sunday morning in September, however, a craving for a view of more complex civilization than that which was his daily portion seized him; he remembered with an uncommon zest that the chef at the Avalon Club was the most distinguished of his profession; and, having scrubbed and scoured his hands and put on a new suit of clothes, he took a trolley car for the city.

The club was an old house on one of the downtown streets, hemmed in now among stores and office buildings, but retaining the dignity that had made it twenty years before the first "mansion" of Avalon. It was a red brick house with a large bay window swelling out on each side of the wide entrance, and with wrought-iron grills curving up to the middle sashes on each of the six lowest windows; between these the passer-by might have a glimpse, at almost any hour, of gentlemen reading newspapers and smoking cigars or looking idly out upon the street. Floyd, approaching, caught sight of two such venerable heads, and for a moment his heart failed him. Then he walked briskly up the steps. The flunky at the door bowed and said, —

" Good-morning, Mr. Halket; walk in, sir."

Floyd had a mild pleasure and pride at finding that the servants already knew him.

He was standing at the long table in the reading-room, turning the pages of a periodical and trying to make up his mind to go over and speak to the two gentlemen in the window, who were eyeing him lazily through the smoke of their cigarettes. Some one came into the room and stepping up behind him, cried, —

" Hello, Floyd, my boy; how are you?"

And turning round, Floyd saw Mr. Dunbar, Lydia's father, holding out his hand.

" Why," said Floyd, " I thought you were at Chester, Mr. Dunbar."

" The rest of the family are there, but I had to come back and work. You're lunching with me, Floyd?"

" Thank you; with pleasure. But " — Floyd laughed — " not at your expense, if you please. I'll tell you why. I came here to get all the things that you don't get in a New Rome boarding-house; I have my mind made up on terrapin or canvas-back or whatever is the most expensive and preposterous thing they provide, and — "

" All right," declared Mr. Dunbar, taking his arm. " I'll eat the same, — the most expensive and preposterous thing they've got. I've been bored to death ever since I've been here — even with my food."

As they went into the dining-room, he told Floyd that he and Lydia had said good-by at the steamer the week before to Stewart, who was sailing to take up his two years' studies abroad.

" Two years?" Floyd asked.

" Yes; that's what they think now. Perhaps he'll become impatient and hurry home after a year, but I hope he'll stick it out. Of course it's pretty hard on Lydia,

— it's been a long engagement, but I objected to her getting married while Stewart was just a student at Technology. Perhaps now she'll go over next spring and be married in Paris — though of course I'd rather have her wait till Stewart is settled down in this country."

"Lydia's still at Chester?"

"Yes, she'll be home in less than a month now. I think she'll be ready to come. Now that Stewart's gone, the summer isn't quite the same for her."

He was a genial, brisk little man, very neat in his frock coat and large blue Ascot tie, with his gray mustache closely clipped and pointed, and his small blunt boots brightly polished; he carried himself with a kindly pompousness toward the young, and an aggressive dignity — demanded by his minuteness — toward men of his own age. Above his shrewd blue eyes towered the benevolent dome of his bald head, to a height of which he was secretly proud and which led him to pay clandestine visits to phrenologists; he preserved the records of these sittings, and sometimes he and Mrs. Dunbar took them out and fondly brooded over them. Had he not achieved success as a manufacturer, distinction had been his in literature; he had a master mind for statesmanship; he possessed mechanical genius which, properly developed, had been prolific in invention. "Never mind, George dear," Mrs. Dunbar had once said to him when with rueful pride he had shown her the most gratifying of all the charts; "if three great men were spoiled in making one good one, I don't begrudge them a bit." And she had bent down over the superb bald head and kissed the three cranial bumps containing the vast undeveloped possibilities, exclaiming as she did so, "There, Poet!" "There, Statesman!" "There, Inventor!" And then she kissed him on the lips, and said, "There, George!" The unfolding to himself of his many-sidedness had perhaps aided in preserving the little man's fresh springiness of step, but with his wife's help he was a sensible and modest soul who hoped humbly that, if he might succeed to Colonel Halket's place in the community, he should not sink much below the stature of that splendid figure. Indeed, he aspired to this eminence not without reason, for he was public-spirited, a director in various boards of which Colonel Halket was president, a liberal contributor to all worthy charities, a man interested in good works, and a willing disciple of the Colonel's in the art of oratory. He was sure that he would receive Colonel Halket's indorsement, — so far, that is, as Colonel Halket might have the privilege of indicating a successor. There was no other man in Avalon for whom Mr. Dunbar had so ardent an admiration; and Colonel Halket for his part was humanly susceptible to loyalty of this kind.

Mr. Dunbar had a friendly interest in Floyd's life at New Rome.

"It's a splendid education for a young fellow, if he has the grit to stay at it; and it will give you a sympathy and understanding of the workmen's point of view. Sympathy and understanding, — it's because they lack it that so many managements of good business go to pieces. Why, take my own case," — he sat closer to the table, folding his short arms upon it confidentially and puffing hard upon his cigar as if to supply himself for a protracted conversational *entr'acte*, — " it's just because my superintendent lacked those qualities that I'm here. He's a first-class man, but arbitrary beyond what's reasonable — got the drillmaster's point of view ingrained in him — and the drillmaster's good for small squads, but he loses himself when he tries to swing anything big.— Not, you understand, that our works are big as yours are — it's the difference between making small castings and steel construction beams; ours is small potatoes, comparatively, — but we have three hundred men on the pay-roll. Well, lately, this new thing, the Affiliated Iron Workers, has been getting after our men — we've always run nonunion — and our superintendent sticks up signs all over the works: 'No Union Men Allowed on these Premises.' Next thing a strike was threatened — even the fellows that had n't joined the Affiliated resented the move as tyranny; the superintendent would n't budge. I had to come on."

"Have you settled the trouble?" Floyd asked.

"Oh, I 'm smoothing it down. The union men came to me; well, I thought they had a real grievance; I told 'em as much; I said it was n't my intention to discriminate against the union, — all I stipulated for was free play for everybody. Then I explained that while I was privately willing to go as far as that I could n't consent to withdraw my support from the superintendent publicly — would n't force him to make a public acknowledgment of defeat, you understand, and take down the offensive signs. But I'd talk the matter over with him and explain my views, and meanwhile it would be understood that if any signs were — accidentally destroyed, they would n't be replaced. So I'm getting the men into a better spirit, the superintendent is kicking, but I'm smoothing him down, too — and it's wonderful how many accidents are happening to those signs."

"The men are joining the union out at New Rome," said Floyd.

"Yes, we 've all got to come to it, I suppose. But up there at New Rome, where there's such a strong family feeling on the part of the workmen for the mills, and where they're in a measure isolated, the union can never get quite such a grip as it's bound to have here."

"I don't know," Floyd said. "When it becomes fashionable to join a thing, a man does n't like to stay out. That's the way it's working with a good many of our people, who don't see any other real advantage in joining."

"That's all right; it's almost as much of a safeguard to have a big discontented element in the union as a big non-union element. And where you have several mills, can't you play 'em off against one another — keep the fashion in some of 'em non-union?"

"That's Mr. Gregg's idea," Floyd answered. "The open-hearth mill, where I'm working now, has a good deal of union spirit; the rod-mill, that I go to next, is almost entirely free from it. And that's the way it is at present; the feeling varies a good deal."

"Some day," Mr. Dunbar laughed at the jocose idea, "we'll have to form an Employers' Union to equalize matters."

They sat talking together for some time, until Mr. Dunbar, looking at his watch, announced that he must go to keep an appointment. "But why should n't you dine with me here to-night?" he said. "You have nothing to do, have you?"

"Nothing except get back to New Rome," Floyd answered, and he accepted the invitation cheerfully.

The more he was with Mr. Dunbar, the more curiously did he find himself reminded of Lydia. No one could have been less like her in appearance than her father, with his large head and pompous little figure, yet every now and then some tone of his voice, or some turn of expression that he used came to recall the girl enchantingly. And remote from her as he was in personal appearance, there was in his presence that honest sturdiness which Floyd instinctively attributed to her character. Floyd was enough of a sentimentalist to be moved by these similarities; once or twice he caught himself almost accepting the little man as an impersonation of Lydia, grotesque yet not unsympathetic. Melancholy descended upon him during the ride back to New Rome that evening. Perhaps while he had been abroad and since the beginning of his apprenticeship he had not exercised himself much with thoughts of her; there was little enough opportunity among the pits and cranes of the open-hearth mill, or even in his tiny room at night, for then, when he was not occupied with letters or reading, he went at once to bed in weariness. But on this Sunday evening the melancholy which possessed him after leaving Mr. Dunbar settled into depression. He recalled the dull pang with which he had, on the May afternoon more than a year before, heard the announcement from Stewart's lips, — the dull pang that had persisted even through his happiness for his friend. But even then he had not understood how utterly he had been robbed that day of some hope that must long have been dormant in him, or how incapable he must be of finding a substitute for that which he had lost. On this night his pain and his understanding became acute.

The next Sunday he went to Avalon and lunched alone at the club; and afterwards walked out a mile beyond his grandfather's to the Dunbar house. It was closed, as he had expected to find it; under two maple-trees by the side entrance the caretaker sat in a hammock reading, and a small fox terrier frisked about her with a ball. Floyd strolled slowly along the sidewalk to which stretched the generous, unfenced lawn; it was odd, he thought, that well as he knew Lydia, or felt he knew her, he had never been inside her house. And yet, he remembered, he had seen her not very many times. It was a pretty, graceful house, with the feminine quality that suited her, — a low, rambling cottage, half brick, half wood, with ivy climbing up the walls and framing the small, diamond-paned windows. When he had reached the fence that separated the Dunbar place from its next neighbor, he turned and went back to the club, and he could not tell himself just what had impelled him to take that walk; he had passed the house often before, and it had never had quite so particular an interest for him.

He thought he should probably be less lonely and melancholy when it was opened again and he could come in occasionally and see Lydia; he was sure that would put him in better spirits.

Letty Bell gave her musical party. Only a few of the

neighbors were invited — Mr. and Mrs. Tustin, who lived next door, Mr. Tibbs, with his two daughters, Miss Lally Gorham, who was Letty's most intimate friend, Hugh Farrell, and Mr. and Mrs. Don McDonald, with their nine-year-old twins, Gertie and Greta, who could not be left at home, and who came in hopes of cake. Floyd felt that his presence was making the affair solemn, but on the arrival and introduction of Mr. and Mrs. Tustin, there ceased to be the necessity for any such impression. Mrs. Tustin, a narrow-eyed, low-browed, dark woman, with a large cleft chin, closed with him at once, and the other guests breathed easier and began to talk.

"Well, I've seen you many's the time going up and down the hill with your lunch-bucket under your arm," Mrs. Tustin said, — and Floyd recognized her voice as that to which he had listened one Saturday evening with so much disgust, — " and I never could believe 't was you, Mr. Halket, lookin' so much like everybody else. But you do now, I declare, and dressed up, too."

" It's queer you should ever have seen me," said Floyd. " This is the first time I've had the pleasure, Mrs. Tuskim."

" Tustin, not Tuskim. Mrs. Bell's never spoke quite clear since she had in false teeth. I can see she's awful thankful you did n't put on more style; of course the Bells live very plain. Must be kind of hard after what you're accustomed to. Ain't a bass viol a ridiculous lookin' instrument!"

Floyd agreed that it was.

" Hugh Farrell and Letty they do everlastingly like to play before a crowd. Some says Hugh is quite a good performer on the bass viol, and I don't know but what he is, only I can't rid my mind of the clumsy way he has of drawin' the bow back and forth. You see if it ain't the clumsiest you ever saw. There now!"

Farrell was producing a few preliminary booms on his instrument.

"'Listen to the Mocking Bird,'" he announced; Letty struck the opening chords, and Hugh sawed away with a pained and anxious face. At the end of the selection there was an embarrassed murmur of applause, but Floyd began to clap his hands heartily, and the others followed his example. "It's great," he cried to the performers; "I don't see how you jiggle out those little notes so fast."

"You kept together splendid," Mrs. Tustin declared.

"It is perfectly *won* — derful," proclaimed Miss Lally Gorham in a languishing, refined voice, and Floyd observed Mrs. Tustin's glare of scorn. Miss Lally sat under the large red shade of the piano-lamp, fanning herself with what looked like a flattened and enlarged powder-puff; she fanned not more than fifteen strokes to the minute. Her gaze wandered over the rest of the company until she was addressing Floyd absently, as a sympathetic soul. "The rhythm is so delightful."

"Such airs!" breathed Mrs. Tustin to herself, yet so that Floyd heard. Farrell and Letty began turning over their music, and there was subdued conversation among the audience. "We was speaking of the Bells," Mrs. Tustin confided in Floyd's ear. "As I was sayin', they've been unfortunate and have to live plain. If you find things ain't comfortable, we'd be glad to have you try our house; there's just Tustin and me, and we keep a girl. Maybe we could make it more homelike for you."

"Thank you, I'm very comfortable here," Floyd answered.

"Well, just in case you ain't. — I think I'll have to send over one of my squarsh pies for you to try; Mrs. Bell tells me I have the knack."

"The next will be a religious piece; 'The Ninety and Nine,' by Ira D. Sankey," Hugh Farrell proclaimed, standing with his bass viol at attention. Mrs. Tustin cleared her throat and after the first bar, to Floyd's astonishment, broke into pious song:

> There were ninety and nine that safely lay
> In the shelter of the fold.

She trilled the words with an eager gusto, closing her eyes; the upper part of her thin face took on a singular look of repose, while the lower part, always emphatic, with its large cleft chin, seemed more than ever masterful and active. The McDonald family followed her lead, and soon her husband, a big, grim-looking man with a square beard, raised a sulky bass — as if under compulsion. At the end of the first stanza she opened her eyes and said to Floyd:

"Don't you know the words?"

"No," Floyd answered. "And I don't sing."

"That's too bad," she said compassionately. "But how you must enjoy listenin'! —

> There were ninety and nine — "

and her eyes had closed again.

Floyd had at first thought that Mrs. Tustin's sudden outburst must disconcert the musicians, but both Farrell and Letty were now singing with complete heartiness. When the last stanza had been finished, Mrs. Tustin turned again to Floyd.

"It always does me good to sing a hymn," she said. "After that I feel ready for anything."

"Oh, it's sweet." Miss Lally Gorham's voice emerged tranquil, deep, and final from among the mutterings, and to Floyd, glancing up, it appeared that, just as before, she was speaking directly to him.

"Oh yes, your turn 'll come," murmured Mrs. Tustin with deep hostility.

"Who is she?" Floyd asked.

"Lally Gorham, and she's had these outlandish airs since she began taking of an elocutionist. She'll speak a piece to-night; you can't stop her. She's planning to be an actress. — I was just thinking; Tustin and me could accommodate you in our regular spare-room — it's got a nice set of yellow ash furniture, new only this spring — and a good bit roomier than anything in this house — "

"'The Blue Danube,' by Strauss," proclaimed Farrell.

And while he came booming in, " *One* — two — three," "*One* — two — three," to Letty's glib tinkle, Mrs. Tustin continued to urge her claims in Floyd's ear. Wearied by the importunate woman, he sat stolid, seeming not to hear a word that she said; and finally with a malicious glance at him she desisted. She was so angry that in the next intermission she did not converse with him at all, but contented herself with crying out, —

" Letty dear, you have the most elegant touch."

Miss Lally Gorham's contralto thrilled across the room, — " It is the most *won* — derful waltz ; " — and Floyd felt transfixed by those hypnotic eyes. He turned from them coldly.

" Aren't you going to sing something for us to-night, Mrs. Tuslim ? " he asked.

She was mollified by the compliment. " Oh, I ain't a singer," she replied, and then she laughed. " You do have a time with my name, don't you? Tustin, not Tuslim. No, I 'm modest about it; I 've got no gifts, except for housekeepin'. That I do pride myself on."

" Well, that's certainly the most important for a woman," Floyd observed with cheerful platitude.

" It seems so to me. Now I would n't trade what I know about squarsh pies and other things for all that Letty knows about that instrument. My knowledge ain't showy and it don't entertain for the moment, like her playin' does — but you stop in one house for a week and then in the other, and you 'll find where cookin' and comfort is, — if I do say it."

" The ' Misereer ' from Verdy's Trovator," announced Hugh Farrell; and while he scraped his strings once or twice to reassure himself for this supreme effort, Mrs. Tustin hastily concluded her remarks to Floyd — " And Tustin often says to me there ain't a better fed nor a comfortabler man in all New Rome."

The Prison Prayer was wailed and thundered passionately; Floyd watched with a certain admiration Letty's strong white hands as they pounced about among the keys while her figure swayed and her cheeks flushed, whether with the heat of the exercise or with emotion, he did not know. Standing behind her, Hugh Farrell, with streaming face and with limp locks of yellow hair hanging over his forehead, contributed a solid, trustworthy accompaniment, a background of gloomy sound against which contrasted Letty's more colored and expressive performance. When in a last gorgeous burst the selection was finished, the audience clapped loudly; and through the open window came the sound of applause from a house on the opposite side of the street. Letty and Farrell responded to the encore, and then Miss Lally Gorham rose from her seat under the piano-lamp and putting her arm about Letty's neck, kissed her, and then stood embracing her with affectionate admiration.

"Always shovin' herself forward, the blarneyin' thing," commented Mrs. Tustin. "Besides bein' next door to an idiot. Asked me once if Letty's hair did n't resemble an oriole. I told her if she thought that she must be color-blind; the only orioles I ever seen were yellow, not red. Letty," and she raised her all-powerful voice, "it don't seem possible, but how you have improved!"

Floyd stepped forward to congratulate Letty upon her playing; "I don't know much about music, but you put a lot of go into it, and that's what I like," he said.

She laughed with honest pleasure at the compliment. "I get really worked up when I play," she answered. "But my fingers are too clumsy; it makes me wild sometimes, the way they seem to hold me back."

"But, Letty," broke in her friend Miss Gorham, with her deep voice, "your technique is grand. Did n't you think it was quite *won*—derful, Mr. Halket?"

She had a way of booming out this adjective with a profound expressiveness.

"Now, Lally, hush, or he'll think you're silly," Miss Bell admonished her. "Mother's provided some light refreshments, and if you'll excuse me, I ought to be helping her. Hugh," — she summoned him from an airy flirtation with the elder Miss Tibbs, — "you come along."

"Isn't she beautiful?" exclaimed Miss Gorham to Floyd, when Letty had gone. "Did you ever see such superb hair! Isn't it just like an aureole?"

"Why," said Floyd gravely, "an oriole's yellow, isn't it, not red?"

"Oh, not that kind; spelled a-u, I mean."

"I don't believe I've ever seen the a-u kind," Floyd said.

"But you've read about it surely, Mr. Halket?"

"I think I should recognize the word."

"And can't you just imagine what it would be — and wouldn't it be like her hair? But I suppose I'm a too imaginative temperament."

"You act, I think I have heard."

"I love it, I adore it; it's my life."

"I wish you might be persuaded to do something to-night."

"Oh, before you I shouldn't dare."

"Why not?"

"Oh, you have seen so much, all the great actors, Booth, and Louis James, and everybody. You would be so critical. — Did you ever see *King John?*"

"Never," said Floyd.

"I do *Constance before the French King* sometimes," remarked Miss Gorham. "If you've never seen anybody in it to compare me with — "

"Of course you must do it," declared Floyd.

"Well, maybe I will if they ask me. I doubt if they will, though; most of those here would not appreciate it. There's Mrs. Tustin and the Tibbs girls; I suppose they never heard of Shakespeare. Letty is so good-natured she

DIVERSIONS OF A WORKINGMAN 109

asks in anybody. I expect you find this quite a queer crowd, Mr. Halket."

"No, not at all. People are pretty much the same, don't you think, Miss Gorham, wherever you find them?"

"Yes, I suppose they are. At least if you say so; you have had such wide experience. But personally I have no sympathy with those who cannot appreciate the great works of literature. Especially Shakespeare. What a master mind he had, Mr. Halket!"

"Yes."

"I am so glad you love him. Then, if you really want me to, I'll do *Constance before the French King* — that is, if you feel like asking for it. But here comes the lemonade; I guess we'd better wait till after that."

Floyd had an opportunity to make himself useful in passing the sponge-cake and so to escape from Miss Gorham and sit down with Tibbs and his two daughters. Tibbs was a man of sixty, with small white side-whiskers and apple-red cheeks, broad of face and broad-shouldered; wearing an amiable, silent smile; his daughters, though not pretty, had a sort of buxom, blowsy bloom, and wore frizzed and flaxen hair. Floyd asked him what mill he worked in, and then how long he had been in New Rome;

"Twenty years, sir, ever since I left Devonshire with them two — little misses they were then."

"Land, Pa! you ought n't to tell a lady's age," sniggered one daughter, while the other giggled and said, "We was young enough anyway not to pick up that awful English accent, was n't we, Sadie?"

"That troubles them quite a bit, sir," Tibbs explained to Floyd. "But Hi tell them Hi'm glad to 'ave something to remind me of the old 'ome."

"I like the Devonshire accent," Floyd said. "Do you or your sister sing, Miss Tibbs?"

"Oh no, sir, not worth mentionin'. Not in public."

"Yes," observed Mr. Tibbs irrelevantly, and in an absent voice, "twenty year 'ave I worked for your grandfather, Mr. 'Alket. And he's a grand man, a grand man."

"It's a pleasure to find that his workmen feel so," Floyd said, "for I'm one, and it's the way I feel. — Miss Tibbs, let me take your glass."

Letty had been consulting with Miss Lally Gorham in a corner. Now she stepped forward and said —

"Lally is going to do a scene from Shakespeare. *Constance before the French King* — from *King John*."

Floyd began to clap his hands, and led the applause. But Miss Lally's face had already assumed a tragic aspect and did not relax.

"Letty, you will have to help me with my hair," she said, drawing out hairpins as she spoke. When all the sustaining articles had been removed, and the hair had tumbled abundantly down over her shoulders, she said, "I must ask you all to move a little farther back; I need more room. — King John has defeated the French King in battle and taken Constance's son, young Arthur, prisoner; Constance, grief-stricken, enters to the French King."

Miss Gorham paused a moment; then, with uplifted shaking arms, started forward, crying violently, —

> No, I defy all counsul, all redress,
> But that which ends all counsul, true redress,
> Death, death. — O emiable, lovely death! — etc.

She stopped her agitated pacing and addressed with absent deliberation the following lines to Mrs. Tustin, —

> And I will kiss thy detestabul bones,
> And put my eyeballs in thy vaulty brows,
> And ring these fingurs with thy household wor-r-ms.

In the pause she made here, Mrs. Tustin inserted a brief, contemptuous, and defiant laugh; Miss Gorham, without altering the direction or intensity of her gaze, continued, —

> And stop this gap of breath with fulsome dust,
> And be a carrion monster like thyself.

Mrs. Tustin whispered to her husband with a great air of bravado and derision, but looked relieved when Miss Gorham turned and took a step or two away from her. The elocutionist not only acted the part of Lady Constance; when necessary, she would step to the opposite side of the room, remark " King Philip " or " Pandulph," and drop her voice a couple of octaves for the speech; then back again to the position of Constance, and shrilling loudly, —

" I am not mad," she cried; " this hair I tear is mine," and she drew her unbound locks in front of her face and pulled them hand over hand. When she had finished Constance's last despairing cry, she staggered back against the wall and leaned there, panting as if exhausted, during the applause.

" Ain't that great! " exclaimed Hugh Farrell. " But say, Lally, you 're wrong in one thing; I 'll bet that old girl was red-headed. Where there 's that much fire, there 's got to be smoke; eh, Let? "

Miss Gorham came up to Floyd, coiling her hair on her head as she approached.

" What a splendid scene that is! Thank you very much," Floyd said cautiously. " It must use you up to do it."

" Yes, I throw myself into it so," she explained. " When once I begin I lose myself entirely; I actually become the person of the play. I just can't help it. I suppose you noticed that? "

" I suppose," Floyd said, evading an answer, " that makes it all the more exhausting."

" Oh my, yes! But that 's what it is to have a temperament, — as of course you know, Mr. Halket."

" No, I 'm afraid I have n't it."

" Oh, I 'm sure you must have. I can always tell by a person's eyes. Your eyes show temperament."

" I guess it 's time, then, for me to be taking to glasses, or they 'll get me into trouble," he said flippantly.

Miss Gorham smiled with gentle indulgence for such levity. "Oh, if I could only persuade you to go in for acting!" she breathed in her low tones. "With your temperament — those eyes — I am sure you would be quite *won*-derful."

Letty came up to them smiling, and her cheerful blue eyes were dancing mischievously. "You see, we nearly all show off here, Mr. Halket," she said. "I'm sure you do something — and we'd appreciate it so if you only would."

"I'm sorry," Floyd answered. "I can't sing or dance or speak a piece. Why, excuse me just a moment, Miss Bell; what is this just coming out of your sleeve? It's caught there, is n't it?" And he reached out, and after three or four gentle tugs drew forth a twenty-five cent piece.

"Oh," cried Letty, clapping her hands, "he's a juggler, he's a juggler! Look here, children," and she pushed the McDonald twins forward. "Watch him do tricks."

So Floyd went through his limited performance: he even brought a silk handkerchief down from his room, showed successfully the magic of the vanishing egg and of the disappearing ring, and then with a pack of cards mystified and delighted his audience.

Only Tustin, who seemed to be a grudging sort of man, looked on with a crooked, contemptuous smile. Floyd had been both interested and repelled by the man's strong and disagreeable face. Now the crooked smile that seemed to deride his own small efforts to entertain the company jarred upon his nerves, and Floyd found himself disliking Tustin even more than his wife. The only time during the evening when Tustin had opened his lips had been to join in the singing of the Sankey hymn, and that had seemed to be under angry protest. But not until Floyd began his sleight-of-hand did Tustin's mouth slant into its crooked smile of scorn.

"Sorehead!" thought Floyd. "Sorehead, all right."

The others, however, were sufficiently appreciative. As for the young ladies, they had no words with which to express their admiration — except Miss Gorham, who ejaculated from time to time "Sorcerer!" or "How *wonderful!*" When the party came to an end, it was evident that Floyd's contribution was more highly regarded than any other feature of the entertainment.

Floyd had enough simplicity and vanity to enjoy such a little triumph, and he was willing always to display his one accomplishment before the unsophisticated audiences that sometimes gathered in Mrs. Bell's parlor. His fame was spread widely by Letty's friends; often in the evenings visitors came in the hope of meeting the distinguished boarder and of seeing him do some of his conjuring. He himself was unconscious or at least thoughtless of the fact that by his geniality and willingness he was winning friends among these humble people — friends whose influence spread out and reached even those who never entered the circle of Mrs. Bell's acquaintances, who never spoke to him or touched his hand.

VIII

LYDIA

ONE evening in the latter part of September, Floyd returning from his work found a letter awaiting him on the table in Mrs. Bell's hall. It was a small blue envelope, with his name and address written across it in an ardent, uneven hand; and because he guessed at once from whom it came he picked it up gingerly in his dirty fingers and laid it unopened on the table in his room. Then he hurried down to his bath, where he was more brief than usual with his splashing and whistling; after which, with clean hands that would not deface the little note, he opened it and smiled at the first words. "Dear Floyd," it began, and he knew from his pleasure that he had feared Lydia would address him more formally, — "I am back in Avalon and I want to see you very much. Papa says you will hardly be able to come over for an evening; but can't you come to luncheon with us next Sunday at one and stay for tea? Do say you will."

Floyd posted his answer before he sat down to Mrs. Bell's supper that evening. His flow of spirits during the meal delighted the landlady, and afterwards, when he insisted on Letty's teaching him to sing, Mrs. Bell sat in the parlor and grew hysterical over his efforts. "Oh, you think it's a bad job, my trying to sing," Floyd cried to them when they were quite speechless with laughter. And he started out boldly upon "Fair Harvard," and in the middle of the second line, Letty broke in upon him, — "Oh, Mr. Halket, that *can't* be right; you're away off," while her mother rocked and rocked, red in the face, unable longer to laugh audibly. "Look at mother; you'll be the death of her," said Letty; and Floyd pretended to be quite petulant and said that everybody was always trying to discourage him. Letty and her mother wondered together that evening what could have happened to make him so gay, and shrewdly decided that the blue letter must have had something to do with it. For they always examined his mail — Mrs. Bell especially — with a respectful curiosity; they were as familiar by this time with Colonel Halket's superscription and that of Mrs. Halket as Floyd was himself; and frequently Mrs. Bell would pick up the letters from these persons for the mere pleasure of holding them in her hand.

When Floyd presented himself the next Sunday at the Dunbars', he was ushered into the room where Lydia sat alone. She was on her feet, waiting for him, and ran forward, crying, "Oh, Floyd, I'm so glad to see you again!" and took his big hand. Then she fell back a step or two, gazing at him and laughing — "You've grown so awfully strong and — *manly* looking," she said. "Sit down and tell me all about yourself."

That was done in a few words — wandering and dull they were, too, for Floyd, sitting on the edge of his chair, was gazing at her and had no other thoughts. He wished that he had the power to make her temporarily inanimate, so that he could stare at her as long as he liked and touch her and walk round and round and examine her. She laughed at him kindly. "You're ever so much more interesting than that," she said. Brown and strong from exposure to the summer sun and winds, she seemed to have developed a new loveliness; her figure that he remembered as girlishly slender had matured, her gray eyes shone with an eager friendly spirit; but that which caught Floyd more than all else with its enchantment was the intermittent quiver of humor over her face — like a light flickering up from lips to temples; it made her seem to him kind and sympathetic and alert with every feminine charm. It was as if the spirit of laughter made quick, frolicsome excursions from the lips where he abode, yet always darted back to them to lie there and look out. Floyd's imagination was touched even by watching her, even by noticing the little details of her dress, the red ribbon against her clear brown throat, the peeping tip of her slipper. At luncheon new sides of her character appeared to him; though he knew instinctively how high her spirit was, he caught, too, a vague perception of her docility, of her innocent, simple humble-mindedness; she sat — and again Floyd's imagination was stirred — through her father's stories with the spirit of laughter lying comfortably in his gateway, issuing spontaneously now to glorify a stupid joke, now to cover the retreat of a crippled one. This last service Floyd felt the more acutely when he bungled in telling something that he had hoped to make amusing.

"Oh, Floyd, have you heard about Stewart?" she cried to him. "You haven't, I'm sure, for my letter came only yesterday. He's got into the *Beaux Arts* right off; isn't he the cleverest thing!"

"But I thought it took years and years!" exclaimed Floyd.

"Oh, it does often; indeed Stewart never expected to get in the first year anyway. But he did, — one of the first ten. Of course he calls it luck — but I knew he was patting himself on the back a good deal, so I wrote to him not to get too vain. But just between ourselves — now that he can't hear — isn't he the cleverest thing?"

"I always thought so," said Floyd.

"And I'm sure you'll be glad of this; he really does think now he'll come here to live — imagine, a Bostonian leaving Boston and coming to Avalon!"

"The inducement would bring the most conservative Bostonian," Floyd declared gallantly.

"Oh," she laughed, "*I'm* not the inducement; he's quite too lordly for that. No, indeed; I'm afraid he's found out how meek I really am. But he has an idea that all the people out here live in wigwams and log cabins, and that they die off by thousands every year because they never heard of open plumbing. And being a Bostonian he has a very strong sense of public duty and is interested in the spread of civilization. And he thinks that architecturally Boston is the last cry of beauty in this country, and that there's not much chance there for a new man to put his stamp on the city the way there is in one of the cruder towns. So if everything goes well, he'll be here in about two years to wage war on the cupola and the mansard roof."

"Yes," said Mrs. Dunbar. "And while he's studying, Lydia is to go about here and say to everybody, ' Of course you don't know, but your house is a perfect fright and all wrong, and you ought to have it torn down and rebuilt, in order to help beautify the city. And if you will put this in the hands of the only competent man for the purpose, it will help him and me so much towards building a nice attractive house of our own.'"

"That's our scheme," said Lydia. "Don't you think you could persuade your grandfather, Floyd, to have his house torn down and let — oh — " and she flushed with embarrassment — " I — I didn't mean what that sounds like — honestly I didn't."

Floyd only laughed, and then she joined him merrily.

Mr. Dunbar gazed at her with an assumption of severity. "When you and your mother get frivolous, Lydia," — he began.

"Mamma, be serious at once," Lydia commanded. "Wait, I'll sober you; I've thought of a joke. Floyd, does pig-iron, when it's made into chains, become sausage?"

"Not legally," Floyd answered. "That would be *forging* a name," and he felt quite elated because this far-fetched effort seemed to amuse Mr. and Mrs. Dunbar and drew a distressed groan from Lydia.

"Dear me!" she said, "to think such brightness is being wasted on the people of New Rome!" And then she cried quite seriously, "Oh, Floyd, it must be awfully forlorn for you out there. Why don't you cut it often and come in here to us? You must be able to do as you please."

"Is anybody?" Floyd asked. "Just think how much more fortunate I am than Stewart. I'll be entering upon what I consider civilization about the time he's quitting his idea of it. When one has to live in Avalon, maybe a term in New Rome is a better preliminary than one in Paris."

"But Stewart will love to be a civilizing influence," said Lydia, laughing. And then she added, "How different you two are! I can't imagine Stewart working out there at New Rome the way you're doing. Tell me, do you really like it?"

"Not altogether," Floyd confessed.

"I never could understand," said Lydia, "why men don't always do the thing they like — when they can. Stewart's doing it; why don't you?"

"Lydia, my dear," interposed her mother, "don't ask impertinent questions."

"Oh, I don't mind answering," Floyd said. "Only, I'm not sure that I've thought out the answer."

"Well, don't bother with it now, for goodness' sake," Lydia urged. "I certainly didn't mean to get you down here to brood on life. — What do you say to a walk this afternoon, — or a ride?"

"I have a new saddle horse that I'd be glad to have you try," said Mr. Dunbar.

"I'm hardly dressed for riding," Floyd answered. "But if you'd just as soon walk — "

"Yes, that's better," Lydia agreed. "Besides, I don't think Mamma quite approves of my riding on Sunday when we're in town."

"Lydia has such nice afterthoughts," said Mrs. Dunbar mildly.

It was a very genial family, Floyd thought; they all liked to tease one another and to be teased, they all seemed in spirits to be of the same age — and that was Lydia's. Mrs.

Bell and Letty had good times together, which Floyd had shared, but he thought of them now compassionately, — "What a pity everybody can't be happy like these people!"

In the afternoon he and Lydia walked along familiar streets; in the grounds about the houses the maples were turning yellow, and the early autumn flowers were in bloom. But Floyd did not notice much along the way. He was absorbed in his consciousness of Lydia — delighting in the fact that she seemed to be revealing herself to him with the freedom of intimacy, delighting, too, in the personality that she revealed. When his eyes were not fixed on her, laughing and admiring, they were directed at the ground, while he mused pleasantly over the always fresh knowledge that they had acquired.

"I hope," she said doubtfully, "you did n't think I was very flippant, speaking of Stewart as I did at luncheon, and laughing a little about his Bostonian ideas?"

"No; of course it's perfectly true," Floyd answered.

"It's just the way I talk to Stewart himself; I feel I can talk about him to you almost as I could to him," she explained. "The — the relations are so — so queer, you know; I must always associate you with him so closely as long as I live. — But you two are very unlike, are n't you? I wish " — she spoke a little timidly — " I wish you would n't always be so heroic, Floyd."

The remark stung him even while he did not understand it.

"What do you mean?" he asked.

"Just what we were speaking of at luncheon," she answered. "I'm sure you're not doing what you want to do. You're being heroic, day after day, up there at New Rome. Why is n't it better to have a good time working, the way Stewart will do, than — oh, you don't mind my talking to you this way, Floyd?"

"But what makes you think I don't have a good time?" he asked her, and there was something of a challenge in his voice.

"The way you look — something in your face — you've changed since I last saw you," said Lydia. "I think I *feel* things about some people, and — you're one."

They walked on in silence for a few moments.

"The trouble is," Floyd said abruptly, "most young fellows have nothing particular they want to do, or if they have, it's not worth doing. Now," and he laughed a little, "I've always been fonder of doing stunts in athletics than anything else — but you wouldn't want me to go in for that, would you?"

"That's not the only thing," Lydia insisted. "Stewart's told me that you're a wonder in chemistry."

"It's good fun playing in a laboratory," Floyd said. "But some time I can have my own laboratory out at the works and do as I please with that. — No," he broke out suddenly, "I won't pretend I'm doing just what I most like. But it's a responsibility I can't dodge. The works are there and I must be trained up to take charge of them some day."

"But why — if you don't want to? Why can't you sell them? — why can't you turn them over to somebody else to run? Why can't you just drop the whole business of steel and become a great chemist, or a college professor, or whatever you want to be?"

"Because there are ten thousand people in New Rome who depend for their living on the Halket works," Floyd answered. "The business has been conducted in a certain way, the men have grown accustomed to expect a certain kind of treatment, perhaps there has been all along an attempt to keep on friendly terms with the men and to do things for their comfort — more than would be done in other places, — and it's a matter not only of pride to me, but of justice to them that there shouldn't be a change. Sell out and there's bound to be a change. A few days ago I heard a labor agitator talking to some of the men, talking about my grandfather. 'He may be wanting to do for labor more than labor wants to do for itself,' said the man. 'But some day, when he's no longer with us, there may be somebody come in who won't want to do for labor more than it wants to do for itself, — but who will want to get out of labor all that it can give for as little as he can give.' I can't blame the men for dreading something of that kind. I'd dread it in their place. It must be worth while to stay and study and work to prevent a change, when so many people are dependent on you. And if it is n't what I'd most like to do, I'd better learn to like it — and I suppose I shall. — How did we happen to get so serious, anyway?"

Lydia did not answer for a moment; her face under her broad blue hat remained serious.

"Oh, I don't see why the nice people who deserve a good time and could do so much good just having it must be saddled with big responsibilities that they don't want," she exclaimed at last. "But I suppose the rest of us would n't admire them half so much if they did n't do such things. And I think you're fine, Floyd, to take it as you do. I like to play and frivol and have fun in life; I'm afraid that's all it means to me."

"So long as you make it mean so much more to somebody else, you need n't worry," said Floyd with a laugh. "And if you'd play with me once in a while, when I can get away from my job—"

"Oh, always" she cried, and her face lighted up quite eagerly. "That's a promise: you'll come here whenever you can; do get off some Saturday afternoon before long, and we can go for a ride out in the country."

"I'll strike for next Saturday," declared Floyd.

"Splendid!" and she clapped her hands. "I'm glad to see you're willing to be something else than heroic all the time."

She chatted then gayly about the people at Chester whom he knew; some of his classmates had been there this summer and had said nice things about him to her, which she now repeated, — to his pleasure and embarrassment. "You don't know," he said to her, "how good it is to hear from that part of the world again."

When they returned to the house, the afternoon light was growing dim; Mr. and Mrs. Dunbar were just coming out for a romp with two small cousins of Lydia's who had arrived a few minutes before. "Who's going to play 'Follow my Leader'?" cried Mr. Dunbar, and the small visitors screamed with delight when Lydia said, "Why, all of us, of course." "They think Papa and Mamma are the most enchanting things," she explained to Floyd; "they wear themselves to a gasp running round with them." The game took place behind the house, where the lawn sloped away from the street, and there was no danger of shocking passers-by. "Now, you must fall in line and all do as I do," said Mr. Dunbar. "Lydia first, and then Laurie and then Aunt Elinor and then Teddy and last of all Mr. Halket."

"Indeed," cried Mrs. Dunbar, laughing, "you don't get me into this game."

"Oh, but you always play, Aunt Elinor," exclaimed Teddy; and Mr. Dunbar said, "Why, of course; Floyd won't be shocked, will you, Floyd? Fall in line, now; all ready? We're off — sneaking Indians."

And he led them, all crouching and taking long slow strides; they circled twice round a bench, three times round a tree, and then trailed about the lawn, ejaculating "Hist!" with every two steps, because that was what the leader was doing. Floyd, from his position at the end of the line had a view of the procession as it swung and turned; Mr. Dunbar, Lydia, her mother, and the two little boys were all doing their part with the utmost seriousness. "Hop-Skip!" cried the leader, straightening up, and at that they all straightened up and hop-skipped, zigzagging about and again circling the bench twice. "Go faster, Aunt Elinor!" cried Teddy, pounding his small fist on his aunt's stout, tight back. "I can't!" she protested, and threw a deprecating glance at Floyd. Lydia, light of foot and graceful in every movement, pranced on, laughing back now at her mother, now at Floyd, who grinned and enjoyed the spectacle; the two small boys were now giggling, and Mr. Dunbar was the only one who remained serious and earnest, going through the motions with a dignified rhythm.

"Positively not another step," gasped Mrs. Dunbar, dropping out of the line, which her husband instantly led round and round her in a derisive circle. Then they all stopped, out of breath and laughing.

"Great exercise," said Mr. Dunbar to Floyd. "I'm not so much winded, am I, for a man of my age and weight; that's because I do dumb-bells every night and morning."

"You didn't jump up on the bench," complained Laurie. "You didn't make Aunt Elinor jump up on the bench the way you always do."

"Aunt Elinor's getting too old and fat for such things," Mrs. Dunbar said to him. "I can't let your uncle drag me round much longer as he's done to-day."

"Your aunt needs training," Mr. Dunbar said. "You boys must come oftener and we'll limber her up again."

"You ought to let Floyd or me lead the procession," said Lydia. "I guess we would wear the kids out."

"Ho! I guess you wouldn't," cried Teddy. "You're nothing but a girl."

She "tagged" him and fled laughing, and he pursued her vainly, while she dodged round a tree and then round Floyd, and then caught Laurie and held him in front of her for defense.

"I think," said Mrs. Dunbar, "this is almost worse for Sunday afternoon than horseback riding. Let's go into the house."

Floyd stayed so late that evening that he had had much less than his usual eight hours of sleep when Letty knocked on his door at half-past five the next morning. He woke to a day of fog; through that week a heavy fog hung in the valley, growing thicker and thicker with each new day of breathless atmosphere, depressed and blended with the weight and filth of smoke. At mid-day the sun was only a pale white disk overhead at which one might stare as harmlessly as at the moon. In the morning Floyd groped his way down the hill toward a void of clamor and sound; at nightfall, when he climbed the hill, the flames and illuminations that gave usually a splendor to New Rome, compensating for the squalor of its day, were blotted out by the damp murkiness, and again out of the invisible rang the harsh noises of the mills. These were more piercing, more continuous than ever; the locomotives, pushing or pulling their little trains with a slow caution, were sending up always their shrill whistles — in spite of which warnings there were two accidents during the week, two Italian laborers caught and run down between trains. An accident always caused a feeling of sullenness in the works; this was now intensified by the gloom of the weather and the increased discomfort of the conditions; the thick and acrid smoke that would not rise, the floating particles of grime that clogged one's breathing-passages, the chill dampness, worse than wind, worse than rain, that greeted the man who went sweating from his furnace to draw a breath of air. But worst of all was the oppression caused by the strange, imperfect sun in the sky, appearing hazily day after day, only to disappear vanquished by the clammy night. Some of the ignorant and superstitious foreigners found portents in this feeble inability of the sun, and stopped work; others went about their tasks cowed and afraid. Among the intelligent there was sullenness without fear, rebellion without animus, a hatred of the work itself, divorced, it seemed, from any feeling against their superiors or against the necessity that compelled them to such work. And in these days and nights the movement to " unionize " the mills advanced as it had not done in a whole month of summer.

Floyd was aware of the changing spirit; the men with

whom he worked made no effort to conceal it from him; Shelton, already a member of the union and its advocate, would discuss it with him in the intermissions, while Tom and Bill and others of the men would sit and listen. Floyd disavowed hostility, but tried to present such arguments as should cause them to hesitate. The day the second Italian was killed, Shelton said to him, —

" It's well enough so long as we all know that if we're hurt or killed at our work the company pays the expense. But supposing the company don't always do that? We want an organization that will — "

"The company will always do it; I can promise that," said Floyd.

"Well," Shelton grumbled, "maybe so. But even so — it might be better for us to feel more independent — "

"You think that joining the union makes men independent?"

"Yes, of some things."

"The generosity of their employers, and what else?"

"Well, even supposing we was to let it go at that. Wouldn't it be more self-respecting?"

"Oh, shucks!" said Floyd with a laugh. "Come and let's pitch quoits."

He never went far in these arguments with any of the men; he admitted to them quite frankly that his inexperience in the subject qualified him to listen rather than to speak. They seemed not to disguise their sentiments in talking before him, and this pleased him. So far as he could judge, even those most outspoken for "organization" had no grievance that they wished redressed, no definite end that they hoped by organizing to accomplish; their argument was simply that they would be putting themselves in a better position to lay complaints, to defend themselves against aggression, to command the granting of their utmost rights. It interested Floyd to learn that Tustin, the grim, silent man with the crooked smile, who was Mrs. Bell's next-door neighbor, was one of the most active and able organizers. But he did not himself come into contact with Tustin.

Floyd was summoned one day to lunch with the company officials in their private room at the New Rome Hotel. Some of the superintendents were there and reported the state of mind prevailing in their mills. Most of them were disposed to regard lightly the union agitation. "There's no real disaffection among the men," said the superintendent of Open-Hearth Number One. "This is one of those periodic simmerings; we've had them before. The union has several times got a foothold here; but it's never been for long."

"I think they mean business now," said Gregg slowly. "The union agents have been working systematically the past two months. Mr. Halket, what is your opinion, from what you see among the men?"

"The men are joining the union a good deal more readily than they were a month ago," Floyd answered. "But it does n't seem to be with any particular end in view."

"There never yet was a beginning but what some end grew out of it," remarked one of the superintendents pessimistically. "I'd fight the movement and choke it before it gets under way."

"That," said Gregg, stroking the prongs of his beard, "is something to consider. — Your grandfather will be back the latter part of the week, Mr. Halket?"

"Yes," said Floyd.

"I guess," observed Gregg, "we'll get an opinion from him before we take steps. Mr. Sharp, has n't Mr. Halket here learned all there is to know about making steel?"

"I was just going to suggest," replied the superintendent of Open-Hearth Number Two, "that he might go on to something else pretty soon. Don't you think so, Mr. Halket?"

"Why," said Floyd, "I feel that I've learned something; if you think it's enough, I'm ready any time for a change."

"Yes," said Gregg. "Next Monday you'd better report at Rod-Mill Number Three. And," — he smiled cheerfully, — "you'd better take a holiday on Saturday to get ready; I guess Mr. Sharp will spare you."

"Thank you," Floyd answered; and he was quite elated at the idea of a holiday — and at not having to ask for the Saturday afternoon which he had promised himself with Lydia.

He went back through the fog to his work with a light step; promotion — or transfer — to the Rod-Mill was his first distinct achievement. It was in Rod-Mill Number Three that Hugh Farrell worked, and Floyd wondered if he would be put on the same turn with him. He hoped so; for in spite of the coolness with which he had treated Farrell since the night when they had separated at the dance-hall, he could not help liking the fellow — both for the merry nature he showed in his relations with Letty and her mother and for the quiet indifference with which he accepted Floyd's coolness.

The men in Floyd's heat at the open-hearth mill seemed honestly sorry to hear that he was leaving them.

"But," cried Shelton, "you and me was such a team with the quoits!"

"I know it," said Floyd regretfully. "Well, we'll have to find new partners and lick each other."

"'T ain't hardly the same thing," Shelton said.

"No," said Tom and Bill, "'t ain't."

They were always men of few words.

On Friday a north wind came down from the hills and cleared away the fog; the sun emerged in a sudden autumnal brilliancy, and Floyd went light-heartedly about his last work at the furnace. He had not been much affected by the general depression; he was getting on with his apprenticeship, his family were soon to be back in Avalon, and he would have a home to go to on Sundays; he looked forward to the ride with Lydia; indeed, he thought of Lydia whenever he had time to think at all; and not in the wistful, melancholy way that he had done before seeing her. Now it was with a certain courageous gladness; for a time at least there might be no Stewart at hand to dispute his devotion, to reduce him to silence and retirement; for a time she would be his frank and glad companion. Now on this last Friday, with the north wind blowing down the promise of fine weather for his holiday, his face must have shown his joyousness, for Shelton would often glance at him wistfully, and Floyd, intent upon his work, or possibly his anticipations, did not notice. When the six o'clock whistle blew, the men gathered round Floyd and shook hands with him, bidding him good-by, and then hurried away, lest they might say too much. But Shelton hung round till the last and walked with Floyd across the bridge. Then, as they were to separate, he said awkwardly, —

"I don't blame you for bein' glad to quit us; I seen it in your face all day."

"No, Shelton," Floyd said, "if I've looked glad, that's not the reason; honestly, it's not. I want to thank you and the other fellows for the way you've treated me."

"Hell!" said Shelton, "'t was nothing. I'm proud to know you, Mr. Halket, — and some day I'll be proud to work for you."

He turned abruptly and walked off; Floyd stood quite speechless. Then his face lighted up and he called, "Shelton! O Shelton!" The man turned back, and they advanced towards each other; Floyd came up and put his hand on Shelton's shoulder.

"There was just one thing I felt I ought to say," he began earnestly. "Now that I'm going away, I can't help having it on my mind. I want you to promise me that you will be very, very careful about the fumes."

Shelton stared into his solemn face and burst into a loud laugh. Then he slapped his hand into Floyd's. "Good-by," he said. "Good-by." And so they parted.

IX

A HOLIDAY

FLOYD slept luxuriously late the next morning; when he came down to breakfast, Letty had already gone to her work at the Library.

"Mrs. Bell," he said, while his landlady waited upon him, "what should you do in my place, getting a sudden holiday like this?"

"Land!" said Mrs. Bell, "I don't know, but I guess I'd get as far away from the works as I could."

"It must be fine out in the country this morning," observed Floyd. "I have to go into the city this afternoon; why would n't it be a good thing to spend the morning in the country?"

"Why, it would so," assented Mrs. Bell.

"What do you do with yourself, mornings?" pursued Floyd. "What do women do after they get the men-folks shipped out of the house?"

"Oh, warsh the dishes and read up the rooms and sweep and mend clothes and bake and put up preserves and get things ready for dinner," Mrs. Bell replied.

"Suppose you take a holiday from all that this morning," Floyd suggested.

"My land! what for?"

"I'll get a team from the livery-stable and we'll go for a drive in the country."

"Oh, my goodness, Mr. Halket!"

"Yes, you go and get yourself ready, and I'll go after the team. I wonder if Letty could n't join us. I'll stop at the Library and see."

"Oh, the idea!" giggled Mrs. Bell. "Well, it certainly will be enjoyable."

She darted upstairs, and when a moment later Floyd went to his room for a box of cigarettes, he found her there, whisking about, making his bed, beating up his pillow.

"Woman!" he cried sternly, "have I not declared a holiday?"

She turned a scared face. "'T won't take me a minute to read up your room," she pleaded. "Besides, if I don't do it now, I'll have to later."

He looked at her with silent scorn while he pocketed his cigarettes.

"I will return anon," he said, as he departed, "with two horses — two." And he heard her tittering with glee as he descended the stairs.

At the Library he found Letty and sent her, quivering with excitement, to ask for a morning off. The librarian of the Halket Library was not inclined to oppose any obstacles to the wishes of a Halket, and Letty came back to Floyd, pinning on her hat, and with her face radiant.

"Oh, and it's such a beautiful day!" she said as they descended the steps of the building. The sun shone, the sky was all blue, even the smoke from the mills seemed clear and bright, going up in smooth, harmonious curls. Letty ran home to get ready for the drive, and Floyd went down the hill to the livery-stable. Here he had to expostulate with the proprietor, who, on finding that his customer knew something about horses, showed a belated eagerness in supplying the best pair in his establishment and the smartest turn-out. When Floyd drove up the hill, Mrs. Bell and her daughter issued promptly from their door; evidently they had been alarmed lest they might keep him waiting. Mrs. Tustin was pottering round in her front yard; Mrs. Bell had found an opportunity before Letty's arrival to dart over and tell her what was about to happen. She came and leaned upon the fence and smiled at Floyd. She watched her neighbors as they were mounting to the back seat of the carriage.

"Are both of you going to sit in there?" Floyd asked. "Somebody ought to be up here to help me in case these spirited horses get beyond my control."

Mrs. Bell was at once for changing her seat obediently, but her daughter laughed and held her back, saying, "Don't you see, Ma, he's only joking?"

Then Mrs. Tustin cried in her most genial voice, —

"My goodness, seein' that extry seat makes me feel almost like invitin' myself along."

Floyd pretended not to hear, flourished the whip and chirruped to the horses, and in another moment had left Mrs. Tustin standing in sour contemplation by her fence.

Up over the crest of the hills and away from the dirty river he laid his course, and before long the country cleared before them, unspoiled and unbegrimed. Woods of hickory, maple, and birch, all in the full glory of their autumn coloring, fringed the small farms and bordered the roadside.

"Oh, look, Mr. Halket, there goes a chipmunk with a nut in his mouth!" cried Letty; and Floyd touched up the horses and raced the squirrel, who went bounding along the top of the rail fence in wild affright.

"My, that's exciting!" said Mrs. Bell, when the horses had settled again to an easy trot. "I was afraid for a while, Mr. Halket, that they'd got away from you."

"Oh, I tell you," bragged Floyd, "there's nothing so good for the muscle as being an iron-worker."

"This is the first carriage ride I've had in — my goodness! I don't know how many years," mused Mrs. Bell aloud.

"I guess it isn't such a new thing to you, Miss Bell," hazarded Floyd.

"Why, I don't know. What makes you think that?" Letty asked.

"Doesn't Hugh Farrell handle the reins now and then?"

Floyd winked perceptibly over his shoulder at Mrs. Bell.

"Now, Mr. Halket, you are the tease!" exclaimed Letty.

Floyd turned round to her with a sober face.

"You'd tell me, wouldn't you, if you really minded?" he said.

"Why, yes, of course — oh, my goodness, what am I to say!" cried Letty. "Well, you certainly are the tease!"

"I suppose," Floyd said to Mrs. Bell, "your daughter would tell us if we are taking a road that's familiar?"

Mrs. Bell began to giggle, and Letty cried in despair, "Well, if you *aren't* the tease!"

Returning home by a different road, they came past the grounds of the Avalon Country Club, and Floyd was pointing out the golf-links and tennis-courts when a young woman driving in a high-wheeled cart dashed through the gateway toward them. It was Lydia, and as Floyd raised his hat her glance of surprise followed hard on that of recognition. She slowed up to say, "You're coming to luncheon?" and to get his answer, "Yes;" then she drove smartly on.

"Funny, isn't it," Floyd remarked to his companions, "that I should meet the lady I'm going to lunch with away out here."

Letty wanted to ask him who the girl was, sure that she must be one of those enviable persons whose names were so familiar to her in the society column of the Avalon Sunday *Eagle*. As she said to her mother afterwards, she was "dying to know," and Mrs. Bell confessed to a like curiosity. But though Floyd could be so free in teasing Letty about Hugh, she did not dare to question him flippantly in the same way — especially when he lapsed for a while into an abstracted silence. It was not, however, long before he resumed his former buoyancy and drove with what seemed to Mrs. Bell a wild carelessness, turning about on his seat and chatting irresponsibly with her and Letty. And afterwards, when he had driven them home and left them, and they were talking over the experi-

A HOLIDAY

ence, they reminded each other of the note in the strange handwriting and of the idiotic gayety that had possessed him that night, and recalled similarities to what Mrs. Bell termed his "nice craziness" on the road. "I'm sure it's that girl we met, Letty," she said, and Letty agreed with her.

Meanwhile Floyd was hurrying in to Avalon. He went to his grandfather's house, where he put on his riding-clothes, and then to the stable, where he mounted his black mare, Kitty. Then, because he was late, he galloped all the way to the Dunbars', and came in to Lydia and her mother flushed and disheveled.

"So you managed to get your Saturday afternoon off," Lydia said to him, with a laugh.

Floyd entered upon an earnest explanation of how his work had suddenly been changed and he had unexpectedly been given the whole day.

"Oh," said Lydia, "I don't think any the worse of you; I'm glad you're willing to take a holiday when you can. It was perfectly splendid to see you enjoying yourself. But I'm afraid after this morning you'll find our ride a very tame affair."

Floyd protested, flushed, and checked himself; he had a feeling that it might be either caddish or priggish to explain to Lydia who his companions had been. He certainly did not mind being teased by her; he wondered why he should seem so embarrassed.

At luncheon Lydia did not altogether drop the subject; she wondered where they would go; she would have to map out a new course, for she had intended to take him where he had been that morning, and it wouldn't do now at all — such associations as he had with it possibly, and so recent — And Floyd, remembering that in similar words he had teased Letty on the drive, broke here into sudden laughter.

"But what is so funny?" Lydia asked. "Do tell us."

Floyd shook his head. "No, it's just a little private

joke of my own," he said, and he went on laughing in the most annoying fashion.

"How mean of you!" exclaimed Lydia. "Mamma, don't you think he might tell us?"

"Lydia," said her mother, "as I have often said, you are consumed by a burning curiosity."

"And yet one would think," observed Floyd, "that a burnt child would dread the fire!"

"Both of you are quite horrid," said Lydia, "and I don't believe I'll read you Stewart's letter."

But after luncheon she relented a little — so far as to read Floyd extracts from it, describing the two French friends he had already acquired and his rooms in the Rue Soufflot. "Why do you skip?" Floyd asked innocently, and was delighted to see her blush and hear her say, "Oh, Stewart gets silly here and it wouldn't interest you."

The horses were brought round; the groom held them while Floyd helped Lydia to mount. In her light, strong spring from his hand he caught as it were a more vital conception and possession of her personality, more vital than had been conveyed by the touch of her hand or the glance of her eyes. That instant he was flooded with the desire and the love that he had until then been trying to suppress.

He mounted and rode along the driveway by her side, silent and with his nerves throbbing. They trotted down to the park behind his grandfather's hill; here there was a bridle-path, and she gave her pony rein and dared him to catch her. With a sudden fierceness, the antidote to his sense of impotence, he gave chase and swept past her, sitting erect and ruthless, not drawing rein until he had distanced her by twenty yards. She cantered up to him, a little hurt and reproachful.

"You might have made it more of a race," she said, with an appealing smile that went to his heart.

"I guess I just forgot myself," he said humbly.

"I don't mean," she explained, "that I wanted you to *let* me win."

He laughed. "I guess I should n't think that of you."

They came out of the park and ambled along country roads, now and then making brief dashes, in which for a few seconds at least Lydia always held her own. After a time she said to him, —

"Floyd, I'm going to be very impertinent. Do you mind telling me who those people were I saw you with this morning? If you do mind, just say so."

"They were Mrs. Bell, my landlady, and her daughter," Floyd answered.

"Oh!" She meditated a moment. "That is just the kind of thing that I should have supposed you 'd do."

"What?"

"Put in part of your holiday giving people a good time."

"I'm sorry I'm making such a failure of the rest of it."

"How disagreeable of you to say that! But you know what I mean. It's because I thought it was something of that kind that I dared to be impertinent. Do you mind if I say right out what I think? It makes me like you better than ever."

Floyd swept off his cap and bowed down to his horse's mane.

"Oh, you need n't take that as a great compliment," Lydia continued. "I'm perfectly illogical. Now, we both know that Stewart would no more do a thing like that than he 'd — well, I give up. But he would n't do it for anything — and just that trait in him is one of the things that makes me care for him. It's so — Bostonian — and so human."

"And I'm neither Bostonian nor human," Floyd said rather sadly.

"You're certainly not Bostonian; you have some tendency to be human, but I shall always think of you as mainly heroic," Lydia pronounced; and she did not know how deeply the definition cut him. "Of course, Stewart *could* do an heroic thing, don't you think so, Floyd?"

"Yes, oh yes, indeed," Floyd hastened to declare.

"If he couldn't," Lydia continued vaguely, "I'm sure he wouldn't be so — so lovable. And everybody feels that he is — don't they, Floyd?"

"Yes, everybody," Floyd answered.

They rode silently together, side by side, and Floyd looked at her with a kind of rage, because she was so beautiful and yet was not for him. He clinched his teeth and his lips and turned away from looking at her. And then in a moment he would glance round again, and she, catching the movement and thinking he was about to speak, would turn towards him with an expectant smile. That smile, so cajoling and so gentle, must soften the most churlish companion. It summed up all the light of fellowship and liking in the gray eyes, all the sweetness and humor of the flexible, light lips, the poetry of the temples, the courage and spirit of the chin; it was Lydia. And the figure of the girl, erect on her horse, outlined beneath the tight-fitting black coat, had something of the same frankness, clearness, and simplicity of beauty as her face, — slim-waisted, deep of chest and bust; and more and more as Floyd rode with her the feeling of her spring from his hand to the saddle tingled through him, making him cognizant of her subtle strength and lightness.

A wish was swelling and stifling in his bosom — a wish to show her that he was no monstrosity of self-immolation, such as she seemed to conceive him, but a man, greedy, selfish, passionate, turbulent, loving — loving — loving. He was close by her side; Stewart — in Paris — intervened. The arrogance of utter conviction possessed Floyd; if he chose to show himself, to make the effort, he could win her from Stewart; he looked at her again, and again the conviction cried out arrogantly within him and urged him on. Conquest would not be his at once, but it would be attained; he had the consciousness of utter desire which is the consciousness — or the delusion — of the ultimate power. Yet his lips were sealed and his power was chained in his breast, and his love must beat itself to death in his brain — all because a man lived whom he had plucked from the depth of the sea.

Again he looked at her; and then, with the sudden imagination that he was riding Stewart down, he struck his horse's flank and shot ahead a little way at a gallop. Then he pulled in and sat with his head dejected, thinking, "It wouldn't be square; it wouldn't be square."

"I'm afraid you're tired," said Lydia sympathetically, riding up. "I ought to have remembered you're not riding as I am every day."

"No, I'm not tired," Floyd answered. "Don't worry about me; I'll ride with you as long as you want."

"I think perhaps we'd better turn back anyway," she said. "It will be dark by the time we get home."

Most of the way they jogged in silence. When they came near the Halket place, Lydia said, "You mustn't bother to ride home with me. Put up your horse and then come over to dinner."

She was so urgent that at last he consented; he was not loath to prolong for an hour an intimacy that in his silent thoughts he had decided to bring to an end.

It did not ease his mind to sit opposite her at dinner that evening; with her arms and shoulders bare, with her dark hair piled thick and glistening and dropping loose tendrils forward about her temples, with her face and neck lighted softly from the shaded candles, she seemed to him even more radiant and entrancing than on horseback. After dinner he took his leave early, though Mrs. Dunbar and Lydia pressed him to pass the night and Sunday with them; he said vaguely that he had things to do at New Rome; no, he could not even come in on Sunday to dinner; he rejected the invitation obstinately, telling himself that no good could come of further dallying.

When he had closed the door of the house behind him, he walked down the driveway with a swelling in his throat and with a miserable feeling of despair. Lydia in Avalon — the presence to which he had looked with expectation and delight — could only be a torture to him — the more maddening the more that he saw her. From this moment he would give up the sight of her if he could not abandon the thought. And then savagely the old, primitive, brutal instincts seized him; he would strangle the thought of her, too. He boarded a car for New Rome and sat brooding and huddled together in a corner. He was not human, was he not? To-night he would carouse with humanity.

He was, however, in a mood which was not easily influenced by drink. In the bar-room in New Rome he sat at a table and consumed whiskey. It could not take his mind from Lydia; he thought of her, with his arms outstretched upon the table, turning his glass slowly round and round in his fingers. Though his head remained clear, his thoughts seemed to grow tainted and corrupt, until suddenly he pushed the glass from him, and sitting with his head bowed on his hands muttered to himself, "God! I was soiling her with my thoughts!" He called for more whiskey and for more; and at last with a sullen, dogged, and inflamed mind he resolved this night to descend to a depth from which he need not again aspire, the memory of which would be a reproach and chastisement to his love. "She's not for me; let's be a man to-night." He betook himself upon slightly unsteady legs to the dance-hall.

A large blonde girl stood near the stairs talking with two men. Floyd approached and said to her abruptly, "Will you dance with me?" She looked round, ready to make some flippant reply, but the expression on his dark face subdued her, and she offered herself without a word. When he had put his arm round her, she tried a little coquettishness. "Now you've got me, don't look so fierce. Can't you smile, old Pain-in-the Face?" He did not answer, but whirled away with her, and if she felt piqued she also felt elated, for she had captured one of the best-looking men in the hall.

Bumping through the crowd, Floyd bumped eventually against Hugh Farrell, who had the same partner as at the former dance, the girl with the pronounced cherry color on lips and cheeks, the silent girl who chewed gum. "Hello!" cried Farrell genially. Floyd looked coolly at him and did not answer. Farrell steered close alongside. "Hello!" he said; and then as Floyd still did not answer, his voice became stern. "I'm speakin' to you," he said. Floyd drew his partner away, and getting over to the other side of the room, stopped.

"That will do for me, thank you," he said; and he abandoned her as abruptly as he had come. He went to the head of the stairs and leaned against the wall.

If his mood had suddenly become virtuous, it was still ugly. He kept his eyes fastened on Farrell and his partner. At the end of the dance they sat down on one of the benches across the room; Farrell threw one arm carelessly over her shoulders, and she nestled up to him and chewed her gum in the serenity of being possessed. Floyd stood looking at them; his vindictive, chastising rage on behalf of virtue simmered harmlessly away, and in its place came the wish to help rather than to punish a friend. He walked across the room unsteadily, conscious and ashamed of his unsteadiness, and as he stood bending down in front of Hugh Farrell, he swayed a little from side to side.

"Hugh Farrell," he said, "I — I didn't answer you. I want to beg your pardon." He put out his hand and leaned on Farrell's shoulder, and then continued, murmuring in his ear, "You — you see how it is — how it is with me. I beg your pardon."

"Oh, sure," said Farrell good-naturedly, reaching up and gripping his hand. "I know how it is, old man; that's all right."

"Thanks. Hugh Farrell, I want just a few minutes'

private talk with you; just a few minutes, Hugh Farrell; tell — tell her."

Farrell spoke to his partner, who released him; then he rose and walked with Floyd across to the stairs.

"Come outside just a moment," Floyd urged. "I — I can't have private talk with you here."

He was losing control over his speech as well as over his legs, but his head was clear. Farrell was quite willing to humor him and descended the stairs. Floyd drew him across the street, and still clinging to him leaned against the fence inclosing a vacant lot.

"Hugh Farrell," he said, "you're a friend of mine — and I like you. You're engaged to a girl that's a friend of mine — and I like her. She loves you, and you've given her to understand that you love her. Now you think I'm drunk — 'nd I am. I can't walk straight — 'nd I can't talk straight — but I can see straight — you — you understand?"

He looked Farrell in the eyes, even while he clung to him, wobbling.

"No," said Farrell doggedly.

"Then — then you must have patience while I explain. You must be patient — for 'n this condition I must pick and choose my words — pick and choose — Look here," Floyd stiffened himself. "A man that loves a girl — and then runs with a woman — he's a cad — and he's a — he's a human skunk —"

Farrell cursed under his breath and tried to shake himself free, but Floyd clung fast.

"I tell you he is," he cried earnestly; "I know, for I have so mighty near been one myself — so mighty near — but I'm not — I swear I'm not! And, Hugh Farrell, I don't want you to be one — for you're my friend, and I like you, and you're a man, a man — and Letty — you know, Hugh Farrell, she loves you and you can have her, she's yours," Floyd burst out with a sudden intense passion and came to a full stop, clutching Farrell's coat and looking steadily into his eyes. " And — you run with that!"

He let go of Farrell and pointed across the street up at the lighted windows of the dance-hall. Farrell stood motionless; he did not move when Floyd turned to him again. This time Floyd staggered and half sank against him.

Farrell stood supporting the drunken man.

"Come along, old boy," he said gently at last. "I guess you need a hand getting home. — Now we're off — that's right — no, need n't bother to thank me; some other day we'll thank each other. I swear," he murmured reflectively under his breath, "if you ain't a gentleman, though."

He piloted Floyd home, and since Mrs. Bell and Letty were already in bed, got him up to his room without creating a scandal in the house.

X

THE END OF AN APPRENTICESHIP

ONE Saturday evening in midwinter Floyd and Mrs. Halket sat alone together in the library before the blazing fire. The fireplace was a large one, in keeping with the size of the room; it had great brass andirons surmounted by horses' heads; and on these andirons, symmetrically placed, were three huge artificial logs, perforated on all sides with little holes from which jets of flame issued. These unconsumable logs were cunningly devised; here and there a red glow would appear upon them and slowly fade, the flame leaped now and then irregularly, and the similitude to a wood fire was improved by the bed of real ashes which had been placed under the logs in the autumn and would be removed in the spring.

"Is n't it a sham!" Mrs. Halket murmured to Floyd.

She sat with her feet resting on a cushion and turned up toward the fire; her left hand hung over the arm of her chair, and the rings on it — opals and diamonds — gleamed and glittered in the light. Her husband liked to have her crowd her fingers with rings before she came to dinner; he considered that with the silver and flowers and glass they helped to make the table more cheerful.

Suddenly she rose, with a shiver, and stood, tall and graceful, with her back to the fire, looking down at Floyd.

"I think I have reached an age when it's more decent to cover one's shoulders," she said; "at least in private. Of course when one has people to dinner or goes to a ball, one must still display one's edifying bones. I suppose it helps to give confidence to the young and shy. I had the

END OF AN APPRENTICESHIP 143

feeling the other night at the Assembly that every young thing in the room was flaunting her youth at me. — And speaking of the Assembly, Floyd, reminds me of something that I've had in my thoughts to say to you for a long time. It troubles me a little, the way you're shutting yourself off from all social life."

"But, good gracious," Floyd answered, "what am I to do? I get home Saturday afternoon and leave Sunday evening; there is n't much chance — "

"You don't seize what there is," objected his grandmother. "Now, your Saturday evenings. Generally after dinner, you call Ted Baldwin or Harry Stevens up on the telephone, and by the way I heard Ted speak of it the other day as the 'phone;' I trust you do not call it that?"

"Never," said Floyd.

"I could n't have borne it if you did. Well, as I was saying, usually on Saturday night you go with one of your friends to what you call a show. Then you drop in at the Avalon Club for something to — "

"Drink," said Floyd. "Yes, quite right, Grandmother."

"Then you come home, go to bed, get up in time for church the next morning — you are very dutiful about that and you please your grandfather very much. Personally I'd rather see you less dutiful, — either sleeping later, or, if you must go to church, now and then accompanying some attractive girl."

"You have such radical ideas," murmured Floyd.

"Radical! Not at all; highly conservative," replied Mrs. Halket. "They date back to my own youth — when Sunday morning, with its question as to who would be my escort, offered one of the chief excitements of the week. If girls are anything like what they used to be, they would be quite thrilled by your proposing to walk to church with them — such an interesting, aloof young man. Then Sunday afternoon, instead of going off again with Ted

Baldwin or Harry Stevens to skate or snowshoe or what not, you ought to thrill a few other young ladies by calling on them. Now and then I would even resign myself to your absence from luncheon or dinner. It's quite wrong for you to be so backward or indifferent, Floyd. After all, to be socially awkward is never anything to a man's credit."

"I'm sorry, Grandmother," Floyd said, quite seriously. "But beside you and Grandfather — well, I am the ugly duckling sure."

"My dear, I refuse to admit it," replied Mrs. Halket, "and even if it were so, you would still be the whole brood. And whether you like it or not, you will some day have social duties to perform. I don't suppose it's very much fun really for me, but it's the penalty of position. Here was this week's programme: Monday, a dinner of twenty old people; Tuesday, a dinner for sixteen young ones, and afterwards the ball that I gave for Ann Phelps's little girl; Wednesday, another small dinner in honor of the New York publisher, Mr. Stark, who spent two days with us; Thursday, the Assembly; Friday, theatre party and supper, besides one or two luncheons and minor episodes. You may as well make up your mind to it, Floyd; some time you'll have to face that sort of thing — or your wife will have to. And you ought, at least, to be getting acquainted with the people of your own town. Why, you know hardly anybody here. Wherever I go, my ears are afflicted with that doleful cry, 'Aren't we ever going to meet Floyd, Mrs. Halket? Isn't he ever going anywhere? Why does he hate us?'"

Floyd laughed. "Only let me have the rest of the year," he said, "and next winter you can treat me like any debutante. When I'm busy through the week at New Rome, I want to spend Sunday in my own way. I don't think I take much interest in girls."

"Possibly that is why they have an interest in you," replied Mrs. Halket dryly. "Well, if you prefer to postpone social duties until next year, I shan't protest. It will make explanations easier when I'm asked the sort of question that Lydia Dunbar put to me to-day."

"What was that?"

"Oh, wondering if she had done anything to offend you, or some such foolishness. 'I've asked him to dinner twice by note and twice over the telephone,' she said, 'and always for a Saturday night. And he's refused every time. He hasn't been near me for two months — and I thought I was going to see a lot of him this winter.' I must say I think you might now and then make an exception in her favor — an engaged girl, with the young man in Paris, is likely to be forlorn."

"Where did you see her?" Floyd asked.

"She came here this afternoon to call. I have an idea she hoped that you would be home early and that she might have a glimpse of you. She said she had things to tell you about Stewart. I asked her to come to luncheon to-morrow, but she had an engagement; she's going out to the Country Club with a party to skate."

"Then I'll probably see her," Floyd said carelessly. "Harry Stevens and I are going out there, too. By the way, speaking of engaged persons, Letty and Hugh Farrell are going to be married in June. Hugh's been promoted to first roller in our turn. They're going to live with Mrs. Bell, so they can't get married till I'm out of the house. I offered to leave at once, but when they found I should be through with the works anyway by June, they insisted I should stay. You'll have to help me on a wedding present for them, Grandmother; I want to give 'em something worth while. I thought of a set of furniture for the parlor, — some time they'll be having a house of their own, — how would that do?"

"You'd better ask them what they would most like," Mrs. Halket suggested. "You must know them well enough for that."

"Oh, do you think so?" Floyd asked, pondering.

"No, I think they'd like it better if I went ahead and picked out the thing that *I* most liked."

Mrs. Halket admitted that he was right; it amused and pleased her to realize that his instinct of courtesy had been surer than hers. Still standing before the fire, she smiled down at him, thinking gayly, "What a good, well-balanced man he'll make!"

"It's funny," Floyd said presently, "to hear you exhorting for society. I don't believe you care about it."

She came and seated herself on the wide arm of his chair and caressed his face with her hand. "All that I really care about, my dear, are you and your grandfather," she said. "At my age nothing else matters much. Your grandfather has had many honorable ambitions which I have tried to further: we have ambitions for you that we want to help you to realize. Your grandfather has won an eminence here that is more than commercial; we want you to retain it and go beyond it. Your position will be one in which you'll be expected — you'll be more useful — if you can bear yourself royally toward women as well as men — without self-consciousness, without awkwardness, without stiffness and the effort to unbend. We want you to have with all the graces all your natural simplicity and kindness; we want you to keep a manner as unaffected always as it is now; we want you to be in the best sense all that an American gentleman may be who has wealth and position and opportunity. *Arbiter elegantiarum* need not be an unworthy office for a man — if he is something more."

"It is a large order," Floyd sighed. "And after all, does it pay? The frills, the formality — "

"Yes, it pays," Mrs. Halket responded firmly. "Of course it is easy to overdo — and excesses, acquired late in life, are not, I fear, to be corrected. We might get along here with a little less — well, flourish of trumpets in our daily routine, — but in a large way I believe your grandfather's idea is sound. This city, where people are acquiring wealth so fast, is especially the place for a man to set a right standard — of how to spend, how to entertain, how to live. What people here need is the example of dignity. Of course it's necessary that you should have the right sort of wife to help you."

"Yes," Floyd said lightly. "It's early to think about that yet."

He observed that his grandmother was on the point of formulating a dissenting opinion, and he welcomed as a diversion Colonel Halket's dignified entrance.

"Grandmother's been giving me a lecture," Floyd said to him.

"Ah — and on what?" asked Colonel Halket. He took up a position before the fire and stood looking down on his wife and grandson with complacent affection.

"Oh, his whole duty to his neighbor," said Mrs. Halket.

"We're quite a family for lecturing, Floyd," observed the Colonel. "Your grandmother does it to me, and I do it to everybody else. It's one of my great pleasures, and I may say I do it rather well, too; the last one I delivered is going to have some very excellent results."

"Going to have!" echoed his wife, and Floyd, more respectful, asked, "What was that, Grandfather?"

"A little talk that I gave Gregg and the superintendents the other day — about the methods of dealing with the labor union sentiment that's taken possession out at New Rome. Gregg and some of the others were in favor of fighting. No, I said; let it work, let it work. This union enthusiasm is a passing fad. We have nothing to fear. The men are contented; they're proud of their connection with Halket & Company; they know they can't get as good treatment or as good pay elsewhere. Why, it's a gratification to me every time I go out to New Rome; I pass a workman on the street and he lifts his hat — no surliness in it, either; I've spent my life reading faces.

Those men like me, Floyd; they have, I believe, a real affection for me; and I'm proud of it, and I'm going to show them that I trust them. I'm writing a thing now that will show them."

"What's the title of it?" Mrs. Halket asked.

Colonel Halket put his hands behind his back and expanded his broad chest braggingly. "It is the Autobiography of a Manufacturer."

"What!" cried Mrs. Halket.

"Exactly," responded her husband. "I am writing my life. It was suggested to me by Mr. Stark, the publisher. He came over from New York to discuss it with me. That was why he was here those two days last week."

"How on earth did he happen to think of such a thing!" Mrs. Halket exclaimed in wonder.

"Why," the Colonel answered with what modesty he could, "he said it was the biggest business of its kind in the United States — built up and controlled by one man — a typical American achievement — a part of American progress of the last forty years. It's known all over the country, — and he believes that people will be interested in hearing the story of it straight from the man who did it. I expect anyway I'll get a good deal of fun out of writing it. Better not speak of it to any one outside," he warned them.

"It's a very nice thing for you to be doing," said Mrs. Halket, with enthusiasm. "Mr. Stark is exactly right; it *is* something that ought to be written up."

Colonel Halket walked to the door of his study and there turned.

"There is one thing," he said, standing in the doorway with his white head thrown back, a figure of oratory; "in thinking back over the whole course of events, in going over records and letters and journals, I find nothing to conceal and nothing that needs apology or excuse. Such success as I have won has been won openly and honestly;

END OF AN APPRENTICESHIP 149

it has n't been bought, it has n't been wrung from the poor or defrauded from the unwary; and if I have made mistakes, they need not shame my conscience. I 'll tell the story truthfully, and if it can help any American boy or young man, I shall be glad."

Expressing this high and solemn hope, he returned to his literary task.

"Dear man," murmured Mrs. Halket to Floyd, with wistfulness saddening her smile. "It 's a splendid thing, Floyd, at seventy-five to be so able to enjoy success."

"Is n't it!" said Floyd. "And, you know, it 's all true — I mean about the men liking him so. When he was out at the works the other day with Mr. Stark, he went round beaming and smiling and nodding to everybody, from a superintendent to a Dago water-boy — and they all loved it. They have a personal feeling for him, which is wonderful in such a big and impersonal concern. He called me from the rolls and introduced me to Mr. Stark and patted me on the back; and when I went back to work again, it was funny, — the difference in the attitude of the men toward me. You see, they kind of forget who I am; generally I 'm just one of them, — but after that — oh, the respect and awe did n't wear off for about an hour." Floyd laughed. "It was quite pleasant. I think I 'll hire Grandfather to come out and speak to me two or three times a week."

"Your grandfather is a very wise man," said Mrs. Halket. "He realizes the value of not displaying himself too often. In that way he retains his dignity, and when he does appear he can be as genial as you say without cheapening himself."

"How cold-blooded of you to analyze it that way!" exclaimed Floyd.

"I think," she continued, with a somewhat cynical humor, "I will ask him if he means to expose that particular bit of wisdom in the autobiography. You know he said he had nothing to conceal." She laughed and patted

Floyd on the head. "Don't be shocked, Floyd; your grandfather likes to be teased — by me."

"Just the same," Floyd said, standing in defense, "he's a big man, Grandmother; he has a grip on things. So don't you tease him too much."

"I won't, Floyd," she promised earnestly, and she added, "I'm glad to hear you talk in this way, my dear. It does me good. I hope I've never had a disloyal thought about your grandfather. Only sometimes — when I've been tired and depressed and cowardly — I've had a sort of fear — very vague, I can hardly describe it — as if something were lying in wait to mock all his serenity and confidence of power, make a ruin of his success and a sham of what had always seemed so real. Perhaps I've been afraid that in his very self-confidence was the germ of delusion and disappointment. It sounds disloyal, Floyd; but I've dreaded this only when I've been morbid and tired — and at least I've never shown my fear to him. It does me good to hear you speak so confidently, — for of course you *know*."

She stroked her grandson's hand for a moment; then she continued: "He has worked so hard, so honestly all his life, Floyd; his success has meant so much to him, and he's going on and on so industriously increasing it — that I don't want him to know tragedy now — the tragedy of failure. After he's attained and built up so much — if it were somehow to be broken down — the work of a long and ardent and patient life — well, he's a *man* and it might not crush his spirit; he'd set to work again. I don't know why I should sometimes have this dread; after the way you've talked I'll try not to be afraid any more."

Floyd did not answer. He had often shared his grandmother's vague apprehensiveness; he had often been made uneasy by Colonel Halket's sincere acceptance of himself as a great figure. That which had become reality to Colonel Halket was doubtless allowed to pass as pleasant fiction by many of his friends, and Floyd had a feeling that if the fiction ceased to be maintained, disaster of some kind would fall. It had been, therefore, with real alarm that he had begged his grandmother not to tease. It had been with some reservations that he had assured her of his grandfather's "grip on things." That fine, showy, picturesque, skillful personage — perhaps he had been stronger once.

Sunday morning Floyd went to the Avalon Country Club to skate. The day was mild, but the ice on the two rinks had not begun to soften. Having a contempt for fancy skating when anything more active was in progress, Floyd joined the hockey game that was beginning on the lower rink. The upper rink, just across the driveway, was reserved for the ladies, and for those of the men who preferred moderate and leisurely exercise. Mindful of the information he had received from his grandmother, Floyd looked for Lydia, but she was not to be seen. In a few moments he became entirely rapt in the excitement of the game; he was of all the players the swiftest skater and the most proficient, and he was easily exhilarated by success. At last, after he had made a long run and shot a goal, he leaned on his hockey-stick to recover his breath. Across the driveway Lydia, with her hands in her muff, was circling about doing the "outer edge" with casual ease and watching him intently.

"Good run!" she called to him, waving her muff.

He touched his cap, and went back into the game. But his enthusiasm had waned; when he was not in the scrimmage or running with the puck, he took his eyes from the play to glance at the lightly sailing figure, that wheeled and spun with such fantastic ease. Lydia seemed as much interested in watching the game as he in watching her, — doing her tricks merely by way of keeping warm. When he saw how intent on the game she was, a hot eagerness to distinguish himself in it again seized him; he dug into the ice with his skates, charged across the rink and, snatching the puck out from a scrimmage, made off with it toward the distant goal. As he approached flying, he heard Lydia's cry ringing out above the clash of skates, — "Go it, Floyd, go it!" — and then the next moment the goal-keeper had blocked his shot, and he had slid up against the bank, chagrined at the failure of his brilliant run.

Lydia swung out upon one foot and called to him as she floated on the long curve, "It's brutal the way you skate. Come and do this with me."

He deserted the game without a word, walked across the driveway on his skates, and stood beside her.

"This way," she said, and dropping her muff and holding out her hands to him she led him upon a long outward roll. In this light partnership, Floyd felt her buoyancy. A swift side glance gave him the dark autumnal color of her cheek, the gentle parting of her lips as she gazed down at the ice with pleased intentness. In that glance, the excitement of the game with which he still was throbbing became a more mad and possessing excitement. They stopped, and at that moment Lydia made the unluckiest speech.

"If you'd only come round, so that we could practice together! Where have you been? Why haven't you been near me — after your promise?"

"Can't you guess?" Floyd cried. He paused, but in the pause he seemed only to gather force to hurl himself more recklessly into the pit. "It's because I care for you too much — and because I know I could make you care for me."

"Oh, Floyd!" They stood facing each other in silence; the dark autumnal color faded from her face, the light of gay-hearted fellowship left her eyes, and Floyd, looking into them unflinchingly, saw there only sad regret.

"I knew I'd tell you if I kept on seeing you," he said gloomily. "I didn't dare trust myself. And now — I've told."

END OF AN APPRENTICESHIP 153

He could not endure the pity in her eyes. It stung his pride; he would have none of it. And so he said deliberately, —

"If I had gone on seeing you, I'd have taken you from Stewart."

Her eyes showed her swift change from pity to wrath, though her voice was low as she asked, —

"And would I have had nothing to say?"

"Nothing," he answered gravely. "And so you need not wonder any more why I stay away from you." He held out his hand. "Good-by, Lydia."

She took his hand and held it a moment, looking at him as if she would give him the opportunity to retract; she did not speak. Then he turned and walked across the driveway. She followed him with her eyes; she saw him take up the hockey-stick that he had laid at the edge of the rink and glide out upon the ice. Some one sent the puck spinning out of a scrimmage; with a whoop he sprang forward to it and raced with it toward the farther goal.

Lydia turned her back; he might go on playing, but as for her she no longer had any heart for skating — for any of her pretty tricks. She sat down and took off her skates and then went, carrying them, forlornly to the club-house. Her eyes were wet with tears of anger and sorrow; but to her grieved, astounded senses Floyd turning from her, not broken-hearted and bowed down, but springing to play a game, — that was the Floyd she could not forgive. He had declared an arrogant confidence in his power over her and then — then he had spurned her!

A month later Floyd had his barren triumph. Lydia went abroad; in February she and Stewart were married. Mr. Dunbar, who journeyed over for the wedding and returned the week after it, announced to his friends lugubriously that his daughter had taken affairs into her own hands; he deplored the impatience that had insisted on a ceremony in a comparatively heathen land and a foreign tongue. At the same time he did not conceal a certain pride in such unconventional independence. "It's romance," he said to Floyd one day, meeting him at luncheon at the club. "They could n't wait. A year's housekeeping in Paris — I suppose an old fellow like me can't see the glamour of it. Mrs. Dunbar's staying over a couple of months to get them started right." He sighed a little over the vanished dream of a wedding at home — a wedding on which, as he said, he would have liked to lay himself out. "I'd almost got her to thinking that was what she wanted, — after another year," he complained. "She changed her mind suddenly."

"She was afraid — she was afraid of me, after all," thought Floyd. And that was his barren triumph.

In June of that year Letty and Hugh Farrell were married; at the wedding-supper at Mrs. Bell's — which Floyd had begged as a great privilege to be allowed to supply — he was the gayest of the party. He proposed the health of the bride and groom in a speech which the New Rome *Gazette* of that week, in its extensive comment upon the affair, declared to be "replete with witticisms." He distributed the rice with which the fleeing couple were pelted, and he himself hurled the slipper that landed on the roof of the carriage as they were driven away.

After the guests had dispersed and Mrs. Bell, who at the last had given way to tears, had been comforted, Floyd went up to his room to finish his packing. He had marked a period in his life. His work as a laborer in the mills was at an end. He was leaving forever the lowly people who had been his companions for a year; his friends they might always be, but never again his companions. He had failed in love; but failure, even in this, must not always cloud his face. The sound of Mrs. Bell moving about below in the lonely house, the thought of Letty and Hugh sitting together in their bedecked carriage made him feel somehow that in friendship at least he had not failed. What he had accomplished or gained, how he advanced to meet the future, he did not know; a year had passed and he had set up before him no definite mark for ambition. Under this deficiency he had sometimes chafed, fearing that it denoted a weakness ; now he went forth to his freedom with humility and blind hope.

XI

MRS. HALKET

THE social life of Avalon, with which Mrs. Halket had threatened him, engulfed Floyd. Unaccustomed to being sought after, he had for a time a pleased wonder over the universal desire for his company, and not even a winter of almost nightly dining out dulled the edge of expectation and excitement with which he set forth upon each small social adventure. But his unsuspicious gratification over his success and his equally unsophisticated conception of a universal, fundamental kindliness did not endure for very long. He had for a partner at the first cotillion of the winter a poisonous young woman who supplied him with information about others in the room.

"It's funny," she observed. "I didn't think Mr. Bergen would get on the list this year. But there he is. I always like to see him and Sally March at the same place; it's so interesting."

"Why?" asked Floyd. "Why shouldn't Bergen have been on the list?"

"Well, you know he's not exactly one of us. Nobody knows much about his father and mother; why, people never even heard of them. They live in a little house off somewhere; they haven't any money. But because Mr. Bergen was such a football player at college some people ask him round. But I didn't suppose he'd get on this list."

"He's a good-looking fellow," said Floyd. "Isn't he a good fellow, as well?"

"I don't suppose he is, quite," replied the girl. "Anyway, he's not one of our crowd. And Sally March can't bear him. You see, she started out by being quite nice to him — for you know how he did distinguish himself at college, and that gave him a start here. Sally invited him to several things — I suppose as much as anything to see what he was like. Girls have to do that sometimes, you know. And then the first thing — he disgusted her by being in love with her. You can imagine how indignant she felt. Inviting a person to your house is one thing — but letting him care for you — when he's a certain kind of person — is another. Sally does n't speak to him now; it's always interesting to see them at the same place together."

"It must be," Floyd said grimly. "But he is n't one of us. Who are the people that make up 'us'? Would I be counted in? Don't be afraid of hurting my feelings."

She was not very intelligent, and she was so absorbed in her own point of view that she quite missed his irony.

"Oh dear, yes," she laughed gayly. "Of course you're in. Why, did n't you see the list of the Hundred and Fifty?"

"The what?"

"The Hundred and Fifty. Avalon is n't big enough, like New York, to have a Four Hundred; so last winter Tom Cary made out a list of the Hundred and Fifty, arranging them in order of precedence — and printed it in his *Gazette;* you know he owns the Avalon *Social Gazette.* He did it more as a joke than anything else, I guess; but it was a pretty fair list and it made some people awfully mad because their names were left off, and others because they came behind somebody else. Tom likes to get up a joke like that; he has the greatest amount of nerve."

"Nerve!" cried Floyd. "I call it impudence. And the fellow that did that is considered one of 'us'?" He stared across the room at Tom Cary, who was gracefully amusing an audience by decking himself with all the favors within reach.

"Oh, Tom can do anything, you know; he's so entertaining," the girl explained. "Besides," she laughed, "you ought n't to feel irritated; your grandfather's name headed the list."

"Indeed!" said Floyd. "They kept it from me. How did Mr. Cary classify himself?"

"Oh, he came in among the first ten. That was fair enough; he is so important socially — always getting up things, you know. — That little girl in pink there — she thinks Tom Cary is a perfect basilisk — is n't that what you call it? He left her out of the list — and she's silly enough to be afraid of him; she'd like more than any one else to be counted in. But of course she does n't belong. She's one of the *nouveaux riches*. I feel halfway sorry for her; she's trying so hard. She and I have the same sewing-school every Saturday morning down at the North Side Settlement, so I see a good deal of her; it's her mother that is trying to push her into everything."

"You teach a sewing-class?" Floyd asked, with some surprise that she should do anything so worthy.

"Yes, every Saturday morning. All the girls do something now; I hate it, but you don't like to drop out of things. Sally March has gone in for nursing; she told me she had to give an old beggar woman a bath the other day; I thought that was about the limit."

Floyd asked with some curiosity, —

"Who are a few of the Hundred and Fifty — besides 'us'?"

"Oh, most of the people in this room. It's easier to pick out those who are n't," she answered, and she enumerated some of the interlopers.

She thought it queer that after what she had just told him he should at the first opportunity dance with the little girl in pink.

Floyd asked his grandmother the next day if she knew a man named Tom Cary.

"Oh, yes," she answered. "Everybody knows him."

"Would you invite him to your house?"

"I have done so."

"And you know what he is?"

"I don't think Tom Cary has very much character to conceal," replied Mrs. Halket. "Yes, I know all about him. But you must remember, Floyd, that his mother is an old friend of mine, and that we've always been very intimate; and if I slighted Tom, it would make trouble between us, and not only between us, but with the Tracys and the Shaws; all the Cary connection are so clannish. I invite him only to the big things, where it would be rude to leave anybody out."

"I don't see," said Floyd in his most downright manner, "how you can have him in the house."

"One must make compromises," Mrs. Halket defended herself. "Besides, in society, it is gratuitous to look beyond manners and into morals."

"It's his manners I object to most. Well, I hope you're not going to give anything 'big.' What snobs girls are, aren't they!"

"It is very hard for a girl to escape being a snob," admitted Mrs. Halket. "But why that observation?"

Floyd repeated to her some of the comments of his partner of the night before. "I won't tell you who she is," he said, "but I guess a good many girls are like that."

"Yes, I'm afraid that at a certain age most of them are snobs," his grandmother replied. "But also most of them outgrow it. Don't judge them as harshly as they judge others. That's part of being young and having been brought up in ignorance of everything except a few paltry external details. In spite of all that, when you come to know them, you will find that some of them, anyway, are pretty nice girls."

"But this one was vulgar as well as snobbish," Floyd insisted.

"Then I think merely that you were unusually unfortunate," declared his grandmother, with spirit. "The girls of this town are as nice as those of any other. It is true that there is a greater variety; society here is changing very fast, the place is growing, and new people are appearing with sudden large fortunes which they have n't been trained to use. But my experience is that most people can acquire some cultivation — enough to be tolerable — in a remarkably short time. And you must n't take a hypercritical attitude about everybody; it won't do; it won't do."

"No," said Floyd stoutly; "it's just the hypercritical attitude in others that I'm protesting against. I went and danced with the little girl in pink who I had been told was *nouveau riche;* and she was a very attractive, nice little girl — much nicer than the one who had told me about her. I think I have a mission in society — to be the wallflowers' friend."

He said it laughingly, but his grandmother seized his wrists in distress.

"Floyd, don't do it, don't," she cried. "If there is anything dangerous and deplorable it is for a man to start out on a career of conscious chivalry."

"I will do it," declared Floyd, smiting his hands together with gleeful emphasis. Then, throwing himself into melodramatic posture, he exclaimed, "I, leader of the Junior Hundred and Fifty, do pledge myself to be the wallflowers' friend."

"If you really are — and won't have anything to do with the nice attractive girls like Marion Clark and Helen Foster and May Pennington," said Mrs. Halket, "I shall be seriously displeased. But I'm not much afraid. You're too human and normal a boy."

Her sense of security was reasonable enough, but she knew nothing of Floyd's feeling for Lydia, which materially altered his outlook upon the world of girls. With a standard in his own heart to which he was silently loyal, the prettiest and most popular left him as cold as the homely and dull; not one of them awakened in him the ardor of pursuit. And if kindness of heart alone would not have prompted the attentions he showed to the forgotten, a certain cynical amusement and pride aided this devotion; he saw that where he turned, others followed, and that if at a party he singled out the plainest girl for his conspicuous attention, within an hour men would be nagging her for dances. The popular girls were piqued and hurt by his neglect of them, but he caused the heart of many a desponding mother to beat high with hope. From the gay months of this winter he derived a compassionate friendliness for those whom he had rescued from neglect and disappointment, a contemptuous friendliness for the young men of society who had shown an eagerness to follow his lead. His grandmother was disturbed and puzzled by the obvious sincerity of his indifference. She knew him to be an emotional boy, a boy who had seen little of girls, a boy who in this first year ought to be even perilously susceptible to feminine charm.

She invited to dinner the eight girls whom she considered the most attractive in Avalon; she placed Floyd between Marion Clark and May Pennington. He called them Marion and May, they called him Floyd, because they had played children's games together twelve years before. In reality Floyd knew them hardly more than if he had just been introduced. Marion made a remark to this effect: "You certainly don't know me," she said, "and I don't believe you know Mrs. Evans."

"Mrs. Who?" asked Floyd.

"Mrs. Evans, — sitting next to you."

May Pennington, hearing the words, turned her head.

"Why, if there is n't my old friend Mrs. Morse!" she exclaimed; and at that both girls giggled a moment to Floyd's bewilderment.

"What's the joke?" he said to Marion.

"Oh, something foolish," she answered. "I suppose it's mean to tell — but I will. Do you know Jim Morse and Lawrence Evans? Well, May thinks Mr. Evans is the biggest stick of all the men in Avalon, and I know that Mr. Morse is the biggest, and several times we've tried to convince each other. A few days ago somebody called me up on the telephone and said, 'Is that you, Mrs. Morse?' and I answered and said, 'Why, it's Mrs. Evans, isn't it?' And then we stood there giggling. And we've been calling each other those names ever since. And when we're alone together, we try to act out the parts. But you mustn't tell anybody this."

"Not even Morse, or Evans?" Floyd asked seriously. "What is it that makes a man a stick?"

"Well," replied Marion, "if instead of saying 'Not even Morse, or Evans' you had said, 'No, indeed, I won't tell a soul,' you would have been a stick."

"Heavens!" exclaimed Floyd. "What a narrow escape! How absolute the girl is!"

"It's the only safe thing for a girl to be," replied Marion calmly. "What do you think of girls? I always like to hear what a man who knows nothing about us thinks of us."

"Why do you ask me?" inquired Floyd.

"Dear me! I never saw a man yet who wouldn't pretend that he knew girls like a book. You are the vainest creatures. Now you know what I think of you; make a fair exchange."

"All right," said Floyd. "I think that girls are terribly hypercritical and prejudiced and sarcastic. And that means, of course, that they are rather shallow and ignorant. At the same time, they are so bright and clever and self-possessed that a man is usually much more afraid of them than he has any right to be, and very much influenced by what he thinks they will think. They are nearly all snobs — until they grow older — and the men who play round with them most are the worst snobs among the men. According to novels and poetry, girls ought to be very tender-hearted, but I believe they take more pleasure in being cruel than boys. I guess they improve as they grow older. A girl of thirty-two is likely to be quite nice."

"I don't wonder you've avoided us," said Marion.

"I was just generalizing," answered Floyd. "Nothing personal."

"Generalizing from my remarks about Mr. Evans and Mr. Morse?"

"Oh, nothing personal."

"But that is the kind of thing in girls that you criticise?" She pressed him honestly for an answer.

"Well, yes. One kind of thing."

"But we only do it in fun."

"You asked me what I thought of girls," said Floyd. "But you can't draw me into an argument. I was n't accusing anybody."

"You say that just as if you meant, 'If the cap fits, put it on.'"

"But anyway," Floyd reminded her, "my opinion was that of one who knew nothing about the subject."

"Oh, yes — but I have to admit that what you say is more or less true. Only, we don't mean to be unkind, or hurt people's feelings; if we 're funny at their expense, we try to arrange it so that it 's behind their backs. That does n't make it any better, does it? And I suppose it does n't really help much if we have quite a lot of kind feeling that we keep to ourselves?" She spoke a little wistfully — in a manner quite out of keeping with her usual positive tone. "All girls are n't the way you think them. The very best of us is n't here this winter."

"Who is she?" asked Floyd.

"Lydia Dunbar — I mean, Lydia Lee; I can't think of her as married. You'd never find her making fun of a man because he was a stick."

"I know her; she *is* a nice girl," said Floyd. Then he looked into Marion Clark's face and laughed. "But after all, she is n't the only nice girl, Marion."

She was a self-possessed young person, not to be upset by

an unexpected compliment, however much it might please her. "Oh, is that meant for me?" she laughed. "Some time, maybe, I'll have a trade for you."

After dinner, when the men withdrew to the smoking-room and the Madeira had been passed round with the cigars, Floyd received a lesson from his grandfather in the art of hospitality. He knew beforehand just how the conversation would go; at all the dinners for young people given by Mrs. Halket, the Colonel pursued the same tactics; he had even tutored Floyd in the art. "It's always an awkward moment when the men are left alone; the host must then embrace all the guests in his conversation — turn quickly from one to another — bringing them all in — and so get things started briskly. It's his duty to show an interest in each individual — to be mindful of them all." So now he began, shooting out his questions with a brisk, masterful, rising inflection — "Well, Mr. Bradford, and what is the largest single fee on record in the legal profession in Avalon?" "They say that in the Lovell case Mr. Scrooby got one hundred and fifty thousand dollars," replied Bradford. "A hundred and fifty thousand! Dr. Torrence, what has the medical profession to say to that? Not much, eh? No use in curing people only to ruin 'em. Ha, ha! that's a good humanitarian view. Mr. Carr, painters haven't got to asking a hundred and fifty thousand dollars yet for a portrait, have they? But the architects nowadays seem pretty prosperous, Mr. Gryson. Mr. Harlan, I guess you and I will both agree that the iron and steel business, though it hasn't such brilliant moments as the law, is a tolerably satisfactory sort of grind."

Thus the old gentleman passed rapidly from one to another of the company, turning his head with each sentence toward some new face. Floyd was drearily aware that this methodical display of geniality was rather overpowering and that the young men sat, as it were, blasted in its path. He had observed the same effects and had

heard the same form if not actually the same substance
of address at other dinners that winter; it was therefore
embarrassing when the Colonel plumed himself on his
social *aplomb* — he used the word — and bade Floyd take
notice of the way in which a host could put his guests at
their ease.

Late that evening when all the guests had gone, Mrs.
Halket called Floyd into her sitting-room.

"Floyd," she said, looking at him, as he thought,
queerly,. "tell me about Mabel Dinsmore."

"Tell you about her?" he asked, puzzled. "What is
there to tell? Why?"

"You have been seeing her a good deal this winter?"

"Yes, at dances and so on."

"She was one of the girls that you devoted yourself to
out of chivalry?"

Floyd laughed. "If you want to call it that. She
never had many partners, and some of the girls even
didn't seem friendly to her; — do you remember my
telling you of how afraid she was of Tom Cary, because
he hadn't put her into the Hundred and Fifty? She's
a timid, nice little thing. Why?"

"And because she has had so few partners, you've been
filling in the gaps — devoting yourself to her more than
to any other girl?"

"For a while I did. But it's a funny thing. When
you devote yourself to a girl that way, by and by other
fellows begin to think there must be something in her
and come up to investigate; and so gradually Miss Dinsmore's got quite popular and hasn't needed my special
care for some time."

"So you've given it to some other unfortunate?"

"Yes," said Floyd, with an uncomfortable laugh.
"What's the trouble?"

"Oh, a tiresome woman," said Mrs. Halket. "I don't
know that it's worth while to bother you with it — but to

show you the peril of deliberate chivalry, I can't resist. Mrs. Dinsmore is stupid and not very well bred. This afternoon she called on me, and after working round to the subject of you and what a standard you would have to live up to, she expressed a fear that you were — were rather inconstant in your friendships. Her daughter had been led to think — your interest seemed to be such — that — that — well, that you cared somewhat for her, and the thought had made her quite happy; and then suddenly you ceased to show an interest — she could not imagine in what way she had been to blame; and she has felt hurt and grieved ever since."

"Oh Lord!" cried Floyd, exasperated and distressed. "What did you say?"

"I was n't able to spare her feelings as much as I should have liked; one can't with a person of that kind. I said that I was sure you had no idea of being in love with any one, — you were hardly more than a boy anyway, — and if you had been attentive to her daughter, it had very likely been because of your kindness of heart; and if you had discontinued your attentions, it had probably been because some one else appeared who needed them even more. Of course I did not put it as brutally as that, but I conveyed to her what was, I am glad to know, the truth."

"What ought I to do?" exclaimed Floyd, sincerely wretched. "It seems as if I ought to go to the girl —"

"Oh dear, no!" cried his grandmother. "Let it drop, and free yourself gently but firmly from any other entanglements that you may have got into through compassion. It was only because it was *you*, Floyd, that this happened. Your friend, Mr. Bergen, who was here to-night, might have acted toward Miss Dinsmore exactly as you have done, and she would not have felt grieved and hurt; the dream of love would not have been awakened in her young heart, and her mother would not have gone to Mrs. Bergen with a complaint. Mr. Bergen has neither money nor position: you have both; it makes some difference with the girls themselves, and a great deal with their mothers."

"It's sickening then," declared Floyd. "Do you mean that they're all mercenary? Why, take Tom Bergen and me. He's a fellow with a lot to him, a gentleman, who's making his own way, and who has a good future ahead of him at the law; good-looking too. But they cut him out right off; and it's everything for me — because I've got the Steel Works behind me, and never mind what else I may be!"

"It is reprehensible but human," replied Mrs. Halket. "After all, if you philosophize a little about such a view, you feel more indulgent toward the person who acts on it. Mrs. Dinsmore has experienced 'love in a cottage,' and probably has no very idyllic recollections; she knows what it is to rub along with one servant, or even none, and keep up appearances and worry about the next month's rent. What has she progressed for if her daughter is simply to drop back and retrace the same old tedious ground? The Dinsmores are not so extravagantly rich; it's a matter of some importance to them whom Mabel marries."

"I will drop the whole thing," Floyd said with decision, — "society I mean, — if I have to feel that I am so different from other fellows, and must inspire such different feelings. I don't like it; it's undignified and humiliating, and it makes me ashamed of people."

"Oh," answered his grandmother, "you need not feel so about society, if you only go into it as other young men do, and not as the chevalier of plain ladies in distress."

"Besides," continued Floyd virtuously, "it's a great waste of time. I've got as much good out of it already as I'm likely to get, and I must learn to omit the unessential. It's time I was thinking about getting things accomplished; this sort of play does n't help at all."

"To choose the right woman for wife may help a good

deal," observed Mrs. Halket; "and going into society should enable you to do that."

Floyd was silent. His grandmother looked at him with her friendly gray eyes and a little smile, but he did not respond, as she hoped he might do, with some shy confidence. She drew near him, and putting one arm about his neck, stood leaning on his shoulder, with her forehead against his cheek.

"I hope you don't think me hard and worldly for the way I've been talking, Floyd," she said. "I don't by any means believe that the women we know are simply on the lookout for advantageous bargains in husbands. Because several women would perhaps like to marry their daughters to my Floyd is no reason for me to attribute purely sordid motives to them. Indeed I shouldn't be sorry to hear that you had a special interest in some one of the girls you know—"

Floyd shook his head. "No, Grandmother, there's nobody," he answered.

"Well," said Mrs. Halket, "it's a very good thing for a young man who can afford it to marry young. Marriage is like life insurance; the longer a man puts it off, the higher premium he has to pay. He can't help feeling in the end that he is a loser for delaying. For one thing, his children don't grow up with him, and when he's sixty and his boy John is twenty, he'll think wistfully, 'Now that John's coming of age, if I were only forty-five! I could be playing tennis with him, and swimming races with him, and going shooting with him, instead of sitting, gouty and rheumatic, and just looking on.' Besides, the man and the woman ought to marry while they're still in the adaptable age; otherwise there will be unhappy friction in the necessary readjustments of life. And finally— well, the only real happiness in the world, to my way of thinking, is married happiness. We're here for a short time at best, and while we're here, don't let us economize on whatever real happiness lies within our reach."

"You want to lose me in a home of my own!" said Floyd reproachfully.

"I don't think of losing you," Mrs. Halket replied. "In what I say — though it's all true — I'm partly urged on by selfishness. You will hardly understand it, Floyd; but when a woman gets to be as old as I am, she doesn't want any loose ends in the affairs of those she cares for. She's like the child who says at the end of the story, 'But you forgot to tell what happened to the bad man after he was arrested and put into prison.' It seems so unsatisfactory to die without an idea of what sort of a life the person you most love is going to have — or who is the person that he will most love. I consider it almost bad art."

"But when you talk about dying — " Floyd protested.

"Ah, I'm an old woman, quite an old woman," his grandmother reminded him with some pride. "Seventy-one my next birthday, Floyd, — seventy-one. Can't you imagine how comfortable it would make such an old person feel to see you settled and happy? Nothing to trouble one then with disturbing speculations and questionings — just let one go off peacefully dozing. Well, — to keep interest in life awake to the end — we want that of course — there might perhaps be a little great-grandchild. Floyd," she said, and it surprised him, looking up, to see that there were tears in her eyes, — "yes, it would really please me very much to have a little great-grandchild."

Her appeal, that he had at first been disposed to regard lightly, he found suddenly touching.

"Grandmother," he said, "I'll have to tell you. I wouldn't have any prejudice against getting married. But the girl I cared about — she married another fellow. It was Lydia Dunbar. I — I can't see any other girl."

"Oh!" There was pain in the gentle exclamation. "Forgive me, Floyd. I didn't know — why did you never tell me? I might have helped."

"No. It's not the sort of thing a man likes to talk

about — better to keep it to himself. But you see that's why — I can't at once oblige you." He tried to cheer himself and her with a flippancy.

"Not at once, Floyd." He felt her embrace tightening with a fresh tenderness. "But it does no good to keep an old wound open. One disappointment must not wither a life. If a man can't have the first woman of his choice, it's better that he should take the second, and if he misses her, the third. Nine times out of ten, he'll be congratulating himself over his luck in marrying as he did. Turn your mind away from Lydia; stop thinking about what you've lost and begin thinking about what's left. She is a nice girl, I know — but are n't there any others that you like especially well?"

"Not in that way. But I suppose there are three or four that strike me as more interesting than the average," Floyd admitted.

"That's it!" cried his grandmother with enthusiasm. "Three or four! Now you pick on one of them — any one — and say to yourself — 'Now suppose I actually *were* thinking of that girl for a wife! How would she do?' Ask yourself that every time you see her. Take the most attractive girl you know — and just bear that in mind with regard to her. Love does n't always spring up full-grown in the human breast. It depends on all kinds of things — suggestion and care and nourishment. You might take any of the girls who were here to-night — May Pennington or Marion Clark, for instance; Marion's pretty and lovable and attractive — and I have an idea you'd find her responsive; I was watching her at dinner. Well, I would recommend this just as an experiment."

For answer, Floyd laughed and shook his head. "Ah no, Grandmother, I can't do it that way; I know how it once came to me, and if I'm ever to have it again it's got to come the same way. I can't force it and manufacture it; maybe some people can, but they could n't if they 'd ever once been taken with it spontaneously. And if you don't mind, I think I 'd better draw out of the social racket. I 've seen enough; this Dinsmore affair is a little too much; and I can make more of my time spending it with men than with girls. — I 'm afraid I 'm disappointing you, Grandmother."

"No, Floyd," she answered. "You may sometimes puzzle me — and surprise me — but I don't fear that you will ever disappoint me."

"That is very handsome of you," he said, and he kissed her.

"But, Floyd," she continued, "let me urge one thing. I 'm sorry — you will believe how sorry — for the way you must feel — over Lydia. But — don't get too sorry for yourself. Don't get to the point where you take a melancholy pleasure in your disappointment and your faithfulness. Don't keep thinking of your one true love. If some spring day you should suddenly find a shy tiny green sprout in some corner of you, don't pounce on it and yell, ' Why, what a miserable little sprout you are compared to that lovely palm-garden that I had to transplant awhile ago! How did you sneak in! Away with you!' No, don't treat it like that, Floyd. Be hospitable to the faintest little inclination toward love — if it 's just the vaguest, that comes from hearing the birds sing and being outdoors in spring. It 's good for the spirit, Floyd — and if something in a girl's voice or eyes comes to you and asks for admittance to the place of pleasant feelings, let it in; don't try to hold the door against it. And some time, perhaps, you 'll find some girl whose voice you 've let in — and then, first thing you know, you 'll have to let in that look she has in her eyes — and next her laugh — and then, it 's funny, but you had n't noticed before what pretty hands she has, and of course there must be a place set aside for them — and when you 've admitted eyes and voice and laugh and hands to the place of pleasant feelings, you 've just about taken in the girl."

"Grandmother!" cried Floyd, holding her off at arms' length. "You're not a man; how do you know so much about it?"

"I've lived a long, long time," she answered. "I'm a very old woman. Seventy-one, Floyd — seventy-one!"

XII

A CLIENT FOR STEWART

FLOYD returned one September from a short vacation in Canada with an unusual expectancy; one of Stewart Lee's infrequent letters had reached him just as he was setting out, and announced that he and Lydia would arrive in Avalon within the month. And no sooner had Floyd run through the accumulation of mail awaiting him than he closed his desk and went across the street to the new building in which Stewart had written that he had rented offices.

The elevator-boy dismissed him on the fourth floor, and he stood facing a door with the lettering — "Stewart Lee, Architect." He felt absurdly excited, and he flung the door open with the shout, "Hello, Stewart!" all ready on his lips. Then he stopped dismayed, for he found himself behind a little gate with only a boy in a long blouse sitting on a stool at a high table and looking at him.

"Is Mr. Lee in?" asked Floyd.

The boy got down from his stool. "What name, please?"

Floyd produced a card, and the boy disappeared into the adjoining room.

Floyd's excitement, momentarily dampened, rose again. And when he heard from within a well-known voice cry, "No, I'll show him in myself," he laughed aloud, kicked open the gate, and met Stewart on the threshold.

"Hurray!" cried Stewart, and "Well! Well!" said Floyd, and each seized the other's hand.

"Come in — 'way in," Stewart said, dragging him. "Ferris, if anybody comes, I'm busy — too busy to see *anybody*, mind!"

"Now don't you start out by turning clients away," Floyd protested.

"I'd turn the President away if he came to ask me to rebuild the White House," Stewart answered, slamming the door. "Now I've got you just where I want you. What the dickens have you done to your face in all these years?"

"I might ask you the same," said Floyd.

Thus they belittled the mustaches with which they had gradually adorned themselves — Floyd's black and drooping, shorn off stiffly above his lip, Stewart's long and light and gracefully twisted and pointed at the tips. In his blue working-blouse, Stewart looked taller, slimmer, more nonchalant than ever; his light blue eyes ran swiftly over Floyd, noting the changes with a kindly humor. Floyd, after the first glance, did not examine Stewart, but looked straight at his face with an uninquiring, complete delight in his presence. Except for the mustache, which gave him a fresh breeziness, he seemed to Floyd exactly the Stewart of old, — as boyish, as negligently gay and graceful, and as lovable to even the most passing glance. Stewart offered him a cigarette and at once Floyd experienced his old interested admiration for those oriental, slender, talented, versatile fingers; they made him conscious of the ugly stubbiness of his own, buried awkwardly in his pockets.

The room was large and well lighted and elaborately if somewhat scantily furnished with old Venetian chairs of walnut, deep, high-backed, covered with mediæval carvings. The table, on which were spread three or four plans, was also a solid old Italian piece, the spoil no doubt of some ancient palace; the walls were paneled in dark oak, and on them were hung four of Ruskin's drawings of the Doge's Palace.

"You see, I'm not half settled yet," Stewart said. "I've hardly opened the shop. I'm going to hire the three rooms across the hall — that will give me six altogether — and I 'm looking round for the best draughtsmen, which takes time; I shan't be in full running order for several months yet. I brought over a lot of things to fit the place up with — these that you see are just a few odds and ends thrown in temporarily. I expect to like it here; there 's a great chance in this town of yours."

"I suppose there is," said Floyd humbly.

"I wonder it 's never been taken advantage of. Why, with these splendid hills — and the three rivers meeting among them — oh, what a place to build a city!"

"But the mills had to be built first," Floyd reminded him.

"Yes, but think of the hilltops! Why, what have you done with your hilltops — ragged, big houses and dreary, unsightly little ones! Oh, there 's a great chance here — if a fellow could only get at it. Honestly, Floyd, just since I 've been here, I 've had more ideas in my head than in all the last year in Paris. It 's stimulating — and I want to be up and at it, instead of sitting here, waiting for clients."

"They 'll come," Floyd assured him.

"Yes, I 'm not worrying much about that. You know, I 'm just drawing the plans for Mr. Dunbar's new house; he 's bought the Keating place, and he 's given me pretty nearly a free hand, to show what I can do, and never mind the expense. Well, that 's a good beginning. And then I have this house of my own to keep me busy."

"Where 's that to be?"

"At the upper end of the Keating place; Mr. Dunbar's presented us with the land. They 're going to be, both of them, in Italian Renaissance. You know, I think that 's the style that ought to be adopted in this place — it 's the thing that is most effective on the hills. Some of the architects have seen it, but sandwiched in are a lot of Colonial houses and Queen Anne houses and big nondescript barns of houses. Well, it takes time for a place to settle down — or grow up — to a right standard."

"I guess you'll hurry it up," said Floyd.

"Oh, I don't know about that," Stewart answered modestly. "But there are a few schemes that have occurred to me already. One is, for building decent-looking, as well as comfortable houses for the working-people. It can be done — and there's no reason for having all these miserably ugly tenements; I'd like nothing better than a chance to get at some workmen's houses."

"Maybe that's where I can help you," said Floyd. "We may be putting up some more before long — and anyway, before I left on my vacation one of our men was telling me he wants to build a house of his own. At one time my grandfather didn't encourage that, but he's grown more liberal. This workman's quite well to do and is after something pretty good. I'll send him to you — his name's Farrell."

"All right; it may be a chance," said Stewart. "And if you people here would only institute some adequate sort of park system — why, you have no idea how beautiful a city you might have — with one street running along the crest of the city, overlooking the Yolin River; that could be the most splendid residence street in the country! I suppose it's having been abroad so long that makes me grieve over these wasted possibilities. But here — I'm so full of my own ideas I haven't asked you a word about yourself; let's hear."

"There's not a great deal to tell," said Floyd. "I'm just busy making beams and things — for you to turn into — what is it? — frozen music — or office buildings."

"And you're not engaged yet or anything?"

Floyd shook his head.

"Ho!" laughed Stewart. "Why, I don't think you've been getting busy at all. Better think about it; married life is the only kind. I tell you, Lydia's the best thing that ever happened to me. She'll be mighty glad to see you again; she ought to be here now any minute. She

A CLIENT FOR STEWART 177

and her father are coming down to go over the plans. Want to see them?"

He spread out the drawings for the two houses — Mr. Dunbar's and his own. Floyd bent over them admiringly.

"They look well on paper," he said.

"They'll look a great deal better in reality," Stewart declared with enthusiasm. "They really will." He began explaining, pointing out the particularly effective features. "This of Mr. Dunbar's — it's to be of Pompeiian brick, with red sandstone cornice and pilasters, red tile roof; this great porch, with the four groups of columns and the terrace extending in front of it and beyond it — that's the thing I like especially. Down some distance below this wide flight of steps there's to be a fountain — wait a moment, I have the design for it here — there, don't you think that's pretty good? Don't you, really?"

He showed it with the most sanguine pride and yet waited for Floyd's verdict with open and sincere anxiety. This combination of ingenuous delight in what he had done and eagerness for another's opinion — or praise — was one of Stewart's winning qualities.

"I think it's immense," said Floyd, and then he laughed. "I know mighty little about architecture, but I know you'll draw the clients, all right."

Stewart was giving a graphic description of the dining-room, "to be in Flemish oak, with the panels of the walls filled in with red leather," when the door opened. It was Lydia; she stood for a moment with her lips parted in surprise; then the light of happy recognition danced over her face and she came forward holding out her hand with the one word "Floyd!" He blessed her for that; ever since Stewart had told him she was coming, he had been indulging a painful curiosity as to how she might treat him; he had sometimes been afraid that in the last parting from her he had given her undying offense. But now, as she looked at him with her gray veil drawn up across her forehead, it was impossible to doubt the honest friendliness in her eyes. She seemed to Floyd not a day older than when he had ridden and skated with her; she was the same slender, graceful figure, and her face wore the same girlish merriment and welcome.

"You have been away a long time," he said. "I'm glad to see this sort of thing," — and he indicated the plans, — "for it looks as if you meant to settle down."

"Oh, I shall never leave Avalon again," Lydia declared. "You can't know — you people who've been staying here — I've been so homesick for all of you! Don't you think we're going to have the prettiest house? Has Stewart shown it to you?"

She pulled out the plan from under the drawings for her father's house and pointed to a second-story window.

"There," she said. "That's to be your room, Floyd — whenever your family desert you — or any other time."

"If you mean that, you'll have me deserting my family,"' said Floyd.

"Of course we mean it," Stewart answered. "You're to come round and keep us from getting lonely. Oh — and I've got you to thank, Floyd, for pushing me into the Avalon Club — you and Mr. Dunbar. I'm much obliged; it gives me a first-rate start."

"You'll lunch with me there to-day?" said Floyd.

"Can't; I have to go with the lady to-day." Stewart hooked his arm affectionately round his wife's neck and stood rocking her with a good-natured rudeness back and forth, while she swayed unsteadily and cried, "Oh Stewart!" "But I'll see you again this afternoon; you're just across the street, are n't you? I'll drop in."

"Come to dinner to-night," said Lydia, while Stewart was still hauling her head back and forth. "There will be just the family. — Stewart, dear!"

"Boo!" said Stewart, releasing her, only to seize her by the arms from behind.

A CLIENT FOR STEWART 179

"Thank you, I'll be delighted," Floyd said, while she stood looking at him helpless and laughing.

"We'll tell you all about our travels — and you'll tell us all the gossip about everybody here. — Stewart, I'll turn on you in just about five seconds."

"Then I'd better be going," said Floyd. He put out his hand, and just as she was about to take it, Stewart jerked back her arm, and twice repeated this, until Floyd made a dive forward and seized the hand; and then Stewart let her go, laughing.

"Of course you know what he is, having roomed with him," Lydia said to Floyd. "Don't be surprised if you hear he has taken to wife-beating next."

Floyd went out of the room with a queer little pang; he would almost rather have had Lydia show some self-consciousness, some awkwardness in the recollection of their last meeting. "She's so happy she's forgotten all about it," he thought. "Well, that's as it should be, I suppose." But all that morning the picture of her and Stewart kept intruding itself before his mind, interfering with his work, making him restless and discontented. He tried to think it was only because of his return from a vacation that he could not at once concentrate his thoughts.

Floyd dined at the Dunbars' often, and always he found Lydia frank and unconstrained; he wondered if she would be so should he some time find her alone. One afternoon, calling on her, he tested this — with some little discomfort to himself; for to be alone with her filled him now, as it had done three years before, with the sense of the inadequacy and imperfection of his momentary happiness. He knew that she was untroubled by any memory; her friendliness was spontaneous and free. Instinctively he felt that in her married security she had not only quite dismissed the thought of the declaration he had once made, but had even taken it for granted that his love had not survived her marriage. There was an innocence in this attitude and in her straightforward treatment of him that he reverenced even while it diminished him unflatteringly. This afternoon, when he rose to go, he said with some awkwardness :

"Lydia, I want to tell you — it's good of you not to lay up anything against me — what I said to you that day we were skating — "

"Oh," she interrupted with a laugh, "that was years ago. We've both got over that — long since."

"Have we?" said Floyd.

"Oh yes; quite." She smiled at him firmly, as they shook hands.

Their close and friendly relations continued unimpaired. But Lydia had awakened to the fact that Floyd had not in all her years of absence ceased to care for her and that he cared for no other woman. She was touched rather than annoyed by this fidelity; she was not annoyed, for she felt as secure in his honor as in her own. In the happiness of her married life, she did not resent his constancy, and she rather liked being the woman of his dreams. She could even have been jealous a little of another woman, should any appear to whom he might turn. Of course she had no desire to intervene between Floyd and happiness — such happiness as she and Stewart knew — but if one finds oneself first in a good man's affection, and the position involves neither risk nor sacrifice, one does not wish to be dethroned. Lydia never went so far as to speculate on what might have happened if Floyd instead of Stewart had been the first to propose marriage; any other arrangement than the actual one was unthinkable; no one was ever happier than she.

Stewart established himself in Avalon with remarkable celerity. At the Avalon Club within a month no member was unknown to him, and with all who frequented the place he was on terms of an easy familiarity; he never had to sit down at a table alone like a stranger. Men liked him and complimented Floyd on his protégé; Floyd was not backward in proclaiming Stewart's qualities.

Only one discordant voice reached him, that of an older man, Bennett, the leading architect of Avalon. "Lee does n't *quite* patronize the rest of us — yet," said Bennett, who felt irritated because Stewart had spirited away his best draughtsman. Floyd protested he was sure that Stewart had not knowingly transgressed the bounds of professional etiquette. "Oh, I don't mind," Bennett said with a cynical tolerance. "I know the boy's young. Let him make his splurge." It wounded Floyd to think that anybody could take such a disparaging view of Stewart.

Hugh Farrell was prospering. He had two babies and he was earning two thousand dollars a year. Five thousand dollars he and Mrs. Bell had saved up between them; now they had decided to leave the little house they had been living in, buy land farther back from the town, and build a dwelling-place commensurate with the increase in their family and fortunes. The remoteness of the site was, as Hugh explained to Floyd, an important consideration; he and Letty wished to have the children grow up with open fields around them. So Floyd sent Hugh — in whom ever since leaving the works he had taken a close and friendly interest — with a note to Stewart Lee. And for Hugh, explaining that he had three thousand dollars with which he wished to build a house, Stewart, with sympathetic imagination, described exactly the house that he wished to build. He took the few definite points that Hugh gave him, improved on them, elaborated them, sketched a house with more and larger rooms, a bigger porch, a handsomer front, and finer materials than any that Hugh had dared to dream of — and said, "That's the sort of house you want? Very well; put everything entirely in my hands, leave everything to me, and I'll build you such a house for three thousand dollars." Hugh signed the contract on the spot and went home in delight to tell Letty of their good fortune.

As for Stewart, he was quite pleased with this opportunity; he did not by any means despise it — even while building a hundred thousand dollar house for his father-in-law.

"The trouble with workingmen's houses," he said to Floyd, " is that they have no dignity. You see a street of workingmen's houses, and you're not impressed with the dignity of labor or the beauty of simplicity; you're only impressed with the dreariness of labor and the squalor of the commonplace. Now that's unnecessary. The laboring-man can have a dignified house, one that will help his self-respect. It's a thing worth working out."

When the people who had been away from Avalon for the summer returned, and the winter gayeties began, Stewart and Lydia became so involved in social interests that Floyd, adhering to his renunciation of such matters, saw much less of them. Now and then his grandmother gave a dinner party, and sometimes he made a casual appearance at the Country Club, but he was known among the young women as the Recluse, the Hermit, the "man too busy to bother with us." The girls invited to Mrs. Halket's dinners underwent each of them a certain hopeful curiosity as to whom Floyd would take down; and because Marion Clark was twice thus honored during the winter, she was much teased by her friends. She herself would have been glad to know whether Floyd had expressed a preference for her society or whether it had been merely a matter of Mrs. Halket's arranging. However that was, she had to confess that Floyd did not follow up his advantage.

Stewart laughed cheerfully when people complained to him, as they often did, about his friend's inaccessibility. "Why, we know you a great deal better than we do him," they would say. "Though he went out all through one winter, I'm afraid he didn't like us. What is the matter? You know him well enough to say." Stewart replied that he guessed Floyd was simply shy and afraid of girls; he said that he had never been able to induce him to go anywhere in Boston. And then he would extol Floyd's virtues, and, "Oh," the young women would cry, "it's maddening to hear that sort of thing about a man who won't look at a girl."

Stewart himself showed no aversion to the society of Avalon, nor did he occupy himself too much with the younger people. The older women liked a young man who could talk to them agreeably about books and pictures, about the French theatre and the German opera; at this time there were not many men in Avalon who were as well informed as Stewart on these subjects, and there were a good many women who had a superficial knowledge of them. Even Mrs. Halket, who scrutinized him narrowly because of his presumption in marrying the girl whom Floyd had loved, found no fault in him; she said to Floyd that in a place where all the young men received a special and technical education that killed off every particle of human interest, it was a relief to have one person of such wide cultivation as Mr. Lee. Such praise from Mrs. Halket meant a great deal for any young man, and it caused Mr. Dunbar a thrill of even more conscious pride in exhibiting his son-in-law.

Meanwhile, the houses that Stewart was building for himself and for Mr. Dunbar rose and drew attention. Outwardly they were indeed unlike most of the Avalon houses; even in their uncompleted state they had a certain winning lightness and grace; Mr. Dunbar's great villa looked down from its hilltop toward Stewart's smaller one with none of the forbidding austerity or cumbrousness of the older Avalon mansions. To be sure, Stewart was not the first to introduce a new style of architecture; Bennett and two or three others had broken away from the unimaginative variations on the "Queen Anne" type that had prevailed; but as it happened, none of them had yet had such a conspicuous opportunity as Mr. Dunbar's new house had offered. Stewart had succeeded at the outset, and on a scale which gave him not merely self-confidence, but the confidence of others. Even before the outcome was so certain, he had gone ahead in the most sanguine way, enlarging his offices and his office force; Avalon had never before known anything like his establishment, part of which was fitted up more like the luxurious apartments of a wealthy dilettante than as a hard-working architect's " shop." He had reached out for more draughtsmen and had raised salaries in a manner that taxed the patience and resources of his brother architects. His theory, which he talked over with his father-in-law, was that if one started in a big way, work in a big way would come; and as he had the money to spare and was not dependent on his profession for a living, he wished to make the experiment. Mr. Dunbar agreed that this was good business. So Stewart continued the methods which he regarded as enterprising and the other architects as ostentatious; Bennett nodded to him coldly in the club, for Bennett was jealous and resented this attempt on the part of a youngster to oust him by mere hue and outcry from his hard-won position of eminence. And when in the same day Bennett heard that Henry Maxwell had asked Lee to draw plans for his new office building and that Mrs. " Tom " Dowling had commissioned him to build her a house, he closed his office early and went home to his wife indignant and depressed. After years of hard work and close economy he had attained the state of keeping three servants and a horse; and in his gloom he believed that he had tasted of luxury only to have it dashed wantonly from his lips. It was pretty disheartening to have young millionaires invade the profession, become the fashion, and throw their money round for sport — driving the old and experienced architects to the wall.

Hugh Farrell's house was finished, to the great delight of the owner and the envy of some of his friends. It was a small Colonial house of red brick with white trimmings and an air of miniature elegance; within it had hardwood floors and oak wainscotings, tiled fireplaces, and carefully designed mantels — "all as good as the best," Letty said

A CLIENT FOR STEWART

with joy. The set of furniture that Floyd had given her for a wedding present, and that had been stored away ever since her marriage, graced the little parlor in a way that made her wonder if such things could really be her own. With this raising of the standard, she took a proud pleasure in the expenditure of the thousand dollars that her mother and her husband had allowed her for fitting up the house. They had been but a few days in the enjoyment of this wonderful perfection when Hugh, returning from work one evening, met the builder on the street. The builder asked if the house was all right, and when Hugh spoke with enthusiasm of it, he remarked, "I'm glad to hear it; I've just mailed the bill to Mr. Lee — and at such a time it's good to know there are no kicks coming."

Hugh asked the amount of the bill, expecting to be told that it was fifty or a hundred dollars in excess of the contract price, and prepared, in view of the result, to pay this excess cheerfully.

"A shade under six thousand dollars," said the builder.

Hugh put out his hand, and grasping a picket of the fence clenched it till its sharp edges cut into his fingers. "You're joking," he said, with an effort to laugh. "Mr. Lee promised it would n't cost but three thousand."

The builder shook his head with a compassionate smile. "Why, you did n't think you were getting all that for three thousand dollars!" He added by way of consolation, "A house generally costs more than it sets out to."

Hugh made no answer; he stood silently gripping the paling and looking off up the hill. After a moment he walked away; his steps lagged and his head was bowed; he was trying to figure in his mind the amount of the mortgage that would be necessary, the interest, the years it would take him to pay off the debt. He did not reveal the ill news that night to Letty, and she was puzzled and distressed by his depression. The next morning, getting leave of absence from the mill superintendent, he went to Avalon to Stewart Lee's office. He insisted on seeing the architect at once, though there were others ahead of him waiting, — women who, he reflected bitterly, had a better right than he to consult so expensive a gentleman. One of the draughtsmen took him into an inner room, and after a moment Stewart, wearing his long gingham blouse, entered.

"Mr. Lee," said Hugh, looking at him gravely, "I told you I had three thousand dollars to spend on a house — not a cent more. The builder tells me it cost six thousand."

"Oh, that's absurd," said Stewart with a laugh. "I haven't had the bill yet, but it won't be anything like that."

"He told me he mailed you the bill last night," Hugh answered.

"Then maybe it's here." Stewart turned to a desk. "I haven't had a chance to look at the morning mail yet. Yes, I guess this may be it."

He tore open an envelope and glanced over the contents with a frown. "Fifty-eight hundred and sixty-five dollars," he said aloud. "Well, that's all wrong, of course; he's made a big mistake. I'll straighten it all out, Mr. Farrell. Don't let it worry you for a moment; three thousand dollars is the cost of that house, and you can take my word for it. Satisfied with it, I hope?"

"Oh, it's fine," said Hugh, whose face had brightened with intense relief. "And you're sure it'll be all right, Mr. Lee?"

"Absolutely," Stewart answered. He gave him a friendly pat on the shoulder. "I guess you were kind of bowled over; I don't wonder. Never mind; I'll have this corrected, and then you won't think me a fraud."

"Thank you," Farrell said heartily. "I'm sorry I had to trouble you — but you see how it was."

"Of course; I'm sorry you had such a scare. Good-by," and Stewart came with him out into the room where waited the well-dressed women, and there shook his hand.

A CLIENT FOR STEWART 187

Later that day he went over the items on the bill and reluctantly verified them; it had not occurred to him that as from time to time he had thought of some new feature to make a workingman's house attractive he was making it so very expensive. His lack of practical knowledge and experience had led him badly astray. He had expected to overrun the estimate by a small amount — so small that Farrell could easily pay it. "I guess I won't get caught that way again," he muttered, as he drew a check for fifty-eight hundred and sixty-five dollars. After doing this he made out a bill to Hugh Farrell for three thousand dollars, and sent it with a note explaining that the mistake had been satisfactorily adjusted.

From the occurrence Stewart derived several lessons, the most important to him personally being these, — that to build dignified houses for the laboring classes is not remunerative business, and that an architect wishing to do really beautiful and artistic work had better confine himself to clients able to pay a good deal larger price than any they had considered in their first calculations. Yet he was not to escape the embarrassments of his indiscretion. Hugh and Letty could not refrain from telling a few of their friends what they had paid for their delightful house; there were a number of men in New Rome who could put three thousand dollars into a house, and several of these men, friends like Joe Shelton, and unfriendly, jealous rivals like Tustin, bought land back on the hill, not far from Hugh, and then went to Stewart Lee. They were hurt or indignant and certainly mystified when he declined to undertake their commissions. "I have so much work to do now," was his excuse, "I simply cannot give my time to this. I am devoting myself, anyway, to an entirely different kind of thing." They understood that he meant to larger matters, and they felt snubbed. One of them, Tustin, expressed himself as willing to have a house built on just the same plans as Farrell's. "That wouldn't cost you any work," Tustin said. "It would not," replied Stewart. "But it is my unalterable rule never to build the same house twice." With cynical amusement, he had advised each of the applicants to go to Bennett, who had lately been quite disagreeable. Those who followed this recommendation were told that it was out of the question to build such a house as they wanted for three thousand dollars. They protested that Mr. Lee had done it, whereupon Bennett referred them again to Lee, saying that as for himself he did n't profess to work miracles.

Each applicant went back to New Rome discouraged and angry. Tustin was especially bitter. He openly attributed Hugh Farrell's good fortune to the fact that he had been befriended and petted by Floyd Halket, who had got this fashionable young architect to build Farrell a fine house as a special favor.

"It's a mighty bad thing when favoritism gets into a concern like this," grumbled Tustin.

His wife was even more resentful; it was she who had given him no rest until he had made the effort to build a house as fine as the Farrells'. An undercurrent of enmity to Hugh began flowing; somebody even started a story that Floyd Halket had presented him with the house. Some one else altered this story into one that drew an unpleasant inference about Floyd's past relations with Letty. But Hugh and Letty and Mrs. Bell occupied their new house and enjoyed their prosperity, unconscious of slur or slander.

XIII

CALLED HOME

THE spring that Hugh and Letty moved into their new house, Floyd Halket went abroad; of the subsequent developments in which Stewart Lee was concerned he knew nothing. The purpose of his trip was to establish if possible a foreign market for the company's steel and to pick up in England and Germany fresh ideas about the manufacture. He spent a month of hard work in Birmingham, and then, feeling that he had accomplished all that was possible, he declared a vacation and joined three of his college friends on a walking trip through the Lake Country; then they went on up into Scotland; and after two weeks there, Floyd's companions insisted that he should not desert them, but should go with them to Paris, and then through Touraine and Brittany. They were over for three months to have a good time; and Floyd, who had hardly taken a vacation since leaving college, yielded to their entreaties. He had almost forgotten what fun it was to be an irresponsible young fellow with congenial idle companions, and he surprised his old friends by his spontaneous gayety. "You're more of a boy than you used to be," one of them said to him seriously. He stayed with the party until October, and then went to Southampton to see them off on the steamer; they had a tremendous dinner together, at the end of which Floyd sang "Fair Harvard" many times over and declared his belief that nothing but prejudice and personal animosity had kept him off the Glee Club in college.

A week later he was in Germany, visiting iron mills and gun factories, studying methods, making notes; for

a month he was traveling from one establishment to
another. At a beam-mill in Frankfort he observed that
the piles made ready for the heating-furnace contained
more than twice as much steel scrap as it was the custom to
use at New Rome. He made a memorandum and a sketch
of one of the piles; and if his trip had produced nothing
else, this casual discovery would, as it afterwards turned
out, have justified it. For when Floyd returned and tried
the new method, he found that it effected a saving in
manufacture of nearly a hundred dollars a day.

He had been in Berlin a little more than two weeks
when a cablegram came from his grandfather saying that
Mrs. Halket was desperately ill and summoning him home
at once.

Floyd caught the Bremen boat the next morning; the
pilot boat that met the steamer in New York harbor a
week later brought him a letter edged with black. His
grandmother had died the day he sailed. "It was pneumonia," Colonel Halket wrote. "She did not suffer much
—after the first; she was unconscious and spoke only once,
an hour before the end, when she murmured something —
asking for you, I think. The funeral service will take
place as soon as you arrive. I shall be very glad to see
you, Floyd."

There was no word to betray his emotion. Floyd had an
equal power of repression. He folded the letter and put
it quietly into his pocket, and no one of those standing
by would have guessed that he had just read the saddest
news that could come to him. But when he had landed
and was sitting in the friendly obscurity and loneliness
of a cab, he dropped his face forward in his hands and
tears trickled through his fingers. He felt miserably forlorn and alone. How much brightness and sweetness and
unselfish, gentle wisdom had gone out of life when his
grandmother had died! Even though in the nature of
things this could not have been many years distant, Floyd
had never really looked forward to life without her. The

affection between the two had been so intimate, the sympathy uniting them so understanding and acute, that now in her loss he felt as if something vital to his own character had been withdrawn. Who would supply him now and fortify him with her humor and imagination, her appreciative praise and blame, her courageous, hopeful spirit? Yet at least he had a dear and very vivid memory that should shine for him always as his star. It was something she could never have known or dreamed — that her waving him at the steamer that bright and brave farewell should always be an incentive toward nobility.

And then, less selfish, his thought turned to his grandfather. Poor old man, with what pride of restraint he had written unemotional statements! What a week it must have been for him! Colonel Halket had never, to Floyd's mind, shown any subtle understanding of his wife; sometimes, even, his obtuseness had engendered in Floyd a sense of resentment; yet he had loved her with constancy and devotion for half a century, and to Floyd his dependence on her had been even more marked than her dependence on him. Floyd suddenly began to appreciate what a cruel thing it must be to be old and alone; in comparison with that, the pathos of being young and alone, on which in his black moments he had sometimes dwelt, was indeed trivial.

It was the middle of a gray November morning when Floyd drove up to his grandfather's house; Colonel Halket had been sitting by a window awaiting him and met him in the hall. He took Floyd's hand silently and holding it walked with him into his study, off the library, and closed the door.

"I'm glad you are here at last, my boy," he said; there was an unaccustomed softness in his voice; his lean brown face, surmounted by the waving plume of white hair, youthful still with its dashing white mustache and imperial, seemed to Floyd only the more handsome and dignified in its expression of grief, and betrayed no evidence of a man broken and overwhelmed — rather it seemed that of one who, utterly sad, was master of himself. "Sit down, Floyd; it has been a hard trip for you. Here is something that you will like to keep."

He opened a drawer of his desk and took out a sheet of paper, half filled with his wife's handwriting.

"It is a letter to you that she began just before she was taken ill — and was never able to finish," said Colonel Halket, and as he gave it to Floyd there were tears in his eyes. "She left it lying on her desk; I found it there and put it away for her — and — and then I put it away for you." Floyd looked up from reading it with wet eyes.

"Thank you, Grandfather," he said. "Have you read what she has written?"

His grandfather nodded. "Yes. I thought you would n't mind."

"She speaks of the weather and of having caught a little cold, and makes light of it," said Floyd. "And passes on from that to warning me to be careful." He smiled sadly. "She never thought of herself for longer than a moment, did she?"

"And all the more reason why some one else should have thought for her," Colonel Halket said. "But I never noticed — I never realized — if I only had! —"

"She was ill only a few days?" Floyd asked.

"Longer than that, I think — if I had only noticed," replied Colonel Halket, with bitter self-reproach. "She had been interested in organizing a Women's Club out at New Rome — she had given money for a building where they should have reading-rooms and gymnasium and everything the men have — your friend Lee is to build it; she made three trips down from Canada during the summer about it, as perhaps you know. And all the fall she had been very busy interesting the women in it and explaining it to them and trying to provide some place as a substitute until the new house should be built. She used to go out to New Rome three or four times a week and spend the day visiting the women who seemed most capable and interested, and arranging matters with them — often spending the whole day and coming back at night tired out. But I never noticed. One morning — it was a cold, rainy day — she told me at breakfast she had a sore throat and laughed about it, saying she hoped her voice would hold out, as she had called a mass meeting of all the women and was to give them an address about the purpose of her scheme; I advised her not to go, but she said she could n't disappoint them. They kept her talking nearly all that afternoon, answering questions, organizing the club; and when she came home she went at once to bed — and never got up from it again. I feel, Floyd, that if I had only been a little more watchful I might have saved her."

"You must n't blame yourself," Floyd answered. "It was in her spirit to do things that way."

"Those women — you must see the letters they have sent me. You will see how they loved her. They sent a wreath — but it's the letters from the poor women that count. Well, they could n't have helped loving her — though I never thought how much. For years she made it a duty to visit every one who had been widowed, every one in affliction — and when it was money that was needed, she knew how to give without hurting any one's pride. And the cases of little crippled children that she'd had treated at her expense — that was always her special charity — and she was so modest and shy about such things she never told even me the way the people felt and expressed themselves; going through her papers, I found some letters from women whose children she'd helped; she kept the letters — but she never showed them to me."

He handed a packet to Floyd.

"I don't know why," he said, and for the first time his voice broke, "but — if it's possible — I love her more for knowing how much others that I never dreamed of loved her."

So he sat talking with Floyd for a long time, recalling little memories of his wife with a simplicity and vividness that made Floyd's eyes fill with tears. "He understood her better than I ever guessed," Floyd thought, remorseful that in his heart he had reproached his grandfather for lack of sympathy. Never before had he come so near to his grandfather's heart; he was to come yet nearer that evening. When the funeral service was over and he and Colonel Halket had returned to the house, they sat in the dark before the small yellow spots of the gas-fire. And suddenly the Colonel leaned over and, resting his arm and head on Floyd's shoulder, sobbed aloud. He had broken down for the first time in the ten days.

Floyd reached up and pressed his hand silently.

"Oh, Floyd," said the old man in a faltering voice, "I don't know what I shall do. We'd been together for fifty years — your grandmother and I — and now — what am I to do!"

"She'd want you to live and work the way you've always done," Floyd answered.

"Yes, that's something. But it's the lonely hours — when the brain can't work or sleep — I have them often now. It's the moments through the day when some little thing reminds me — and I stop and stare and think of her. I've never thought much of death; a few days ago I was going on as unconscious of it as if I had all of life before me. And now I don't care much about life; I feel that I'm through."

"She wouldn't have you feel that way, Grandfather."

"No; you're right, she wouldn't. It was nothing but her faith that kept me going when your father died. She pulled me through that. But — I'm older now — and I haven't got her. — 'When with the morn those angel faces smile' — they sang that at your father's funeral too, Floyd. If one could only believe it!"

"I thought you did," Floyd said.

"I've tried hard. I've gone to church — and heard

all they could say, and tried to believe. But here's the thing I could never get out of the way — and if I only could! If my soul is immortal, why did it have a beginning? If I'm to know eternal life, why don't I reach out to infinity behind as well as before? How can a thing be immortal that has its moment of birth? I've asked; they tell me I've always existed — in the consciousness of God. But *I* don't know it — and according to that theory I may go out of this existence into another with no recollection of this, no recognition of the angel faces that are dear to me — no, they can't answer that question, Floyd, they can't answer it — they have to fall back on quibbles. It's a beautiful, beautiful myth — that God might have made true. It's done a great work in the world; it's made men better and kinder to one another — but it's only a beautiful myth. And I'd rather have it so; rather than believe that I'm to be transmuted from one personality to another, never allowed to see again the two faces that I love — rather than that I'd ask for everlasting sleep."

Floyd was silent for a while. "I've never thought much about it," he said at last. "Until now, nothing has ever brought it home to me personally. But it seems to me that that line of the hymn — 'When with the morn those angel faces smile' — illustrates the most beautiful thought that the human race has ever worked out. It's just as you say — you have the feeling that nothing could be more beautiful than that — if it were a fact. Now why shouldn't the Supreme Power of the universe actually achieve the thing that we grasp as most beautiful in our thoughts? It seems to me unlikely that He should fall short of our own highest conception; it's more probable that He's worked out an arrangement that's even better and more beautiful. Of course if you deny the existence of a Supreme Power, it's different — but I haven't got to that. As for an immortal soul — a thing that's to have no end — having a definite beginning, that's an inconsistency I can't fathom. But just the same I fall back on my argument; if there is a Supreme Power, — and I suppose there is, — the mind of man can't conceive anything too beautiful or desirable for Him to execute. That's probably not orthodox, but it satisfies me."

Colonel Halket stroked the young man's hand. "There's a good deal of your grandmother in you, Floyd," he said. "I can almost imagine that would be the way she'd talk. You have the right idea in one way anyhow, — for it means courage and hope; and there's no doubt about it, a man must have those qualities if he's to make anything of life. Only — it's a good deal harder for an old and lonely man to have them than for a young fellow starting in. But I'll try, Floyd; I'll try." He patted his grandson on the shoulder with affection and respect.

They fell then to talking quite cheerfully of more practical things — cheerfully yet with reverence, for that which they discussed was the fulfillment of what they had reason to believe would have been Mrs. Halket's wishes and the carrying out of her plans. Colonel Halket had in the days before Floyd came drawn up a schedule of her charities and subscriptions, so far as he could find records of them; he and Floyd sat together till late that evening following clues that were indicated by hasty memoranda, tabulating, and planning for the systematic development of her unfinished personal work.

XIV

A FAILURE AND A SUCCESS

DURING the next few months Floyd for the first time came into business relations with his friend Stewart Lee. He found that beyond stating in a general way her desires, his grandmother had given the architect no definite instructions about the club building; she had asked him to submit plans which should embody certain features and which should represent a building that could be constructed for a certain sum.

Stewart, who was very busy, did not get the plans ready until the end of January. He was building a church, half a dozen large houses, two office buildings, and three country houses; he was at work on plans for many other things, and with them all he had been reckless in his promises. When at last he had the plans for the clubhouse ready, he submitted them to Floyd with a gay confidence. "I think the ladies will find that is just about the sort of building they want," he said. "Artistically, I have n't done anything better."

Floyd and his grandfather studied the plans for several evenings, and the more Floyd studied them the less satisfied with them he became. His grandfather did not so readily visualize the defects; he acknowledged them, however, when Floyd pointed them out. "I think," Floyd said to Colonel Halket at last, "as long as this is to be a club for women we had better get a woman's opinion on it." He consulted his grandmother's friend, Mrs. Hubert Clark; her criticism confirmed the judgment he had already formed of the plans.

Stewart was not very hospitable to suggestions concerning his work. When Floyd called his attention to the awkwardness of having the bathrooms so remote from the dressing-rooms, Stewart answered, "You can't place them any other way and keep the colonnade." "Then I guess we'd better dispense with the colonnade," said Floyd. Stewart demurred frostily. The colonnade was the detail which gave character to the building. His theory was that what women living in poor ugly houses would most appreciate and find restful in the club was its æsthetic quality, and he had made all else secondary to that. None of the points that Floyd criticised could be altered without radical impairment of the beauty and harmony of the design. Floyd was firm; he said that his grandmother's purpose had been practical rather than æsthetic, and he wished to carry it out as she herself would have done. He did not believe that the æsthetic was so irreconcilable with the practical. If Stewart said that it was in this set of plans, he would have to take his word for it; but of course fresh drawings could be made.

Stewart grumbled a little about the inability of laymen to appreciate the first principles of architecture, and said that if they could only realize how capricious their desires and criticisms usually were, they would give the architect a freer hand. He promised, however, to make the changes without delay. He had drawn the plans himself, wishing to do something especially good for Floyd; the next day he gave them to his chief draughtsman, telling him what objections had been raised, and asking him to make the necessary changes. The draughtsman was a clever fellow in his way; and when Floyd received the revised plans, he was gratified to note how successfully the old difficulties had been eliminated and with what little loss of beauty. He congratulated Stewart on this, and Stewart answered with resignation, "Yes, it looks so to you — but the building is not really the same."

Stewart's pride had been touched by the fact that Floyd, quite unknowingly, had preferred the draughtsman's revision to his own carefully finished plans, and to that as well as to the other demands on him may be attributed the indifference and negligence which marked his attitude toward the work. In the first place, though the site chosen was on the edge of a marsh, he neglected to take borings; in the second place, the measurements for the granite foundation and limestone superstructure which he made personally while his draughtsman was enjoying a vacation were discovered, after the foundation had been laid, not to agree, and there was a long and vexatious delay. When at last, six months late, the club-house was finished, it did not long retain the first favorable opinions that it won; in the spring, when the frost was out of the ground, it began to settle and crack and leak amazingly. Cracks appeared in the plaster, the rain came through the roof, and in the reading-room the paneling swelled, the mantelpieces started away from their fireplaces, the doors refused to close. Stewart blamed the contractor, but the contractor inculpated Stewart, who had to make the humiliating confession that he had not thought it necessary to take borings and that if he had done so he might possibly have prevented such a settling of the building. To Floyd, who had been anxious to have this one thing done especially well, the result was a great disappointment; he felt that somehow he had failed in a labor of love, and in his loyalty to a friend it was even more painful since he could not exonerate Stewart. "I suppose," he said to himself when he had at last attained a cooler temper, "everybody sometimes makes a botch — even the best of men. Every now and then a crack painter does a daub, and a good man writes a poor book, and a real humorist gets cheap, and a great statesman flies off the handle. But I wish it had been something else than just this that had been Stewart's off job."

Although Floyd did not yet know it, Stewart was having a good many "off jobs" at about this time. Up till now he had been prospering in his work; a few blunders about which disgruntled sufferers made some talk had not been treasured up against him; of course, people said, an architect so young and inexperienced was bound to make mistakes. But there was no one else who grasped an idea so sympathetically, touched it up with so nice an imagination; his work had, said the ladies, distinction and charm — and it was a pleasure to work with him. On a rapidly spreading reputation of this kind, he had himself spread out; that is, he had thrown more rooms into his office and had called to his aid more men. But on his chief draughtsman he had come more and more to rely; he was the man who had the knowledge of petty and tedious detail for which Stewart himself had no patience; it was he whose mathematical calculations were unerring, and who moreover had an astonishing practical sense that could devise a forgotten cupboard or a staircase in the most compact plans. This man Stewart had taken from Bennett, and Stewart flattered himself that he had taught him much and that the man was humbly grateful.

But Bennett had been keeping a close watch upon his young rival's career. He had never shown any resentment toward Durant, the draughtsman, because of his desertion; rather, his friendly interest in him was as marked as his cold disapproval of Stewart. Sometimes he invited Durant to luncheon, and by perfectly natural and indirect methods led him to discourse of his employer's peculiar bent and abilities. He knew Durant, — a modest, unassertive man of unusual competence, always contented to occupy a second place and work laboriously. And one day he astonished him with a proposal that they should go into partnership together.

Durant, who was poor and so conscientious a plodder that he had never dreamed of such an achievement except as possibly crowning his old age, was thrilled by the suggestion. The firm name, "Bennett & Durant, Architects," glowed in his imagination. He told his employer of the proposal and admitted that he was greatly tempted.

Stewart was considerate and kindly, and Durant was humble before condescension. "Of course," Stewart said to him, "I believe that this office is the place for a young man. It has a future before it; we're going to lead every one else. For that reason I can't honestly advise any young man who looks to the future to leave. But if you are more inclined to consider the immediate present, — I'm free to say I can't make you such an attractive offer as Mr. Bennett has done. And I don't want to put any obstacles in the way of your doing what seems to you best."

Durant was torn with perplexity; for a day or two he was of a most unhappy, vacillating mind. He had never before faced a problem of such immense seriousness. Hitherto his services had been at the command of the highest bidder, — but now, urged to consider the future and impressed by his employer's confidence and resources, he wondered if it would not be wise for him to reject the glittering opportunity. Bennett drew from him an account of the conversation that had set him so adrift. Durant's faithful report caused Bennett to rage inwardly and to think more than ever of Stewart Lee as an impudent, patronizing young upstart, but he was too discreet to explode such sentiments. Instead he attempted to infuse into Durant a proper self-confidence and to reason with him. He took a tolerant, humane view of Stewart. "It's natural a young man like that should be over-sanguine," he said. "He has money and pull, and everything at the start has seemed to come his way. And I'll concede that he has a very pretty talent for certain things. But don't you see, Durant, he needs a man like you to fill him out here and a fellow like Burke to pad him there; and yet he wants to be the whole thing himself. Why, you're more important to him than he realizes; you're the balance-wheel of the whole establishment. I'll go so far as to say I did n't know myself how important you were till I'd lost you. With our combined energy, with your head for practical detail and my general knowledge and experience, Bennett & Durant can snap their fingers at all the amateurs and dilettanti that ever left Paris."

By such persuasion Durant was convinced; and a month later a new shingle was hung on the door of Bennett's office. Within the next half-year Stewart lost two more competent men; one, having inherited some money, "set up" for himself; the other went to New York. Affairs in Stewart's office were muddled; he was not a good organizer, and what with trying both to get effective results from his office force and to do all the creative work himself, and what with his lack of practical experience, he made a poor showing. His clients first murmured and then expressed outright dissatisfaction; they said he promised but did not perform, was careless and expensive, could make plans that were attractive, but was unable to build a house that fulfilled the promise of the plans. His contracts were never executed on time. There came a slack season in which he succeeded in gathering together the loose ends of his work; and because he knew that it was a slack season in all the offices, he did not appreciate how widely disappointment over what he had done was simmering.

Lydia was more sensitive to intimations of this, which somehow reached her. She asked Stewart if he was not too rushed with work, and said she wished he would take a partner and so relieve himself of some of the worry and responsibility. But Stewart would not listen to this advice. He had an odd personal vanity on just that point; he wished to stand alone. When his reward and reputation were established, there should be no one to share and diminish the credit. "Stewart Lee, Architect," was to remain his sign until the end; he had started in with a mind definitely, obstinately made up to that. He was conscious of his deficiencies, but belittled them, as those which inferior men were created to supply. He tried hard enough to secure the right kind of inferior

A FAILURE AND A SUCCESS 203

men; he engaged one after another in Durant's place, but none of them proved, like Durant, fundamentally amenable and patient. The office was in a state of continual flux and change; it was never after Durant left really organized.

One evening when Floyd had come to dinner, Lydia remarked that she had never been inside the Women's Club at New Rome; she said she liked to see the things that Stewart had done, and asked how she might secure permission to visit it.

"Oh, you don't want to see it, Lydia," Stewart said, with an uncomfortable laugh. "That's one of the things that ought to have turned out better than it did."

"Nothing turns out quite as you'd like to have it," replied Lydia. "I know enough of architecture to know that. I want to see it anyway. Do you suppose it could be arranged, Floyd?"

"Of course," he answered. "I have to go out to the works to-morrow morning; if you care to come too, I will get one of the members of the club to show you round."

To Stewart's annoyance the arrangement was made. Floyd drove Lydia out to New Rome the next morning; he took her first to Hugh Farrell's house, of which he was glad to be able to speak handsomely.

"I was hoping he'd build a lot more such houses out here," Floyd said. "But of course he has so many larger things to do."

Letty was at home, and came to the door, with a red-haired infant in her arms and another clinging to her dress. She was delighted to meet the lady whom Floyd introduced as "Your architect's wife, Letty." To show Mrs. Lee over the club-house would be, she declared earnestly, a pleasure; she would just run upstairs and ask her mother to take care of the babies while she was gone.

"Let me keep this little fellow until you come down," Lydia said, patting the head of the older boy.

Letty laughed and slipped out of the room.

"What gorgeous hair!" Lydia said to Floyd. She lifted the little boy up on her lap and smiled at him and shook her head and stroked his cheek. "Is n't that woman the happy looking soul!" she added.

Floyd suddenly caught a pathos in the exclamation, and in the wistful and tender look in Lydia's eyes as she played with the little boy. It occurred to him for the first time that her happiness with Stewart was not complete, and he felt a pang of sympathy and sorrow. What a mother she would make, he thought, and how truly sad if children should be denied her!

The little boy slid down from her knee when his mother reëntered the room.

"He's shy of strangers," Letty explained, caressing his head. "Run upstairs to Grandma, Hughie. — Is n't it too bad, Mr. Halket," she said, turning to Floyd with her bright smile, "that we did n't have this house when you were boarding with us? My! you'd have been so much more comfortable! And" — her eyes twinkled — "the bathroom here is enough to make a person sing for joy — really sing," she added mischievously.

Floyd laughed. "Mrs. Lee does n't know about that joke," he said. "If you don't mind, I 'll leave you to explain it to her. Good-by, Letty. I 'll call for you at the club in half an hour, Lydia."

At the company's offices important matters engaged his attention. A new wage-scale had to be prepared and submitted to the men to sign.

"It 's going to cause trouble," Gregg said. "Especially if you 're still of a mind to promote Farrell and make him foreman."

Floyd folded up the superintendent's schedule and put it in his pocket. "I 'll study this," he said, "and go over it with you in a day or two. What 's the trouble about Farrell?"

"Nothing; he 's a good man; that 's it; he 's too good.

A FAILURE AND A SUCCESS

The Affiliated crowd are down on him; he's been so opposed to the union and all it stands for; there's a faction, headed by Tustin and a half-dozen others, that are bitter against him. Tustin's chairman of the Affiliated, and the radicals generally are in control. And if you put Farrell in — I think they'll make a fight for what they'll call a 'principle.'"

"I'm afraid that fight cannot be indefinitely postponed," Floyd said. "Is there any other objection to Farrell except that he's non-union?"

"Yes," said Gregg. "It's claimed that he's too young — at least that there are older men who've been working in the rod-mill longer than he and who ought to be preferred —"

"I have worked in that mill myself," Floyd interrupted. "With those men. And I have formed a perfectly definite opinion as to how competent they are, any of them, to fill an executive position."

"Here's a document," proceeded Gregg, taking a paper up from his desk. "Kind of a curious thing — just came to me this evening. I have n't done anything about it yet."

It was a paper signed by six of the workmen at the rod-mill, "taking the liberty to recommend," in case the place of foreman was to be vacant, as they had heard, Jacob Schneider for the position.

Floyd looked at his watch. "Could you get those men up here for me within ten minutes?" he asked.

Gregg sent for them.

"I don't want to appropriate one of your duties — or privileges, Mr. Gregg," Floyd said, with a smile. "But as I am personally familiar with the conditions in this case, perhaps you'll let me talk to the men?"

"I don't mind at all having a job of that kind taken off my hands," Gregg replied. "Would you like to see them alone?"

"It might be better."

Gregg left the room; in a few moments the delegation from the rod-mill entered.

Floyd nodded to them gravely as they stood bunched by the door with uncertain, anxious faces.

"I have read your recommendation," he said. "I know of no business in which it is customary for the employees to furnish advice, unsolicited, concerning the management. I will ask you to observe the usual custom. When we feel ourselves in need of advice and think that you can supply it, we will appeal to you. That is all I wanted to say."

He nodded to them again abruptly and turned aside to the desk. They left the room in silence.

Half an hour later he was driving Lydia back along the road to Avalon. She seemed constrained and disinclined to make any reference to the building which she had come to see, and Floyd, understanding plainly enough the cause of this, talked of Letty and described the parties that used to be held in Mrs. Bell's parlor. "I wish you could have met Miss Lally Gorham," he said. "She used to do Shakespeare. One day not long ago I was passing the Women's Club; they had a big sign out announcing that she would give a 'dramatic recital' the next Saturday afternoon. If men had been allowed, I'd have gone to hear her."

"Was she funny?" Lydia asked.

"Funny! No, indeed. Tragic, passionate. She was intending to go on the stage, but perhaps the club gives her sufficient opportunity to display her talent. I should hardly think it would; she had self-confidence for anything."

"I suppose it's always gratifying to see a cock-sure person fail," Lydia observed.

"That's the most cynical speech I ever heard you make," said Floyd.

She turned her face toward him for a moment and he saw that tears stood in her eyes.

A FAILURE AND A SUCCESS 207

"No, I don't really think that, Floyd," she answered. "I was just thinking, indeed, of — of what a pity it is when other people have been cock-sure too."

"Is it only for the others? Haven't you any sympathy for the poor devil himself?" Floyd asked.

"Oh, I hope so," she answered, and caught her breath.

He realized then how bitter and surprising the disappointment of the building had been to her; he imagined that it was the first time she had been confronted with such inferiority in her husband's work. And if he had known, the greatest pain to her came from the feeling that Stewart had failed in the thing that he should for reasons of sentiment and friendship have done best.

That evening when Floyd went home, Colonel Halket welcomed him with an eager excitement.

"Come in here, Floyd," he said. "I've got something to show you." Then he stopped at the door of the library and looked at his grandson sharply. "Have you seen the new *Contemporary Review?* — the one that's out to-day?"

"Not yet," Floyd answered.

Colonel Halket walked to the library table and took up a magazine which he handed to Floyd. "Glance your eye down the table of contents," he said.

"Hello!" Floyd exclaimed. "You're pretty secret about doing things, aren't you? You never told me you were writing for the magazines."

"I thought I'd surprise you," chuckled his grandfather. "It's not many writers, I guess, whose first contribution is accepted by the *Contemporary*. Maybe I mistook my vocation, and should have been a literary man!" He laughed gayly; it was a long time since Floyd had seen him so youthful and so pleased. "Read it, Floyd, and tell me what you think of it."

The article was entitled "The Employer and the Union." It began informally: "For many years I have been a large employer of labor, and I have the happiness of feeling that I am regarded by my workmen as a friend. In the security of this feeling, I have never been able, like many of my neighbors in business, to regard the growing power and development of the labor union as a menace. In the words of the poet, —

> 'Should banded unions persecute
> Opinion and induce a time
> When single thought is civil crime
> And individual freedom mute,' —

my attitude might change; but I have very little fear."

He sketched the history of the Halket Steel Company blandly, describing the original patriarchal nature of the establishment, and expressing the belief that even in the great enlargement of the plant the unity of sentiment animating all connected with it had not been weakened. Then he passed to an account of the first effort of the union to obtain a lodgment. "Organization was in the air; it became epidemic; the contagion extended to the mills at New Rome. The first symptoms were observed during a summer when I was away. Not unnaturally, the management was alarmed. The union had its secret agents and missionaries at work, a fact which seemed no doubt to imply a sinister purpose. With capital everywhere agitated and frightened by the sudden looming up of a new power, the power of labor, it is not surprising that the cool heads in control at New Rome should almost instinctively have accepted the situation as ominous and critical. In that spirit they were prepared to resist the union from the start, — to prevent it from getting a start, — to exterminate it if it had got a start.

"As I have said, I was absent at the time. Possibly it was that fact which gave me a better and truer perspective of the whole matter than that enjoyed by those who were close at hand. Certainly I do not take any special credit to myself for being able to view the issue from a different angle than that of the usually cool but now agitated heads at the works. Finding that a crisis actually

A FAILURE AND A SUCCESS

was at hand, I returned to New Rome and inaugurated a policy quite unlike the combative one that had been proposed. It was the policy of *laissez faire* — to which I have always adhered, to which, I trust, I shall always adhere. 'Organize?' I said to the men. 'Why, certainly. An excellent thing for you to do if you want to. It will mean for you certain sick and death benefits — not that you're in need of them, for, as you know, the company always tries to do the right thing at such times — and also it may give you more of a feeling of brotherhood — which of course is to be encouraged.'

"That was the way I met the union, and since then I have always been on the friendliest terms with it. As it happens, I have been able to pay my men somewhat better wages than those required by the union scale in other mills. I find my union men are as willing as my non-union men to accept this better rate. They have arranged it with their parent organization so that they are permitted to accept my scale. Some of the mills at New Rome are union, others non-union, others half and half. There is no difference in smoothness and efficiency, there is no visible friction. I have not had a strike at New Rome in twenty years."

He passed on here to the subject of strikes, and became more general, ceasing to draw from his own personal experience. His tolerance was comprehensive; he believed that if all the strikes were analyzed, employers and workmen would be found to share about equally the blame. As to the charges of violence and lawlessness made against strikers, it was only fair to consider the temptation which often confronted them. "When a man is out of work and has a family starving on his hands and sees another man employed to fill his place, he is perhaps not fully accountable for his actions; at least he should not be judged with the harshness that rightly attaches to an ordinary case of assault. After all, when men are sacrificing themselves for a principle, — even admitting it may be a wrong principle, — it does n't seem the most worthy act for others to step in and invalidate their sacrifice. The law that is often heard quoted among workmen has almost the moral force of a commandment from the Decalogue — 'Thou shalt not take thy neighbor's job.'"

In closing he admitted that other employers of labor might not subscribe to such leniency. "It will be said doubtless that I write as one who has never had experience of the horrors of a protracted strike. I cannot regret my immunity. It is a satisfaction to me to feel that while I have been tolerably successful in business, I have never been obliged to quell a spirit of discontent among my men. I have found that if one yields to human nature's just demands, and makes only just demands of it, human nature will respond. And I hope and believe that in the years that are left to me I shall never be led to adopt a more rigorous policy toward my men or they to decline in their friendly feeling toward me."

Floyd, after he had finished reading the article, did not for some moments raise his eyes from the magazine, though he was aware that his grandfather was eagerly awaiting his comment. He was trying to think how he could disguise his opinion that the essay was most unfortunate and indiscreet. At last he looked up with a smile.

"Well, Grandfather," he said, "you 've come out pretty strong."

"Not a bit too strong," replied Colonel Halket. "If, after all my years of life, I ever had a message to the world, that comes pretty near being it." He spoke with the gayety of a man who has really freed himself from a burden. "But what do you think of the way it 's written, Floyd? Does n't that quotation from Tennyson come in pretty pat?"

"First-rate," Floyd admitted, and his grandfather laughed with a proud pleasure. "But why did n't you let me know you were writing it — why did n't you let me go over it with you?"

"Why? You don't find any mistakes in the English, do you?" Colonel Halket asked anxiously.

"No, oh no. It's very well written. But I should have liked to talk it over with you beforehand."

"I thought there could n't have been any mistakes," Colonel Halket said, with great relief. "You know, when they sent me the proof of it and I read it in print for the first time, I could hardly believe I 'd written it; it seemed too — well, too smooth and professional. I said to myself, 'I guess the editor's fixed it up a bit.' So I compared the manuscript with it — and not a word had been changed — not a word. I tell you, I was surprised."

An old man exulting in the discovery of a new thing that he could do, a new achievement — Floyd could not blow cold upon his pleasure now. He looked at his watch and exclaimed, —

"By Jove! Your article was so interesting I had no idea it was as late as this! We 'd better be dressing for dinner, had n't we?"

In the interval, Floyd secured a clearer view of the manner in which his grandfather's published article might complicate the situation at the mills. It was conceivable that Gregg and the other superintendents might resent the somewhat patronizing reference to their "usually cool but now agitated heads;" they might resent being made a text for a public preachment. They would certainly feel that much of their work had been undone, for, notwithstanding Colonel Halket's declaration of a *laissez faire* policy, his subordinates had for a long time in small ways been endeavoring to discourage the spread of unionism in the mills. Now this authoritative utterance must advance victoriously the cause that Floyd himself had come to regard as dangerous and to be opposed. His contemplated promotion of Hugh Farrell, his rebuke that day to the union delegation from the rod-mill occurred to him as but two out of a multitude of matters which had suddenly been transformed — by the stroke of his grandfather's pen — from petty details to large issues and embarrassments.

When he came down to dinner it was hard to meet his grandfather's unsatisfied appetite for comment and appreciation.

"I suppose you didn't hear anything said about it downtown to-day?" Colonel Halket asked. "Of course the magazine was out only this morning, but I thought somebody might have read it. You heard nothing at the club at noon? Well, I guess in a few days it will make some talk."

"Oh, you'll hear from it," Floyd assured him. "The newspapers here will be reprinting it — and you'll hear from it — from all sides."

"Not altogether favorably, you think, eh? Well, there's nothing I like better than to stir people up now and then. I've spoken out the truth as I've learned it from a long apprenticeship; and other people can learn from it or not — as they please."

"You haven't told me yet why you wouldn't let me see the article when it was written," Floyd said, returning to his first question.

"Oh, I just wanted to surprise you — in case it was good enough to print; and if it wasn't, I didn't want to be mortified by showing it to any one," laughed Colonel Halket; he was in a merry mood.

"I hope you don't intend to be so secretive with the Autobiography," Floyd said.

"I think it's quite likely," replied his grandfather.

"But I might perhaps be able to make suggestions," Floyd urged.

"I don't want them. I want the thing to be my own — down to the last word. I don't want even you — or anybody — to read it till it's all done and in print. It's pretty nearly done, too."

A FAILURE AND A SUCCESS 213

The announcement — in which, before the appearance of the magazine article, Floyd would have rejoiced — smote now upon his ears like a threat. He foresaw for himself weeks of patient diplomacy and scheming; in the light of the published article, it seemed nothing less than essential that he should read and revise the manuscript of the book.

After dinner, when they sat smoking together in the library, Floyd suddenly put a question.

"Grandfather, you 've made me general manager of the company. Does that mean that I 'm to act on my own judgment in deciding questions that come before me, even though I 'm pretty sure that my judgment would run counter to yours?"

"No," said Colonel Halket decisively. "When you think you 're probably differing from me, you 'd better refer the matter to me. What is this thing that you feel so experimental about?"

"The appointment of foreman in Rod-Mill Number Three. A fellow named Farrell is by all odds the most efficient man there, and I want to give him the place. He 's younger than many of the men; he 's antagonized some of them because he 's always steadily set his face against the union. If he 's promoted instead of one of the older men, the union is likely to regard it as an affront; and I may as well admit that, although I consider Farrell the most efficient man, I also consider it important to take a step of this kind for the very purpose of restricting the union."

"No, sir." Colonel Halket shook his head with vigorous emphasis. "It won't do. Why, it 's going against the very principles I 've laid down in that magazine article; it 's using the policy of compulsion instead of that of conciliation. I won't hear of it, Floyd. If your appointment of a young man is going to affront a large body of our old and experienced workmen, you must appoint some one else; a slight loss in the individual efficiency of the foreman will be more than made up by the general efficiency that comes from harmony and contentment. No, we're not in business to fight the union; let other firms do that for us if they want to. Why, to go back to that verse, —

> 'Should banded unions persecute
> Opinion and induce a time
> When single thought is civil crime,
> And individual freedom mute,' —

then you could think about restricting them, not till then. That's wisdom and humanity, my boy."

"I only hope we shall never see the time," Floyd remarked.

"We never shall — at New Rome," his grandfather responded, with a confident, reassuring smile.

Floyd telephoned to Gregg the next morning that he had decided to appoint Jacob Schneider foreman of the rod-mill; he offered the superintendent no explanation. But all that day it galled him to think that the six men whom he had censured for their impertinence were no doubt crediting themselves with a victory and laughing at his rebuke as a "weak bluff."

XV

THE AUTOBIOGRAPHER

OWING to Floyd's considerate care, hardly the echoes of the disturbance created by the article in the *Contemporary Review* reached Colonel Halket's ears. To be sure, the Colonel read with great enjoyment the editorial comment in two of the three Avalon newspapers — comment so respectful, courteous, and sympathetic that a man who was the subject of it could not avoid thinking better both of himself and of the press. As for the officials of the mills, Floyd had called them together and explained his grandfather's attitude. The explanation made them very gloomy.

"I tell you this, Mr. Halket," said one of the men, bringing his fist down on the table, "if that's the Colonel's position, then it means disaster."

"I hope not," Floyd answered. "My grandfather's been in this business a good while, and it's quite likely he's wiser about it than any of us. Anyway we've got to accept his view, whether we sympathize with it or not, — all the more because he's gone on record publicly. Has anybody here seen the *Contemporary Review* for this month?"

No one had seen it, and Floyd prepared them for the article as tactfully as possible; but in spite of that, when he met Gregg again the next day, he found him injured, aggrieved, and discouraged.

"A thing like that can just about undo ten years' work," Gregg said dejectedly. "It is n't the implications against my judgment and management — it is n't those so much that I mind; but it's the fact that Colonel Halket has got so far away from the real crux of the whole situation. He doesn't seem to understand what we're up against, and yet he's directing us just as if he'd never got out of touch with things." He pulled at his beard desperately. "I swear it's enough to make me feel like resigning. Here I've been building the best I knew, as I thought, to the interests of my employer; and now he tells me to pull down the whole shebang. I've turned down half a dozen good offers because I've had a certain feeling about this place — having grown up with it, you get a kind of sentiment and interest about it, you know; but this is pretty near the limit."

Floyd admitted a sympathy with his feelings, but tried to inspirit him. "It will be a little rough, altering our tactics at first, but after a while we'll probably find it easy to carry on this new policy."

Gregg shook his head. "It's almost a betrayal of those men who've been the company's best friends," he said; "the fellows that have stood out against the union. They'll read that magazine article, and they'll say, 'So that's the way he feels about it! Well, what is there in it for us?' That's what they'll say; see if they don't. And the union men will read the article too, and get after them with a sharp stick — drive 'em into the union or out of the mills, one or the other."

"I'm afraid you're right," said Floyd. He meditated for a moment and then said, "I think we'd better not attack the subject of a new wage-scale for a few days — until we see what effect the publication of that article has in the works."

Reports from the various mills showed that it had a very marked effect. There was jubilation among the radical union men, there was gloom at the mills that had been holding out as non-union. Gregg's prediction was immediately verified; murmurs of anger and despair rose from the men who felt they had been abandoned by their employer. There was a stampede suddenly to join the union;

within two weeks there was not a skilled iron worker in New Rome who was not a member of the Affiliated. Hugh Farrell had been among the last to surrender. Floyd, going through the works one day, passed into the rod-mill, where Schneider, the new foreman, had just taken charge. He passed near Farrell, who was at the old work of drawing out the long steel rods with the tongs, stepping back and forth with the same active grace which had impressed Floyd years before; and Farrell returned only a curt, unsmiling nod to his greeting. The unfriendliness of it hurt Floyd, even though he knew that he could not escape the suspicion of holding his grandfather's ideas.

Hitherto the men at the New Rome works had been paid by tonnage. Improvements in machinery had, however, so enlarged the output of certain workmen that their earnings had grown out of all proportion to those of the machinists, tool-dressers, and others, and were indeed so great as to eat into the profits of the business. In many other mills the sliding scale of wages had been adopted to counteract this difficulty, but the conservative management of the Halket Company had been reluctant to inaugurate a change of custom. When the skilled mechanics who built the improved machines were earning only a sixth or an eighth as much as the men who pulled the levers, and when steel workers who were exceptionally fortunate in their branch of employment were some of them practicing the luxurious habit of driving to and from their work in carriages, the necessity for reform was imminent. "It's all right for them to make good earnings," Floyd said in one of his conferences with Gregg, "but we can't increase the percentage all along the line without running the mills at a tremendous loss. As it is now, the expert machinists are sore at seeing some of these other fellows, who are really less skilled than they, making so much more money. Another thing that makes for trouble is that the machinists are ineligible for membership in the Affiliated, and from all accounts they feel they're being doubly discriminated against. Now that we've given the union the encouragement of a magazine article, we've got to force them to accept reasonable terms."

Therefore the sliding scale was drawn up and submitted to the executive committee of the union, of which Tustin was chairman.

At first, appreciating the cut in earnings that it would involve for a large number of men, the committee positively declined to consider it; they declared they would never accept the sliding scale. On this point their position was quite untenable; their association had accepted the principle in almost every other mill in the country. Floyd, who conducted the negotiations personally, replied that as to the principle there could be no debate; that would be enforced or the works would be closed. Then the committee shifted their ground and fought for better terms in the scale that was submitted. The principle of the sliding scale was this: that wages should move up or down, following the advance or decline in the price of steel, but that there should be a minimum price below which they should not decline. Floyd proposed that this minimum price for steel billets should be twenty-five dollars a ton; and the men insisted that it should be twenty-six dollars. On this point, as on the principle itself, Floyd was unyielding; on what seemed the minor points, to which the committee of the steel workers retreated, he was less exacting. Prices of steel were at this time high; by the agreement that was finally made, and that was to endure for two years, the rate of wages was to be fixed by the prevailing price and was to continue for six months. Floyd had proposed a monthly adjustment, but had not held out for what seemed to him then an unimportant detail. There were other details which seemed comparatively insignificant, — provisions giving committees of the union a voice in arranging the "turns," opportunity to

THE AUTOBIOGRAPHER 219

pass upon the installation of new machinery, the privilege of making visits of inspection and presenting grievances to the superintendents of the mills. During the next two years these committees were incessantly active — often for the sole purpose of keeping their authority in evidence. The mill superintendents came to regard them as pestilential nuisances whose inflictions it was an indignity to bear; more than one superintendent resigned during this period rather than submit to the constant harassments of these committees. And quite apart from the special arrangements made with the union in this two years' agreement were the provisions in the constitution of the union itself, which took note of the smallest details and assumed jurisdiction over the lives of its members to a degree that meant regulation of the business of their employers. The daily output of each man was defined and was not to be exceeded; limits were set to the instruction of other workmen and of apprentices; the constitution bristled with restrictive and mandatory clauses, such, for instance, as the rule that seniority of service should always receive preference in promotion. The recognition of the union by the management meant the conforming to these and countless other irksome requirements.

Floyd carried the burden of the ensuing perplexities, reluctant for two reasons to let his grandfather share it; he wished to spare the old man anxiety and worry and to preserve in him his optimistic, contented spirit; and he was also honestly afraid that any interference on his grandfather's part would produce confusion worse confounded. Colonel Halket's humane liberality and tolerance on all matters pertaining to labor alarmed Floyd and seemed to him to foreshadow a weakening. More than ever did the Colonel welcome any opportunity to hold forth at a public meeting and preach the gospel of tolerance, human kindness, and friendliness in business relations; it delighted him to feel that he was, as a presiding officer introducing him once put it, " the best-loved man in Avalon." It gratified him to find that his reputation was extending beyond the city limits; certain political honors came to him unsought; he was chosen delegate-at-large to the Republican National Convention, and there he made the speech nominating for the presidency the "favorite son" of the state, who on the first ballot received the complimentary vote of his state and no other. Experiences like this caused Colonel Halket to renew his youth; he aspired to an eminence broader, greater than any that had yet engaged him — in short, to an eminence that should be national. His mills were known all over the country; what he now dreamed of and set his mind upon was that his personality should likewise be known and esteemed. The noble, public-spirited citizen, the generous employer, the polished, cultivated gentleman, the pioneer of a more humane and kindly era, the lovable man — these were a few sides of his character of which he was profoundly conscious and for which he desired wider recognition. To that end, he no longer confined his benefactions to Avalon; he contributed to various good causes in various parts of the country, traveled far to make speeches, enjoyed hearing the eulogies pronounced upon him by presiding officers, enjoyed bowing to the applause. Sometimes he thought of identifying himself with some political issue and lending his influence and voice to the championship of some public cause, but there was none that appealed with sufficient strength to his dramatic sense; no doubt he was wise in restricting himself to the enunciation of excellent generalities and championing nothing more definite than humanity.

Meanwhile, his autobiography was progressing. Floyd made repeated efforts to secure a reading of it, but Colonel Halket was firm; no one should see the manuscript except the publisher. Floyd felt that he could mark the stages in its development by the reminiscences which his grandfather occasionally let fall; from dealing with the remote past, they were now approaching perilously near the im-

THE AUTOBIOGRAPHER 221

mediate present, and Floyd felt that the conclusion of the work was imminent.

During the first six months of the sliding scale agreement, the price of steel remained high — billets sold at thirty-five dollars a ton — and the mills were running at a good profit. The monthly reports from the superintendents, which Colonel Halket scrutinized with care, were very favorable, in comparison with those which had been made during the previous year under the tonnage system of wages; therefore Colonel Halket triumphantly called the attention of Floyd and of the other officers to the fact that the union had been allowed to establish itself and nothing serious had happened. It was in the last month of this profitable period that his book was issued; in a short time it went through several editions. Floyd read, with rapid alternations of feeling, the copy in which his grandfather had inscribed his handsomest signature, of the old-fashioned, florid type. Some chapters were so unconsciously egotistical and complacent that Floyd squirmed in reading them; it mortified him to think that his grandfather had exposed himself thus to the laughter of the multitude — or worse, of the discriminating. Other passages filled him with pain and concern because of the frankness with which they criticised certain of the associates and subordinates who had helped in the building up of the company; the author's opinions of his own greater wisdom at various crises were as thinly veiled as they had been in the magazine article, which reappeared without change, as a chapter of the book. The utterances on the freedom of labor to arrange its own affairs were more pronounced, the declarations that the employer had nothing to fear from permitting such freedom were more assured than any the author had heretofore made public, and this chapter of theorizing, Floyd felt instinctively, would be prolific of misfortune. On the other hand, there were pages that were generous and not misguided, in which Colonel Halket had recounted some of the fine acts

of heroism and self-sacrifice that had been brought out in
the daily life at the mills; these descriptions were vivid
and real and introduced a likable human quality into the
midst of what was often dull and pretentious. And one
chapter moved Floyd deeply, the last; it was called "My
Wife," and it told, simply and without sentimentality,
what part Mrs. Halket had taken in building up New
Rome and helping the women of the town. In this most
difficult chapter of all there was no violation of taste, no
undignified airing of the writer's love and bereavement;
intimacies were not exposed, and yet no reader could miss
the tenderness and reverence behind the words, or the
self-contained, unasking sorrow. Floyd laid the book down
with a different feeling from that which had possessed him
when he was in the midst of it. "The end redeems all its
mistakes," he thought — "for me at least." He awaited
with more cheerfulness the disagreeable events that he
believed certain to follow.

They did not come at once; even the dissatisfaction
among the officers of the works was less than he had
expected to find it; rather, it was resignation; their feeling seemed to be that the magazine article had already
done all the harm that it was possible for a printed thing
to do. The comment of the press was, with but few excep-
tions, respectful and favorable. In Avalon one graceless
newspaper, to be sure, which was a scoffer at all things
established and decent, paid the book the compliment of
a sarcastic review. "An adept at solitaire performances
with bouquets," it began, "Colonel Halket is here exhibited in the act of presenting himself with the choicest
nosegays of his collection. The Colonel's reminiscences
have what might be called an old-world charm in their
ambrosial fragrance and cloying sweetness. We confess
that after lounging the better part of a day in the Colonel's garden and observing him as he decks himself all
down the front with boutonnières, we have a hankering
to see him take a hoe out behind the barn and grub up

burdocks. We have an idea that if the Colonel keeps on attending to the business of personal decoration, the burdocks will get a good start out at New Rome."

This, however, was almost the only carping note in the grand chorus of reviews that teemed from the Atlantic to the Pacific. Colonel Halket hoarded them in a scrap-book and dwelt upon them with admiration. He treasured likewise editorial discussions based on his volume and even newspaper clippings that quoted passages from it. The titles of these gave him pleasure, for he figured in them very often, — "A Golden Rule Manufacturer," "A Pioneer of Industry," "The Best Type of Capitalist," "The Portrait of a True American." A man of seventy-eight might spend his last days less pleasantly than in brooding over such definitions of himself.

With the popular success of his book, he felt that he had achieved that which he had coveted, — a national reputation for *himself*, not merely for his steel. It was a fitting achievement to crown his life; he had taken rank now and was recognized as one of the influential men of the country, a power in the industrial world, a leader in action and in thought. "Perhaps no man of this generation," said the Avalon Sunday *Times*, "has been more actively identified with the country's development than Colonel Robert Halket of this city." Perhaps not, thought Colonel Halket.

Having bemused himself with these pleasant notions, he was quite entertained to learn that his utterances had shocked some of his brother manufacturers severely. It was the privilege of the first citizen of Avalon, a leading citizen of the United States, to shock smaller men; it was in fact a duty; and as for their murmuring criticism and dissent, it was truly ludicrous. Who among them had achieved one tenth of his success? He was giving his immediate neighbors — more than them, the whole country — a demonstration of the fact that a gigantic industrial concern can be run with absolutely no friction, with tremendous profit, and to the complete satisfaction of employer and employee. For convincing proof he had but to turn to his monthly balance-sheet.

"Floyd," he said to his grandson one day, "what should you consider a fair price for the works?"

"Are you thinking of selling them?" Floyd asked, in surprise.

"No, no, indeed. I was just wondering how nearly our ideas of the value would correspond."

"Twenty millions?" Floyd spoke dubiously.

"Twenty! My dear boy, I would n't consider an offer of fifty millions, cash down. I would n't think of it!"

"I don't believe you 'll ever be offered it," Floyd said, with a smile.

"Oh, I 'm not so sure," responded the old man. "It would be a good bargain at that figure for a man who understood the business and appreciated what it was to have a force of workmen in such thorough harmony with the employer as ours now are. With the perfection to which we 've at last brought our organization and policy, there should be no limit to our growth."

Floyd was so surfeited with this kind of talk that for once in his weariness he spoke out incautiously.

"Sometimes I don't feel so sure of the harmony," he said. "I find I don't harmonize with the Knights of Labor for a cent. I can worry along with the Affiliated, but when the 'parent organization,' as the Knights loves to call itself, makes demands on me, I object."

"What trouble has there been?" Colonel Halket asked.

"Oh, nothing much, and there won't be. A committee of the Knights waited on me to-day with the most preposterous demand I 've ever had presented. It seems there 's an old fellow named Tibbs, who 's been with us more than twenty years; he was one of the last to join the union and he did it reluctantly. Some of those unwilling members the union is apparently trying to freeze out; anyway it looks as if they had it in for Tibbs. His two daughters have been employed in a laundry, and the Knights have ordered all the laundresses out on strike because of some question of wages. The Misses Tibbs declined to quit and are still working, and because of that, the Knights came down on me with the demand that I discharge the old man! They'd been to Gregg and he'd kicked them out of the office; I naturally did the same."

Colonel Halket frowned and shook his head. "The demand may have seemed unreasonable," he said. "But I hope you did not treat them rudely; there is a way of getting along with such men, and no doubt to their minds there was nothing unreasonable in what they asked."

"But, Grandfather—"

Colonel Halket raised his hand.

"Conciliation is never wasted in business. Violence in speech or act never yet served any good purpose. The policy that I have enunciated in my book should be your guide in small matters as in large."

Floyd stared in silence. The vague feeling which he occasionally had experienced, that sometimes his grandfather's moods bordered on insanity, stirred again within him.

Three days later Colonel Halket told Floyd that he had been visited by the committee of the Knights of Labor. "They came to see me about the Tibbs case," he said.

"Did they have anything new to say?" Floyd asked, with a sinking of the heart.

"They made clear to me that they had been treated with insufficient consideration," replied his grandfather severely. "As I was inclined to suspect, there is some reason in their contention. Their aim — a very proper aim — is to harmonize labor. Unfortunately, this can only be done by weeding out the inharmonious elements. Tibbs is an irritation and must go. Otherwise, they will call a strike, and that we cannot afford."

"But the principle, Grandfather—" began Floyd.

"We cannot afford a strike for a principle," declared Colonel Halket. "The men realize perfectly that this would be an advantageous time to strike — when we are making large profits and cannot fill all our orders." But he was thinking of the possible loss to his national prestige rather than of the pecuniary loss that a strike would entail. He had boasted of his security against strikes and of the affection of his men; the threat of the Knights of Labor committee had frightened him with its unwelcome possibilities. "We must preserve harmony among our men. I am sorry to order the discharge of an old employee like Tibbs, I am willing even that he should be pensioned; but under the circumstances he must go. I have promised it. You will issue the order for his discharge and at the same time convey to him the information that a suitable pension will be paid him."

Floyd, sitting forward in his chair, leaned over and laid his hand on Colonel Halket's knee.

"Grandfather," he said, and there was earnest appeal in his voice, "I've got to mutiny. I can't issue any such order. Tibbs is a good man, and I simply will not be a party to turning him out of his job because his daughters are trying to earn an honest living. Why, good God, Grandfather!" — indignation suddenly swept him out of discretion — "What do you and the Knights of Labor want to do — drive the man's girls out on the streets?"

"Floyd!" Colonel Halket rose to his feet, stood clinching his hands, and looked down at his grandson with flashing eyes.

"I beg your pardon, sir," Floyd said, rising. "But though that remark was uncalled for, I feel that what you command is a great injustice to an innocent and faithful workman. It seems to me unworthy of such an establishment as yours, and likely, moreover, to do untold harm. Rather than issue such an order, I will resign my position."

Colonel Halket put his hands on Floyd's shoulders and looked at him steadily. "Do you mean it, Floyd?"

THE AUTOBIOGRAPHER 227

"I do."

The old man stood for a moment, looking into his eyes. Then he said, —

"Very well. I will not ask you to issue the order, Floyd."

This mildness made Floyd ashamed of his outburst, made him feel uncomfortable, as if he had been striking an attitude and spouting heroics. He laughed apologetically.

"You and I never before came so near to having a row, did we, Grandfather?" he said. "I did n't mean to be disrespectful. But honestly I can't help feeling this way about it all." And while Colonel Halket still stood with his hand on the young man's shoulder, smiling faintly and with only a trace of austerity, Floyd amplified his ideas about "the principle of the thing." He spoke now with no defiance in his manner, but confidentially, explaining the views that he held and that he was happy to think had this time prevailed. It encouraged him to believe that his grandfather was after all so amenable to reason, was truly so liberal and open-minded. Not many a man of seventy-eight would have been so tolerant of a rebuke from a grandson, so able to see the justice of it.

Three days later, when Floyd paid his next visit to New Rome, he was informed by Gregg that Tibbs's discharge had been ordered. Floyd expressed incredulity, and Gregg handed him the note from Colonel Halket.

"I never made a worse mouth over anything," said the superintendent. "I don't know as I can stand this sort of thing indefinitely, Mr. Halket; that's a fact."

Floyd was too stunned by the evidence of his grandfather's duplicity to make any remonstrance. He was still looking stupidly at the note.

"Have you done anything about it?" he asked.

"Yes, I've done it," Gregg replied. "I notified him that he'd draw a pension of fifty dollars a month. But he's a sturdy old fellow. He said he'd have none of it.

'Keep your conscience money for them that needs it,' he said."

Floyd sat down in a chair and laid the note with slow bewilderment on the table. "It beats me," he murmured. "It beats me."

He could not fathom his grandfather's motive, he could not believe his grandfather was so poor a craven as to yield this point simply because he dreaded the calling of a strike and the temporary loss that would result. Colonel Halket had hidden successfully from every one, even from Floyd, his ambition of late birth, his anxiety to shine as a national figure, as the great industrial peacemaker of the modern world. And Floyd in his simplicity had never perceived what had become the ruling purpose of his grandfather's life.

"I wish," he said after a moment of vain meditation, "that you'd keep track of Tibbs for me, Mr. Gregg, so that I'll know where to find him if I ever want him — and how he gets along. Maybe we'll get him back again. There will have to be a change of policy some time. I hope you will stand by us till then, Mr. Gregg. Your advice will be needed."

"The fight will have to come pretty soon," declared Gregg. "This victory of the Knights will encourage all sorts of extreme demands. And they'll likely carry them all straight to the Colonel."

"Maybe they will find that he has conceded as much as he is prepared to concede," Floyd answered. "Well, we must wait and see."

Perhaps the union was unwilling to jeopardize the effect of its unexpected victory by making another instant demand and possibly meeting defeat; perhaps no issue at once presented itself to the minds of the leaders. At any rate the pressure which Floyd anticipated was not applied, and in a few weeks the conditions had been so altered that it was hardly to be dreaded. For the price of steel began now to decline rapidly, and with the prospect of

THE AUTOBIOGRAPHER 229

running the mills at a loss, the threat of a strike, had it been made, would have had no terrors.

During this period depression overcame Colonel Halket. It was midsummer, and his great house in Canada remained closed. "I dread going to it somehow," he said to Floyd. "I can live on here — but to go back there and have all the memories of last summer recalled — it would make me feel too lonely and forlorn. I have got now to be with people."

In the end he chartered a steam yacht and sailed restlessly up and down the coast, stopping here and there, now for a day, now for a week. Floyd and the Dunbars and Stewart and Lydia Lee were with him for a time, and when they left him he secured other friends to keep him company, aged business men and lawyers from Avalon who were often seasick, talked tediously of the money and stock markets, and when they were more than a day at sea felt the lack of their newspaper. He sat with them at interminable games of cards and smoked too many cigars, and after a time the aimlessness of this vacation weighed on his spirits. When he had rid himself of the last of his guests, he finished his cruise and went home, though his charter of the yacht had still a month to run.

He was himself at a loss to account for the dejection which often now oppressed him. He felt perhaps that after issuing so gloriously into sudden national prominence he had ceased to make headway. How indeed was he to proceed? That was the question which confronted him. He could not write another autobiography, and the completion of that work had left him in a sense without an occupation, without an intimate personal interest, had left him more acutely conscious than before of his loneliness, his bereavement, his age. And from this weary consciousness he would start hopefully at any sign of public interest or favor, any invitation to speak at a banquet or to address a meeting; his appointment as chairman of the State Board of Arbitration gratified him, and the newspaper editorial articles commending the appointment he read and reread and treasured in volume X of his scrap-book. But events such as these were only intermittent flashes. If he had been a younger man, he might easily have become governor or gone to the Senate; he began mournfully to reflect on what he might have done had he not modestly confined himself for so long to winning merely local recognition. The truth emerged upon him with gradual distinctness: he had after all attained the ambition of his latter days so far as it was attainable; he stood, a figure known and admired throughout the land for his industrial achievement and progressive ideas. And the realization that he had gone as far and gained as much as would ever be possible for him deepened his melancholy. "It seems that when a man finishes his autobiography, he's practically finished his life too," he thought. "That had never occurred to me."

Only one occupation remained for him — that unlovely one of sitting tight and seeing that he lost not one inch of place that he had gained. He must live up to his reputation to the end; what people thought him, that must he be and seem. He had outlived the close and eager interest in his business; he had outlived the sense of individual justice; he was absorbed in larger things.

XVI

STEWART ACQUIRES SOME NEW INTERESTS

THE same conditions which depressed the steel manufacturers caused slackness and gloom among the architects. First, strikes in the building trades, and then the pinch of hard times had caused stagnation in Stewart Lee's office. This would have given him little concern, had it not been apparent to him that Bennett & Durant were getting more work than he. It was to no purpose that he maintained downtown an air of great activity, that he walked at full speed into the club at luncheon-time, and after luncheon went from the dining-room into the reading-room with the excessively brisk step that he had adopted at the outset of his promising career. Bennett from his table in the corner noted it and smiled cynically.

Stewart's pride was such that to no one but his wife would he confess that he had really nothing to do. From her he made little effort to conceal his discontent. He railed against the town — her native place. "For a man who's not so busy that he hasn't time to think, Avalon is the devil," he would grumble. To ride out in the country that had once been so beautiful and was now marred by the blight of human industry afflicted his spirits. It was late autumn. To play golf bored him. To sit at home in front of the monotonous natural gas fire was of all things the dullest. Boston became a word that knelled in Lydia's ears. It was not that he was unmanly in his complaining; he exhibited his dissatisfaction on the whole in very cheerful witticisms, and when he was really bitter it would be in an extravagant diatribe that was not meant to be taken too seriously — that one could, if one chose, regard as an exercise of voice and vocabulary. As a husband he could not have been more devoted. When he and Lydia walked together on the street, he would place himself between her and the curb as scrupulously as he had always done in his courtship, and if they crossed the street, he would at once slip round behind her and again take the outside. His faithful, constant chivalry in small things such as this made his unhappiness in the larger order of his life the more poignant to Lydia.

She loved her native town in spite of its ugliness, in spite of its disregard of charm as a necessary element for well-being. "The people, anyway," she laughed back at one of Stewart's flashes of censure, — "I don't see how you can help liking the people." Stewart did not reply that he found them less interesting and attractive since they had receded from their first ready welcome of him as the long-expected architect of Avalon. But he had certainly cooled toward them in a degree corresponding to that by which they were pruning their first exuberance about his work.

Lydia fell into a long silence one evening after Stewart had been exercising his wit at the expense of the natural gas fire which burned in the library grate, and before which they sat. She usually laughed back at his attacks and kept alive a spirit of light-heartedness. But now he realized after a few moments that she was pained. He rose and seated himself on the arm of her chair.

"Look here, dear," he said, taking her hands, "you're not hurt by my remarks about the old fire, are you? There wasn't anything personal intended, you know."

She smiled up at him affectionately. "Oh, I understand, Stewart," she said. "I wasn't feeling hurt — just sorry because — because you aren't happier. Why wouldn't it be a good thing for you to move away from Avalon, since you don't like it? Wouldn't you be better satisfied to live in New York — or Boston?"

"But you would n't!" he exclaimed.

"Oh, I like living here, of course," she answered simply. "But that's nothing. I want to live where you'll be happiest."

He kissed her. "When you talk like that, you make me perfectly — uxorious!" he declared. "Foolishly fond of my wife — according to the dictionaries. They don't know much; how could anybody be foolishly fond of such a wife!"

He drew her head round under his arm, and with the other hand stroked the soft brown hair and pinched the little ear.

"I do want you to be happy, Stewart," she murmured. "I'm wedded to you — not to a town."

A reluctance to speak fell upon him; in the presence of his wife he found himself suddenly not knowing what to say — not knowing even what his own inclinations were. There was no reason that he could give for not preferring New York or Boston to Avalon. Yet he knew that however more congenial to his tastes these cities might be they could neither of them hold out to him any more happiness.

"Oh, I just like to growl sometimes," he said. "I'm all right; I like the place — and I'm not going to quit beaten. I want to fight it out, and get on top of the whole bunch here, and some time have my own way in things and build up the town."

A manly declaration served to cloak a coward consciousness. His own soul told him that he had slipped back and back, that in the competition of the larger, older cities he could not win a place and must lag behind with the undistinguished. And doing that, he would never be happy. It would be more easy for him to regain what he had lost here in Avalon, where the competition was of men whom he did not fear, than to hew out his niche in New York among men of whom in his secret heart he was afraid.

But he could not say this to his wife. She admired him because of his determination to make the dismal, uphill fight. With a new consideration for her, he tried to refrain from the little jeers which had distressed her.

Floyd came to him one day that autumn with a proposal that they should join a shooting party in Tennessee. To Stewart, who had not been on such an expedition since his marriage, the idea was exhilarating. Lydia was delighted. "It will be just the thing for you," she said.

"You don't mind my going off and leaving you?" Stewart asked.

She was pleased by such anxiety. "I'll content myself by being just as gay as I can while you're away," she answered. "You won't let him forget me, will you, Floyd?"

She said it laughing, heedlessly, and then something in Floyd's eyes reminded her of that which she had forgotten. She flushed, and there was an awkwardness that Stewart felt without understanding.

The two weeks' shooting had a very soothing influence on Stewart's mind. He was the crack shot of the party, and no one was ever happier than Stewart when he was able to excel. The weather was good, game plentiful, the life not too rough; and he returned North knowing that he was admired by his companions as a marksman, a clever and accomplished gentleman, and a good fellow. He was ready to have another fling at architecture and be admired for his skill in that.

At the little suburban station on the edge of Avalon, Lydia was waiting for him. He had his first glimpse of her through the window — sitting expectant on the high seat of the trap and holding the reins over the cobs that had been his birthday present to her. The cobs were restless, rocking the trap back and forth, and she was steadying them with a competent hand, and at the same time looking eagerly towards the train. Then for just a moment he lost sight of her; but when he appeared on the platform she waved her whip in salute and laughed; and he silently cursed the fat man in front of him who was so slow in getting down the steps.

When he climbed up into the seat beside his wife and kissed her, he felt, with the sympathetic sensitiveness that was his peculiar endowment, that something wonderful and important to them both had taken place.

"Oh, Stewart!" she said, and then, with a smile on her lips and tears in her eyes, she was silent. She turned the horses round; they wanted to trot, but she held them in and made them walk along the maple-bordered street, though they tossed their heads protestingly. Then she spoke, with a tremor of exultation in her voice. "I wanted to tell you at once — I could hardly wait — I wanted to write it to you — but somehow it wasn't anything I *could* write — Stewart!"

He looked at her oddly, wondering.

"What is it, dear?" he asked.

"Can't you guess? Oh, Stewart — we're going to be so much happier!"

He put his arm round her and murmured into her ear.

"Yes," she answered. "Oh, I'm so glad! Stewart, aren't you glad?"

He made no reply, but he pressed her more tightly with his arm. After a moment he said soberly, —

"I believe that's what I've been wanting all along — only I didn't know —"

"*I* knew," she answered. "It was because of that you were so unhappy, dear."

She looked round at him with a serene confidence in her explanation, and an unselfish gladness that she was able to bring him this happiness. He understood it and was touched. It drew from him a boyish expression of love, and even the levity with which he followed it was caressing and tender.

"How terribly handsome you are, Lydia!" he said, and then he added, with a smile, "I'll bet the little one will be a peach!"

She laughed, touched the horses with the whip, and let them run. Then as she sat erect, holding the reins taut and looking ahead with steady eyes, but with the warm blood still reddening her cheeks, Stewart leaned back comfortably. He wondered why he should ever have been discontented.

His new interest in life did not at once lapse, even though he had come home to find his office work as light and unpromising as ever. He got out his paint brushes and palette and easel, and set himself to making a portrait of Lydia. She was delighted with this revival of an old talent. His enthusiasm in exercising it seemed to have been intensified by long disuse; he worked with an absorption that quite awed Lydia into silence. She admired the picture when it was finished; even Stewart admitted he thought it was rather good, considering. "I wish I'd gone in for painting," he sighed. "That's what I really was cut out for." He extended to himself the complacent, indulgent pity of a man who idly meditates on what great things he might have done had he only been led into the right career. When he had painted Lydia's portrait and hung it in the dining-room, he painted her father and then her mother. They were very tolerable amateur portraits, and Stewart looked on them all with an indulgent eye.

"Yes," he said again one day to Lydia, "I almost wish I'd gone in for painting instead of architecture."

"You have a lot of talent," she answered. "Why can't you do both things?"

"Well, I will," he declared. "But I wish I'd studied."

Floyd, looking at the pictures one Sunday, suggested, with a laugh, that Stewart owed him a portrait. "For that college caricature you once did of me. Remember, Stewart?"

Stewart remembered, in some embarrassment. "It wouldn't be that kind of a picture," he said. "I wish you would give me a few sittings, Floyd."

"Grandfather's going to have his portrait painted by a Frenchman that he's bringing over for the purpose," Floyd announced. "I'll tell him that I'm disappointed in him; he's always professed to stand for the protection of home industries. When can we get together, Stewart?"

They arranged to have the sittings on Sunday mornings in the music-room at Floyd's house, the room in which Colonel Halket was to sit for his portrait before the eminent Frenchman. But after the first two meetings, Stewart was discouraged. "I'll never finish it this way," he said. "Couldn't you get off, Floyd, at noon two or three days this week and come up here for an hour or so? I'll manage it if you can." Floyd good-naturedly managed it, and Stewart in three consecutive sittings almost finished the picture. While he was working on it, he neglected his office duties; they annoyed him. "There's no fun equal to that of doing what you like when you ought to be doing things you don't care about," he said to Floyd. "I suppose I ought to be building stables and warehouses at this moment; they may go to the devil."

Having had his burst of speed and nearly finished the portrait, he could get no further with it; Floyd could not see wherein it was unfinished, but it made Stewart so impatient merely to suggest this idea that Floyd after suggesting it held his tongue. Under the artist's persuasion Floyd, at some inconvenience, made two more trips uptown at noon, only to see Stewart putter and dawdle and hear him murmur under his breath. He bore this amiably enough, but at the end of the second day he told Stewart that they had better go back to their Sunday mornings.

"Oh, all right," said the painter moodily. "You're not of much use to me now, anyway. I've got to work the thing out for myself."

Temporarily, it was the one piece of work on which his enthusiasm was set, and he was restless thinking about it; he slid through his day or his half-day at the office and hurried away to study his canvas. There was never any one to bother him; and he was free to go and come in the Halket house. But one morning when he was entering the door of the music-room he stopped short. Colonel Halket and a short thick-set man were walking down toward the farther end where his painting rested on its easel. Suddenly the stranger threw both hands up and out in a gesture of light disdain, towards the canvas, and twice he repeated this gesture, laughing merrily. With a question to Colonel Halket and another laugh, he went forward and deliberately turned the easel round until the picture faced the wall. Then he flung out both hands to Colonel Halket, chattering gayly as if he were rejoicing in his childish performance.

Stewart compressed his lips for an instant, and walked with great dignity down the long room. Colonel Halket, seeing him, looked for one moment confused; but he raised his hands and placed his thumbs in the armholes of his waistcoat, an attitude which at least gave him the appearance of his usual calm. He awaited Stewart thus with a swelling blandness.

"I am very glad you've come, Mr. Lee," he said. "It gives me an opportunity to present you to my friend, M. Sevier — Mr. Lee."

"I regret I had not heard M. Sevier was coming to-day," Stewart said, as he and the Frenchman shook hands. He addressed M. Sevier directly in French. He had had the reputation while abroad of being one of three Americans who spoke French like a Parisian. He pointed at his picture with a smile. "I should not have left my amateur work where it would offend M. Sevier."

"Ah, Mr. Lee," said the painter deprecatingly, "pardon an impertinence. But — artists are a jealous breed — is it not so, Mr. Lee?" He offered Stewart an appealing and apologetic smile.

"M. Sevier does me the honor to suggest that he is jealous. It is a compliment that I shall cherish. It is a thing to remember with affection, — that in jealousy

M. Sevier once turned the poor amateur's uncompleted picture toward the wall."

He spoke as sardonically as was compatible with the polite utterance of his faultless French. M. Sevier understood that his offense was unpardonable; he looked at Stewart piteously.

"Pardon," he said, and bowed.

"I don't get more than half of it," struck in Colonel Halket amiably, "but I gather that you two gentlemen are paying each other compliments. Maybe M. Sevier will be willing for you to come in and watch him paint, seeing you're so interested and have a talent for it, Mr. Lee."

The Frenchman sent a conciliatory glance to accompany this ill-timed suggestion, but Stewart was inexorable.

"Thank you, Colonel Halket," he replied, and as he spoke he took down his canvas from the easel. "But I'm afraid I shouldn't have time; in fact I shall have to finish this picture of my own at home in odd moments. Good-by, Colonel Halket. Please tell Floyd I'll have it ready for him before long. Good-by, M. Sevier."

He bowed and walked out, carrying his picture. Nor did he have one qualm of compunction for the severity with which he had treated the unfortunate painter. A slight to his dignity, an affront to his importance he resented with a wholeheartedness that always drove him to excessive efforts for retaliation. Now, when he arrived at home with the picture, he sat down and worked until the failing afternoon light put a stop to his labors. "It's more nearly right now," he said to himself, as he washed his brushes. He was quite sure that he knew why Sevier had been so displeased with the picture; the colors needed toning down, a small fault. He did not feel disheartened by the criticism of an academic Frenchman, who, however well he painted in a conventional method, was obviously unable to recognize the superiority of a great natural gift over mere technique. Thus Stewart met scorn with scorn.

Floyd was sufficiently appreciative, and on being told

that the picture was now finished thought he saw how greatly it had been improved. "I tell you," Stewart said to him, as they stood in front of it, "there's a field for painters here that has never been touched. Here's the place to paint the laboring-man — the type of American labor and industry. By George! it's a great idea — and the chance for picturesqueness in the backgrounds — mills and forges and lurid lights and red-hot iron and all kinds of things! You know, it's just occurred to me; I think I'll have to try my hand at it!"

"I'll find you subjects enough," said Floyd. "Come out to our mills; you'll see all kinds of faces there."

"I'll do it," declared Stewart. "Business is light downtown; I can get away now and then —"

"You might come out some evening; it's more picturesque at night."

"That's a good idea; an iron mill at night — a splendid subject!" Stewart's sudden enthusiasm had kindled his imagination. "Labor in the fields has been represented by painters — but not the labor of the mills; it's a chance for an artist — a great chance. Yes, sir, I'll try my hand at it and make a date with you right now."

Floyd made the "date" and carried home his picture. He set it up against the wall in his study, and looked at it with a scrutiny which was at first impersonal, but gradually became meditative and melancholy. His own appearance had always been exceedingly vague and nebulous to him; the thought of himself had never called up a distinct image in his mind; it carried with it only the suggestion of a dark, loutish young man pushing a sullen way through a crowd. Stewart's picture represented him as not so ill-looking as the creature of his mind, yet as wholly aggressive, black, and hard. He sighed after a while, concluding that he must impress people as such an inexorable and pushing person, and took the picture into the library that his grandfather might see it. M. Sevier was there also, having just finished the day's sitting.

"I've been having my portrait painted too, M. Sevier," Floyd said to him innocently, setting Stewart's masterpiece up against the book-shelves.

M. Sevier bowed and smiled. Colonel Halket put on his glasses and paced off to get the range.

"Ah — yes," he said conservatively, "he's caught a likeness — eh, M. Sevier? Eh" — he added in a more doubtful tone as the Frenchman did not answer — "eh, M. Sevier?"

"Of a blue cravat and a pearl pin — yes," agreed M. Sevier politely.

"You don't think much of it?" Floyd asked.

M. Sevier shrugged his shoulders and spread out his palms. "What can I say?"

"Of course it's only by an amateur painter," Floyd explained. "Isn't it pretty good for an amateur?"

Again M. Sevier shrugged his shoulders. "Oh — perhaps."

"M. Sevier has seen it before," Colonel Halket said. "It was here when he first came — and," he added, with a faint smile, "he felt obliged to turn it to the wall."

"Pardon," said the Frenchman, bowing to Floyd. "Yes, I so far forgot myself."

Floyd laughed. "Well — it must hurt to look at a face like that. But — if you don't mind telling me — what's out about it, M. Sevier?"

"It is not you — and it is not a picture, Mr. Halket," replied the painter. "Therefore it is not good. But see — the face, it is of wood, and stares; it is of no interest, it is nothing. But it is a very careful coat — and flower in the button-hole, and pearl pin, and cravat. They are all of an interest equal with the face."

"But," insisted Floyd, "doesn't it really show a lot of talent — in an amateur?"

"It would have shown more — not to paint it."

Floyd thought of Stewart's large ambition expressed that afternoon, to be the painter of Labor, and looked again at the picture. Perhaps, if M. Sevier was right, the stupid, aggressive hardness of that face was not really characteristic, but was attributable to technical deficiency on the part of the artist. It was such a cheerful thought that Floyd could not spare much sympathy for Stewart in the predestined failure of his large designs.

M. Sevier of course spoke with authority, and yet before accepting his judgment upon Stewart as final, Floyd waited to see for himself something of the Frenchman's work. The portrait of Colonel Halket was finished and hung in the hall of the house, and Floyd no longer doubted M. Sevier's authority. It seemed to him almost a cruel thing that the painter had done, yet his grandfather was proud and delighted. To Floyd the picture of Colonel Halket standing with his left hand in his trousers pocket and holding a roll of manuscript in his right suggested all his pompousness and love of prominence and oratorical display; and what was worse, Floyd seemed to see in the admirable painting of the old man's handsome head the subtle showing of his selfishness and foolishness and shrewdness, which Floyd had come by slow degrees to understand and yet was striving all the time to deny.

"This portrait, Floyd," Colonel Halket said to him, "I want always to stay in the family. It may be," — he spoke with a certain self-conscious modesty, — " of course I hardly expect it, but some time there might be a — a general desire to have a portrait of me in some public institution of the city. If any such desire should ever be expressed — and you felt inclined to gratify it, I should prefer that you would do so with the portrait which Theobald Smith painted of me four years ago — the one that hangs in the hall upstairs. This one I want always to be preserved as the family portrait."

"I'll see to that," Floyd assured him. "And if I should die, and the mayor should want a picture of me to hang in the city hall, why here's this one of Stewart Lee's. It's the only one I've got, and it will be hard for you to part with it, but you 're so public-spirited, Grandfather, that if the people do clamor to have it where they can see it — "

"Young man," said Colonel Halket stiffly, though his lip was twitching, " don't be impudent." He turned away to conceal a grin. It was only of late that his grandson had adopted the occasional habit of chaffing him, and his dignity did not permit him openly to encourage it. But he owned to himself that he liked it now and then; it was a thing that he had missed since his wife had died. No one else ever ventured upon it.

Indeed, he was remarkably cheerful in these days. Floyd noticed it and was pleased even while he wondered what new mischief was brewing. His grandfather was in a remarkably studious mood; he sat at home and collated statistics of the iron trade. He seemed to Floyd to have grown once more dangerously non-communicative. But the situation at the mills was reassuring, the men were quiet, and business was picking up; therefore Floyd did not waste much time in speculating on what would be the next source of trouble.

He had not forgotten the promise he had made to Stewart, and he had several times taken the budding painter out to New Rome and put him in the way of finding material. Floyd had thought that Hugh Farrell would be a promising subject for a painter, and he called Stewart's attention to him with the remark that there was the most picturesque figure in the mills. "The best type of laboring-man, too," Floyd added. But the sight of Hugh only awoke in Stewart the recollection of his immature and costly effort to build ideal houses for working-men, and he could not dwell with any satisfaction upon one who evoked such an unpleasant memory. Much to Floyd's surprise and somewhat to his disappointment, Stewart found in Tustin sitting at the great slab-mill a more worthy subject for his brush. "No, he 's not beautiful," Stewart said, as they stood watching him, " but he 's splendidly grim. Now, he's really a man," and Stewart laughed, "of whom it might be said that the iron has entered into his soul. Not like that fellow Farrell, who's too lively and genial-looking; this man's much more my idea of the typical iron-worker."

Tustin ignored them, sitting with his two helpers beside the rolls of which he had charge. He kept his right hand on the lever that controlled the great hammer and gazed sullenly at the white-hot slab that was being thinned and elongated before his eyes. A pipe held in one corner of his mouth contributed to the dogged, meditative sourness of his expression. He was a powerfully built man; his suspenders, crossed upon his blue flannel shirt, marked out the thick muscles of his shoulders.

At the end of the building was a row of furnaces in front of which passed a car, a great leviathan with a long arm which it would stretch forward into a red-hot furnace mouth. In a moment this arm would be withdrawn, clutching a huge white-hot slab of steel, which the leviathan would rapidly carry on to a great double hook suspended by a traveling chain. The hook would then swing forward and lay the slab on the series of cylinders before which Tustin sat. The cylinders would be set in motion, passing the white-hot slab back and forth under a hammer that squeezed down on it, gradually flattening and elongating it. Three times at least was the slab passed back and forth and sometimes four; this was decided by Tustin, who after the third passage would leave his seat and test the edge of the steel with a pair of tongs. After the slab had been under the hammer twice, one of the helpers would turn on the water-cocks of the engine and spray it; clouds of steam would hiss up, and the streams of water would be illuminated, turning green, purple, and orange, as the hot metal came groaning under them. And when this point was reached, the great double hook was always waiting with another white-hot slab in its clutch, holding it patiently till it should be time to lay it on the rolls.

"Oh, if one could only paint light and fire!" cried Stewart. "Nobody can really do it — but I'm going to try."

And one clear November night when Floyd had taken him up to the hilltop that overlooked the mills and the river, Stewart was for a long time silent. "I didn't know it was anything like this," he said presently, and then was silent again. Two miles of iron works lay before him, vast, shadowy forms of buildings weirdly illuminated by irregular leaps and jets of flame. The trains bearing the hot ingots crawled about through the yards like huge glow-worms. Flags of fire sprang out of tall chimneys, signaled for a moment, and died away. At intervals from heights in mid-air caldrons of metal were spilled with a roar, and the shower of vari-colored fire and flame sent sparks soaring skyward even after it had been itself licked up by the night. The steady red glow of open furnaces, the red shuttling of beams on the rollers in the plate-mills and of rods in the rod-mills, and the gigantic flow of molten metal at blast furnaces and converter made a spectacular and dramatic display that appealed deeply to Stewart. "Oh, but this is the real thing!" he exclaimed at last. "I had no idea it was so gorgeous and magnificent. If a man could only paint this — but he'd need a mile of canvas! But parts of it — there, those three figures down there in the light of that furnace, Floyd! Just little glimpses like that — wouldn't they be pictures!"

In the way of painting such nocturnes, indeed, in the way of painting any pictures at the mills, there were practical difficulties to be surmounted. Some things had to be worked up at home from rough pencil sketches and memory. Others Stewart, with the enterprise of enthusiasm, determined to paint upon the spot. In two or three visits on which Floyd did not accompany him, he succeeded in breaking down Tustin's antipathy. When Stewart deliberately set out to win a man, he never failed. By the use of judicious speech he not only secured permission from Tustin to paint him as he sat at the rolls, but he pleased him by making the request. Soon after that was to be observed the unprecedented spectacle in the New Rome mills of a painter at work with easel and palette and canvas. The other men joked Tustin about sitting for his portrait; but he was clever enough to see that they regarded it as a distinction. It contributed in a small way to his eminence among them. When he found that Stewart had a great idea of the sufferings, privations, and hardships of iron-workers, he lost no time in confirming the impression. He uttered no personal complaints; his incidental anecdotes, delivered in a calm, matter-of-fact way and showing how pitiable was the life of an iron-worker, filled Stewart with sympathetic indignation. He went to Floyd with a protest, but Floyd was provokingly cool and undisturbed, and either belittled or laughed at Tustin's charges. "Of course it's a hard life," he said. "It can't be anything else. But the men get the very best wages that skilled labor gets anywhere, and we do all we can for their comfort." As to specific cases that Stewart cited, Floyd thought they were very likely misrepresentations. Still he would look into them. Stewart felt that Floyd as an employer of labor might not be much better than many others; he felt after hearing Tustin talk that iron manufacturers were a sinister class.

His vague ideas of doing a great missionary work through his painting took a stronger hold upon his imagination. He saw himself as possibly the Verestchagin of Labor, the painter who should awaken the apathetic public to a consciousness of the dramatic horrors of a wage-earner's life. To be sure, in his portrait of Tustin, a sturdy man sitting comfortably with his hand upon a lever, this purpose was not realized; and he was dissatisfied, not with the picture, but with the impossibility of expressing in painting the true inward misery of such employment. There were opportunities enough, though, to portray strained faces and contorted muscles, and violent effort, at the blast furnaces, and in the open-hearth and rolling-mills. A series of subjects took form in his mind.

With this new enterprise to occupy him, he found it possible to spend only the mornings at his office. But there was not work enough coming in to keep him busy, and what he had was of an uninteresting character, hedged in by restrictions of the clients, — the sort of work that in Stewart's opinion could be done perfunctorily as well as in any other way. His father-in-law, Mr. Dunbar, was disposed to question the wisdom of such indifference, but Stewart naturally enough reflected that Mr. Dunbar was merely a business man, a Philistine.

"But what is there in painting, Stewart?" Mr. Dunbar asked. "It's well enough as a recreation, but you can't follow a profession for just half the time this way, or soon you'll have none to follow. You're sacrificing it, are n't you, for a recreation? Or if you are n't, what is there in painting?"

Stewart replied that he did not look at it as altogether a recreation, but as a profession that he could pursue along with that of architecture. It was not necessarily unremunerative; painters of merit received large prices for their work. And quite apart from pecuniary considerations, he felt that this was something he must do; he had ideas to express and he should not be happy until they were expressed.

"And so far from being a drawback," Stewart concluded, "if I get a reputation as a painter, it will help me as an architect."

Mr. Dunbar bowed to the young man's superior wisdom. Art and architecture were matters of which he had little knowledge.

XVII

LARGE IDEA OF A PHILANTHROPIST

COLONEL HALKET surveyed the table with satisfaction. His reflection that the twenty guests represented a total capital of nearly two hundred million dollars was gratifying to his vanity; they had all been glad to come at his bidding. Except for Kerr, the New York banker, all were iron and steel manufacturers of Avalon; Colonel Halket had invited them to dinner to discuss a financial scheme and they had come impelled by an interest greater than that of curiosity, greater than that of sympathy — self-interest. Floyd was the only man in the room who was quite ignorant of the purpose of the dinner.

When the dinner was at an end, Colonel Halket rose from his chair.

"Gentlemen," he said, "I suggest that we adjourn to the library."

He led the way and at the door stood aside to let the others enter. Floyd came last, and when he saw the chairs arranged at the farther end of the room in two stiff rows of ten each, he stopped and looked at his grandfather.

"What's the show?" he asked.

"I am," said Colonel Halket. "Get along in with you."

The guests walked across the room and seated themselves in the two rows of chairs with what seemed to Floyd uncanny promptness. But then they had come prepared to hear a speech. Colonel Halket stood before them with the tips of the fingers of his right hand resting on the table, with the thumb of his left hand caught negligently in the arm-hole of his waistcoat. In this attitude he took several puffs of his cigar even after the others had

A PHILANTHROPIST'S IDEA

settled into an expectant silence. Then he removed his cigar and began to unfold his scheme for consolidating all the iron and steel plants of the region into one immense corporation.

The amazement with which Floyd listened was not shown by any of the others. They were all paying the careful, unsurprised attention of men who had already been made cognizant of the plan. Colonel Halket was expressing correct sentiments, to the effect that in union there is strength, that united we stand, divided we fall, etc. " Think of the waste entailed by the competition among us who are gathered in this room ! " he urged. " Waste effort, waste labor, waste product. I have figures here to show that by joining forces we can so diminish the cost of production and so increase profits that our earnings will in four years equal our total fixed capital."

After reading these figures, he brought forward his main proposition, which was that on the basis of these prospective earnings they should capitalize the new organization at five times the actual capital of the mills which should compose it, sell the stock at par, and do a great thing for the industry, the public, and themselves.

" Eventually," he said, " we shall find ourselves strong enough to extend our organization. Avalon is already the most vital spot, industrially, in America. It is already the great radiating centre of manufactures. Gradually and naturally we shall absorb all the iron-mills of importance in the country ; we shall control the iron industry of the continent."

He dwelt with fond oratory upon the benefits to be derived by the public and by the workingmen from such a consolidation, and during this part of his speech the studious, concentrated expression on the faces of his auditors became more marked. He brought in one or two apt quotations — one about the truly good citizen who cares not to be great but as he saves and serves the state — " and for the word great we might substitute rich," declared Colonel Halket loftily. He felt as he stood before these twenty eminent citizens that he had never addressed a body of men in a higher or more ennobling vein, or been more eloquent. "Bear with me if I seem didactic," he begged them with the complacent confidence of the orator who appeals for indulgence most when he feels most assured that he is about to be interesting. Only Colonel Halket deluded himself and misjudged his audience; they admired his polished utterance of fine sentiment, but were impatient for him to descend again to practical facts and figures. This before long he did, with another apology; and Floyd began then to understand the purpose of his grandfather's laborious study of statistics during the past months. The audience was once more interested and impressed.

Colonel Halket spoke continuously for an hour. When he had finished no one seemed at once ready to meet him in argument. After a moment he called on Kerr, the New York banker, for an opinion as to the financing of the scheme.

"I am willing to undertake it," said Kerr. "On condition that it appears that Colonel Halket is to be president of the new corporation."

"That is a condition, gentlemen, that I should not have thought of naming," said Colonel Halket genially. "I dare say Mr. Kerr, at any sign of opposition, will be willing to withdraw the compliment."

"On the contrary," said Mr. Kerr. He was a serious-looking man, bald except for a few long wisps of sandy hair laid across the peak of his head; his reddish mustache drooped, his ears were big and protuberant; he was a homely man, but an impressive by reason of his cool, calm eyes. His shrewd foresight passed among the unimaginative men of his world for constructive imagination; his prestige was enormous at this time, for he had had several large successes in getting together the properties of other men and putting them into the hands of his friends; he had met with no failures; articles appeared about him, therefore, in the supplements of the Sunday newspapers, from Boston to San Francisco, with pictures, more or less genuine, of his country house and his steam yacht and his family; in these articles he was usually referred to at least once either as "the Napoleon of finance" or as "the master mind of Wall Street." An enterprise fathered by Kerr at this period was sure of a joyful, care-free, blooming infancy — however friendless and forsaken might be its old age.

For these reasons nineteen men listened submissively and one listened proudly when Kerr said in his deliberate and pregnant voice, "On the condition that I have named and on that alone will I undertake the matter; and on that condition I shall be glad to undertake it."

Mr. Dunbar spoke. "If we sell out, do I understand that we mill-owners are definitely retired from business — given no active management either in the affairs of the corporation or in the mills which have been ours?"

"Some of you will be asked to take part in the management and others will not," replied Kerr. "Some of you will necessarily find yourselves gentlemen of leisure — with three or four or eight or ten times your present income. You will receive your pay for your mills in bonds and preferred stock on which dividends are certain or which may be sold for a price. The public will absorb the common stock — on which dividends are probable. We may be extravagant in paying for the mills which shall form our nucleus — but when we have demonstrated our power" — an ungenial smile crossed his face — "we shall be able to recoup by acquiring other properties at bargain prices."

The manufacturers smiled at this agreeably sinister suggestion, and the solemnity with which they had been listening was dissipated very soon in jokes and laughter, and then in practical questions and answers. Floyd sat overlooked in a corner of the room, absorbed in a slow,

burning wonder and disgust. Nineteen men, who had for
years been reasonably honest, single-minded producers of
useful materials, were being transformed before his eyes
into as many chaffering hucksters whose only aim was to
find for what multiple of its worth they might sell their
property to the ignorant and gullible. His grandfather
and the banker had evidently arranged even small details
of the scheme; it was hardly the fault of the other men
that they should exhibit such eagerness to profit by it.
The power of the two leaders was great enough to compel
submission, even had there been no temptation. The
breadth and scope of his grandfather's plan, which had
been worked out so quietly and patiently, with the assistance of but one man, the one man in the country whose
coöperation at this stage was essential, left Floyd aghast
with unwilling admiration. There was something both
superb and revolting in this insatiate greed for power on
the part of an old man who was approaching his eightieth
year.

When the guests had all departed, Colonel Halket returned from the hall where he had hospitably been bidding the last of them good-by, and found his grandson
sitting on the corner of the big table, swinging one leg
and gazing at the floor moodily.

"Have another cigar, Floyd," said Colonel Halket,
pushing the box toward him. "Sit down properly and be
comfortable; I want to talk with you."

Floyd took a cigar and bit off the end of it, although his
grandfather was offering him his cigar-cutter. The small
crudeness of this preference annoyed Colonel Halket;
occasionally Floyd did something of about this quality
which led his grandfather to think that he had not fully
profited by his advantages.

"I'm comfortable enough," said Floyd. "I'll walk
round; I'm tired of sitting down."

"No," said Colonel Halket, with a slight asperity. "*I'm*
tired of sitting down. *I* want to talk to you — and walk

A PHILANTHROPIST'S IDEA 253

round. Please sit down and, besides *being* comfortable, do your best to look it."

Floyd understood that Colonel Halket was in an exacting mood and submitted. When he had settled himself in an armchair by the fire-place and had lighted the cigar, his grandfather began to pace slowly back and forth with his thumbs hooked in the arm-holes of his waistcoat.

"Floyd," he said at last, "this night marks the crowning achievement of my life. I think I may say without vanity that all I have ever heretofore done — and it has not been little — is as nothing in its possibilities for beneficent and far-reaching results compared to what I have this evening accomplished. It is a thing that I have long dreamed of, and I thank God that I have been spared to consummate it. To-night you have seen taken — you have witnessed with your very eyes — the grandest step, as I believe, to advance the cause of labor that has been made in half a century."

"Labor!" cried Floyd, taking his cigar from his mouth and staring. "Labor!"

"Labor," repeated Colonel Halket, and his sonorous utterance seemed to breathe into the word all the nobility that should by tradition be associated with it. "For a time I felt that having brought about in my own mills a relation between capital and labor which I may go so far as to term ideal, and having published my book, my philosophy of an employer's life, I had contributed my utmost to the cause of industrial civilization. I felt that my work was finished, and that men might learn from me, so to speak, both by example and by precept — if they would. But, Floyd, a man is not happy when he feels that his work is done. I chafed under the feeling; and then one day there flashed upon me this idea for further work and usefulness."

"How did it come?" asked Floyd; his grandfather's pause seemed to demand some remark. "What suggested it?"

"I think it was reading in a newspaper one morning of the strikes in the rolling-mills at Warrenton and Leetsburg," replied Colonel Halket. "It started me thinking. I said to myself, 'I never have strikes in my mills; why should these men have them in theirs?' The answer was simple; my methods, my organization, my system of dealing with my men were based on correct principles; theirs were at fault. And then it occurred to me; if my methods could be applied to all the steel mills of this vicinity, under my personal supervision, there would be a harmonizing at once of interests which have been conflicting — a harmonizing and humanizing, to speak in epigram. It was the idea of so harmonizing and humanizing the relations of capital and labor, of giving a sense of stability to the workingman as well as to the employer that suggested the gathering together of all the mills in the valley under my control. From that, the next generalization is logical enough. If one can combine the iron industries of the valley, one can, almost as easily, combine those of the country. It will be done by gradual, inevitable accretion. It was first my mission to introduce a more enlightened and liberal policy towards labor into my own mills; it is now my mission to propagate this wherever the industry flourishes; in another decade, if I am spared to set this work properly on its feet, the condition of the iron-worker will be improved a hundred per cent., and a strike in the iron and steel business will be as unlikely as an earthquake in New York."

Floyd found himself for the moment with nothing to say. The idea that his grandfather had evolved this prodigious scheme in the interests of the laboring-man seemed to him unspeakably astounding and grotesque. It indicated a monstrous delusion as to the situation in the New Rome mills, where there was greater disaffection and discontent than there had ever been. It indicated a development of the visionary side of Colonel Halket's nature which Floyd had hardly suspected.

A PHILANTHROPIST'S IDEA

"It strikes me as queer," Floyd said at last quite bluntly. "Here is a plan conceived in the interests of the laboring-men — and all the definite provisions it makes are for the instant and enormous profits of the employers. Where does labor come in?"

"In a thousand ways," declared Colonel Halket. "My dear Floyd, you seem to have the uneducated theory of most men — that if something is done for the profit of the capitalist, it is at the expense of the laborer. Not at all; the prosperity of the one is the prosperity of the other. It is true that my plan provides for the realizing of large profits immediately by those who enter into it; but it is also true that in the larger, ultimate sense the great benefits resulting from its adoption will fall to labor. For it will mean the cessation of erratic, feverish competition, over-production, under-selling, periods of depression when men are laid off or discharged; those days will be at an end; there will come into existence an era of steady, equable employment for all. In comparison with so great and beneficent an achievement, what are the profits of a few hundred thousand, a few million dollars made by a handful of individuals?"

"Your reasoning almost turns my head, but it does n't get hold of me," Floyd said, with a laugh. "I think the beneficent results to labor that you see so clearly are very dim and doubtful. I think that the iron-workers themselves will distrust this move and regard it as a conspiracy to oppress them. So far from causing better feeling among them, I think you will make the feeling worse. And even granting that the ultimate end will be as you say; it seems to me you and Mr. Kerr are planning to achieve it by unjustifiable means."

"Perhaps you will be good enough to instruct me," said Colonel Halket, with tolerant sarcasm for this juvenile moralist.

"It was intimated pretty plainly in Mr. Kerr's remarks," Floyd answered. "You men who go into the combination first sell your mills at five times what they are worth. The public pays the price. Then you hope to pay dividends by acquiring other mills at bargain prices — and how will you do that? Your combination means to invade the field of every private manufacturer of importance and under-sell him and drive him to the wall — until he will give his plant up to you at the unjust price you dictate. That is the only method by which you can ever extend such an organization, and the only method by which you can win. It is practically committing highway robbery with a club."

"Nonsense!" cried Colonel Halket. "Even assuming the truth of your rash statements — which I don't for a moment admit — it would be merely applying the principle of competition —"

"There's fair competition and there's unfair competition," broke in Floyd. "It's fair when it's a permanent endeavor to make the best product at the cheapest price compatible with a profit. It's unfair when, simply because of greater resources and staying power, one manufacturer makes an assault on another's business, temporarily produces at a loss in order to drive his rival out of the market, and having accomplished that, pushes up the price again and recoups himself for his loss."

"Oh, you're splitting hairs, splitting hairs," Colonel Halket declared, with an impatient gesture. "Competition's the life of trade — and everybody's fighting everybody else. Of course after I close up the combination, that will no longer be true, — and it will be better for every one, — but meanwhile, no doubt, some one will have to suffer. There are always sacrifices in the path of human progress."

"It does not seem to me," said Floyd, "that it is the part of a humane and just man to profit by them."

"Profit by them!" exclaimed Colonel Halket, sweeping one hand through his hair in exasperation at this crass misconception and misstatement of his aims. "I tell you

A PHILANTHROPIST'S IDEA

that any profit that accrues to me is merely incidental; it isn't that that I'm after. It's the profit to the cause of labor that I think of — that has inspired my plan. Kindly bear that in mind, — and you will not accuse me of injustice or inhumanity."

The futility of argument became apparent to Floyd. He bade his grandfather good-night and went up to his room, but when he was undressed he sat for a long time before the fire, pondering on the situation that would be created for him by the adoption of Colonel Halket's plans. It was not difficult for him to realize what that situation would be, though it was difficult enough to decide how he should face it.

The business of making and selling steel beams, armor-plate, rods, axles, and all the multiform products of the New Rome mills had not grown more attractive to Floyd in the years which he had given to it. The one department that held for him a personal interest was the chemist's laboratory; in the tests and analyses and experiments to improve the quality of steel he found the element of play that distinguishes work from drudgery. As for the general management of the mills and all the various small and large responsibilities that it entailed, he viewed it with an odd mingling of distaste and unconcern. His training had been so thorough and his natural methods were so direct and simple that it did not take him long to acquire confidence in his ability to fill the position; but the performance of his executive duties became, as he soon learned, largely a matter of routine, and it irked him to give his attention to them instead of to the discovery of new formulas. He would have preferred not to be in the steel business at all; being in it, he would have chosen, had there been any freedom of choice for him, to be the chemist for the company; instead, he had not been permitted to specialize, but had been compelled to prepare himself for the general supervision of the works.

He had looked forward to a certain human interest in

this which might compensate him for the loss of that scientific interest to which his mind naturally turned. The one thing that seemed to him to give value to what his grandfather was doing, to what he would eventually have to do, was the burden of other lives which the work imposed on him. To guard the happiness and prosperity of ten thousand dependent people would be work enough and interest enough for anybody, — at least he had gradually and willingly been coming to this conclusion. In his awakening interest in the opportunities of such a position, he had already begun to diverge from his grandfather's views; he felt that there would have to be a radical readjustment to make happiness and prosperity permanent. Bit by bit, and more or less unconsciously, ideas for reconstruction had been taking shape in his own mind, — ideas which might perhaps have their fulfillment some time when he should be the commanding figure of Halket & Company.

Now at the intimation that this time was never coming he felt little disappointment. His expectations had long been merely an impersonal and rather reluctant acceptance of a matter of fact. Indeed, for himself there now emerged from the plan proposed an attractive vision of escape from the exacting responsibilities for which he had been laboriously preparing. He might be his own master, and not the master of other men — a relation for which, with a sensitiveness that few suspected, he had a real distaste. The thought that here suddenly his path was open, away from the mills, back to the academic laboratory, was a temptation.

"But the people out at New Rome when they hear of it!" Sitting on the edge of the bed, he pictured the consternation that would run through all the grades of employees, from the superintendents down. There would be among them all, he felt instinctively, but one thought, — that their employer had sold and betrayed them. Perhaps, so long as Colonel Halket lived and was president of the

A PHILANTHROPIST'S IDEA

great new corporation, they would not suffer; but after his term had passed there would be a gradual leveling. The works at New Rome might always perhaps retain a certain prestige, but their independence was doomed, and in time there would be inevitably a scaling down of men and of wages. Floyd imagined the dismay in thousands of families when they should learn that the paternal care of a generous and indulgent employer was to be exchanged for the iron rule of a corporation to which there could never be any human appeal.

Colonel Halket moved quickly. The newspapers the next morning contained an outline of the "rumored" combination, mentioning three or four of the most important works that would be included, pointing out equally the advantages to capitalist and to employee. " The Halket Steel Works," said the article, " will of course form the backbone of the new organization — of which it may not be premature to assert that Colonel Halket will be president. The total capital of this stupendous combine will run up into the hundreds of millions."

Floyd went that morning to New Rome. He had business with the superintendent; when it was finished Gregg leaned back and said, —

"Mr. Halket, did you read the paper this morning?"

His face was anxious.

"Yes," said Floyd.

"Can you tell me if there's anything in that report — about a big steel combine which is to take in Halket & Company?"

"I knew nothing about it till last night," Floyd answered. "Then I had a talk with my grandfather. Yes, I think what is in the paper is substantially true. Of course the plan is only under contemplation. It may never be tried, — though I'm inclined to think it will be."

Gregg rolled a little cylinder of paper and turned it round and round in his fingers.

"Well," he said slowly, "it will make the old man

some richer. I don't know as it will make him much happier."

He tossed the cylinder of paper into his waste-basket, and touched a bell summoning a stenographer. Floyd rose to go, and Gregg said with his infrequent, mild smile, "Of course, Mr. Halket, you understand I'm not advising any man how to run his business."

"Oh, no!" Floyd laughed. "But a person may sometimes pass an observation."

As he went out he did not guess that the chagrin and disappointment which had shown so distinctly on Gregg's face had been mainly for him; yet it was indeed an indignation over an act which was depriving Floyd of his expected rights that had seized the superintendent most forcibly. It seemed to Gregg a piece of injustice to bring a boy up to the steel business, put him through a hard apprenticeship, and then, when he was at last fully prepared, to sell his inheritance over his head and deprive him of the opportunity to practice what he had learned.

"Of course he'll have a big fortune," Gregg reflected to himself. "But a young man ought to have his chance to do what he's expected and studied to do. It's not fair to him to take away the chance."

He felt a certain dull resentment toward Colonel Halket in behalf of himself, in behalf of all the employees of the works. Their positions were probably secure; and yet it seemed a rather disloyal thing that Colonel Halket had done, especially to those who had spent long lives in his service.

Floyd, leaving the superintendent's office, passed on into the works, where he wished to inspect some new machinery that had been set up that week. Just inside the doorway of Open-Hearth Number Two he came upon a curious sight, — Stewart Lee in light overcoat and cap painting at an easel. "Hello, Stewart," he said, and the painter turned suddenly. "What are you at now?"

"Just a sketch to work from," Stewart explained. It

was a rough picture of Shelton and another man standing aloft emptying one of the ladles of molten metal into the ingot moulds. " Of course I can't paint the picture here; I make just the rough sketch, and then work it up at home as well as I can from memory and imagination. I guess the men think I'm all kinds of a lunatic, but they don't mind me any more."

" You ought to show them a finished copy," Floyd said. " Then they'd be more sympathetic."

" Oh, they're all right," Stewart answered. " I get on with them very well. I did have one of them come in to my studio and see the picture I'd made of him — Tustin his name was. He was quite pleased, considering what a saturnine cuss he is."

" I'm glad you've got a more pleasant subject this time," Floyd said. " I recognize my old friend Joe Shelton." He waved his hand. " Hello, Shelton," he called; and Shelton waved in reply. A moment later, having emptied his ladle, he descended from his perch.

" I never expected an artist would want to make a picture of me," he said, looking at the canvas curiously. " I don't come out very clear in it yet, do I?" he asked Stewart with disappointment.

" Not yet, but you will," Stewart assured him.

" That's good. When a man has his picture done just once in a lifetime, he wants it so's folks will know it's him. Mr. Halket, there ain't any truth in that newspaper yarn this morning, is there?"

" If you read that, you know just about as much concerning it as I do," Floyd answered.

He felt temporarily comforted when Shelton interpreted this evasive reply as a frank assurance that there was no truth in the story.

" I guessed it was a fake," Shelton said. " What would Colonel Halket be wanting to use us that way for — and you too? Do you mind, Mr. Halket, I told you once I'd be proud to be working for you? and so I will."

"Well," said Floyd cheerfully, "we used to work together pretty well; I guess our team play would still be good."

"Say, that's right," Shelton answered with a chuckle. "The boys'll be glad to know it's nothing but newspaper talk, what they read this morning. They're a good bit worked up about it."

"I'm sorry to hear that."

"Yes, but when they know it's all right— Say, Mr. Halket, it would n't be a bad thing if the Colonel or somebody was to come out in the newspapers and nail it, you know."

"I understand," said Floyd. "No doubt there will be some definite statement before long."

He left Shelton and Stewart and continued on through the works. It seemed to him that passing workmen looked at him with anxiety and mute questioning and that those who stood talking together were depressed. He himself felt distinctly pessimistic. He had not liked to give Shelton the evasive, misleading answers, and yet it was not time to confirm the man in his fears.

Half an hour later, when Floyd was leaving, he was joined by Stewart, who had finished his sketch. They returned to Avalon together, and Stewart told him that some time he meant to have a small private exhibition of his pictures; he would soon have enough of them. But it would n't be for some little time. More important things were on the eve of happening at his house. Floyd had been aware of this; he felt it would have been more delicate if he could have shown surprise at the news. The subject imposed constraint on him, though Stewart spoke freely enough and in a happy frame of mind even invited him to express an opinion as to the comparative desirability of boy or girl. He himself declared he had not enough of a preference to be disappointed whatever the result. And he ended with an exhortation to Floyd to get married.

A PHILANTHROPIST'S IDEA

"You'll think first that getting engaged is the most exciting thing you've ever done — and the best fun," he assured him. "And then you'll find that is n't anything to getting married. And now I'm finding that is n't anything to this. It's the whole of life, my boy."

"I think perhaps you're right," Floyd said gravely.

"Then cheer up and look about you." Stewart clapped him inspiritingly on the back and they parted.

Floyd went to his office and sat down at his desk, but energy carried him no further; he let the morning's mail lie unopened at his hand. Swinging round towards the window he looked out on the grimy roofs of the city and abandoned himself to idle dreams, if those dreams may be called idle which sometimes make vital moments in a man's development. Stewart was right. Floyd, looking down unconsciously upon a city block that he possessed, knew that he was missing life — the whole of life. How unsatisfactory and barren was his existence, stolid, comfortable, monotonous, diversified only by occasional poignant memories and regrets, bearing only such responsibilities as his grandfather chose to dole out to him. Stewart and other fellows of his own age had plunged in and were fulfilling their destiny; he, patiently waiting for something that could never be his, with a kind of dull fidelity to a hopeless and foolish love, was wasting his youth and narrowing the interest of his maturer years. They were not so far distant now; that morning while shaving he had noted how conspicuous the gray hairs had become among the black. It was so easy to slip on from year to year, thinking always that there was yet time and that happiness and the fuller life were just round the corner — and then at last one would suddenly realize that there was no longer time and that one had never stepped round the corner to meet the good angels. A man might be to blame, certainly he could not be happy, if he locked up his heart against the charm of women. At the thought a longing for feminine society and companionship seized him; he passed in quick review the girls of his acquaintance — Marion Clark and May Pennington and Helen Foster especially, wondering why he should always have been so indifferent to these three, whom most men found attractive and whom his grandmother had urged upon his attention. It instantly occurred to him now that with any one of them he might pass a profitable and consoling half hour. That afternoon he called upon them, one after another, beginning with Marion Clark, ending with Helen Foster; they were none of them at home. He had brought his mind into a condition receptive for pleasant impressions; with each disappointment at the door he cooled into his attitude of former indifference.

Then, when he was turning away from the last house, he met Marion Clark.

"Oh," she said when he had told her of his unsuccessful attempt, "I'm going home now; please come with me, please! I'll give you a cup of tea."

"Thank you," he said. He turned and walked with her. "I was beginning to lose hope of getting one anywhere."

"I always suspected," she remarked, "that men were a predatory race whose afternoon excursions were prompted by a desire for tea. But I never met one before who so frankly acknowledged it."

"It's the first excursion I've made this year."

"That demands an excuse instead of being one," she answered.

Walking with her, he brightened unconsciously into a gayety of spirit. She was of a robuster type than Lydia Lee, fair-haired, with blue-gray eyes that took one in at a kindly glance and then lighted up humorously if the person pleased her. They were not eyes like Lydia's, which alternated musing with their sprightliness; they expressed a vitality too abundant ever to give place to a deeper, meditative curiosity. A swift practical sense of values which her extravagant speech did not disguise, an eager if passing interest in things and people, and a certain fearlessness which accompanied the restless glancing of her mind established Marion Clark's leadership among girls and made her fascinating to most men. She was amusing, they thought, and reckless and individual; and if she had not had these charms men must still have admired "the Scandinavian beauty," as Stewart Lee termed her. She and Stewart were close friends; she had in fact started the exchange of amenities by praising the color scheme of his marriage. So he had retorted upon her, and Lydia had laughed at them both.

"I 've had a hard day," Marion said, as she sat behind her tea-cups. "I 'd just come from the most acrimonious meeting of our Discussion Club when I met you."

"Your what?"

"Our Discussion Club. Stewart Lee is responsible for it. The girls in Boston have them, and he told Lydia, and so she started one here. We meet every two weeks."

"What do you discuss?"

"Fine moral questions mostly. We 're terribly ethical. To-day the subject was, 'When is a man justified in asking a girl to marry him.'"

"When he 's sure he 's in love with her," Floyd suggested promptly.

"Oh, it 's not so simple as that. That 's where Adelaide Ward and I got into trouble; that 's what we said in our unthinking young way. May Pennington pointed out to us that a cab-driver might fall in love with the lady who was in the habit of employing him when she went shopping, but that he would n't be justified in proposing marriage. And —"

"Oh, within reasonable limits, of course," said Floyd.

"Yes, it all came down to a question of defining reasonable limits. That was where everybody got earnest. We decided that class distinctions had to be made somehow. I was in favor of letting in pretty much anybody who could read and write, and Geraldine Fitz-Gerald thought that no one who did not belong to the Brahmin caste should aspire to marry one who did. She was great on the Brahmin caste."

"It would be quite a job to define the Brahmin caste of Avalon," said Floyd.

"We simply could n't bother with it. We 'd have to leave it to Tom Cary. And that, of course, was the great objection to Geraldine's solution."

"I suppose the question really narrowed down very soon to this: 'When is a man justified in asking one of us to marry him.'"

"Certainly," said Marion. "Almost immediately. And being a coarse, indelicate person I was for letting pretty much anybody speak, so long as he was in love. But most of the others agreed that one had to consider the man's social position and income. Here in Avalon you can't talk very long without getting on the subject of money. Most of the girls decided that a man had no business to mention marriage until he actually had enough money to marry on. Then the real debate began. What was enough to marry on — what income? Everybody was afraid to show her hand — they all wanted to draw one another out; of course nobody wanted to seem willing to be bid in for less than her neighbor."

"I see," said Floyd, with a laugh. "But are n't you all terribly hard on the men? Has a fellow got to bring his check-book in his pocket when he comes to propose to a girl? Can't he take it for granted that if she cares for him, she 'll be willing to wait a while?"

"Oh, when you ask me, I 'm an anarchist on the subject. And Adelaide Ward seemed sort of glad that I felt as I did; you know Jim Henderson's been attentive to Adelaide, and Jim has n't a cent. But the others were all pronounced in favor of the income. The minimum that any one seemed willing to accept was five thousand a year."

"Supposing the girl had some money of her own,"

A PHILANTHROPIST'S IDEA

said Floyd. "Must the man show up five thousand then or forever hold his tongue?"

"We went into that quite thoroughly," Marion replied. "Adelaide pleaded hard that he should be let off for two thousand at least, but the others were quite firm. The girl's condition shouldn't and wouldn't influence any right-feeling man one way or the other, they decided; there was only one course that he could feel justified in pursuing in any circumstances. Adelaide Ward got quite indignant and said everybody was vulgarly commercial, and Geraldine reproved her for making such charges, when, as every one knew, they were only trying to take the highest ethical position. Adelaide was quite worked up by that time and said she didn't care, she didn't believe a single one of them had ever been in love or they wouldn't talk so; and then there was a great commotion, and I backed up Adelaide, — she seemed so alone in the world; and altogether it was one of the liveliest meetings the Discussion Club has had. Adelaide went away almost in tears, and I went away cross; and the last I heard was Helen Foster and May Pennington off in one corner discussing whether a man was ever justified in proposing by letter. May insisted that nothing but great distance could excuse this; she declared she wouldn't consider a proposal in writing from anywhere nearer than Salt Lake City — and probably not from there, as it might be a Mormon; and Helen thought there might be cases — some men might do it so much more prettily that way — it might be allowable."

"It seems a pity that the only persons to whom your debate might have been profitable were excluded," said Floyd.

"Men? Oh, it wouldn't have done them any good — only bewildered and scared them. They wouldn't have understood the intellectual dishonesty and moral cowardice of a lot of girls when they're gathered together and called on to express convictions. It was such a vital thing to Adelaide she had to speak out; it was n't to any of the others and so they could afford to pose; and my backing up Adelaide did n't hurt me any, for I 'm simply regarded as the irreverent scoffer. What I like most about men is that they never seem to puzzle themselves with fine ethical questions the way women do. 'They do not make me sick discussing their duty towards God,' — as Walt Whitman says of the animals."

"You think that's a poor practice?" Floyd asked.

"Yes, rather contemptible — does n't it seem so to you? It has a belittling effect on the mind — for girls take small subjects and treat them with such a big seriousness."

"That's a very novel and interesting view of girls," said Floyd. "I always thought of them as taking large subjects and treating them frivolously — at least with a light touch."

"Of course those are the nice girls that do that," replied Marion. "The nice and most useful."

"I 'll concede they 're the nicest," Floyd said. "It seems hardly right they should be useful, too."

"But they are; it 's that light touch that makes them so," Marion cried. "Why, I 'll show you — only you 've got to use your imagination. You 're a man and you 've done a hard day's work, and one of your thumbs is all sore and blistered from it, and you sit down by the road and tear a strip off your handkerchief to make a bandage. Then you try to put the bandage on your sore thumb, and you can't get it tied, though you try and try and try, with hand and teeth. And finally, you throw away the rag in despair and go on limping home, just as you are —"

"Why do I limp?" Floyd asked. "I thought it was my thumb that was sore."

"I told you that you 'd have to use your imagination," she answered. "You limp; I don't know why. You go limping home, now holding your thumb this way with your

A PHILANTHROPIST'S IDEA

other hand, and now putting it up to your mouth to breathe upon it — so, — and altogether you're about the most forlorn and wretched spectacle of a man — "

"Yes, I know," said Floyd sympathetically. "Never mind that part."

" — You're so forlorn and wretched looking that another tired old wayfarer that you meet stops and offers to help you. So you stop and hold out your poor thumb to him — so — and he takes out of his pocket a lot of twine and cotton waste and oiled rags such as a man usually carries in his pocket, and he bandages your thumb with it. Then, because you are really a nice man, in spite of being so forlorn and wretched looking, you thank him politely and seem just as grateful! But the moment you've turned a bend in the road, you sit down and begin pulling off his bandage, for it's too clumsy and dirty and uncomfortable. And then, while you're just sitting there looking and wondering how you are ever going to get home with such a poor sore thumb, a beautiful stately girl in a pink organdie, with white kid slippers and wearing pearl ear-rings — "

"You might dwell a little on her," Floyd interrupted.

— "And bare-headed, but with one white rose nestling in the coils of her nut-brown hair," continued Marion, "comes down the road. As she's passing, she glances at you and at once exclaims in the sweetest voice you had ever heard, 'Ah, the poor thumb!' She takes out the roll of sterilized gauze bandage that she always carries, — for she has taken a course in District Nursing and is as good as she is beautiful. She bandages your thumb until it feels all new and smooth and clean; and you hate to have her stop; you like the way her cool little finger-tips just touch your hand and play over it; you begin to have an idea that if she'd only keep it up a little longer your poor sore thumb would turn into a musical instrument and suddenly begin to give forth beautiful sounds. And when she gets through with you, you feel so well that you go striding home along the road without any limp, you have your dinner and are able to thumb your guitar, and you spend a pleasant evening thinking about the girl in the pink organdie who fell in love with you while she was putting on a bandage — for that's what a man always thinks of any woman who does anything for him, isn't it?"

"I'm afraid you're cynical," Floyd answered.

"Not of the girl with the light touch, anyway," Marion said. "For, see what she's done; she's healed your thumb and sent you home in high spirits and made you happy for the rest of the day — and without any such selfish motive as that of love, which you, in a man's egotistical way, are beginning to impute to her, and just because, being a cheerful soul with a light touch, she couldn't help it. And the light touch is the same useful thing when applied to mental troubles as to sore thumbs."

"I am quite sure of it," said Floyd.

"Then, do you see why girls with the light touch are the most useful as well as the nicest?"

Floyd rose to go. "I should indeed be stupid," he said, "if I did not see — in the face of two such lessons."

"Two?" She looked at him, puzzled.

"Two." He held out his hand.

Her cheerful laugh of comprehension followed him as he left the room.

He went away, conscious of a distinct improvement in his spirits. He allowed his mind, usually curbed and bitted for the most cautious and conventional processes, to take one of those random, daring leaps, which its real vitality, chafing under such close control, sometimes demanded. It put him with a startling suddenness into a fascinated, half-alarmed contemplation of marriage. Perhaps, if one could but present an open mind towards women, one would discover that not all one's capacity for love had been exhausted upon a vain object.

It occurred to Floyd that it might at least be a healthy mental attitude, provided one could assume it. If one could consider every woman one met with a view to her possibilities as a wife, it would surely make women much more interesting. It was perhaps because he had never viewed them in this way that they had interested him so little. Looking at Marion Clark in the light of such a hypothetical relation, he found her quite a new person — quite agreeable. He wondered how it would be to live with such buoyancy always in the house — a little wearing perhaps; she had, he thought, a masculine sureness about herself, and he believed he liked better a quality of uncertainty and elusiveness in women. He wondered vaguely what he did most prefer in them. He could not explain Lydia's attraction. Marion Clark was a very good-looking girl — quite as good-looking as Lydia, perhaps; there was really no reason why she should not appeal to him in the same way. Then he strayed off to wonder if a man's susceptibility to certain colors might not determine the sort of person with whom he should fall in love. He doubted if a man whose first wife was very dark could have any intrinsic interest in taking for a second wife a high-colored blonde. It had happened, of course; but probably with some slight insincerity. If one's natural inclinations towards an albino were thwarted, one could surely never develop an equal passion for the most beautiful and intellectual Cuban.

Inquiring into his own tastes, he concluded that fair hair and blue eyes were in general distinctly less attractive to him than brown. Yet though it was an inferior class, he was disposed to place Marion Clark quite at the top of her class. He admitted in her case a warmth of temperament which in most blue-eyed and fair-haired persons was unpleasingly lacking. She had a certain originality and humor, too — qualities which he attributed to the blue-eyed class rather than to the brown. It occurred to him that she might very likely illuminate these subtleties herself in discussion, and he determined some time to put them before her. But she was masculinely sure of herself and decisive — a virtue which he applauded and abhorred.

Floyd's meditative, whimsical mood was wiped out in an instant when he turned in at his grandfather's driveway and met, just as it was leaving, a carriage in which sat Kerr, the New York banker.

XVIII

TWO AMATEURS

COLONEL HALKET pursued his habitual policy of reticence.
Any one who intimated to him disapproval of his plans was
excluded from further confidences on the subject. Since
the night of his dinner party, when he had found Floyd
unsympathetic, he had never discussed with him the
scheme of the great combination, and Floyd for his part
had evinced no curiosity. It seemed to him that if his
grandfather cared to volunteer nothing, his own most
effective protest must be by the indifference of silence.
The old man was, however, waiting for his grandson to
make advances and grew vexed when they did not come.
To have the most important designs of his life ignored in
this manner, treated day after day as if they were visionary notions which after a first enthusiasm had been abandoned, exasperated Colonel Halket and set him more
obstinately than ever to the task of carrying them out.
Floyd was not kept in ignorance of their development;
Mr. Dunbar and Mr. Ackerman and others of the manufacturers who were included in the arrangement consulted
him casually from time to time, taking his interest for
granted.

At the proper season Colonel Halket resorted to his
customary channels — the local newspapers. On each of
them he conferred a carefully written statement: "It
is now said, on the highest authority, that the mammoth
combination of iron and steel mills to which reference has
previously been made in these columns will comprise
among others the works of Halket & Co., Dunbar & Co.,
Ackerman & Jones, — etc. This vast corporation will

undoubtedly be successful in controlling the steel output of all this section; and its further growth is not easy to forecast. Its main objects, in the words of one who is high in the councils of the organizers, are to cheapen steel for the consumer, prevent over-production, advance all legitimate economies, and to harmonize and unify the interests of labor as well as those of capital. . . . The company is to be capitalized at two hundred millions of dollars — one hundred millions of preferred stock, and an equal amount of common. A certain amount of these shares, not yet determined, may be subscribed for by the public; definite announcement with regard to this is deferred for a few weeks. It is the confident expectation of the large interests behind the scheme that the new corporation will begin operations the first of next October, and that its first quarterly dividend will be paid at the beginning of the new year."

Floyd did not see the article until he arrived at his office. He was interrupted in the middle of his reading by a telephone message from Gregg; the superintendent was disturbed; anxiety in New Rome over this announcement had become a "scare;" already the men were wondering which mills were going to be shut down and how much of a cut in wages would be made at the start.

"Tell them," said Floyd bluntly, "that from your point of view the persons to be alarmed are the officers, not the men."

He had hardly hung up the receiver and resumed his reading when he was again interrupted by a telephone call. Mr. Samuel Tustin, chairman of the executive committee of the Affiliated Iron Workers, and two members of the committee desired an appointment with him that afternoon. "Come in at three," Floyd said. "But if it's in connection with what is published in this morning's newspaper, I can tell you nothing."

At intervals that morning he was harassed by clerks and salesmen and other employees of the company's offices coming to him with a timorous desire to be reassured. They were afraid that when this big combination was organized, the office force might be reduced.

"I hope there will be no change in the policy," Floyd said to each one in turn. "I shall certainly use all the influence I have to prevent a change."

They thanked him and departed confidently; he wished there was better ground for their confidence. His influence with his grandfather! Floyd felt that Colonel Halket would listen neither to argument nor to appeal. Never yet had he suffered Floyd's advice to deflect him from a purpose; and though he might be silenced by argument, he always remained, as Floyd had found, undaunted and unshaken.

Tustin, Shelton, and a man named Caskey, representing the executive committee of the Affiliated, called that afternoon. Tustin explained that on behalf of the men they wished to inquire if the changes of which the newspapers had given the first warning foreshadowed a change in policy toward employees.

"I can express nothing but a personal opinion," replied Floyd. "That is, that the workmen at New Rome have nothing to fear. If you wish for any more definite expression, I must refer you to headquarters — to Colonel Halket. And I cannot promise that even then you will get anything more definite."

Tustin, who was a suspicious and distrustful man, looked at him with narrow eyes. The other two delegates were silent. At last Shelton, with an effort, said:

"I — I kind of thought, Mr. Halket, from the way you spoke to me a while ago that there was no danger of this thing going through."

"At that time I was not at liberty to speak freely," Floyd answered. "I am very sorry if what I said misled you. But I think that the workmen at New Rome are in no danger of suffering by the proposed change."

"I've worked," said Shelton, "for Colonel Halket a

good many years; I was expecting to work for you a good many more, — and no kick coming. Working for a man that you like and respect, that's one thing; but working for a trust that you don't know nothing about, that's another; and I don't relish the change. And it seems hardly fair, Mr. Halket, to transfer a whole lot of men that have kind of grown up with one order, so to speak, just by a stroke of the pen, to another order — and never giving them no say about it at all."

"No doubt they will be less affected by the change than they fear," Floyd answered. "Although I don't yet know all the details of the plan, I do know this — that in what he is doing, Colonel Halket has the welfare of the people at New Rome very much at heart."

The words had a hypocritical sound, and Floyd felt that Tustin at least believed he was a hypocrite. It would not have surprised him could he have known that when the men had departed Tustin denounced him bitterly to the two others as a double-dealer, and that Shelton had not the heart or the ability to undertake his defense. And because he was conscious of the impression which he had necessarily made, the interview left him depressed.

The telephone call sounded; Floyd's ungracious "Hello" was succeeded by a more amiable tone. "Oh, is that you, Stewart?" He detected an unusual excitement in Stewart's voice, even before he deciphered the announcement, "It's a boy!" Stewart was crying to him; and then it seemed to Floyd that he felt the elation traveling over the wires. "A great, fat, bald-headed little kid. Born early this morning. — Yes, Lydia's as well as can be — and so's the baby. I wanted to let you know about it at once; we're going to call him — if you don't mind — Floyd Halket."

"*What?*" Floyd cried into the telephone.

"Floyd Halket — H-a-l-k-e-t. Got it? That's to be his name. Lydia suggested it — but I want some credit for seconding a good idea.".

"I'm overcome," said Floyd. "Thank you both; thank Lydia for me. I feel like a father myself. Look here; when can I come round and see my namesake?"

"Oh, I don't know — I don't know much about such things yet. But I guess any time; stop in to-morrow. The christening's to be in three weeks; you'll be on hand?"

"I'll be sure. Wait. What kind of a present would appeal to him most?"

"Oh, you mustn't begin right off giving him presents. You'll spoil him."

"You've got to risk that from godfathers," said Floyd.

He put on his hat and went out to inspect spoons, napkin-rings, and mugs; he decided finally that nothing could be more satisfactory than a mug, properly inscribed. The mug suggested other things; returning to the office, he called up his grandfather's farm and gave orders that the prize Jersey should be sent at once to Mr. Floyd Halket Lee.

The fact that Lydia was the mother of a boy drove all depressing business cares from Floyd's mind. He alternated, in thinking of it, between elation and a shadowed kind of happiness. Her wish to name her son after him revived his failing romance; the fact that she had a son seemed somehow to exhibit more pitilessly to his mind than anything yet the folly of his romance. He felt vaguely that the birth of the boy meant the gradual withdrawal of her intimate interest in himself — an interest which so long as she had only Stewart she was able to give, but which now must be very intermittent. Her wish to name the child for him pleased him — yet as he thought, even it had its tantalizing incompleteness; if he could only feel that it had been prompted by the desire to please and commemorate the man whom next to her husband she loved, and not by a grateful sense that it was proper so to honor one who had saved her husband's life! Then he knew that there must have been in her thoughts something of both these motives; and in this belief he was content.

Lydia was a mother; the fact moved him to a gentler tenderness. There followed with this a melancholy reflection; Stewart and Lydia were living life in its fullness; he was not. The man who had no wife to cherish, no children to train and love, was a petty, pinching fellow; inglorious middle age would wait upon his wasted youth, and would in turn be followed by lonely and unblest senility. Hitherto there had been a certain pride with which Floyd had measured himself up to the stature of one whom Lydia might have loved; now he was of a humble mind.

Colonel Halket was mildly interested at hearing the news from Floyd.

"We'll have Dunbar over here every day now," he grumbled, "telling us what it's like to be a grandfather. He'll kick up more row about it in a week than I've done in all the years I've been one. He's got no sense of proportion, that man. Boy or girl, did you say?"

"Boy," Floyd answered. "You'll be glad to hear, I think," he added modestly, "that they're going to name the baby Halket."

"You don't say so!" exclaimed Colonel Halket, with real interest. "Well, well! Of course I always knew George Dunbar was an admirer of mine, but I certainly would n't have expected him to make his daughter name her child for me! Well, well!" The old man laughed with the most candid pleasure. "Dunbar's a good fellow; he certainly is, — and I'll remember it."

"I'm afraid I did n't explain," Floyd said. "The baby's named Floyd Halket Lee; I guess Stewart and Lydia did it without consulting Mr. Dunbar."

The satisfaction had left Colonel Halket's face. He said with sharpness, —

"Why did n't you make it clear — instead of leaving me to think? — "

Then he walked away quite in a dudgeon. He got as far as the door, and Floyd could not make up his mind whether to laugh or to be disturbed at such feeling over the matter. But at the door Colonel Halket turned and came back.

"Well," he said, and there was a twinkle in his eyes that betokened returning good humor, "they've given him a good name anyhow — and I'm willing my own should be reserved for your first-born."

"Thank you, Grandfather," Floyd said.

"So they've named him after you instead of me," continued the old man, still with a tinge of displeasure. "Well, wasn't I just telling you that Dunbar had no sense of proportion? I don't care whether he had a hand in it or not; it's just what I should expect of him; oh, I don't begrudge you the honor; I've had babies named for me in my time — and I'll have more. When the new combine gets to working, about one in every ten babies in New Rome will be Robert Halket Something-or-other. See if they aren't."

This vaunt contained a challenge that Floyd could not pass over in silence.

"I don't see any signs of that now," he said. "I received a delegation from the works to-day, and I don't believe, Grandfather, that they contemplate naming their children after you. Until you can reassure them with a statement of your real purposes, I am afraid they will distrust you. It may even go so far that nothing you can do or say will reassure them."

"I'll speak when I'm ready," Colonel Halket answered irritably. "My plans are working out — but I don't hurry them. I know you don't sympathize; you are no doubt glad to see any obstruction placed in the way. But the movement cannot be checked; and when it is explained to the people they will welcome it — as much as Ackerman and Dunbar have welcomed it."

"And other manufacturers who lacked a sense of proportion where the value of their property was concerned," Floyd said cynically.

"Floyd," Colonel Halket answered, "you must be more receptive; you must endeavor to cultivate and imbibe more progressive ideas. Otherwise — I must tell you frankly — you will be unable to hold the commanding position which should be yours. To control successfully a tremendous enterprise, such as ours now is, a man must be abreast of modern business methods — and ahead of them. Always a pioneer — that is the motto for a young man; it has been my motto as an old one. I have heard men say, 'Pioneering does n't pay;' I have found it contains all kinds of rewards, and most satisfactory of all, the consciousness of improving upon conditions, of creative achievement. When you stand off and instead of coöperating in a great movement affect to belittle it and question the motives behind it, you show a flaw in your character, a most serious flaw, a wretched dilettantism for which in the industrial world there is no place, and a carping spirit of criticism that is, to say the least, most unbecoming. And I repeat: if you have no other pride or ambition in the matter — if only for your own good — it is essential that you try to stand for advanced policies and break away from this benumbing conservatism; for the place which I hold and to which you should sometime succeed is not one where a man may sit still; it demands of him activity and progress, and if he does not respond, it will demand some one who will."

"You think I am trying to place obstacles in your way because I try to represent to you the true sentiment of your workmen," Floyd said. "I believe when you come into actual contact with them yourself on this matter, you will be surprised; you may find it advisable to modify your plans."

"I have been used to handling men all my life," Colonel Halket declared haughtily. "I have never had any trouble with them; and I do not expect to have any now."

A few days later he came to Floyd with a triumphant expression on his face and said, "Here is an object-lesson in how to handle men."

He gave Floyd the draft of a proclamation addressed "To the Employees of Halket & Company."

"I'm going to have big broadsides struck off and posted up all about the works," he explained.

The proclamation was brief.

"On October 1st, Halket & Company and other steel manufacturing companies will be united, forming the Central Steel Company. The individuality of the Halket works will, however, be preserved. On Thursday evening, May 15th, at 8 o'clock, Colonel Robert Halket will address employees of the company in the auditorium of the Halket Library. As the purpose of this address is to remove any misconception as to the effect of the new merger upon employees of these works, a full attendance is desired."

"Well," said Floyd, "it's good as far as it goes. The important thing of course is the address."

"I'll take care of that," Colonel Halket replied confidently.

"It's worth working over," Floyd warned him. "I'm afraid it won't be an easy victory; you've got to convince men who, because of the delay in giving them your confidence, have grown distrustful and afraid. They don't like the scheme; you've got to give them mighty good reasons to make them like it."

"Floyd," his grandfather said, and though he began patiently he soon grew irritable, "I don't know what has turned you into such a pessimist; it is deplorable in so young a man. It annoys me; it annoys me exceedingly. After my experience of all these years in handling men — my men — this constant nagging advice on your part is presumptuous — impertinent. I — it seems to me I am entitled to your support, not your criticism. I — it annoys me — it annoys me exceedingly."

He folded up the manifesto with fingers that trembled, and turned away.

"Oh, look here, Grandfather! Don't take it that way." Colonel Halket stood irresolute. "You know I don't mean just to be fault-finding when I differ with you; but I feel I'm a little more in touch with the men out at New Rome than you are — and I can't help seeing —"

"You can't help seeing nightmares," broke in Colonel Halket peevishly. "You are in touch with the men; very well; so have my superintendents been in touch with the men, and often they have come to me afraid — afraid — and always because they were in touch with the men! But their fears never influenced me; I held to my own course; I may not have been in touch with the men — but I knew my power over them. And I know my power over them now. I tell you, Floyd, I have borne with timorous, complaining superintendents, who were always volunteering warnings and advice; but never till now have I had to live with that sort of thing in my own house, — and I don't like it — I won't have it! It seems hard that a man at my age should be persecuted constantly by such dismal croakings in his own house — at his very elbow — from one whom he wishes to look on as his right hand."

During the latter part of this speech he had been walking to and fro across the room with increasing agitation, and his voice had grown unsteady; having finished, he seemed to feel that he could control himself no longer, for he turned abruptly and went out of the door.

Floyd was left with a feeling of helplessness and pity. He had not needed this fresh evidence of his grandfather's failing powers, of a decline which had been ominously rapid. A comparatively short time before, the note of querulousness had never been heard in Colonel Halket's voice; now it seemed to Floyd almost as frequent as his tone of assurance and self-confidence. His vanity seemed to have grown more childish and apparent, his mental outlook seemed to have been narrowed; and the tremor of his hands when he was agitated, his lack of self-control, and the readiness with which he became agitated, all marked the swift progress of decay. That in this condition he should be burdening himself with first the construction and then the administration of a greater business enterprise than any upon which he had hitherto embarked seemed to Floyd lamentable; it could only, he thought, damage his grandfather in health and reputation and prove costly to all who were concerned in it — except perhaps the small group of mill-owners and financiers. Moreover, the situation made Floyd unhappy on his own account; after having lived in intimate relations with his grandfather for so many years, it was hard for him to feel that they were no longer sympathetic, and that Colonel Halket, instead of confiding in him as formerly, now took precautions to keep him in ignorance, fearing his criticism.

In a few days Colonel Halket's " broadsides " were printed and posted on the mill offices, on the stockade surrounding the works, in the street cars, in the Halket Public Library, on telegraph poles. The notices provoked little comment beyond an expression of curiosity as to what Colonel Halket would have to say. That the proclamation had not the completely disarming effect anticipated by its author was evident to Floyd when Gregg reported to him the proceedings at the meeting of the union on the Sunday after it was posted. The hall was crowded, though it was a warm, clear afternoon such as would ordinarily have denoted a slim attendance. Tustin addressed the meeting from the chair; he urged every member of the union to be on hand when Colonel Halket made his speech.

"This conspiracy of capital is going through," Tustin cried in his harangue, " and what laboring-man has been consulted? Your allegiance is to be transferred, your services are to be disposed of, you are yourselves in fact to be sold — it is not too strong a word — sold like chattels — sold like cattle. Here in this proclamation" — he held it up dramatically — " we have Colonel Halket's word for it; the deal is all but consummated, the terms are being arranged — and when they are settled, he will kindly come here and tell you all about it and let you know what you will get out of it! There is little enough in the situation as we know it to encourage us. But I will ask you to mark one thing. *Colonel Halket will kindly come and explain to us.* Fellow workers, it is the first time that Colonel Halket has ever felt obliged to come here and formally *explain* to us his policy. Before this, he has always been willing to let it speak for itself. Why does he feel obliged to speak for it now? I will tell you; it is because he knows it is on the face of it against the best interests of the laboring-man, and he hopes by smooth words to persuade you to accept it without a protest. It is because his eyes have been opened to your discontent and he has been made afraid. He will try to put you off with plausible words, and it will be your last chance to pin him down to facts. I call upon you all to attend that meeting, and to demand from Colonel Halket his pledge for the preservation of the union and for stability of wages and employment in these works."

Floyd read the stenographic report of the speech, which Gregg had sent him, and after some deliberation placed it on his grandfather's desk. An hour later, when he came down to dinner, Colonel Halket confronted him with the paper in his hand.

" Did you put this on my desk? " Colonel Halket demanded in an angry voice.

" Yes, sir."

" Why did you not come to me in person with it and discuss it? You are too ingenious at inventing expedients to harass me — laying traps for me all about my house. Nothing is more offensive, more despicable than such underhand procedure — "

"Grandfather," cried Floyd appealingly, "I did n't mean to be underhand; you know I did n't. I thought you preferred to avoid discussion of the subject with me entirely; and here was something that came into my hands and that I thought you ought to see — something that I thought might help you in the preparation of your speech."

"Or something that you thought might discourage me from making my speech," Colonel Halket replied cynically.

"I am sorry you have so little kindness toward me as to think that," said Floyd.

"What else am I to think?" asked his grandfather. "Your hand has been against me, all through this affair. The hand of every one seems against me, every one on whom I had reason to count. This very document — why, this man Tustin is head of the union that I welcomed into my mills when others were fighting it. But ungrateful as my employees are, I shall persist in my efforts to advance their interests; I shall persist even though I am opposed at home. And when once they have heard me speak, they will be convinced of my sincerity — even though I have not been able to convince you."

"I have never expressed a doubt of your sincerity," Floyd said.

"I am glad to hear it," Colonel Halket replied, but his tone was inexorable. "Dinner is ready; will you walk out?"

"Yes, I will," cried Floyd, with a laugh, seizing his grandfather by the arm. "And don't let's go in to dinner mad; I don't want to sit glowering at you across the table, and I certainly don't want to have you glaring at me."

Colonel Halket relented at this appeal to his good humor, though with some reluctance and only as far as seemed to him compatible with his dignity. The constraint of politeness and consideration with which he treated

Floyd did not wear off for some time. And although henceforth Floyd avoided expressing any opinion or criticism that might irritate his grandfather and tried to show him only his gayest, most light-hearted, and affectionate feelings, he knew that between them there was hardly more than a pretense of intimacy. Colonel Halket knew it too; Floyd might be as cheerful and lively as he pleased, but he did not sympathize with the crowning purpose and ambition of Colonel Halket's life; and not all the incidental gentleness and playfulness and affection in the world could atone for this essential disloyalty.

Floyd attended the christening of Lydia's baby and after the ceremony was over was allowed to hold the infant in his arms. It was a fat, hairless child, with an unblinking eye, and after looking up at its godfather for some moments it contorted its whole little frame in a chuckle of silent laughter; it was a most agreeable baby. Floyd restored it to the arms of its nurse with an unchristian envy of Stewart's happiness. Stewart stood by, bland, satisfied, smiling; Floyd thought it an impertinence to nature that a man should so soon grow complacent over so wonderful a gift and accept it as a matter of course.

Two weeks later Stewart gave a private exhibition of his "Pictures of Industrial Life," in the Art Room of the Avalon Club. As private views go, it was a success, for the room was so crowded with friends of the painter as to make a critical inspection of the pictures impossible. The visitors all possessed themselves of the neatly printed little catalogues which were piled on a table by the door, and holding these open in their hands went about connecting each picture with its title; after this casual examination they would seize their opportunity to compliment Stewart on his work, and would then form little groups for general talk and gossip. Lydia was there; it was the first time that Floyd had seen her since the baby was born, and he went up to her at once and said that he was glad she was out again. Then he wondered if that was an awkward thing for him to have said, but she answered quite frankly that she was glad to be out again. She asked him if he had seen all the pictures, and when he said he had not, she took him up to three or four that she liked best. While she was describing one of them, she suddenly broke off with —

"Oh, it was so lovely of you to have thought of sending that cow for my baby! But — is n't it sad! — the doctor won't let him have the milk from it. The milk of a Jersey is n't good for babies; they must have only the common cow."

"I never knew that before," said Floyd.

"I did n't either," she admitted. "It's astonishing how ignorant a person can be about babies and yet bring them into the world. I'm not going to send your cow back to you, Floyd; I'm going to keep it till the little Floyd gets old enough to appreciate it."

"Thank you," Floyd said. "Meanwhile it will give me pleasure to send round a most ordinary cow."

"Oh no, you really must n't. Besides, we have no place for it. But it's good of you, Floyd, to think of it; thank you."

She turned again to the picture and resumed her interpretation of it, but, as it seemed to Floyd, with a certain indifference — at least as contrasted with the frank enthusiasm of her digression. Floyd had a flash of insight; Stewart had lost her. Not absolutely, to be sure; but the place he had held since the beginning of his married life was no longer his; there was something henceforth more vital to her than his work and his play; perhaps in the unselfishness of fatherhood he would resign himself to this withdrawal of interest and even rejoice in it. However this might be, the important fact which Floyd clearly recognized was that hereafter she must be more remote from him, as well as from her husband. She stood before him as much a girl as ever, in appearance, — as slender, as laughing, as young; yet her girlhood now lay behind her, and its gentle interests must henceforth be subdued in the gentler, quieter duties of a mother. Such a casual kindness as she was now showing him, in singling him out from a crowd and explaining to him the good points of her husband's pictures, was as much as he might in future expect to receive; he could not have formulated a statement of what, more than this, he had ever received or expected; yet the fact that she was a mother made her seem to him definitely far more distant and unapproachable than she had ever been as merely a wife.

The conclusion was not one at which he arrived by any instantaneous process; but after he had moved away and stood alone watching her, it slowly became clear in his mind. He was roused from his moody, solitary musing by a low voice at his ear — "Why, oh, why do you let him do it?"

Floyd turned and saw Marion Clark looking at him with an expression of whimsical distress.

"Do what?" he asked.

"I hear that they are nearly all painted out at your mills, and so you must be partly responsible," she said. "It's a shame."

"Is it? Really as bad as that?"

She nodded. "In my opinion. And I'm morally sure I'm right. They say he's thinking of giving up his profession — in which I suppose he's pretty good. You mustn't let him; he must be mad."

"I guess I won't undertake to instruct Stewart as to his proper calling," Floyd said dryly.

"Why, you're his best friend, aren't you? And it's no more than friendly to keep him from making a fool of himself."

Floyd contested the point. "Oh, if it were that. But I don't believe the pictures are so bad as you make out. Lydia called my attention to one especially and had a good deal to say for it that I thought all right."

"Well, I don't want to come into conflict with Lydia," Marion said. "But the drawing is enough to make one scream — to say nothing of the composition."

"He will probably improve," Floyd urged.

"He's not the kind that improves," she answered.

"Are n't you rather — positive?"

"You think I 'm hard on people; I know I have that reputation. I dare say I see their faults generally. I 'm sure I see Stewart's — as a painter. It seems to me almost a duty for his friends to organize a rescue league."

"And you hate ethical girls!"

"I 'm not ethical; I just have a regard for art," she declared spiritedly. — "There's your grandfather; I hope he won't set the fashion by liking the pictures."

Colonel Halket had just entered the room; his tall figure, lean brown face and white hair showed above the group by the doorway, where he stood for a moment looking round for the painter. Then, as he saw Stewart and caught his eye, he threw his head back with the restrained smile of recognition which he bestowed on acquaintances in large gatherings. Also he moved toward Stewart with a leading citizen's majesty; and at once the path seemed to be made clear for him, even those who had been talking busily with backs turned, receiving some mysterious intimation of his approach and moving respectfully to one side. It would have been a greater man than Stewart who could have awaited hardily Colonel Halket's advance and pretended to be unconscious of it; Stewart attempted nothing so daring, but came forward at once, with outstretched hand. Indeed he was flattered by Colonel Halket's presence, even though he did not expect the manufacturer to approve of the message contained in the pictures. Marion and Floyd, who were standing near by, heard him offer to conduct his distinguished visitor on a tour of the room.

"No, thank you," Colonel Halket replied. "I must not claim so much of your attention. I will examine the pictures myself, and when I have done so, I will come back and report."

In his slow progress round the room he lost gradually the erect and steady bearing with which he had made his entrance; when he paused, his shoulders drooped, and when he moved on again they did not stiffen up to quite the old angle, which seemed always to denote the most complete confidence and self-respect. His face had grown pinched and withered in the last year; its hard brown muscles had slackened, and under his jaws hung loose folds of skin. The observation was made by more than one person that at last Colonel Halket was beginning to show his age; Marion Clark commented on it to Floyd.

"I'm afraid he's not well," she said.

"If he isn't, he's the most active sick man I ever saw," Floyd answered, preferring not to betray his own anxiety.

"There are so many things besides health that can make a man active," she remarked.

Floyd shared a common prejudice against being told that either he or a member of his family "was not looking well." Marion's resort to the brutal banality jarred on him and put him in a contentious mood. It implied a lack of Lydia's gentler sensitiveness; Lydia would never have roused one in so crude a way to an unpleasant fact. Yet why he should feel disappointment because Marion lacked something that Lydia had he could not understand; that had always been perfectly obvious. Possibly the disappointment came from an unconscious effort on his part to fit Marion immediately, even in the smallest details, into Lydia's place.

"I foresee," said Marion, with a humorous glance from Colonel Halket to Floyd, "that your grandfather's opinion is going to be favorable."

"You regard that as damaging?" he asked.

"No, not necessarily; I only regard it as final. In this

case I am afraid it will be damaging. If he approves,— especially in pictures of such subjects,— it will be the fashion to admire; and Stewart will have a career thrust upon him. Of course he and Lydia have enough to live on, so he can be a dilettante all his life if he wants to, and no great harm done — if he's only obscure enough. A person who dabbles in an art and stays thoroughly obscure is usually all right — unspoiled, sincere, humble-minded, and, if not more interesting than other people, at least likely to be more than usually interested in other people — which is always attractive. But a person who dabbles in an art and has a second-rate success — or a fourth or fifth-rate success, such as Stewart will be sure to have — did you ever know one who didn't become egotistical, puffed-up, self-centred and arrogant over his accomplishment, — in fact generally insufferable?"

"I have never known one at all," Floyd confessed.

"I've known at least half a dozen," Marion said. "And I'm convinced that if Stewart were put in the way of it, he would grow to be just like them — especially here where he'd be the only real live artist."

"I doubt," said Floyd, "if Stewart would give up his profession merely because people liked the pictures that he painted by way of recreation."

"He would fly off at a tangent," said Marion slowly, "at any moment and at anything that promised a temporary distinction."

"That's a pretty shrewd statement," Floyd admitted. "But I must say again that you're rather positive."

"It comes," said Marion, "from being so often right." And then she laughed in a way that redeemed the conceit of the remark. "It would have been so much more valuable if only you had said that," she added.

"If I could only say half the things that you do, my conversation would be very much more valuable," he replied.

She was pleased and said, "You're not like Stewart."

"I don't understand."

"I said he is not the kind that improves."

Floyd laughed and dropped his eyes before Marion's candid, humorous, and yet somehow embarrassingly admiring gaze. He did not feel at all contentious now.

Some one touched his arm; he turned and found his grandfather at his elbow.

"Ah — how do you do, Marion?" Colonel Halket said, taking and holding her hand in a way that he had with young girls. Marion felt old enough to be excused from it. "Capital, are n't they — capital! Quite like life; I recognize everything very distinctly. That one in particular — " he pointed to the largest painting in the room, a picture showing the blast furnace with the liquid metal streaming out and three men spooning it along the troughs, — "it's quite remarkable the way those figures stand out, and the way he's given character to that stream of metal — the consistency, the feeling of heat, and all. Lee! Lee!"

Still holding Marion's hand, of which he had by this time presumably become unconscious, he waved his other arm, summoning Stewart from a group of women to whom he was talking. Stewart hurriedly excused himself and obeyed the summons. Two feeble-looking men and a shabbily dressed woman with a masculine face under a mannish gray felt hat, over which drooped a black feather, drew near also and then turned to look at the nearest picture. Floyd had noticed these persons occasionally jotting down notes on their catalogues and at other times hovering round Stewart, and had concluded that they were the representatives of the press.

"Lee," said Colonel Halket in a public voice, "how is it? Are these pictures for sale?"

"If anybody wants to buy them," Stewart answered, with a laugh.

"No doubt about that — no doubt whatever. You have quite a gift for depicting dramatic action. But what I especially like about the paintings is that they all bring out the dignity of labor; they show the laboring-man as he is, performing his task, industrious and happy."

Stewart gave an imperceptible start; Marion availed herself of the opportunity to withdraw her hand from Colonel Halket's grasp, which he had relaxed in his earnestness. Floyd had an uncomfortable idea that the notes which the three newspaper persons were making in front of the picture did not concern the picture at all.

"Yes," continued Colonel Halket, "I think I have never seen anything so well calculated to illustrate the pride of the good workman in his work and his joy in it as these pictures. It seems to me a high testimonial to your skill, Lee, that I recognize so distinctly the idea that you have put into your painting — the animating motive and expression, if I may call it that. And I am pleased that it should be so; if I am not mistaken, it is the characteristic of the great artist to seize unerringly and portray the salient and significant truth. I wish to congratulate you, sir, on your insight as well as on your technical skill."

Stewart had a struggle to conceal his anger and contempt.

"Damned old fool! — old humbug!" was the exclamation that was passionate in his mind. He had an impulse to reject the inane commendation with the scorn it deserved. But he restrained himself; prudence as well as good manners imposed endurance upon him. It would be folly to offend and turn away a possible purchaser, especially one like Colonel Halket who might not only pay an absurd price, but who might also more than any one else direct toward his work the current of popular appreciation and demand. "The work is good — it's art; there are no compromises in it," Stewart thought to himself proudly. "Well then, where's the harm in — in using methods to get it before the public? They won't many of them take such an asinine view of it."

Colonel Halket interrupted his vague murmured words

of gratitude as indications of a modest and retiring spirit. "Don't undervalue your work, my boy," he urged him; "don't be afraid to set a price on it." — (" I 'll set a price on it," Stewart thought to himself vindictively.) — "I want you to put four of them aside for me. Mark four of them 'sold.'" Colonel Halket consulted his catalogue and read off the titles, pointing to each picture as he did so. "Six: The Forges of Tubal Cain. Eight: The Wire-Drawers. Thirteen: The Blast. Two: Tapping the Heat. I will present two of them to the Library out at New Rome; they can be hung in the Auditorium and they will serve as a stimulus, a source of pride to every working-man who sees them. The other two I want to enjoy for my own personal satisfaction in my own house. Sometime we will discuss the matter of terms; but in any event please remember that those four have been sold."

"I 'll send you a bill for them to-morrow," Stewart said. "They 're yours at any time."

Colonel Halket's appreciative speech and proposition to buy the four pictures had not been heard by Stewart and Floyd and Marion alone, for they had been sonorously delivered and had drawn groups of apparently inattentive persons who were in reality pricking their ears. Stewart was quite aware of this, and in his glance around thought he saw several among the listeners who would seek to emulate Colonel Halket in securing possession of one or more paintings of "Industrial Life." Meanwhile, the two men and the masculine-looking woman stood before "The Forges of Tubal Cain," taking notes with entire single-mindedness.

Marion and Floyd strolled away.

"It's too easy," said Marion.

"To be really success?" Floyd asked.

"Yes. Don't you think so?"

"I don't know anything about painting," he answered.

"You know a little about success."

"The last man in the world one would appeal to for

first-hand information on the subject," he said, rather bitterly.

"You will know more some day," she assured him.

"The thought will recur — you are pretty positive," he replied.

"It comes," she repeated, "from finding that I am always right. Good-by; I must say a word to Lydia and be off."

She left him; and he found himself thinking that her air of perfect confidence was not so jarring after all, but rather pleasant. It occurred to him that although when he was with her she usually did or said something that jarred on him, she always left him, when they separated, feeling rather pleasant.

Stewart reaped the fruits of inexperience the next morning; he had invited the representatives of the three principal Avalon newspapers to his exhibition, but he had not provided them with an abstract of what they were to say. Therefore he was annoyed beyond measure to read in two newspapers criticisms which were indeed extremely laudatory, but which took the point of view of Colonel Halket and were strangely reminiscent of his words. It made Stewart sick at heart to think that the serious purpose which had animated his painting should be so stupidly misinterpreted and perverted, and a false account of it given to the world. He could take no pleasure in praise that was coupled with such unintelligent misunderstanding. It sickened him still more to find that each review concluded in this manner: "Among those present were noticed Colonel Robert Halket, Mr. and Mrs. George Dunbar," etc. ("Among those present we noticed," said the *Eagle;* its reviewer had a less impersonal, more chatty and engaging style.)

There was still one chance remaining; possibly the critic of the third newspaper, the *Evening Telegram*, might show himself — or herself, for Stewart remembered that she had been a woman — more perceptive and truly appreciative than her companions. He awaited the *Evening Telegram* with impatience. When it came, in one respect at least it did not disappoint him. It did not present an insipid rehash of Colonel Halket's opinions and commendations. The *Evening Telegram* was the newspaper which had waxed merry and scornful at the expense of Colonel Halket's Autobiography. It was a cynical and irreverent paper, and was recklessly Democratic in Avalon — a town where the really orthodox believed no less in a high protective tariff and the Republican party than in the doctrines of the Presbyterian Church. Its normal attitude was one of defiance, and the respectable persons of the community, who read it because it was too trenchant and aggressive to be ignored, felt that it never gave its support to the good, the true, the beautiful. It was "breezy" and frankly scurrilous; and hitherto no one had found it more amusing than Stewart.

"Mr. Stewart Lee held his exhibition of amateur paintings at the Avalon Club yesterday," said the *Evening Telegram*. "We say amateur advisedly; we do not suppose that Mr. Lee would care to have any professional standard of criticism applied to his work, and it would be needless as well as unprofitable cruelty to break a butterfly upon the wheel. The well-known littérateur and philanthropist, Colonel Halket, was on hand, pointing out various imaginary merits and beauties to those within reach of his voice. It is rumored that Colonel Halket contemplates purchasing and suppressing the entire collection. The others present were Tom Cary and his Hundred and Forty-Nine, and the three representatives of the *Press*, the *Eagle*, and the *Telegram*."

Stewart's face burned while he read the paragraph.

"What do they say, dear?" asked Lydia.

He held the newspaper out to her, and after a first frown or two she broke into a laugh.

"Good Heaven! you can laugh at that!" cried Stewart in disgust.

"Why it is n't worth being angry about," said Lydia. "And the last touch is rather funny."

Stewart expressed with sarcasm his inability to appreciate such humor. He wrote Colonel Halket a note that evening, setting a price on the pictures; the reviews in the three newspapers had made him reckless and ruthless, and he felt a vindictive pleasure in holding the manufacturer to account for his crass misunderstanding of an artist's purpose. The bill came to forty-five hundred dollars: fifteen hundred dollars for "The Forges of Tubal Cain" and a thousand dollars for each of the three others. Two days later he received a check for the amount together with a printed receipt to which he might affix his signature. The absence of any personal note or comment was perhaps significant.

Stewart, however, in cashing the check had somewhat the feeling of one who is compelled to sell out an investment at a loss. He had thrown all his energy and talent into the execution of a noble idea, which had been coldly received, and with no perception of its nobility. Defeated by such unexpected apathy and obtuseness, he could not pursue his great work to fulfillment; he was disappointed, but he could not afford to spend the best years of his life in the unselfish effort to convince a dull public; therefore he felt, as he cashed Colonel Halket's check, that he was closing out a generous, glowing impulse at something less than cost.

He sold no more pictures of Industrial Life; nor did he ever paint another.

XIX

COLONEL HALKET ADDRESSES AN AUDIENCE

ON the evening of the fifteenth of May there was more purpose of movement in the streets of New Rome than was customary in the late and lingering twilight of a May day. The yellow Halket Library, with its Moorish towers and arches, standing on the smoky hill-top, gathered to itself the rays from the sun expiring across the river; they shone out from a suddenly blazing ember of cloud, tinseled for a moment a few little houses on the lower slope, and then, fading slowly upward, brightened the terraced steps and yellow walls and red tiled roof of the building that, as Colonel Halket said, crowned New Rome. And at the hour when the building seemed thus to be drawing and concentrating to itself the dwindling light, it was also summoning the toilers from all parts of the town. From the side streets they flowed into the main ascending thoroughfare that usually in the evening reclined quiet and empty against the slope of the hill; they mounted slowly to the terraced steps, and there the women and children who sometimes accompanied the men stood aside or strolled about on the green lawn, while the men continued on upwards and disappeared into one of the dark Moorish arches.

The occasion was one of some ceremony, for nearly all the men wore coats, even though it was a warm evening, and many of them had gone home from the works an hour before displaying undershirt and suspenders. Collars were less frequent than cutaways, however, — as if, having made a concession in one matter, a man was entitled to insist upon an equivalent in another. One might have remarked a grim, an almost intentional lack of refinement,

COLONEL HALKET'S ADDRESS 299

a grim prejudice against compromise that seemed on this evening especially characteristic of these men. They approached the Halket Library with sullen reluctance and apprehension.

Inside the doors of the Auditorium there was the subdued atmosphere of a church. At ten minutes to eight o'clock, men were sitting in the aisles and standing at the back of the hall, and their talk was all in murmurs. The only disturbing sounds proceeded from without, as constantly increasing numbers of people tried to enter. Perhaps one reason for the constraint which lay upon the great room was to be found in the presence of the reception committee on the platform — six men, seated in a formal semi-circle, with a chilling gap in the middle, where was placed an empty, significant chair. There was a vacant chair also on the extreme right for Tustin, the organizer of this committee, who was in the dressing-room awaiting the arrival of the speaker. His associates he had sent out on the platform to impart dignity to the meeting. He had written to Colonel Halket that the iron-workers desired to show him some special mark of respect on the occasion of his address and proposed, if it was not distasteful to him, that it should take the form of a committee of welcome. Colonel Halket, after returning heartfelt thanks for the proposed honor, had exhibited Tustin's letter to Floyd triumphantly.

"That shows!" he had cried. "And this Tustin's the fellow that a few days ago, according to your account, was trying to inflame the people against me! I knew that all they needed was time to think things over, and they'd come round."

"Well," said Floyd, "I'm perfectly willing to come round."

Because of this acquiescence and his own rising good humor over the turn that affairs had taken, Colonel Halket had at the last moment invited the young man to accompany him to the meeting and witness his triumph.

They alighted from their carriage at a side entrance a few minutes before the hour and went into the ante-room. Tustin had been sitting there alone with his hat on, studying a dirty little memorandum book, which he now replaced in his pocket. He rose and took off his hat.

"My name's Tustin, Colonel Halket," he said, "and I'm to have the privilege of introducing you to-night."

Colonel Halket laid his silk hat on the table and advancing toward Tustin with a smile held out his hand.

"Glad to meet you, Mr. Tustin, — glad to have your help in getting myself before this audience. Mr. Tustin, my grandson, Mr. Halket."

Floyd nodded. "We've met before," he said; and Tustin shot him a remembering, unfriendly glance.

"We were n't looking for any one extra," Tustin said, with his eyes still on Floyd. "You did n't mention about bringing any one, Colonel, so we've got chairs just for the committee and yourself."

"I suppose a chair could be taken out from this room," Floyd remarked.

"Yes," Tustin admitted reluctantly. "There's hardly space on the platform for another chair, — that is," he hastened to add, "as it's arranged."

"Then I'll go down and sit below the platform or stand against the wall; I don't want to upset the arrangements," Floyd said, — "unless you prefer to have me sit with you, Grandfather."

It was an intimation to Tustin that he and his committee might very easily and conveniently be ignored. But Colonel Halket said, —

"No, no; I'm in the hands of my friends here; I don't need any family support. I'd rather have you down in the audience."

So Floyd followed a narrow passageway and came into one of the side aisles just below the platform. To get a seat was impossible; he squeezed in against the wall between two workingmen, who recognized him and made room.

Something in the atmosphere, as he looked about on the assemblage, filled him with apprehension. The suppressed, expectant quiet, the lack of laughter in so large a body of men, were not normal. When he turned his eyes toward the platform he found nothing to reassure him. The reception committee was the executive committee of the Affiliated Iron-Workers — the men who had been active in circulating persistent, annoying demands, inventing small causes of controversy, thrusting themselves forward at all times as the conservators of the rights of Labor. By such means they had contrived to bustle into positions of prominence; the majority of the workingmen had accepted them as leaders. Floyd felt sure that their welcome of his grandfather would be a sinister one; to his mind they represented a tribunal assembled to sit in judgment.

The door at the rear of the platform opened and Tustin came out, followed by Colonel Halket. The six members of the reception committee rose and stood while Tustin led Colonel Halket forward to the chair in the centre. There was no applause; the murmurous quiet of the room had subsided into a deep hush. Colonel Halket, after hesitating a moment, sat down; the six committeemen did the same. Tustin advanced to the edge of the platform.

"Friends," he said, "I introduce to you Colonel Halket."

There was still no applause, though Colonel Halket waited a moment before rising, and so gave every opportunity for a demonstration. Tustin after uttering his brief sentence stepped aside, and going straight to his chair sat down, apparently without noticing Colonel Halket's bow of acknowledgment.

Colonel Halket was disconcerted by the bluntness of the introduction and by the utter lack of applause. He bowed to his audience, but there was no responsive courtesy. Floyd's pulse quickened angrily; standing well to the front, he could see the changing expression on his grandfather's face, and he was indignant that these men should deny their old employer a show of common respect.

"Friends and fellow workmen," Colonel Halket began in a deep, appealing voice, and then waited, this time not in vain. From somewhere in front spurted a vigorous sound of applause — applause rendered by two single hands, which persevered defiantly and woke thin, desultory responses in various spots about the room; and then the mighty rebuking "Sh-h!" of the audience rose and quelled it. But it had answered its purpose. Colonel Halket smiled.

"You are kind," he said, "to grant me your attention; but you are more kind to make this display of feeling for me."

At this there was some laughter, rather loud and sarcastic, in the front part of the room. Floyd stood straight and stared round at the taunting faces unflinchingly; yes, he had applauded his grandfather, and if it would help him any, he would do it again. At the same time he felt a certain sickness of heart; he had not supposed that simply because of a little clapping the old man would make such a foolish remark. Clearly it was a sentence that Colonel Halket had prepared expecting a great ovation and that he had been unwilling to sacrifice. He was proceeding, with characteristic confidence of pose and voice.

"I bring no manuscript to read to you, no oration to deliver, no carefully prepared address to recite. I have come simply to talk to you in a careless, off-hand, frank way about my business, — our business, — I have come to talk to friends."

There was opportunity here for Floyd to insert a little more applause had he dared to do so; but he began to appreciate now that in the temper of the audience a second such effort on his part might provoke a violent counter-demonstration against the speaker.

"Now, it has been reported to me," continued Colonel Halket, "that the proposed merger of the New Rome

Works with others into one great corporation has excited some alarm among the employees of Halket & Company. How far that report is true I do not know; but I believe that probably the apprehension of my friends has been diminishing as they have given more thought to the matter. It was perhaps natural that they should feel some alarm. They were enjoying prosperity; they had been in the enjoyment of prosperity for many years; they could not at once see any advantage to them in a change; they were quite contented to have things go as they were. Indeed, I may confess frankly that my own greatest pride has been in their prosperity and in the comfort they all took in their prosperity."

Floyd suppressed a groan. About him he heard low murmurs of dissatisfaction. He wondered what more unfortunate thing his grandfather could have done than to extol the prosperity of men who had assembled with a grievance. Colonel Halket, however, did not hear the murmurs; he was attentive only to his own line of thought and to the choice of words which might best express it.

"When I come to New Rome and observe its commodious and well-kept homes, and see the bright, happy faces of its women and children, and mark upon its streets the confident, manly tread of its men, and note the many elevating and refining influences with which it has been supplied by the admirable spirit of its citizens, can I wonder that your prosperity is dear to you, and that you must view with suspicion any policy that might tend to derange it? Can I wonder that you wish to cling to a condition that is happy beyond that of other workingmen "— (Floyd detected an exchange of smiles and shrugs among the members of the reception committee, and observed that one sombre, continuous nudge seemed to traverse the audience) — "a condition that you yourselves have created? — For though much has been done for you, you have done even more for yourselves."

Here again Colonel Halket hesitated a moment, and was visibly nonplussed when so magnanimous an admission failed to evoke the anticipated applause.

"No, I do not wonder at it. And I am glad to be here to-night to explain to you all that in my judgment the arrangement by which the Halket Mills are to form the nucleus of a vast new corporation, so far from being detrimental to your interests, is the most beneficent and progressive step that an employer has ever taken on behalf of his employees. I will tell you why I believe this. What we aim at in this new organization is nothing less than the control of the whole iron and steel manufacture in the United States. This once accomplished, what follows? There will be no fluctuation of prices, no inequality of demand and supply, no periods of pressure followed by periods of idleness, but with this greater stability a high, steady level of remuneration for all, which can be depended on as certainly as the rising and the setting of the sun. The spectre of hard times will never stalk upon your streets.

"Now let me tell you something about the nature of this organization." He proceeded with some care to sketch the important features; he recited the various companies that had "come in," and showed that their coöperation insured the success of the plan; then he explained the method of financing the undertaking, and announced with a good deal of impressiveness and enthusiasm a detail which had hitherto not been given out, and which provided that employees of any of the constituent companies should have the privilege of subscribing for a certain amount of stock at a less price than that at which it was afterwards to be offered to the public. "In this manner you may not only make a profitable investment, but you are given an opportunity to become yourselves employers of labor and to share in the profits of the great enterprise which you have helped to build up. It will be an incentive to thrift and a permanent source of satisfaction."

"Not only has there been this just and generous provision made; I may go further and state to you here and as it were privately that you iron-workers of New Rome are to be the favored people in this new combination.

"I hope, as your employer, to lead you into the promised land of labor, into Canaan — or, as I may say, recalling the name of the first iron-worker and venturing upon a pun, into the land of Tubal Cainaan." This *jeu d'esprit* met with no favor whatever. But Colonel Halket, in spite of the discouraging dullness of his audience, continued bravely, "You are, as I have said, to form the nucleus. These works are now, as you all know, the most important of their kind in the country, and in combination with other mills they must always hold a position of leadership. This position is one in which the workmen will inevitably share. This means that the advantages of opportunity will all lie with you. There is no reason why your advancement should not be rapid and sure; there is no reason why any faithful and competent workman among you should not end his days as mill foreman or better. I do not want you to feel that because I am devoting my energies to a larger, a national problem, I shall cease to regard you with the particular interest which I have always felt in your welfare. You will always be to me 'mine own people,' and I trust I shall ever prove myself to you what I have earnestly striven to be all my life — your true and loyal friend.

"If any one among you has any questions to ask, I shall be most happy to answer them."

As he sat down, there was a thin, perfunctory flutter of applause which expired quickly.

Tustin rose and came forward to the edge of the platform.

"Colonel Halket will answer questions," he stated. "Any questions from the floor?"

He stood looking round inquiringly. Floyd resented his assumption of control over the meeting. It was impudent and gratuitous, and he had a hot-headed impulse to challenge it. Then, before he could act so foolishly, the challenge was taken out of his mouth.

"Colonel Halket!" cried a voice, and Floyd, turning his head, saw Hugh Farrell on his feet in the midst of the audience. "Colonel Halket — kindly step one side, Mr. Tustin; I'm addressing Colonel Halket."

He held out a hand, motioning to Tustin to sit down. Tustin stood leaning forward, looking at him with a crooked smile.

"Mr. Farrell has the floor and will address a question to Colonel Halket," he announced. "Let me recommend you to be brief, Mr. Farrell; others desire to speak."

"I don't recognize your authority, Mr. Tustin," cried Farrell hotly. "If you choose to stand there, stand; what I have to say can just as well be said in your face. It concerns you and your gang; stand and take your medicine, or sit down and take it; I don't care."

At this there was a commotion, the scraping of chairs and stamping of feet as men turned to see the speaker, and instantly an ominously general hissing which swept down upon the few scattered outbreaks of applause. The two men stood facing each other angrily; behind Tustin Colonel Halket rose and then hesitated, irresolute and confused.

When he could be heard, Tustin shouted in a defiant voice, "I'll give you every advantage, Mr. Farrell; I'll sit down."

He returned to his chair, and seating himself, crossed his legs, thrust his hands into his pockets, and looked carelessly up at the ceiling all through Farrell's speech. And all through it Colonel Halket stood, puzzled, irresolute.

"Colonel Halket," said Hugh, speaking very fast, but clearly and incisively, "once before you've forced some of us into a combination against our will. The Affiliated Iron-Workers came along and you opened wide the gates, and they rushed in and affiliated us. We had to join them or lose our jobs. You told us then that combination was great for us, in union there was strength, and all that. How did it work out? Bad. We ain't allowed to do as much as we can, we ain't allowed to earn as much as we can, we ain't allowed to get ahead as far or as fast as we can. We're leveled down to an average. I don't turn out as many rods in a day as I used to, because I ain't allowed; I don't have as much money in my pocket at the end of the week as I used to, partly because I ain't earning as much and partly because Tustin and that gang sitting round you there has to have their rake-off. We fellows that ain't leaders have no liberty; and the only leadership we have is the leadership of the hindmost. They set the pace and the rest of us go limping along in step. Now you want to put us into another kind of union. The way it looks to me, the same thing will happen. You say these mills here are the best and will set the pace. But when they're in a union with a lot of others, they can't run away from the rest. The little lazy ones have got to be humored, they'll have all kinds of a pull; the ones here mustn't work too hard or the others will have to be shut down entirely, and that will never do. So the mills here will have to be kind of scaled down to the level of the little lazy mills in the combine — just the way the good clever men have to be scaled down to the level of the little lazy men in the union. And that will mean shutting off some of the men here from work and economizing on the plant, running three quarters instead of full, and half instead of three quarters — and there won't be as much prosperity then in New Rome as there is now — and there ain't as much now as there was six years ago."

"Your allusions to the situation here are beside the point and quite absurd," declared Colonel Halket testily. "And your ideas about the management of a great corporation are utterly erroneous and illogical. Let me say now, once for all, that there will be no scaling down of the efficiency of these mills."

"Colonel Halket, I protest on behalf of the men that believe as I do and are afraid to speak," cried Farrell, with vehemence, and he went on rapidly, though Tustin had risen and was whispering in Colonel Halket's ear. "They're sitting in this room now — more of them than anybody knows — afraid to speak for fear they'll· be persecuted by the union and lose their jobs. They feel as I do about the present and they're afraid of the future. Especially if — "

"You are right, Mr. Tustin," Colonel Halket cut in peremptorily in a voice directed at Farrell. He held out a stern and silencing hand. "The gentleman has spoken long enough; others must be given an opportunity. I have answered your question, sir; kindly sit down."

Farrell bowed and obeyed; there was a convulsive start of applause, whether to celebrate Farrell's effort or his summary suppression Floyd was uncertain. He was himself divided between sympathy for Hugh and anxiety for his grandfather. For all Colonel Halket's boldly dominating attitude and majestic, rebuking voice, Floyd detected an unwonted and disturbing excitement in the old man's face; he was near enough to see the uncontrollable tremor of his outstretched hand. Colonel Halket had been roused to passionate indignation against an individual workman who had dared to question and oppose his views; his stern, majestic indignation was fortified by a sense that the men behind him on the platform and the mass of the audience were as indignant as he, and as fervent as he in holding to his beliefs. Floyd feared the effect of the imminent disclosure of the truth.

Tustin nodded to one of the committee, a short, bow-legged man with immensely broad, sloping shoulders and a broad head, to which the ears were attached at such an angle that they accentuated the breadth; his face was red and above it grew a stiff standing crop of red hair.

COLONEL HALKET'S ADDRESS

"Mr. Caskey has the floor," Tustin announced.

Caskey stood where he rose and clasped his hands behind his back.

"I've got nothing in common with the man that's just spoke," he said. "He ain't representative, he ain't for anything, or anybody except himself, first, last, and all the time. But I am for the workingman, Colonel Halket, and on behalf of the workingman I am opposed to this combination idea, without reference to anything the speaker before me has said. I am opposed to the combination for this reason. You give us to understand it will be all right for us because you will be running it and will give the mills here the best show. Well, we've got to look ahead. You're quite an old man and not so strong as you once was; maybe you won't last so long as you think. And when you go most likely some other interest will get control, and some other mill will have the pull. Whereas if these mills stay independent, your dying won't make such a great deal of difference to us."

"Sir," said Colonel Halket, with a trembling voice, "it is not necessary to introduce the subject of my death into this discussion."

"We have got to be prepared," Caskey returned brutally. "And not even the best of us lives forever. I am opposed to the combination."

"And what if you are!" cried Colonel Halket, suddenly flaming out with fury. "What business is it of yours? What will you do about it? Oppose it; go ahead; oppose it." He shook his finger scoldingly at the squat, unyielding figure. "I'm not going to die — and if I were, my mills will go on. You are a demagogue — an agitator; sit down, sir; sit down! You oppose my idea, do you? — and what do I care? Oppose it then; what can you do? What can you do?"

"A good many things," Caskey replied. "Not me personally, — but all of us. That's what you've got to reckon with, Colonel Halket — all of us."

Then from the audience, which had sat tense and excited all through the sharp colloquy between the two men, there was a wild outburst of applause. Caskey stood until it had subsided.

"You see," he said, and sat down.

Colonel Halket stood speechless, moving his eyes in a bewildered way across the audience. He turned to the committee behind him and put out his hand as if in a gesture of entreaty, as if he were about to utter an appeal; and then he dropped his hand without speaking, for there was no responsive look on any face. And again he sent his wavering gaze out upon the audience; they all let him stand thus, silent and helpless, and did not make a sound; and Floyd suffered under the cruelty of it.

Then Tustin came forward and began to speak with a suavity, which, Floyd felt sure, veiled a malignant intention.

"Mr. Caskey's given to a plain way of stating things," he said in a conciliatory voice. "But you see how it is, Colonel Halket; there ain't a shadow of a doubt but that just about every workman in New Rome is unanimous against your idea. You see how it is; they've thought it over and they've heard what you have to say for it, and they haven't changed their minds."

"That's right!" interrupted a voice loudly, and that seemed a signal for other approving cries throughout the audience. Then, before Tustin could go on, some one began to clap and stamp, and instantly there was an uproar of applause. Tustin allowed it to last for a few moments; then he put out his controlling hand.

He smiled with a triumphant friendliness and familiarity at Colonel Halket, who stood with his hands clasped behind his back, his head bowed, and his face gloomy and dejected — apparently in the attitude of surrender.

"Colonel Halket," Tustin said, "we do not for a moment question the purpose with which you lent your influence to the scheme of combination. We don't doubt that you foresaw for us many advantages, and that you wished to give us the benefit. But these men here are convinced that there is another side to the shield. They may be wrong — but they are so convinced that no argument of yours or any one's can move them. And so the most generous message you can bring them, the message that would be received with enthusiasm and acclaim, and that would cause the heart of every workingman here to beat high with thankfulness, would be the announcement that the Halket Mills would not enter the combination."

He bowed to Colonel Halket and sat down, and another great outburst of applause swept forward through the hall. Floyd's eyes were fixed on his grandfather with a critical sympathy. The old man suddenly turned his back on Tustin and flung out one hand towards the audience with an effective violence.

"Men," he cried, and the appealing, outstretched hand quivered like his voice, "you have followed me here — you have followed my leadership for many years. Have I been harsh with you? Have I been intolerant or unjust? I have led you onward into prosperity and happiness, I have given you liberty and liberality, I — I have not interfered with your personal freedom — you have organized, you have chosen your own guides — not always wisely, if one may judge from what has been spoken here to-night. Now I ask you — when I have laid a proposition before you, when I have asserted my leadership over you for a definite end, has it not always resulted to your advantage? Will you trust these short-sighted leaders of a day rather than me, your leader of a lifetime? Do you believe me either unable or unwilling to carry out my promises to you? I appeal to you against the speeches that have been made from this platform — I appeal to you not to let yourselves be led astray; I appeal not only to your sense of what is just and generous to me, but also to your sense of what is for your own best interests. And finally I say and I declare " — and Floyd was himself thrilled by the passionate intensity and power which suddenly rose and broke in his grandfather's voice — "that however you or your leaders respond to my appeal, this combination is going through."

He stood for one moment a majestic and commanding figure, but his defiant declaration drew from his audience no faintest echo of applause. He turned to leave the platform, but Tustin had risen, and with one arm outstretched prevented him.

"Colonel Halket," Tustin cried, "there is one thing more to say." He advanced slowly to the edge of the platform, and Colonel Halket, responding unconsciously, advanced with him, watching his face. "I want to say," Tustin proclaimed, lifting up his voice, "that Colonel Halket has been given every opportunity this evening. We did n't want to hurt his feelings. We let him have the chance to retire gracefully. He did n't need to lose anything by giving in. But he has rejected the opportunity. He tramples on the wishes of this audience, he spits upon the will of the people of New Rome. The time for consideration is past. Colonel Halket has given his ultimatum; he will now hear ours."

Suddenly men were on their feet, cheering and waving their arms; and in an instant their enthusiasm had spread over the whole audience; the room was in an uproar of acclamation for Tustin's dramatic defiance. Colonel Halket folded his arms, advanced one foot, and gazed upwards; but his lips were compressed and Floyd was near enough to see that the stern old jaw was quivering.

"Colonel Halket says he has given us liberty, and treated us with liberality," cried Tustin in an envenomed voice. "He dares to say this on the very night when he invites us to sell ourselves into slavery, — and to contribute from our earnings part of the purchase price. That is all that his generous provision for our buying stock in his new corporation means. Does he offer to sell us bonds? Oh, no; he holds the bonds, and all the profits of the business will go to pay the interest on the bonds, and the stock is worthless, and after you have taken your share of it off the hands of the promoters — will *you* get any dividends? — Will the price go above the price *you* paid? No; you 're sold into slavery — and you 're stripped before you 're sold ! "

" Stop ! " shouted Colonel Halket, turning upon him with a sudden, surprising vigor. " You — you — dare ! " Breath and words together failed him; he stood gasping, shaking a clenched fist at Tustin. Floyd had started forward at the moment of his grandfather's interruption; now he sprang upon the platform and stepped abruptly between Colonel Halket and the labor leader. He took his grandfather's trembling arm and held it in a firm yet gentle grasp; Tustin stood silent, sneering at him.

Floyd faced the audience.

" Gentlemen, this meeting is at an end," he said in a clear, decisive voice.

" Keep your seats ! " Tustin commanded, holding the audience down with a gesture of both hands. " I 've got more to say."

He moved toward Floyd and Colonel Halket. Floyd turned his back upon him and tried to lead his grandfather from the platform, but the old man threw Floyd's hand off impatiently.

" You talk to us, Colonel Halket, about our liberty. We 've got our liberty and we mean to keep it. We don't propose to risk it selling ourselves to a corporation. We 're afraid of that corporation of yours, Colonel Halket. We 're afraid that the first move it would make would be against the source of all our liberty — which is not *you*, Colonel Halket, but the union. We believe that you and the other men with you are organizing your scheme to crush out the union — the thing that makes it possible for me to talk to you as I am talking now without fear of the consequences — the thing that has at last enabled the laboring-man to talk to the employer as the employer has talked to the laboring-man for two thousand years — the thing with whose power behind me I now demand, Colonel Halket, that here and now you announce the Halket Steel Company will not be a party to any combination."

Men climbed on the seats and shouted, waving their hats; everywhere throughout the hall men were standing, cheering and stamping; it was applause that came up to Colonel Halket like the roar of merciless wild beasts. Tustin stood looking, with his crooked smile, out upon the throbbing, tossing tumult; Colonel Halket stood waiting with bowed head, resisting only Floyd, who plucked entreatingly at his arm. At last Tustin raised both hands above his head and waved them out and down, out and down, until he had hushed the audience to a sullen grumble.

"We are waiting to hear you speak, Colonel Halket," he said; and almost instantly the hall became still.

"And if I refuse?" said Colonel Halket, without raising his head, and in a voice so low that only those in the front part of the hall could hear.

"If you refuse!" repeated Tustin in his loud, triumphant voice. "That moment I proclaim a strike, and you will see how all these men respond." Another roar of applause broke out, but Tustin quelled it before it had risen to its height. "A strike, Colonel Halket; and where will your combination be? Who will buy your stock? A strike now, Colonel Halket, and we will force you to confess publicly failure and defeat."

"Tell them to strike and be damned!" Floyd shouted the counsel in his grandfather's ear while the audience raised again its intimidating applause.

But Colonel Halket stood silent and dazed, murmuring aloud, "If I refuse! Told that I want to cheat my men! Threatened with a strike! If I refuse!" He stood murmuring such disjointed, feeble exclamations to himself even when quiet had fallen on the audience. Sharp cries of "Answer!" "Answer!" broke from the hall.

"We must have your answer," cried Tustin. "Colonel Halket, will you withdraw your plan?"

Colonel Halket raised his head feebly and looked out on the audience.

"I — I suppose so," he said in a faint voice, and then he turned and walked slowly from the platform, while the storm of applause acclaimed his surrender and retreat. He walked firmly enough until he reached the ante-room; then he leaned a little on Floyd's arm.

"Get me home, Floyd, get me home," he said feebly.

Floyd helped him in silence down the steps to the street, where the carriage was in waiting. For one moment they were in the peaceful silence of the May night, a silence across which even the grim diapason from the dragon-like mills below quivered not so ungently; then suddenly there burst from the main portico of the building a clamor of voices that seemed to the old man brutal, ferocious even, as with the thirst of pursuit. Floyd felt his hand tremble and heard him say, "Hurry, hurry!" They sat in the open carriage and drove slowly down the hill, while beside them, along the steps of the main entrance, along the sidewalk, and dimly illuminated by the yellow-globed electric lights of the portico above, streamed the crowd, boisterous, cheering, hooting. While the carriage passed, Colonel Halket sat erect, gazing ahead in the darkness as sternly as a soldier; but when the crowd had been left behind and there was no one but his grandson to see, he sank back and closed his eyes.

XX

LAST WORDS

THE day after he had delivered his address to his workmen, Colonel Halket suffered a collapse from which he never rallied. A paralysis seized him, and he lay helpless in his bed, able to move his arms, able to turn his head and speak; but beyond that motionless.

"I am not going to get well," he said to the doctor. "Shall I be like this for long?"

There was a consultation of doctors, and when they told him that it would not be long, he seemed relieved.

They said to Floyd, more definitely, that the end was near.

"It's like counting off the minutes on a clock that has almost run down. It's not a bad way to die — peaceful and painless," said one of the doctors to Floyd.

Every morning Colonel Halket was moved to a couch in his sitting-room, where he could recline on pillows close by the window and look down the steep slope of his grounds upon the city park. There was an orchard of apple-trees on this slope, much frequented by birds; and the ivy that was massed against all that side of the house was a nesting-place for sparrows; for a week or two Colonel Halket amused himself arranging morsels of food along the window-sill with which to tempt the little creatures; day by day, having spread out his crumbs, he would watch and wait patiently.

"They never come," he said one day to Floyd rather wistfully. "I think I should feel quite a good deal better if only one would come. — I never cared before about birds."

"They don't know you yet; when they know you, they'll come," Floyd assured him.

"Ah, but how are they going to know me?" Colonel Halket asked. "I keep changing so from day to day; I can hardly expect a human being, let alone a bird, to recognize me."

One day a sparrow did hop on the window-sill and peck at the crumbs, and Colonel Halket described the episode to Floyd with more animation than he had shown during his illness.

"I think I have heard they like caraway seeds," he remarked. "Something or some one must like caraway seeds. I will try them to-morrow for the birds."

So daily he planned and watched; this little thing which he had never done before had now become the chief occupation of his days. He did not care to have people read to him, he did not care to have people sit with him and talk, he manifested no interest in business or in the situation which had developed as the outcome of his surrender at New Rome; and so long as he remained indifferent, Floyd had not the slightest desire to inform him. The accounts in the newspapers had been sufficiently sensational, and there had been some rather unpleasant correspondence with Kerr the banker, as well as interviews with disappointed manufacturers who had been prepared to realize a large profit on the sale of their works to the corporation and were disposed to blame any one of the house of Halket now that the plan was frustrated; Floyd did not concern himself much with these complaints. But he made a special effort to conciliate the workmen at New Rome, and to bring about a better feeling in the mills; it seemed to him that any concession might be justified which would permit Colonel Halket to die in tranquillity. So he received the delegations and committees and told them he was convinced the only serious question that had for some time been at issue and had provoked a sense of general distrust was that of the combination;

he assured them that Colonel Halket had withdrawn from that freely and entirely, realizing what a mistake he had contemplated, and chagrined at having failed to comprehend more immediately the attitude of the people. Floyd begged them to believe that the spirit of their employer towards them was as friendly as it had ever been, and asked them to be patient, since, during Colonel Halket's illness, he himself must assume all the responsibilities. Tustin kept himself in the background, and this made Floyd's conciliatory attitude more possible. He wondered somewhat at Tustin's restraint, and began to conceive a greater respect for the man's shrewdness and judgment; he expected to hear almost any day a demand from the union for Farrell's discharge. But so far as he could learn, Hugh did not suffer so much as a threat in consequence of his defiant speech; Floyd continued to wonder at Tustin's moderation. He spoke of it to Gregg; the superintendent was skeptical.

"They may not think it's the time for it now, but they'll knife him one of these days," Gregg said. "They've got their share of vindictiveness, — and they're schemers."

"Well," Floyd answered, "I have n't any great confidence in Tustin; but we don't need to worry — as long as Farrell does n't."

The hours when he was not at the office, attending to business, Floyd spent in his grandfather's room or within call; although the physicians had predicted no danger of a sudden sinking, Colonel Halket seemed better satisfied if Floyd was at hand. As the days went by, he grew too weak to be propped up at the window, and his pastime of feeding the birds and looking down on the park was denied him. Then he asked for Floyd more often.

"It must bore you, I know," he said one afternoon, "but I'd rather have you sitting in the room with me than the nurse. She's a good woman, but her cheerful incredulity whenever I mention my approaching end annoys me sometimes — a little, not much; nothing could annoy me much. It seems to me that when a man's dying, he's entitled to have everybody agree with him on everything — for once in his life. Instead of being disputed so obstinately on one or two minor points. You don't dispute me — that's why I get you in here so often and bore you."

"Oh, you don't bore me," Floyd said, with a laugh. "It's so calm and restful sitting here with you that I like it. In fact I think I like you sick better than well, Grandfather."

"I believe I agree with you; I like myself better," Colonel Halket said.

"We never used to be able to sit together idly this way," Floyd continued. "We were always too much preoccupied and bothered, and we had too many details to discuss — and differ about. But taking things easy and sort of dreaming along together — yes, I think you improve quite a lot on acquaintance."

"It's dying that does it," Colonel Halket replied philosophically. "I feel better myself — morally, that is — better pleased with myself. I've got so docile and submissive; and when you haven't been that way for years and years, it makes you feel virtuous. And another thing that makes you feel virtuous is knowing that your condition is bringing out the best in the people round you — I mean sympathy and compassion and all that sort of thing; and that gives you a human kind of pleasure, too. It seems to me that dying is just a gradual refining away of a man; there's less and less left of him every day, but what there is grows infinitely contented."

"Of course," said Floyd, "if it's good to live, it must also be good to die. For if it were n't, there would be a hideous, universal cruelty in the scheme of things that one simply can't believe."

"There's no cruelty," Colonel Halket answered. "It's all good. It's good if you fail — for then you give yourself up with relief to a pleasant resignation. It must be good if you succeed; for then you must know you've done what was implanted in you to do, you've fulfilled some inscrutable purpose, you're tired and sink comfortably down to rest. I've succeeded a little and failed a good bit — so I get a double satisfaction out of dying."

He smiled with an abstracted amusement and without any conscious glance inviting Floyd to share it.

"Grandmother was always afraid that you would some time have the disappointment of failure," Floyd observed. "She would be proud of you if she could only see the way you've met it."

"Ah, it's the serenity of dying," his grandfather answered. "And to think what a dread of death I've had all my life! Whenever a hearse has passed in the street, I've thought with a chill of the day when I should be lying in it; whenever I've been to a funeral I've always imagined it to be my funeral — and that always made it so much sadder! I've been a good churchman, but when I knelt to pray, it was with the heart of an agnostic; and when I thought of death, I was always afraid. But now — I'm as much an agnostic as ever, I suppose, but I don't feel afraid. At the very worst I'm only going to lay myself down close by my wife's side and sleep. It was good to do that in life, — and I haven't any fear — of lying asleep by her side forever."

He was silent for a few moments; then he asked, —

"What are your plans, Floyd?"

"My plans?" Floyd repeated, not understanding.

"Yes — when you have your freedom. For of course you haven't ever yet been free. It's going to be quite different for you now."

"I'll try to keep the mills running," Floyd answered. "That's as far as I've got with my plans."

"Ah, I don't mean the mills — I wasn't thinking of them. I've been thinking how little I know about you except in relation to the mills. I'm afraid I've never bothered myself much about your personal designs and desires."

"They've hardly been worth troubling anybody but myself with," Floyd said modestly.

"Oh, perhaps not well people," remarked Colonel Halket. "But sick people — might n't they be good enough to amuse sick people with?" he asked whimsically. "If I knew more about you, I might construct some sort of future for you in my imagination. — Are you interested in any girl?"

"Grandmother asked me that," Floyd answered. "And I had to tell her no."

"But the situation may have changed since then."

"Not materially." Floyd saw that his grandfather looked disappointed, and it at once seemed to him rather ungenerous to give the old man such negative replies. It was no doubt true that he wished employment for his mind and fancy, and if one could help him by supplying anything to build on, it was hardly less than a duty to do so. Prompted by this filial feeling, Floyd after a moment said awkwardly, "I suppose I know Marion Clark rather well. I like her very much — but I would n't say more than that."

"Marion Clark was a great favorite of your grandmother's," Colonel Halket said. "In fact, your grandmother mentioned her more than once to me in — in this connection." He smiled. "There was no better judge of women, Floyd."

"I daresay we shall never be more than friends," Floyd said cautiously. "Very likely I'll never have more than the friendly interest in her I have now; or very likely she would n't respond to anything more than that. I just meant that I knew her on the whole better than any other girl."

"You're a shy fellow; I don't believe you'd reveal to any one just what you really felt," Colonel Halket observed. "But you can't deceive me by any such old-man's talk about a friendly interest! You're not a cold-blooded youth to weigh the merits of a girl before deciding whether to fall in love with her or not. You've got too much healthy impetuosity for that, thank heaven."

"I wonder if I have, any longer!" Floyd thought moodily; he made no answer to his grandfather's comment, and presently Colonel Halket continued in a voice that was for him quite unusually sympathetic, —

"I'm glad to have this confidence, Floyd. It makes it easier — and more interesting for me."

Floyd, with an effort, assumed a humorous gayety. "You mustn't run round talking about it to people," he said. "For it hasn't got so far as that."

"I won't," Colonel Halket promised with a faint smile. "If there's any way of hurrying it up, though — it would be a special favor."

"I'm afraid there's not very much hope of that."

"Why not? You're certainly in a better position to get married than most men of your age — and you don't need to feel there's any uncertainty about your future. Everything that's mine is to be yours — practically everything; of course there are some bequests; I was sure you wouldn't begrudge them."

"I'd rather you wouldn't leave me so much," said Floyd.

"You'll soon get used to managing it — and I can trust you to manage it well. Better to put it in the hands of one thoroughly responsible, competent person — who's not selfish — than spread it out among a lot of charities and institutions that I'll no longer be alive to watch. I'll be criticised, of course — but I haven't used my money entirely for myself — and leaving it to you won't be shutting it up in the family — though it may seem so. Well, there is one public bequest — a large one — that may stop the cynic's mouth — though God knows that's not its purpose." The old man, lying still on the pillow, winked away sudden tears. "I'm counting on you to give your attention to that, too," he said. " It's something you will be glad to do."

" Do you want to talk it over with me so that I may know what your idea is ? " Floyd asked.

" No. I haven't developed it in any detail. I've had a lawyer collect for me all the data that I needed ; it was Barstow ; he's accurate ; you'll be working on it with him and another. There's no use in my telling you about it now — any more than there is of my giving you advice about the works. I'd rather have you go at it without any hint from me ; it will be better done."

" You don't need to feel such a sad certainty about that," Floyd said, with a laugh.

" I'm not sad because I'm so certain. I'm rather proud because I could have at the very end so big an idea ; the idea's a fine one ; even the conservative Barstow admits that. But it's better that I should rest contented with the idea. Besides, if it goes through we should both want to share in it; your share shall be in executing it."

" Considering the way I have frowned on some of your ideas in the past, I am very proud to be intrusted with the execution of this," said Floyd.

" Ah, this is different, quite different ; you won't frown on this," Colonel Halket assured him. " I shouldn't take chances intrusting it to anybody about whose sympathy I couldn't feel sure. — And Marion Clark would be a help, too," he added craftily. " Sympathetic and efficient ; I shouldn't wonder, Floyd, if she had a touch of your grandmother's quality."

" Is the idea one that can afford to wait indefinitely ? "

" Nonsense ; why should it ? You can afford not to wait. I see I'll have to make a codicil to the will — and offer you a bonus if you get married within a certain time. — Only I don't believe I can reach you by appealing to avarice. — Look here, Floyd," — his playful tone turned more gentle and serious, — " perhaps you've got some little delicacy of feeling in mind, that you ought n't immediately, you know, it would be more respectful to wait — that sort of sentiment, maybe. I hope you won't be influenced by that. I never have believed much in holding up the business — or even the amusements — of the world out of respect to the dead — and when it comes to delaying such a thing as marriage — it should n't be allowed; married life is always too short, anyway. I hope, Floyd, you 'll respect my wishes, my sentiment, in this rather than a convention."

"I shall try to do that always," said Floyd, "whenever I am confronted with such a choice."

This ambiguous assurance seemed to satisfy Colonel Halket, who now turned his head away and looked silently out of the window.

"It 's curious," he said after a while, "how interested one is in the affairs of life up to within a few hours of the moment when one passes into eternal ignorance — or " — he added faintly — " or — knowledge."

"That," Floyd said gently, "shows the nobility and courage of the man."

Colonel Halket did not seem to hear; by and by he began murmuring fragments of verse to himself — "' So sad, so fresh — That sinks with all we love below the verge — ' How does it go?" he asked. "Those lines — Ah, wait: this is the part," and he repeated in a low voice, almost drowsily, —

> "' As in dark summer dawns
> The earliest pipe of half-awakened birds
> To dying ears, when unto dying eyes
> The casement slowly grows a glimmering square — '

Ah, yes — dawn is the time — and let death come to me so!"

He lay for a long time quiet, with his face turned towards the window; he lay so still that at last Floyd thought he must be asleep. Floyd rose to tip-toe out of the room and summon the nurse. He had hardly taken a step when there was a movement on the pillow and his grandfather was looking up at him with wide-open eyes.

"Floyd," Colonel Halket said with a calm distinctness, "it would please me very much if some time you would bring Marion Clark in here to me — so that I could give you both my blessing."

"Oh, if we should ever get as far as that!" Floyd replied, with embarrassment.

"It would please me very much," Colonel Halket repeated obstinately. Then he added in a tired voice, "I think I will go to sleep."

Floyd left the room, feeling mortified at the position in which he had placed not only himself but also a girl. He was not in love with Marion Clark; he had merely thought to provide his grandfather with a little harmless interest by giving him her name; and instantly Colonel Halket had jumped to conclusions which it was not the least use to refute. Indeed Floyd had frankly to confess that his naming a girl at all was misleading; if you are n't in love with her, what are you, why do you mention her? he could imagine his grandfather's exclamation. Now Colonel Halket seemed cunningly determined to drive the matter to an issue, to perform one last friendly act for his grandson, who was exhibiting a pardonable want of self-confidence. Floyd feared lest his inability — or reluctance — to produce Marion for the bestowal of the proposed blessing might be construed by his grandfather as an ungrateful neglect of a dying man's wish; he feared the coercion of a last appeal to his sympathy. Obviously it would have to be denied, cruel though the denial might seem; he regretted now the mistaken kindness of furnishing Colonel Halket with a vain clue.

That had been done impulsively; the freedom of the act puzzled him. He would not have been so wanton as to suggest to his grandfather an attachment for which no foundation existed in fact; he admitted that at times the idea of substituting Marion for Lydia as an object of affectionate regard had possessed him speculatively; it had appealed to him at various moments by reason perhaps of its superior availability. At other times this had seemed a sufficient reason for its rejection; and then he had only to imagine the positive yes with which, if Marion were well disposed, she would accept a proposal of marriage, — and the very idea was unpleasant. Even when he had been most hospitably and considerately inclined towards it, he believed that the idea had for him mainly the value of a lay figure, on which he occasionally gave himself the pleasure of disposing and arranging at their best his most virtuous and domesticated sentiments; he believed that his interest was devoted to these trappings, which were his own possession, and to making a good show of them, rather than to the figure which all unawares participated in the display. He believed that he was exercising and airing his agreeable sentiments just as one might at intervals wear a long-folded suit of clothes merely to keep it always fresh.

He was disturbed to think that he could have recklessly intimated an interest in a girl when he had so cynical a conception of the depth and permanence of his feeling for her. It was almost as if he had committed himself by an insincere avowal of affection. It annoyed and perplexed him to think how naturally and spontaneously, in response to his grandfather's pressure, Marion's name had rushed to his lips.

After all, Floyd was destined to escape without further awkwardness from the difficulty of the situation which he had created. Colonel Halket made only one reference to Marion after the conversation which has been described. This was two days later, when he remarked that he thought Floyd was spending too much time at home with him and was neglecting somebody more interesting. "There isn't a great deal more time," he added. "I hope you will hurry up; I'm sure you need n't feel backward. It would be a pleasure to me, Floyd."

The wistfulness of the suggestion wrung the young man's heart; he could make no answer, and Colonel Halket did not press him further.

The next morning Colonel Halket began to fail rapidly; in twenty-four hours he had passed into a doze from which he was never wholly roused; and three days later he died, as he had hoped, at dawn.

XXI

THE GREAT OPPORTUNITY

STEWART LEE had received a fresh impetus toward architecture; it seemed to him that at last his decisive opportunity had come. For a week there had been industrious activity among the draughtsmen in his office, and two evenings he had kept them working there with him until after eleven o'clock, an almost unprecedented happening. One of these evenings he took them to dine with him at the club and the other at the hotel, and he paid them well for their time besides; they responded with an honest zeal to their employer's sudden animation. Stewart himself was working with a mysterious energy. He had spent a morning walking over the wide open lots that lay opposite the entrance to the Halket Park of Avalon. There were thirty acres reaching up to the summit of the low hill, the bare ridge of which marked for one passing in the street the nearest horizon line. Standing on this ridge, one might look over a slant of little houses down upon the Yolin River and its fringe of furnaces. Facing the opposite way, one saw spread out in all the green luxuriance of midsummer the great park, with its gardens and hedges and fountains; its winding drives and avenues of trees. This vacant stretch of thirty acres lay between two populous sections of the city; on one side of it was a schoolhouse; on the other it adjoined a wealthy merchant's estate. Although the taxes on it had in the last few years been heavily increased, no advertisement of it for sale had ever been displayed and no improvement of it had even been attempted. For some time people had been wondering why Colonel Halket clung to it without making an

THE GREAT OPPORTUNITY 329

effort to develop its value. Now it was about to become the property of the city.

Stewart Lee walked about on it, studying the outlook from all points; he walked up and down the street and sat in the park, viewing the stretch of open land with a critical interest, and now and then making a sketch in a note-book. A method of dealing with the problem sprang suddenly into his mind; a few swift pencil strokes gave him more distinctly the visual image. From that ardent moment he never questioned that he had conceived the arrangement ideally adapted to the site. His eyes sparkled and he closed the note-book with a snap, congratulating himself on the flash of insight that had presented the solution so immediately. Indeed he tingled with the ecstatic conviction of creation; instead of groping in discouragement for days for a fundamental motive, he had suddenly developed, as by an unconscious involuntary mental process, a complete architectural plan which he saw vividly and which filled him with delight. His first impulse was to reward himself for this inspiration by taking a holiday and playing golf all the afternoon; but a spirit of unusual sternness ruled him; he returned hastily to his office, meaning to proceed at once to work; then he spread out a lot of photographs and looked at them idly for a couple of hours, turning them over and whistling in vast contentment. The next day he threw himself with energy into the patient contriving of detail; he began to read up on hospitals; for practical advice he went to an eminent family physican; he personally consulted builders, steam-fitters, electricians, stone-cutters, and plumbers about matters which he usually left in the hands of Ayres, his first assistant.

Stewart did not confide the purpose of all this enterprise to Lydia until several days of it had made him thoroughly sanguine. Then one evening after dinner, as they sat together on the vine-screened piazza, he said to her, —

"Lydia, you remember that Women's Club-House I built a couple of years ago out at New Rome?"

"Yes," she said. "Why?"

"I did n't do a good job with that," he answered. "I've never liked to confess it — but I did n't. And I've always thought I should like to make it up somehow to Floyd."

"I'm glad to hear you say that, dear. I can tell you now; that was one of the few times when you ever disappointed me."

"Yes, and I want to redeem myself. And I've got my chance. Lydia, I've been working on plans for the Halket Hospitals."

Lydia uttered a low exclamation. "Have you been chosen?" she asked. "Papa has n't said a word to me about it."

"No, I have n't been chosen — yet," Stewart answered. "But I think I can show good reason now why I should be. And with your father and Floyd for me, I guess there won't be any opposition from Mr. Barstow; he's the third trustee, you remember."

"And what makes you think that Papa and Floyd will want to have you for architect? It is n't as if it were just a little house that one would naturally ask a friend to build; three great hospitals, that are to belong to the city, and to cost two million dollars!—"

"Ah, but when they see my plans!" Stewart exclaimed in gay assurance. "Lydia, a fellow knows when he's got a positive inspiration. It came to me as I sat in the park the other day, looking up at the site; it came to me slowly, as if it were emerging from a dream; — but at last it was all as distinct in my mind as a little foreign picture of something I had seen. A sort of Grecian effect and atmosphere — that was the thing for hospitals — to give the serenity, the calm and quiet, having some soothing charm; I began to see there was nothing for this but Greek. And then, as I say, the picture began to emerge. More than halfway up the slope, lying parallel with the ridge, the General Hospital, the largest of the three buildings, white marble, with Doric columns, and lower down, flanking it and facing each other, the Children's and the Incurables'; — white marble, too, though smaller — the lines of each one perfect in themselves, yet made to conform and harmonize with those of the others — yes, I think the lines are really perfect, Lydia."

She smiled at him, though the moonlight flickering through the vines hardly revealed it. "So soon, Stewart? — perfect so soon?"

"It was inspiration, really," he protested. "I could work a lifetime and never get anything more perfect than those lines. I saw it, Lydia; I saw it! And then, one will view them brokenly — through a little grove of oaks and maybe a garden, in the court; I tell you, Lydia, it will be so beautiful it will be a place to get well in."

"I suppose Colonel Halket had an idea of that sort in mind," said Lydia, "when he made a bequest of that site looking down on the park — it's the prettiest view in Avalon — what sick people ought to have. — You're not going to shut it off from them with your grove of oaks, are you?" she asked with a smile.

"Oh, that won't shut it off much — and, anyway, it will be just as beautiful itself. It's going to be simply the loveliest thing in this part of the world. And when it's done — well, there will be other things — a new city hall and a new court-house sometime — and I'll have got my start at last."

Lydia was silent for a few moments. Then she said, —

"Stewart, it all may be as beautiful as you have planned it. But are you sure you can execute it? — are you sure you can make it something else than a mental picture? You wouldn't want to disappoint Floyd again."

"Oh, I'm sure," Stewart declared. "Why, I've been driving my men on it; the scheme is being worked out in detail. To-morrow I'll be able to show some of the plans to your father."

"Do architects walk right up to people that way and *ask* for commissions, Stewart?"

"Why, I'm not doing that — just showing some plans as possibilities. Besides, to your father, Lydia — and to Floyd!" His tone was reproachful; he felt that Lydia had charged him with an indelicacy.

"Oh, I suppose in this case it would be all right," she conceded, though somewhat doubtfully. "So long as you don't seem to suggest anything too openly. Of course I don't know what the ethics of your profession are, and you do."

"Of course," he agreed, with a laugh. "Well, I'll tell you one thing anyway that there can't be any ethical question about, and that is the right of an architect's wife to use her influence with her father. You'll see him to-morrow before I will, Lydia; you might sort of prepare him for what I'm doing — and get him into a state of mind where he'll be ready to look at the plans."

This seemed an innocent enough intrigue, and the next morning when Stewart had gone to his office, Lydia telephoned to her father and asked him to lunch with her. His own house was closed, and he had been living at the club; a week before he had left his Chester house upon receiving Floyd's message and had hurried back to Avalon to serve as one of the pall-bearers at Colonel Halket's funeral. He had then been gratified to learn that Colonel Halket had named him co-executor with Floyd and Barstow; his duties in settling the estate were now detaining him in Avalon. The most important part of his work was still before him — the duties required of him by the Rebecca Halket Hospital bequest. Colonel Halket had been very definite and precise in his will in determining the names by which the buildings should be known; they were not to be called simply the Halket Hospitals; they were to be the Rebecca Halket Hospital for Children, the Rebecca

Halket Hospital for Incurables, the Rebecca Halket General Hospital. By an odd provision, which in the eyes of many showed acute forethought and distrust of the methods prevailing in municipal affairs, the executors were charged with the responsibility of building the three hospitals, at an expense of not more than two million dollars, and then turning them and the thirty acres of land over to the city, together with a two million dollar endowment. Mr. Dunbar had felt a grave, exalted pleasure not only at being chosen an agent in so great a work, but also in being exhibited publicly as Colonel Halket's intimate, trusted friend. The bequest was one for which even the scoffing, unsympathetic newspaper that had so often twitted Colonel Halket during his life had only charity and a sort of remorseful admiration.

Lydia did not find it difficult to enlist her father's interest in Stewart's plans; Mr. Dunbar had a curious pride and ambition for his son-in-law. "No nepotism, Lydia, no nepotism!" he declared. But secretly he was pleased by the unusual enterprise Stewart had displayed in going immediately to work and producing something to meet the necessities of the case in advance of any other architect.

"I did n't credit him with so much business sense," he said to Lydia, with a laugh. "Of course artistically he 'd do a good job — and if he means business this way — well, I 'll see what he has to say for himself."

Stewart was never deficient when it came to urging his own claims, though he could do this so tactfully as almost to disguise his purpose. When his father-in-law questioned him rather quizzically as to what work his office was now doing, Stewart burst forth into an eloquent statement of the way in which Colonel Halket's bequest had seized upon his imagination. "I 've put everything that I could temporarily to one side," he said. "It is n't only the glory and reputation I 'd get that appeals to me, — though that does appeal, of course, — but it 's the idea of having a hand in such a splendid monument — and of winning the power through it to do other splendid things. In all the work I've ever done, I've never had anything like the conviction of my power to do it right that I have now about this — to do it really nobly; — that sounds conceited, but nevertheless the conviction has been growing on me all along as I've studied out the problems. Hospitals have been a sort of hobby of mine in architecture, — not that I've ever built any, but I've been interested for a long time in the special problems that they offer; most of them are so monotonous, so obviously utilitarian — barracks for the sick; — and I've studied in a desultory way the best work of that kind that's been done, and I've thought about it a good deal. And since Colonel Halket's will has been made public, I've consulted doctors and surgeons to make sure of meeting all the practical requirements. Did Lydia tell you how the plan for the whole thing came to me one afternoon while I was sitting in the park?"

"She mentioned that that was the historic spot," replied Mr. Dunbar facetiously.

"Ah well," Stewart laughed, "I don't mean to make too much of my inspirations. I have them seldom enough; I ought to be allowed to be enthusiastic over them when they come. And this was one of my best; I'm afraid I never shall surpass it. Would you look at some of my drawings? I brought them home; of course they're rather undeveloped, but they'll give you an idea."

Mr. Dunbar was densely ignorant of the principles of architecture; but because the buildings of Stewart's plans seemed to him to suggest the Capitol at Washington — without the dome — a resemblance which he did not venture to mention for fear of being told that it did not exist — he concluded that they were good. He allowed Stewart to explain at length all the arrangements and beauties, but after a short time he ceased to listen. Stewart was a thoroughly competent architect; that fact anyway was beyond dispute — as was the fact that he was the best educated architect in Avalon. No doubt there were men of greater resource and experience in New York — though probably none of greater talent. Certainly with a man of such exceptional ability at home, it was not necessary to send to New York for architects. Colonel Halket had always supported the principle which he himself had phrased — " Avalon should be built from within rather than from without." It was this wise fostering of home industry which had made Avalon so prosperous and self-respecting a community.

Stewart was expatiating on his plans long after Mr. Dunbar had made up his mind that it would be false modesty and false delicacy not to push the claims of the best man simply because the best man happened to be his son-in-law.

" Yes," he said finally, " I like your scheme ; I like it very much. I shall feel at liberty to recommend it ; perhaps the best thing would be for me to speak about it to Floyd."

" I think so," said Stewart. " I'd rather he should hear of it first from you than from me. I don't want to seem even to Floyd, old friend though he is, to be pushing myself."

" Quite right, quite right. I have no doubt that Floyd will be hospitable to the idea — and between us we can manage Barstow."

Mr. Dunbar laughed at the idea of such a droll little conspiracy.

" You might let Floyd know that I'm ready at any time to show him my plans," suggested Stewart.

" Yes ; he'll hardly hold out against them. — In another week we ought to get the matter definitely closed up ; I expect I shall be detained here a week longer at least. If you should be awarded the job, Stewart, I suppose it would mean your staying in Avalon and working all the rest of the summer."

"Yes, probably," Stewart said. "But Lydia and the baby have got to clear out — soon, too. I've objected to their staying here so late as this — but Lydia's been insisting that she wouldn't go till I did — "

"She shall go to Chester when I go," said her father decisively. "Her mother wants her and your mother wants her, and I want the baby, and — "

"Oh, I'm going, I'm going," cried Lydia. "Only I can't leave until this hospital matter is settled one way or the other; I'm too excited over it, and I shouldn't be able to sleep away from home."

"Well, it will be settled," said her father, with the dignified assurance that was becoming to Colonel Halket's successor.

The next day Mr. Dunbar visited Floyd in his office.

"I had some rather unexpected light on the hospital matter yesterday," he began. "I thought I'd let you know about it at once. It appears that as soon as the announcement was made, Stewart — my son-in-law — began trying his hand — in just a tentative way at first — at some plans."

Floyd frowned at his blotter and turned his desk-key back and forth, back and forth nervously. But Mr. Dunbar did not observe his disturbed expression; finding it rather difficult to continue in the most tactful manner, he was looking temporarily out of the window for suggestion.

"Well," he resumed, "from having gone into the thing just to see what he could do with such a problem, Stewart seems to me really to have arrived — as the French say. I was looking at his plans last night, and they're really extraordinary — both from the æsthetic and utilitarian point of view. I never knew before what a thorough study the boy has made of hospitals — they've been a kind of hobby of his in an architectural way, it appears — and the composition of the buildings — I dare say that's not the right term, but you know what I mean — the general effect — is beautiful — so restful and serene — just

THE GREAT OPPORTUNITY 337

what would seem the ideal effect to aim at in a hospital. Now I thought if some time you would take a look at the drawings — "

"Mr. Dunbar," Floyd interrupted, "in a matter of this kind — a public matter — I am convinced that our only proper course is to invite a competition of the most distinguished architects. It seems to me out of the question that we should choose an architect arbitrarily — on our own responsibility."

"But if you could see Stewart's plans," Mr. Dunbar argued earnestly, "I am sure you would not think so. When you have a thing so perfectly adapted in every way, why go to the needless expense and delay that would be involved by a competition?"

"I have also made up my mind," Floyd said, not directly answering Mr. Dunbar's plea, "that three men like ourselves could n't possibly pass on architectural matters. Mr. Barstow is of my opinion. My idea is that we should invite eight or ten of the best architects in New York and Philadelphia and Boston, and also Stewart and Bennett & Durant to represent Avalon; I 'd allow them three months in which to prepare their plans; and then I should have the award made by a committee of three — an architect, a doctor, and — " Floyd hesitated in visible embarrassment, and then added firmly — "myself."

Mr. Dunbar sat for a moment in displeased silence.

"By the terms of the will the executors are instructed to keep this matter in charge until the buildings are completed and turned over to the city," he said.

"Yes; but that does not prevent them from assigning the arrangement of certain details to a sub-committee of their own appointing," Floyd replied. "The duty of the executors is, I think, to put the award in the hands of the persons most competent to render it, and themselves to deal with all financial transactions arising in the course of the work. You probably think it odd that I should name myself on the committee; why I should specify an architect and a doctor is clear enough, of course. Well, I think that my grandfather and my grandmother should have their personal representative in this affair. It is n't just because of sentiment, but I think it's right that so far as the views they might have held don't conflict with those of the doctor and the architect, they should be adopted."

"If you think it would be your grandfather's wish that the men he named as executors should be reduced to mere — mere figureheads," commented Mr. Dunbar rather bitterly.

"Oh, you won't be a figurehead, Mr. Dunbar; we won't allow you to be," Floyd assured him, with a laugh. "But," he added, "Mr. Barstow approves of what I've just suggested; he thinks it's the right way to manage."

"Well, why won't you look at Stewart's plans anyway?" insisted Mr. Dunbar. "I know they're good; I think maybe if you looked at them they'd convince you it would be a waste of time and effort to look any further."

"I can't look at anybody's plans — Stewart's or anybody else's," Floyd answered. "If the competition is to be fairly conducted, as I intend it shall be, no member of the committee should have any knowledge as to the authorship of the plans submitted."

Mr. Dunbar rose to go, his usual good humor seriously impaired.

"It seems to me that it would be showing no more than a friendly interest to glance at a man's drawings," he said. "However, I'll spare you any further urging."

He was so chagrined over his failure that he could not be induced to give any full account of it, even to Stewart. All he would say was that Floyd seemed bent on having a competition and running it all himself, and that he apparently had no interest in having Stewart chosen architect or even in examining his plans. Stewart was not meek in accepting a rebuff. It seemed too improbable that Floyd could have rejected him outright, and he attributed the ill success of the interview to his father-in-law's want of tact. He decided to make an appeal to Floyd in person; in a matter of this importance one had to pocket one's pride.

Arming himself with some of his drawings one morning, he set out for Floyd's office. He had seen Floyd once before since Colonel Halket's death, and had thought then that the sadness of his friend's face was only a passing expression. Now, though Floyd came forward to welcome him with a smile, it was with the same air of sadness, and it chilled Stewart a little; he began to feel that it was a permanent habit of mind which had fastened on Floyd, and which somehow would render him less accessible. In black, too, Floyd seemed more sophisticated than Stewart had liked to think him; formerly his careless way of wearing his clothes had borne out Stewart's conception of him as still not much more than a raw, undeveloped boy. But in black he seemed very different; he seemed not only to have aged in experience but also to have gained in grace. Altogether the undisturbed confidence with which he led his visitor to a seat and said, " Well, Stewart, what's the news to-day?" was not reassuring.

Stewart nevertheless plunged into the subject at once.

"I'm afraid my father-in-law made rather a mess of things," he said. "As nearly as I can make out, he must have represented me as bidding for the job of architect of the hospitals; he seems to have made himself a sort of advance agent for my boom. When I found it out, Floyd, I wanted to come and clear myself of the suspicion of having tried to work you."

"Oh, that's all right," Floyd said. "I know Mr. Dunbar; and I didn't suppose you were trying to work me."

"The fact is, I may as well tell you frankly," Stewart proceeded, "that ever since I built that Women's Club at New Rome, I've had it on my mind. You were good to say so little about it — but I appreciated just the same what a great disappointment it was to you; I can tell you it was a bitter mortification to me, and I hope it taught me a lesson. A thing you were doing for your grandmother — not to do it well — I felt sore enough at myself, you can believe. And when I heard of the hospitals that your grandfather had committed to you to build as a memorial to her, I set to work making plans — not because I had the least expectation of being given the work after my other performance, but just from the feeling that if by any toss-up or turn of chance whatever I should have something to do with it, I should be prepared to do it decently — perhaps well enough to atone in some measure for the other thing. You see I'm making a perfectly clean breast of it, Floyd."

"Oh, that's all right," Floyd answered. He was a little embarrassed by Stewart's unusual self-abasement.

"Well, that's the way it started," continued Stewart. "Then I got more and more interested in the matter; finally I could n't think of anything else, and I practically threw over all my other work to give all my time to developing the hospital scheme that had come to me. Why," — he laughed, — "I used to work downtown till midnight, and kept my draughtsmen working too, I got so interested. But there was n't ever any idea on my part of coming to you and asking you out of friendship to give me the job."

"Oh, I understand," Floyd said. "I understand perfectly. You don't need to feel obliged to explain anything, Stewart."

"Ah, but I must, to satisfy my New England conscience if not you," Stewart insisted genially. "Well, the trouble all resulted from my getting too enthusiastic over my plans and showing them to Mr. Dunbar. He became even more enthusiastic than I was, and rushed off to you — to urge my claims. Of course I should n't have made any such appeal — much as I should like to have the opportunity of redeeming myself in your eyes for that fiasco, and confident as I feel that this would square me. But Mr. Dunbar tells me that you mean to place the decision

THE GREAT OPPORTUNITY 341

in the hands of a committee — an architect, a doctor, and possibly yourself — was n't that it?"

"Yes," Floyd acknowledged. He was again nervously turning the key of his desk, as he had done the day before when he began to perceive the drift of Mr. Dunbar's argument.

"Well, then I confess the idea did enter my head that you might be willing to let me submit my plans to this committee; they 'd advise you whether they were suitable and had distinction; it would n't be as if you were acting entirely on your own judgment; here you 'd be guided by experts — and it would be easy enough to turn me down. If the committee were really enthusiastic about the plans — more than enthusiastic — you could feel safe in following such a recommendation, could n't you? Oh, you don't know how I hate to be thrusting myself on your attention this way, Floyd; I only do it for two reasons — because I really have such complete confidence in my plans, and because I want to do personally this thing for you — this memorial — and make it as fine as the other one was contemptible. It's just because I want to do this thing well and for you."

Stewart derived emotion from the mere utterance of an appeal, and when he finished his plea, there was a gentle, wistful look in his eyes that declared his sincerity. Floyd, clicking the lock of his desk back and forth, did not glance up; his brows were knitted in a frown.

"Thank you, Stewart," he said after a moment. "We need n't talk about the other building; you 've squared yourself all right. But about the hospitals — I don't see how we can manage matters as you 'd like."

He hesitated, and Stewart's face hardened instantly, as if no concession had been granted him. But his voice was still soft as he asked, "Why not?"

"Because," Floyd answered, "I want the buildings to be the best attainable. Your plans may be so very good that they 'd convince a committee right off — but unless we'd seen what the best architects of the country — the other best architects of the country," he corrected himself, with a smile — "can suggest, we could n't be sure that we had got the most suitable thing. We must have a competition, and of course it would n't do for the committee to have advance knowledge of any competitor's work. I hope you'll win the competition, Stewart; I'm almost sure you will, since you feel so confident yourself."

"I did n't say anything about feeling confident of winning a competition," declared Stewart testily. He was sitting with his legs crossed; now he began to swing one foot in sharp, angry excitement. "I have no use for competitions; half the time the award is a matter of chance, half the time it's the result of a compromise. The architect on your committee has a bias towards one style of building; your doctor has a personal bias about some matter of arrangement, and together they'll vote every time for an inferior set of plans if only it hits their particular prejudice. That's why I'm anxious to have my plans considered without a competition. I know that in themselves they're so good that no mere individual prejudice could reject them — so long as they're not being compared with something of which individual prejudice may be enamoured. Do you see my point?"

"I think you overestimate the danger of prejudice," said Floyd. "I believe that generally in an architectural competition, as well as in other competitions, the best man wins. Anyway this seems to me a matter that requires a competition."

"Very well," said Stewart, and he rose from his chair with his lips compressed; his fingers trembled as they tightened upon the plans which he had so vainly brought. "I shall enter your competition, and I shall doubtless have the pleasure of seeing an inferior contribution receive the award." He stood for a moment looking down on Floyd, and then his light eyes flashed with sudden anger. "I don't wish to strain our relations unnecessarily, — but perhaps it is just as well that I should say what is in my mind. I came here — you allowed me to acknowledge to you that I had been at fault in the past — you made no effort out of consideration for me to prevent my acknowledgment — and then, when I appealed to you for the chance to redeem myself, you denied me. It is an unpleasant thing to do — unpleasant for me as well as for you — but I cannot help recalling that episode of our college days when you allowed my overwhelming obligation to you to be always a rankling memory to me. And I regard it as a damned nasty trait of character which finds satisfaction in holding a friend at a disadvantage — in never giving him the chance to get upon even terms or to repair his fault — in keeping the upper hand over a friend."

He turned sharply and left the room. Floyd, sunk low in his chair, continued to fumble absently at the key; after a time he sighed, and sitting up addressed himself to his work.

XXII

DIFFICULTIES OF A MAN OF TASTE

Soon after Stewart's call upon Floyd, he received a formal invitation to submit plans in the competition for the Rebecca Halket Hospitals. The invitation was signed by the three executors of Colonel Halket's estate; it specified the last day of September as the time when the competition would be closed. This allowed a little more than three months for the preparation of plans. The evening newspapers announced the names of the architects to whom invitations had been sent; Stewart read the list with displeasure. There were four in New York, two in Boston, two in Philadelphia, all of the highest eminence in the profession. In Avalon there had been invited besides himself the firm of Bennett & Durant — the only firm, he acknowledged to himself, that he could feel absolutely confident of beating, notwithstanding all his confidence in his plans. Even in the moment of making this secret acknowledgment, he did not acquit Floyd of an intention both unfriendly and ungenerous.

The invitation to submit plans was accompanied by the announcement of the committee who would make the award. The architect was one of the New York men most eminent in the profession; the surgeon was Dr. Edwards of Avalon, who had the largest general practice in the city; Floyd was the third member. Stewart sought out Lydia's cousin, Bob Dunbar, who was a promising young physician, and asked for information about Dr. Edwards.

"Oh, he's a splendid man," Dunbar said. "Absolutely the best that could have been chosen. He's progressive and painstaking, and sure to insist on having things done in the most modern and approved way. He won't be content with what he himself knows about the requirements — though that's a lot; — he'll get the advice of experts. I hear that he and Floyd are going on to New York next week to consult the superintendents and staff officers of hospitals there; that's the right way to deal with such a thing as this. Uncle George and the other executors made a wise move when they put Edwards on the committee."

"In short, he's intensely practical," said Stewart, with disgust.

What with her father's chagrin and her husband's sense of grievance, Lydia was made sufficiently aware of the altered feeling in the family toward Floyd. Of the two men her father was the more outspoken. He declared that nothing but a sense of duty to a trust detained him at a task in the execution of which he was often overruled and humiliated. He had been slighted by Floyd; Barstow had supported Floyd — "for with Barstow it's off with the old master, on with the new," said Mr. Dunbar cynically. "Floyd thinks he can at once fill Colonel Halket's shoes," he added. "But Colonel Halket was a good deal bigger man than his grandson will ever grow to be." Mr. Dunbar was in fact smarting under disappointment. His modest, worthy ambition to wear the mantle of the first citizen of Avalon, which had so long adorned Colonel Halket's shoulders, seemed now unlikely of fulfillment — and Floyd was the obstacle. Floyd was depriving him of the importance and eminence which as the senior executor of Colonel Halket's estate he should have enjoyed. If he had been permitted, as in the ordinary decencies of life he should have been, to display himself as the principal figure in disposing of Colonel Halket's benefactions, it would have harmed no one and it would have been to his own innocent aggrandizement. But egotism or jealousy or some such petty motive had denied him this — denied him a place on the committee of judges; Floyd had installed himself there instead. Mr. Dunbar had long been preparing to shine forth some day the patron of the arts and the apostle of progress; now he felt that the opportunity which his old friend had kindly left him as a legacy was being ruthlessly closed by the machinations of a selfish and ambitious man of a younger generation. In the family circle his bitterness was not to be disguised; and though it seemed mainly to derive its source from the ill treatment which had been accorded to Stewart, it concerned itself in fact with his own hard usage.

Stewart, although more guarded in expression, exhibited his wound to Lydia if not to others. She could do nothing to heal it, and the daily inspection of it caused her pain. Stewart perceived this, but a subtle motive impelled him nevertheless to keep the wound open. He wished her to share his bitterness, his sense of resentment. The demand that she should not nourish a warmer friendship for any man than that which he himself entertained was one that his pride imposed upon her; he watched her silently to make sure that she was acceding to it. Her liking for Floyd had never awakened any jealousy in his heart, and it was no such personal motive as jealousy that now prompted his suspicious surveillance. He was inspired merely by a high sensitiveness to convention; should she try to create for Floyd a different atmosphere from that which he tacitly prescribed, she would be putting either herself or him in the wrong. To Stewart it seemed axiomatic that a wife should never excel her husband in devotion to his friends. Lydia's conduct hardly satisfied Stewart's rigorous requirements.

She sympathized with him in his disappointment; that was well enough. But he desired that she should commit herself to the support of his grievance by some outspoken word against Floyd. He had himself given her the opportunity when he had said to her, "I never thought that Floyd could treat a friend so shabbily." She had made no answer, and he was not altogether displeased at that.

He knew that her gratitude for what Floyd had done years before had been enshrined in her heart as a sacred sentiment and that a word in Floyd's disparagement was not to be easily drawn from her lips. That a woman should be reluctant to admit a flaw in the character of one to whom she owed all and to whom she had been steadfast in her loyalty, was fitting — especially when the man was he whose name she had given to her own little son. The delicacy of such reluctance was a feminine quality that Stewart prized. But he waited for the time when the devotion of the wife to the husband should break down this loyalty of the woman to the friend and permit the utterance of a word in censure — though it were only the lightest; this ultimately must be required to show that she held the friend in error and not the husband; this Stewart required as a definite demonstration that her devotion to him transcended the most sacred of her other sentiments. But she never spoke the word for which he watched and waited.

"Stewart, dear, think how much greater satisfaction it will be to you to win the award in competition," she said to him one day when he had been airing his grievance in the hope that she would respond. "For you will win it, I know — when you feel so sure of your plans."

"No thanks to Floyd if I win," muttered Stewart cheerlessly.

"Ah, but that's what you want, is n't it?" said Lydia, laying a light hand upon his. "You've been talking, have n't you, of the unpleasantness of being under obligations — feeling you're at a disadvantage because of them — and of course if Floyd had given you this commission right off, there would have been one more thank you to say — a thing which you seem to hate, in spite of your generally good manners. But when you win the competition you won't have obligations to anybody."

"Yes — when I win the competition!" Stewart said sarcastically. "Here I've got to stay in town all the rest of the summer — just to touch up my plans for a competition that they will be too good to win. Yes, exactly that. Whereas, if I'd been given the chance that I had a right to expect, — I could have allowed myself a decent vacation and elaborated my plans at leisure."

"I'm perfectly ready to stay here and keep house for you, Stewart, if that would make it a little more pleasant for you."

"No, I shouldn't think of it. You'll go next week — and I'll stay and be as miserable as I can, slaving for a thing that there's no possibility of my winning."

"Oh, if you talk that way! Faint heart ne'er won fair competition."

"There's no such thing as a fair competition," declared Stewart. "It's always one of three things that determines the award in a competition. It's prejudice or compromise or ignorance. It's never merit. It's a fact; I've never known the best set of plans to win a competition."

"Then spend the summer making yours just bad enough to win," suggested Lydia. She laughed and kissed him, and then stood by his chair and passed her hand back and forth over his forehead. "Now we've smoothed it out," she said after a moment, in a tone of triumph. "*Now* we've chased away the frown."

Stewart accepted the consolations of her humorous spirit, and at the same time felt they were not the best that she could have bestowed. If she had taken this matter seriously and shown a little animus, it would have been more sympathetic. Since the most that she could do for his relief was to urge him on lightly to the competition, he began to suspect that she held Floyd justified in his refusal and that she had, therefore, not cooled by the fraction of a degree in her friendship for Floyd. This unseemly tenacity of hers, as he regarded it, irritated him as much as the exoneration of Floyd which it presupposed. When Stewart was with his wife her personal charm could indeed operate to smooth out the frown; but away from the influence of this he was possessed often by a glum reproach of her for her failure to judge justly and to sympathize with her whole heart. It was the first time since his marriage that he had felt a lingering soreness against his wife.

She had at least — so far as he knew — been guilty of no overt act of friendship for Floyd since the rupture. She had had the good taste, for instance, not to suggest asking Floyd to come in and dine with them some evening before she should go away. Stewart felt a certain relief at having fixed so early a date for her departure; it was a safeguard against any unduly premature attempt on her part to renew the informal hospitality to Floyd which had for so long been the habit of the household, and which, now that Floyd was left alone, would naturally be offered more freely than ever. Stewart was not in favor of permanently doing away with these friendly relations, but he was sternly of the opinion that for a period of probation Floyd should be held at arm's length. And instinctively he felt that Lydia's withdrawal from the scene at this juncture might prevent a disagreeable domestic clash.

The day before Lydia and her father were to leave, Stewart came home from his office earlier than usual. Lydia called to him from the drawing-room, and he entered, to find Floyd sitting beside her on the sofa, with one finger in the grasp of the baby, whom she was holding.

"Hello, Stewart," said Floyd cheerfully. "I can't get up, you see."

"How are you, Floyd?" Stewart replied. The lack of cordiality in his greeting and the stiff manner in which he stood, with his hands clasped behind him, caused both Lydia and Floyd to flush. Floyd moved a little and Lydia unclasped the baby's hand from his finger, saying quietly, "Let go of uncle, baby." "Uncle" was the term of address for Floyd that the baby was being brought up to adopt.

Floyd rose and said, "Mr. Dunbar told me that Lydia

and he and the small boy were leaving to-morrow. I thought I'd drop in to bid them good-by." He gently pinched the wide-eyed baby's cheek. " Good-by, little one. Good-by, Lydia."

She rose and gave him her hand. "Good-by, Floyd."

"I don't need to say good-by to you, Stewart? You're going to stay a while?"

"Yes," said Stewart coldly. "I have some work to do for a competition."

"I wish you luck," Floyd answered. "Good-by, Lydia."

After he had passed out, Lydia stood for a moment looking at her husband reproachfully. Then with the baby in her arms she walked up to him and laid her hand on his shoulder. He met her look of appeal rather sullenly, more discomfited by it than he would have been by a flash of temper.

"Stewart," she said, "ah, Stewart! Be magnanimous!"

She did not wait for him to reply; she patted his shoulder gently with her hand and then left the room.

Stewart's glance fell on a baby's plaything lying on the table beside the sofa — a bright new jumping-jack, collapsed now in helpless dislocation. Stewart picked it up and jerked the strings idly, causing it to dance; he was engaged in this employment when Lydia returned, having given the baby in charge of the nurse. She stood by for a moment, watching the gyrations of the wooden figure.

"Floyd brought it this afternoon," she said presently. "He said he was afraid the baby would be bored by the journey — so he brought this to amuse him."

"Oh," said Stewart. He laid the toy down, and as he did so his eyes fell upon a book, a specially and handsomely bound book, which struck him as unfamiliar. He picked it up; it was a copy of Keats.

"Did Floyd bring this also to keep the baby from being bored on the journey?" he asked.

A MAN OF TASTE 351

A sharp light sprang from Lydia's gray eyes. "Stewart," she said, "your tone and your manner make that question very offensive — though you may have meant it to be amusing. Floyd brought me the book; I had no intention of concealing the fact from you."

"I think," Stewart said, and his voice was quiet and deliberate, "that as matters stand it would have been in better taste for Floyd not to make any gifts."

She looked at him; the flash of anger had faded from her face, leaving surprised and scornful contempt.

"Stewart! How can you be so bitter — so unfair! It hurts me to go away knowing that there is such unkindness in your heart."

"There is no unkindness in my heart," replied Stewart. "But when I have had reason to expect generosity and receive instead injustice and injury, I cannot dissemble what I feel and think. You urge me to be magnanimous; that is easy when one has the upper hand. But when one has been unkindly dealt with, it is not well to be too readily magnanimous, for then it is not magnanimity at all; it is just a mean and cringing spirit. I would suggest, my dear, that you examine the matter a little more carefully before you make sure that your sympathy is properly bestowed."

Lydia did not reply; she felt that to protract the discussion could only enlarge the possibilities for unhappiness, and already it had made her unhappy enough. It was a forlorn and silent dinner through which the husband and wife sat, and it was an uncomfortable evening that followed. At last Lydia kissed Stewart good-night and went up to bed; when some time later, he entered the room, he found her lying still awake. She asked him to come to her, and then when he was sitting by her side, she reached up and put her arm about his neck. Her gentle soul had yielded under the pressure of her unhappiness.

"Stewart, dear," she said, "I can't go away feeling that there is something rankling between us. It would spoil my summer — and if anything should happen and you or I should have to remember always that we had parted without — without as much affection as we might have shown, — I — should never forgive myself. Stewart, dear," — he bent down at the gentle pressure and kissed her, and she murmured, — "I'm sorry if I've said anything to hurt you — I'm sorry if I haven't seemed to sympathize."

"It's all right, dear," said Stewart, caressing her. "I'm sorry, too, if I've seemed touchy. But you must know I love you just as much as ever — I love you more every day — and when it comes to your going away from me to-morrow — instead of my being too angry to say good-by, as you seem to be afraid, it's — it's a good deal more likely that I shan't be able to trust my voice to speak."

He said this with an emotional little laugh that touched her heart, and her own voice trembled as she answered, —

"I feel very happy now, Stewart. Now I can go to sleep."

The next morning Stewart bade Mr. Dunbar and Lydia good-by at the station, and, looking into her face bright with love yet sad too at the parting, he felt how much he should miss her; tears filled his eyes.

"I — I told you I shouldn't be able to trust my voice," he said, with a faint smile. He kissed her quickly and then the baby, and hurried away.

He lunched and dined at the club and delayed till late in the evening the return to his house; he feared the first forlorn chill of its loneliness. When he entered it finally, he turned on the lights in the drawing-room and stood dismally surveying the orderly arrangement of swathed furniture and pictures which Lydia had left for him. The room seemed to hold the spirit of her active, cheerful personality even in this dormant state; the books on the table were disarranged as if at the last moment she had scattered them in a hasty search. Moved by a sudden curiosity, Stewart looked over them; the copy of Keats was not there, nor was the wooden toy.

Stewart turned out the lights and went upstairs to his room, stung by a disappointment and chagrin that dulled the softer sense of melancholy. Lydia, in spite of what had seemed her repentant and appealing surrender, had taken with her the book and the toy that Floyd had given to beguile the tedium of the journey. If she had declined to avail herself of his gifts, she would have shown, Stewart felt, a better spirit, a more loyal support of her husband. The discovery made clear to him the fact which he had ignored — that, after all, his difference with Lydia had not been settled, but merely glossed over at their parting.

Stewart set himself rather leisurely to the task of completing his plans. Three months seemed plenty of time in which to elaborate ideas already definite; besides, he had a good start over the other competitors. He felt, therefore, that the important thing was to keep himself from going stale, not to work with a feverish haste, but to take his time and keep his mind free, and not neglect exercise; there was nothing to be gained by risking a break-down in the hot weather. So for the first month he left the office early in the afternoons and played golf or billiards, or sat in the club at the game of poker that was fairly continuous there. "Great Scott, Lee," one of his friends observed one day, "if I had your leisure, I'd go away for the summer."

"I do more work than you think," Stewart replied in an injured tone. "But I've been so steadily at it for weeks that I've got to have a little relaxation, — or I'd simply get fat-witted. Midsummer is the deuce of a time to hold a competition."

If it had not been for his constant meetings with Floyd and Bennett, this bachelor summer would have been quite tolerable; but the encounters with these two men, which took place nearly every day at one club or the other, kept Stewart in a state of intermittent irritation. To Floyd it became quite clear that he was still under the ban of Stewart's displeasure. After asking Stewart twice to come home and dine with him — and he put the invitation rather wistfully, — and being repulsed with the thin excuse that Stewart liked to dine downtown every night in order to be able afterwards to drop into his office and work on his plans, Floyd desisted from conciliatory efforts. He began to think that the only thing which could terminate Stewart's ill feeling towards him would be a favorable issue to the competition. Floyd hoped for this with all his heart; but the more he saw of Stewart sitting in the club or tramping upon the golf links and the more he considered the manner in which his friend's character was revealing itself, the less promising did Stewart's chance of success appear. And though Floyd was innocent both of the intention and of the fact, he seemed to Stewart the embodiment of the spirit of reproach — mild, sorrowful, uncomplaining, altogether maddening.

Bennett, toward whom Stewart had always maintained an air of cold reserve, was disagreeably good-natured and insistent upon the establishment of friendlier relations, now that they were rivals in an important competition. He would sit down at Stewart's table at the club and smoke a cigar and chat about the problems involved; and Stewart was so much on his dignity at these moments that he never observed the shrewd, cynical eyes with which Bennett was studying him or the meditative smile that slanted upward from Bennett's cigar.

"I suppose," Bennett said to him once, "we're both of us fools — wasting our summer here in this way. With all that New York talent entered, a local man does n't stand much chance — and we might as well make up our minds to it now, you and I, that we're going to have our labor for our pains."

"It's something of an advantage to be on the ground," Stewart said indifferently.

"Well, I don't see how you can work a pull in a competition like this," Bennett remarked crudely, but with subtle intention. He was amused by Stewart's look of disdain and his reply.

" When I spoke of the advantage of being on the ground, I had no reference to 'a pull.' I was n't considering the increased facilities for using underhand methods. I simply meant, of course, the obvious thing — that there is an advantage in being thoroughly familiar with the site."

" Oh yes, I suppose maybe we ought to throw ourselves into the spirit of the thing a little better than the outsiders," Bennett agreed. " By the way, I can't thank you enough, Lee, for letting go of Durant; that fellow's a whole team; at least I find him so. Funny thing how men run, is n't it — how a fellow will be of absolutely no use to one man and the long-lost brother to another?"

" I'm glad to hear Durant is doing so well — succeeding so well," said Stewart, rising from the table. " I feel a certain interest in his career; you remember, Mr. Bennett," and he smiled quite good-naturedly, " you never found him so useful until after he 'd been with me."

" Oh, there's no doubt about it; your training was an excellent thing for him — excellent," Bennett conceded. " You put a polish on him that he would n't have acquired otherwise — and his resourcefulness in matters of detail has developed amazingly. I 'm very much tickled over a little inspiration of his, last week — in these competition drawings; it cleared up a difficulty that we 'd been bothering over for days — and made that plan as clean as a whistle. Sorry I can't tell you just what it was — I think you 'd be amused by the cleverness of it."

" Yes, he's a clever fellow," Stewart said.

He separated himself from this man, who both bored and annoyed him, and went back to his office. Bennett had chosen a particularly unfortunate moment to enlarge on Durant's peculiar gifts, — a moment when Stewart was finding himself very much in need of those faculties for neat economical arrangement which his former draughtsman possessed. The drawings which Stewart had brooded over with such affection and confidence had been only those for the exterior general scheme of the buildings, and he had allowed a month to glide by without bringing them much nearer completion. The straightening out of little difficulties which confronted him at the outset seemed too tedious and mechanical a task for him to undertake; and he had assigned this work to his assistants. Now after a month of labor they had brought him results that plainly would not do; and after severely censuring them for the glaring imperfections and hearing their defense, which was that the restrictions he had imposed made awkwardness, inconvenience, and wastefulness of arrangement necessary, he had set about solving by his own ingenuity the perplexities for which his assistants were unequal. It was uncongenial work, and more difficult than he had supposed. Although he had no doubt of his ultimate ability, it was unpleasant at this juncture to be reminded of the knack of his former draughtsman of whom he had been despoiled. Bennett, however, had means of keeping in touch with what took place in Stewart's office and could judge very nicely the most effective moment for administering a prick. His son was one of his draughtsmen and was a friend of one of Stewart's assistants.

The summer wore on, and Stewart felt at last that he had extricated himself creditably from his difficulties — the more creditably since he had depended on no one but himself. He knew that there were one or two weak spots, but they did not seem to him important; and the original beauty of the design had been preserved. So sure was he that only minor points remained to be dealt with that he wrote to Lydia saying that in a week or ten days she would see him at Chester. She sent him a letter in reply, rejoicing over the news and especially over the indication that he had finished his work and found it so satisfactory. "And now that it's all done, I'm sure it will win," she wrote.

In order that he might meet any small technical objection that could be raised against his plans, Stewart asked Bob Dunbar to examine them. Dunbar gave up a morning to the task, and Stewart went over the plans with him in detail. He was rather discouraged at the number of Dunbar's running criticisms; he was dismayed at the end when the doctor said, —

"Of course it's hard for me to speak definitely — just from seeing the plans; but it seems to me, Stewart, that while the buildings will be very good to look at, they'll be pretty impracticable. You haven't made nearly enough provision for light in any of the buildings; the first requisite of a hospital nowadays is light, and your windows are too small and too few to be adequate. You ought to have double the number in the wards. Then in the General Hospital you've given the amphitheatre the wrong exposure; the amphitheatre ought always to have a north light, and it's quite a serious matter when you put it on the south side as you've done. It's not only a matter of light; there's the heat in summer to be considered; it's a very important thing."

So he went on, pointing out one defect after another, while Stewart sat by gloomily.

"Dr. Parsons, whom I consulted, never mentioned any of these things as essential," Stewart said at last.

"Oh, well, Parsons is an old-fashioned family doctor; he has very little hospital work; he's a good man, but he'd hardly be up to date in such matters."

"I've studied a good many hospitals," Stewart said, "and the interior arrangement of a number of them is much like mine."

"It's faulty, though; there are lots of hospitals that aren't fit to be hospitals, they're so inconveniently planned," declared Dunbar.

"I should think doctors and nurses could put up with a little inconvenience without great cost of life," was Stewart's sarcastic comment.

"Oh, I don't know about cost of life," replied Dunbar cheerfully.. "But a hospital's the last place where one ought to put up with inconvenience."

"As for enlarging the windows or increasing the number of them, that would simply ruin the buildings architecturally," said Stewart. "More light is out of the question."

"There isn't enough," insisted Dunbar.

"I suppose I can perhaps make some alterations," Stewart continued reluctantly. "But I've worked over these things till I'm sick of them; I'd been looking forward to joining Lydia next week and giving myself a good month's rest. From an architectural point of view the plans are all right, just as they are; I couldn't improve them if I worked over them the rest of my life. — But you think that for practical reasons they couldn't be adopted?"

"I should feel almost certain that there would be more practical plans submitted," said Dunbar. "I don't know how the judges will feel; they may not regard the utmost practicability as essential. With a man like Edwards on the committee, though, I should think you'd better sit up nights — even about such matters as wash-bowls and chandeliers and ventilating-shafts."

That evening two windows on the twelfth floor of the great building glowed until after midnight, the loftiest lights in the city street. Within the one illuminated room, above all the dark and empty tiers of offices, Stewart sat at his great drawing-table with plans spread out before him and others lying beside his chair on the floor. He was without coat or collar; his shirt was open at the throat, his sleeves were rolled up above his elbows. He had begun one sketch after another, and pushed them all aside unfinished, and now with his head on his hands he sat wearily looking at the work of which he had been so proud. And as he gazed at it, the beauty of it all became to him more than ever convincing; he saw in his mind those buildings all completed, with the embellishment given by trees and gardens. They seemed to him as beautiful as the Greek temples from which they were derived; and the thought that he might forever be debarred from expressing in stone and marble this noble conception came upon him in his loneliness after the profitless labors of the night and filled him with a sudden anger and grief.

"To have created that — only to carry it in my brain — the best work I've ever done, the best I'll ever do!"

Floyd's inexorable figure interposed itself between him and fruition. A committee of architects, a committee of two architects and one doctor might make an award without being unduly influenced by the stern demands of the practical; but upon the committee of Floyd's choice beauty and nobility of design would be sacrificed. Floyd and the doctor would be found allied on every contention; the member of the committee who understood architecture would be overruled. Floyd was a Philistine and a materialist; his few years at college — where he had pursued only the most utilitarian studies — had done little for his development. And Floyd would be more impressed by an argument showing the inadequate size of wash-bowls than by one demonstrating that the lines of the proposed building had the grace of the Parthenon.

Stewart, sitting discouraged in the midst of his futile efforts at revision, asked himself what he should do. Should he hand in his drawings as they were, doomed to be rejected, and, with the consciousness that he had done his best, free himself from the drudgery which was chafing him, from a place which had grown hateful, and go to his wife and the sea for the rest that he had earned? Or should he with a stubborn spirit bend himself day after day, night after night, upon the dreary task of trying to improve that which could not be improved, even of building up a whole new set of plans, which could not, like these, be inspired — should he work till the last hour simply to satisfy the spirit of fight which had awakened in him, and to hold out till the end assailing the impossible? He rose and went to the open window and stood looking out upon the flashing city below him and upon the diadem of lights that rimmed the encircling hills. He was conscious now of what in his absorbed solitude he had not before heard, though it must have been continuous all through the night and drumming gently on his senses — the faint reverberation of the mighty hammers pounding, pounding in the forges, urged on from time to time in their drudging task by the shrill, stimulating whistle of steam. Dull, patient, and persistent — that was the spirit of the place; by night as well as by day its cumbrous potency was fashioning tools for the world from the sternest of metals. On Stewart standing at the window and listening to the sluggish reverberation of the pounding hammers and the driving, derisive shriek of steam, the spirit that was vital in the place laid its hand; he turned after a time from the window in sullen, unrecognizing obedience.

He seated himself again at the table, but not to work; he wrote a short letter to his wife, saying that he should not leave Avalon until the competition was closed. "Bob Dunbar finds fault with some details in my plans, and I shall stay and see if I can render them more practical. Now that I am in for it, no matter how poor my chances are, I have decided that my only course is to work on the job up to the very end."

He prided himself on the avoidance of heroics, but he hoped that Lydia would show a consciousness of his martyrdom. In this she did not disappoint him; her next letter to him expressed her admiration. "I shall miss you awfully, Stewart, dear," she wrote; "especially since I've been counting on seeing you so soon. And I can't help feeling sorry for you; it must be so forlorn! But still I'm glad; it's splendid for you to show so much determination. And I'm more sure than ever that you'll win; with the plans all that they were before and the little improvements in detail that Bob can suggest to you and that

A MAN OF TASTE

you can make in a month, I *know* you'll win. And won't it be fun to have you triumphing over all those New York architects! I'm sure Floyd will be just as glad as I if you get it; you feel a little better towards Floyd now, don't you? How is he? Don't let him get lonely, Stewart; this summer he must be pretty sad."

Stewart felt that an undue proportion of Lydia's sympathy was directed to Floyd.

He had tabulated all the small details which Dunbar had specified, and distributed them among his draughtsmen for revision and remedy. The more fundamental difficulties, such as the unsuitable arrangement of the amphitheatre in the General Hospital and the lack of sufficient light in the wards of the three buildings, he had reserved to grapple with himself. His draughtsmen did not know what problem he was working over; they could not imagine what defect in the plans kept him night after night in the office after they had gone. They only knew that he was growing more irritable and returned to them with sour censure their bungling attempts to provide substitutes for the details that had to be sacrificed. Twice one of these harassed assistants had undertaken to spend the evening working over the rejected effort, but each time he had been dismissed. "I want to have the office to myself this evening, Hopkins," Stewart had said. "If you are very anxious to work, you may take your drawings home."

Day by day, night by night, Stewart pored over the plans, and no helpful suggestion came to his mind. It was apparent to him that to give the amphitheatre the proper exposure would mean reversing entirely the scheme of the building, and this seemed impossible. Equally out of the question was it to provide more windows for the wards; they would make the buildings grotesque and ridiculous. An intolerable restlessness seized him after he had thus been confronted all day long and every night with problems to which his mind could offer no solution; it was a restlessness not to be assuaged by pacing round and round the littered table, or even by going outdoors and walking the streets. In his impotence he had always the impulse to establish himself somehow by violence; unprofitable toil produced in him, not peace of mind, but an ugly wrath, which could be loosed upon no object; there were moments when he felt it not improbable that he should sometime fill himself with rum and take three or four days off forgetting his troubles. He knew that in a violent, prolonged debauch he might find relief; but in his married life he had in that respect been above reproach, and his pride was strong enough to curb the reckless impulse. His bitterness, however, gained intensity from repression. Occasionally Lydia's letters applauded his persistence and determination; one such letter he tore to pieces on the spot. "Persistence! Determination!" he thought savagely. "People prate about its improving influence on character! My God, how people prate!"

One afternoon early in September he was gazing from his high window when there seemed to float into his mind a tangible idea relating to the arrangement of the amphitheatre. He sat down at his table and tried to seize and examine the elusive thought. It involved the reconstruction of the interior with no external alteration, and he was yielding to an excited hope that this was practicable when his office boy entered with a card. It bore the name of Mr. Andrew Delafield, whom Stewart knew as a man of position, a retired merchant of considerable wealth. With some annoyance at the interruption, Stewart consented to see Mr. Delafield. The visitor stated that he was about to invest a hundred thousand dollars in building a storage warehouse on some land which he owned, and that he wished to retain Stewart as architect. "A good, substantial, useful building is what I want," he said. "I don't want to spend money on the outside."

Stewart considered a moment; then he replied, "I'm sorry, Mr. Delafield, but I don't do that sort of work. I don't build warehouses; I may say frankly I don't care to build them; they don't interest me. If you'll allow me, I would suggest that you go to Bennett & Durant; it's the sort of work that they're best qualified to undertake."

"But I'd rather have you do it," said Mr. Delafield.

"Thank you; I appreciate your wish; I'm sorry I can't respond. But I have decided to do nothing of that kind."

"Why, it's simple enough, — it ought to be!" cried the client in perplexity. "You *can* do it, I know, if you want to, — and there's no disgrace in building a warehouse, is there? And the commission ought to be worth while."

"It isn't a matter of being able to do it, or even of the commission; it's merely that the idea doesn't interest me, and I'm making it a rule only to work on things that do."

Mr. Delafield good-naturedly expressed his inability to understand such a point of view, "especially when you have this large office force to work for you. But it's very creditable to your conscience, I'm sure, to refuse all work in which you can't feel a personal interest. And you'd recommend Bennett & Durant?"

"For work of this kind, yes. If you are good enough, you might say to Bennett that I made the suggestion."

They parted amiably; the visitor showed himself sensible of Stewart's courtesy, and expressed again his respect for so high a standard of professional conduct as that which the architect displayed. "Sometime maybe I'll be wanting to build something that you'll think is worth while," he suggested genially.

"Thank you," said Stewart, — "if you care to give me another chance. And if you will mention my name to Bennett — "

Mr. Delafield promised as he passed out and left Stewart to the enjoyment of malicious glee. How wrathful Bennett would be to learn that Stewart had contemptuously put aside a hundred thousand dollar job and recommended him for it, — as a fairly competent warehouse architect!

Stewart returned to his work with some unction. But the idea which to his vague apprehension had seemed so promising only led him from one difficulty into a worse, and at the end of a trying afternoon he had nothing more hopeful to gaze upon than his original plans.

Two days later Bennett came over to him as he sat at luncheon in the club.

"I believe I'm indebted to you for a client, Lee," Bennett said. "Mr. Andrew Delafield; he'd gone to you, he told me, but you were too busy or something — with the hospital competition, I presume."

"No, not too busy," Stewart answered. "I told him that warehouses were not in my line and I believed they were in yours; that was all."

"It's true," laughed Bennett; "I never turned up my nose at any kind of a job yet, and never expect to. As it happens, this thing fits in very nicely; we've just about finished our competition drawings and we're quite ready for the next big job. So I'm much obliged; do the same thing for you some time."

Stewart was irritated to find that Bennett could take a thrust with so good a grace. He more than half wished now that he had kept the warehouse for himself, especially as the glimmer of light which had temporarily illumined the hospital plans had faded. It would at least have been something to do in which he could mark progress; and he was feeling the need of this desperately.

The twenty-third of September came and passed; one week was left him in which to meet the practical objections to his plans.

XXIII

FORCING THE ISSUE

IN company with Dr. Edwards, Floyd spent a week in New York, acquainting himself with the requirements of a modern hospital. This was at the end of July. It was the only holiday that he proposed to allow himself. As a holiday, it was not very satisfying; he was so thorough in his investigations that he had not even time to look up the three or four college friends whom he was accustomed to see whenever he visited New York. One day, as he was coming out of St. Luke's, he met Bennett entering. "Hello!" he exclaimed in surprise, and they shook hands.

"I'm hot on the trail," Bennett said. "You see, when there are so many New York men in the competition, a fellow has to meet them on their own ground."

Floyd complimented him on his enterprise and wondered, somewhat anxiously, if Stewart would take similar precautions. It seemed to him improbable. Stewart was a theoretical kind of fellow who was too apt to get his knowledge of practical affairs at second-hand. It occurred to Floyd that when he returned to Avalon he might give Stewart a hint by telling him that Bennett had been inspecting New York hospitals and that it was a sensible proceeding. But he instantly decided that to drop such a hint as this would be unworthy of one who wished to be an impartial judge. Stewart, like the other competitors, must work out his own problems; it was not for one of the judges of the contest to supply him with initiative. Indeed, in his inhospitable frame of mind he would be more than likely to resent any suggestion that Floyd might put forward.

Floyd returned from New York with a definite idea of the needs of a modern hospital. He worked with Dr. Edwards tabulating the results of his inquiries, drawing up notes of matters to be considered in the specifications. These were arranged under the four heads: "Indispensable," "Important," "Desirable," "Small Details." It had pleased Floyd to observe the growth of the doctor's enthusiasm.

"With the money, with such a choice of architects, with such judges — in all due modesty," Dr. Edwards declared, "Avalon ought to have the finest hospitals in the country. And speaking of the judges, you 'll allow me to say, Mr. Halket, that I have never before known a layman who has shown in medical matters such intelligence or taken such pains to inform himself as you have done in this. It 's a pleasure to be associated with you. I confess at first I thought you would probably just make trouble; but you 're a credit to your grandfather, sir."

Floyd was touched by this tribute from the old surgeon. It was one of the few pleasant things that brightened a sad summer. Not only the loneliness of his life in these days oppressed him; there was also the anxiety over an ominous condition at the mills. Almost the first instructions which Floyd in his new capacity as president of the company had sent to the superintendent had included a request for a report on the occupation and circumstances of Tibbs, the man whom Colonel Halket had discharged at the union's request. Learning from Gregg's reply that Tibbs was employed in a rolling-mill in East Liverpool, Ohio, Floyd wrote the old workman a personal letter, offering to reinstate him in his former position and expressing the hope that in spite of what had happened he would feel disposed to return. Tibbs answered the letter in person, and the next day reported to the foreman of his old mill for duty. Three hours later, Tustin and Caskey arrived at the Halket Company's offices in Avalon

FORCING THE ISSUE

and asked to see the president. They pointed out to Floyd the enormity of his offense in restoring a man to the pay-roll who had been dropped by the previous management because he was personally obnoxious to his fellow workmen; and they again demanded Tibbs's discharge. They asserted that sentiment in New Rome concerning this matter had already reached "the boiling-point."

"Very well," Floyd replied. "Let it boil. Some time it will boil away."

Caskey began to threaten, and Floyd rose.

"See here," he said, "if you fellows want to make an issue of this matter and call a strike, you'll find me ready. I don't know any issue on which I'd rather go before the public. Good-day to you."

"But, Mr. Halket," interposed Tustin, "just a moment. There's a difficulty about Tibbs that I think you'll be fair enough to see. Tibbs has been dropped from the union — and as you know, it's been long understood that the works employ only union men."

"The answer to that is easy," said Floyd. "Reinstate him. Now I want to hear nothing more on this matter — from now on."

His tone was as peremptory as his words; and when his visitors did not immediately rise to depart, but sat with stubborn hostility showing in their faces, he pressed a bell. A young woman appeared at the door.

"Miss Rand, I'm ready for dictation," Floyd said, and she entered and stood with her note-book hesitatingly. Floyd stood also in silence, looking down on the two men. After a moment Tustin got to his feet, shrugging his shoulders with a sort of insolent good nature and smiling crookedly.

"Oh, very well," he said, and walked toward the door, Caskey following. At the door Tustin turned for a parting word. "I tell you, Mr. Halket, you take the wrong tone toward us."

Floyd understood a few days later from Gregg that Tibbs had been reinstated in the union and that there seemed to be no sign of trouble.

"It beats me," Gregg said. "Tustin's not the man to knuckle under without a fight."

"I think it's simply that he does n't want to risk a fight on a minor issue," said Floyd. "Now I'll tell you what I'm going to do. I'm going to push him all along the line. I'm going to put one small issue after another up to him, and he's got to swallow one after another, in which case his influence with the men will be slowly undermined, or he's got to make a fight on some one small grievance — and then it will be easy to beat him. I'm going to dethrone Tustin, Mr. Gregg. If Hugh Farrell were running the union it would n't be a bad thing; with Tustin running it, it's a curse. Now the next move I make is this: you know how Tustin and Caskey and the others of that executive committee are always cutting loose from their job to come and interview me with some kick or other, and how they're always paid full time, same as if they were working instead of stirring up trouble? Well, I want you to give it out that hereafter they'll be docked for such absences, just like other men. Post your notices in all the mills, so that all the men can read them; and word them so that all the men will understand. A little public humiliation for Tustin will be a good thing."

The immediate result of posting this notice was another visit to Floyd of an angry delegation, which did not, however, include Tustin; he had sent two other members of the committee, and Floyd received these men genially.

"Well, it may seem a little hard to you at first," he said to them, "but try to look at it a moment from the management's point of view. Why, some of your representatives, notably Mr. Tustin, have got into the way of cooking up complaints just for the sake of having a day

FORCING THE ISSUE 369

off; they keep coming here about all kinds of trivial matters, wasting my time as well as their own, and not doing the cause of the union the least good in the world. Now I don't want to shut off just complaints. But when a man cuts his work to come in here in the interest of the union, why shouldn't I cut his pay, and why shouldn't the union make it up to him? If the union did this, it would also see that he didn't cut his work just for the sake of a holiday; it wouldn't care to pay for such holidays. Don't you think that's a reasonable position for the management to take?"

Two of the men seemed wavering; at least neither of them had any counter argument. The third, who was Caskey, talked incoherently to the effect that the union was poor and the management rich, and that this scheme was just robbing the poor workingman in two ways.

Floyd ignored Caskey and addressed the other two men. "The rule is not designed to work hardship to any one except the chronic kickers," he said. "The union should cooperate with me in discouraging them. I will say, since the remarks have already become somewhat personal, that Mr. Caskey here is precisely one of the men who should be discouraged."

Caskey blinked at him angrily with his little eyes, but said nothing, and after a further unprofitable interchange the delegation withdrew.

Floyd had reasoned rightly that an affront to the executive committee, especially one so well deserved, could not be made to rouse any unanimous or dangerous sentiment in the large body of workmen, however offensive it might be to a few individuals like Tustin and Caskey. But Gregg informed him that at "headquarters" the men were much incensed; "they feel you're looking for trouble, and they're getting ready to give it to you," he said.

"That's exactly the mood I want to have them in," Floyd replied. "They may do something rash, and then we can break the power of that Tustin-Caskey gang once for all. Let me know if you hear of any special kind of trouble being planned."

It was not till the middle of September that Gregg was able to lay specific information before his chief. Then it was to the effect that the local lodge of the union had held a meeting and voted that at the next meeting the name of Hugh Farrell should be dropped from the rolls.

"It was mighty cleverly done," Gregg said. "That man Tustin's a shrewd one; he's got a fine Italian hand that he showed in this. The whole thing was so reluctant; they were very loath to take action — that sort of tone, you know; they'd delayed dealing with the case so that they could approach it in a truly fair and judicial spirit; why, even Farrell's best friends might have been persuaded into thinking he'd got the squarest deal possible. More in sorrow than in anger it was shown that he had n't been truly loyal to the union — his speech at the mass meeting was something that could n't be overlooked — and now that the union was threatened with the subtlest forms of persecution and subject to covert attack from without, it was necessary for its own existence that it should strengthen itself from within. The thing was done with real art — so moderate and so full of innuendo about the purposes of the new management."

"So Farrell's to go," Floyd said. "I suppose of course the news has been broken to him?"

"I understand he was n't at the meeting. But of course he knows."

"I think," Floyd remarked after a moment with a grave smile, "that the time has come for making Farrell foreman of the rod-mill."

Gregg held out his hand and his eyes sparkled with satisfaction. "That's just what I was hoping you might say," and after shaking Floyd's hand he brushed out the prongs of his beard with a sort of nervous contentment. "I don't know that I'm often spoiling for a fight — but

I guess there's considerable of an accumulation in me by now."

"I have an idea that on this matter the fight will come," Floyd replied. "Of course Schneider as foreman is quite unsatisfactory; he has no business in that place, and Farrell has — but we can't expect Tustin and his crowd to admit it. I wish you'd send Farrell to me, Mr. Gregg; it's only fair to give him the chance of declining an unpleasant job if he wants to — but I don't believe he'll want to."

"No," said Gregg. "I'm sure of that."

Hugh Farrell declared himself quite ready to incur whatever odium might attend his exaltation to the position of foreman. Thereupon Floyd sent word to the superintendent of Rod-Mill Number Three to give Schneider his week's notice and to announce that Farrell would go in as foreman on Monday, September twenty-third.

The morning after this announcement was made, Floyd received through the mail the following letter:

MR. FLOYD HALKET:

SIR, — I am venturing to address you in writing, since it seems to be of no good when I visit you in person. I have this A. M. been informed of your orders to put in Mr. Farrell in charge of Number 3. I would say that feeling regarding this matter is already intense, and while deprecating all violence it would seem from opinions expressed by many that it would be safe for Mr. Farrell not to accept such position but to retire permanently from the works. Have so advised him and would be pleased to have your cooperation in the matter. If appointment is adhered to, it will of course be necessary to call all employees of the works out on strike. Trusting the above meets with your approval, I remain,

Very respectfully yours,
SAM'L TUSTIN,
President Chap. 4, A. I. W.

To this Floyd dictated an immediate answer:

Mr. Sam'l Tustin,
   President Chap. 4, A. I. W.

Sir, — In reply to your communication just received, let me say that any interference with Mr. Hugh Farrell, either in the discharge of his duties or in the exercise of his rights outside the works, will be promptly and properly punished. Should a general strike be ordered, as you threaten, *or should the management for any reason find it necessary to declare a lock-out*, no workman will be readmitted to employment at the Halket Mills so long as he remains a member of a union.

Very truly yours,
Floyd Halket,
President Halket Steel Company.

Gregg telephoned that night to Floyd that in New Rome the feeling was indeed, as Tustin had expressed it, intense. The news had been spread among the men with surprising rapidity that the management was to make a fight for the extermination of the union. A mass meeting had been called for the next night.

"All right," Floyd answered. "Keep yourself as clear of trouble as you can, Gregg. Put the opprobrium for Farrell's promotion on me — and any other trouble that comes up. Are they doing things to Farrell?"

"A crowd followed him and jeered him all the way home this evening. He's not having a pleasant time."

"Any signs of his backing out?"

"Oh, you bet, no!"

"Be ready to have all the men paid off at a moment's notice. I'll be out in the morning. Telephone me if anything turns up."

Floyd's visit to New Rome the next day convinced him that there was nothing for him to do but stand by his declaration to Tustin and await developments.

"It's pretty rough on Hugh Farrell to have put him into such a position," he admitted to the superintendent. "But I don't know anybody who could give a better account of himself."

"Yes," said Gregg. "And it isn't as if he stood absolutely alone; he's got plenty of sympathizers — if they only dared to show themselves. I don't know, Mr. Halket, but what some damage may be done at that mass meeting to-night."

"I don't know that the men can do any more than decide to go on strike," Floyd said.

"That's bad enough with all the orders we're working to fill."

"We've got to make some sacrifices, of course, to get this union matter settled as we want it. And we might as well make them now as later. I'd like to go up and see Mrs. Farrell — see if there's anything I could do to make things easier for her — but I suppose it wouldn't be wise."

"Look too much like favoritism," commented Gregg. "They think it's all that now. Better just write her a note. And I'll call you up to-night again and let you know what happens at the meeting."

The report of this did not indicate a yielding disposition on the part of the men. Whether the promotion of Farrell had at first been universally unpopular or not, it seemed now to have become so. Tustin, who had a native gift for forcible speaking and enjoyed using it, inflamed his audience; he swung them from fury to enthusiasm and back again to fury. He urged them to do nothing lawless, and yet to think upon this traitor who had grown up among them and who now had been bought to make an issue for a harsh employer against the union. This man, whose expressed disloyalty had been treated with so much indulgence by his comrades, had stooped to an even lower betrayal of their interests; no one knew by what intrigue he had undermined a faithful old employee, by what cowardly subservience and abasement he had won his master's favor. It was an insult to the workmen in Number Three to put such a man over them; it was an insult that every brother workman in New Rome was bound to resent. It was indeed a matter of self-protection to resent it. For however much favoritism there was in Farrell's promotion, it was folly to pretend that it was due to favoritism alone. This was the first step in a campaign to root out unionism in New Rome, to make the laboring-man a defenseless dependent upon the generosity of an ungenerous employer, to rob him of the bulwark of his rights, the sense of freedom, the feeling that instead of writhing naked and helpless in the clutch of a cormorant capitalist, he stood armed by the weight of thousands at his back to battle for a living. The union had given to the laboring-man this most priceless spirit, and the laboring-man must guard the union as he would guard his soul. And when he beheld one who had traduced and betrayed it, — "I ask ye," shouted Tustin, raising aloft his clenched fist and holding it there quivering, — "I ask ye, shall ye suffer him? Shall ye suffer him to be your master? I advocate no violence, but I say to you now that this man should be made to see that to his neighbors he is a curse and a stench, and that in the estimation of the world he were better dead than thriving at the expense of their liberty. And if he is so rash as not to be deterred by that which he may read in the face of every man, then we must strike, — strike for the principle that gives us life, and strike — hard!"

It was a great triumph for Tustin; the meeting had broken up in cheers, the men had poured shouting and cheering into the streets. Some one had cried, "Let's show Farrell now, the — — —!" and a couple of hundred men and boys, taking up the cry, had marched to Farrell's house on the outskirts of the town. There they had stayed in the middle of the road, hooting and yelling and cursing, calling on him to show himself; at last some

FORCING THE ISSUE

one had thrown a stone, breaking a window. Letty had opened the door and with the light from within streaming upon her confronted the mob. After a few cries they quieted down and she said in a voice tremulous with indignation, —

"My husband is not at home. You — "

"Where is he?" demanded voices in the crowd.

"You are frightening my little children and my mother," Letty said; and at that some one jeered, —

"How about yourself?"

There was a laugh, and when it quieted down, Letty answered in her clear voice, —

"If you were brave men, I shouldn't be frightened. But I don't know what cowards may do."

The remark called forth an inarticulate cry of protest. Letty followed up her advantage.

"Will you please go away so that I can put my children to sleep?"

"We ain't hurting anybody's children," some one made sullen answer; and then there were exclamations, "Come on, fellows," "He ain't here," "Let her be." Gradually the crowd dispersed.

But the next afternoon Letty came in to the Avalon offices of the Halket Company and called on Floyd. She was agitated and determined and she wasted no time in stating her purpose.

"Mr. Halket," she said, "I know you thought you were doing Hugh and me a kindness. But I've got to ask you not to let Hugh have that promotion. Something will happen to him. I dread having him out of the house; there is such a feeling against him. It's against all of us. My little boy was called 'Scab' to-day by the neighbor's child — five years old. 'Scab! Scab!' she called at him across the fence. Down at the grocer's they don't like to wait on me. I don't mind that — but " — her eyes filled with tears and her face colored sensitively, — "oh, Mr. Halket, they're working up an awful feeling against

Hugh. And if it comes to putting him in as foreman, there will be a riot; I know there will be — and he'll be killed!"

"What does Hugh think about it? Does he want to give it up?" Floyd asked.

"Oh, Hugh! You know what Hugh is, Mr. Halket; I've begged him, but he won't give in. He keeps saying there's no danger, and even if there is, he's not going to let it worry him; he says he's not going to be browbeaten out of his job by every man in New Rome. Of course Hugh wouldn't give up." She declared this proudly in spite of her distress. "But, Mr. Halket, I don't believe you know — if you insist on putting Hugh in as foreman — the morning he goes to his work — they'll beat him to death!"

"The only chance that your husband has now, Letty, lies in our wiping out the union and the gang who are running it," Floyd answered soberly. "What sort of a life do you think that you and he will lead if we surrender in this matter? He's a marked man anyway. You will all of you have to leave New Rome — where you've built your house, where you have begun to see good things ahead of you. If we fight it out — yes, I admit there's danger. I don't believe it can actually come to what you dread — but it may be bad enough. Fighting it out, our side will win in the end, — I promise you that. If we give in — what is there for Hugh but to seek a new home and a new start in life?"

"There's life!" cried Letty passionately.

Floyd was silent. At last he said with a smile, —

"Letty, we won't run that risk. We won't put Hugh in as foreman until the men are ready to have him. But we'll try to hurry that time up in coming."

She did not understand at all what he meant, but she trusted the look in his face and thanked him.

The next morning the employees of the Halket Mills on their way to work were confronted at the bridge by

FORCING THE ISSUE

locked gates and the notice, "Closed. These mills will run hereafter non-union. Employees may sign at the company's offices on that basis. Until a sufficient operating force is secured, the works will remain closed."

After the first stupefaction created by this placard, most of the men turned away laughing, rejoicing in an unexpected holiday.

This was the twenty-third of September.

XXIV

A LETTER TO A NEWSPAPER

ON the morning of September twenty-fourth Stewart Lee called his draughtsmen and assistants into his private office and announced to them that the plans for the Hospitals would be submitted in their original form without further delay.

"You have all been very faithful and earnest in working over this matter," he said to them, "and you've done your best to remedy some impossible conditions." He smiled cheerfully; his serenity and good humor in making this premature confession of defeat bewildered his men. They had attributed to his entire absorption in the competition the impatience, sharpness, and ill temper which had this summer made him a hard taskmaster. Only the day before he had given them some fresh instructions to carry out and had been insistent on improving certain details over which they had all long ago despaired. Now he vouchsafed no explanation for this sudden smiling abandonment of the purpose to which he had apparently dedicated himself.

"I want to thank you all," he continued, "and I think after the way we've been working ourselves to death we'd better declare a holiday. And if you'd each of you do me the favor to take one of these envelopes," — he passed them round as he spoke, — "maybe you draw a prize, maybe you draw a blank. Life's a lottery."

By his manner and by some subtle quality of charm he had the power to win back in a moment the affections of men whom he had gradually been alienating for a year. They tried awkwardly to express their appreciation of his

A LETTER TO A NEWSPAPER

kindness and their hope that the drawings would receive the award.

"It won't be your fault if they don't," Stewart answered. "But I shan't be disappointed however the judges decide."

Stewart paced up and down his small room after the office force had departed on their holiday. He was brimming with a generous excitement, an unselfish indignation. In a good cause he had sacrificed the last days in which he might have found the solution to the hospital problems for which he had been fumbling. It was a generous thought; it was a generous thought that possessed him for a moment now—those boys starting out on their sudden holiday, opening in the street their little envelopes and finding the fifty dollar bill that was his gift to each. He could imagine their delighted amazement; he knew they had never expected any such warm-hearted and lavish reward of their impotent efforts. He gave himself a moment's gratification in contrasting his treatment of his men with that which the employees of the Halket Steel Company received.

The night before, when he had gone to the club to dine, he had read in the *Evening Telegram* of the lock-out at the Halket Mills. Hitherto he had scanned with little interest the occasional newspaper reports of the friction existing between the men and the management at New Rome; they had seemed to concern trivial and technical matters. But the news of "LOCK-OUT!" spread sensationally upon the first page of the newspaper at once absorbed him. The article recited various small matters of dispute between the union and the management and stated that the notice posted on the gate that morning was merely the culmination of a purpose which Mr. Floyd Halket, since his accession to the presidency of the company, had been steadily working to achieve. The *Telegram* was an ardent champion of the workingman; its history of the causes which had led up to the clash at New Rome was unfavorable to Floyd. It represented him as a cold-blooded and deliberate young man who looked upon his vast inheritance as a profitable field to be more thoroughly exploited. The *Telegram* had always railed at Colonel Halket, but now it extolled him; with all his faults he had — up to the time of his last great mistake, which was no doubt attributable to old age — held the affection of his people and striven to benefit them as well as to enrich himself. Since his death, however, the management had ceased to have such a twofold aim. It had wantonly provoked and antagonized the leaders among the men, — for the sake, perhaps, of showing that its iron hand wore no velvet glove. To invite and then to crush opposition had been its policy. And now it had cynically flung aside all pretense and revealed its ultimate purpose — to reduce its workmen to their former position of helpless dependence, to deny them the right to organize in defense of their interests and in defiance of unjust oppression. The new head of the company, with a rashness appropriate to his youth, had committed the unprecedented act of closing down the mills and declaring a lock-out when there was no vital principle at issue — at the most nothing but small differences which could be settled amicably by fair-minded discussion. He had chosen to set up an ultimatum which meant a return to mediævalism, and he was trying to starve his people into surrender.

The newspaper report and the editorial comment set Stewart aflame. There were two manufacturers dining at the club that evening; they happened to be men whose interests had been adversely affected by the union uprising at New Rome and the consequent failure of the great merger which Colonel Halket had planned. Stewart sought an opinion from them, and when they replied that it was a pretty bold move on Halket's part, but that they hoped he would win, Stewart expressed his disapproval of such sentiments. He declared that old friend as he was of Floyd's, he could not sympathize with him in this high-

A LETTER TO A NEWSPAPER

handed and tyrannical proceeding. One of the ironmasters asked him if he knew anything about the facts of the case, and Stewart replied that no facts could justify the measure which Floyd had taken. It was an offense to civilization; it was revolting to the spirit of liberty. The manufacturers resented Stewart's instructive utterances, and there was an acrimonious debate. They refused to accept Stewart's assertion that Avalon was one of the most benighted places in the country and that its capitalists and not its laboring classes needed education. In argument Stewart's manner was never persuasive, but if his eloquence usually failed to convince others, it always gave intense satisfaction to his own convictions. His designation now of the Avalon capitalists as "satraps" struck him as particularly happy, and he harped upon it to the increasing irritation of the two gentlemen whom he thus classified. They assured him after a time with emphasis that he was talking nonsense and intimated that he was the sort of person who might naturally be expected to talk nonsense.

Stewart went home with his mind stimulated and his passions and emotions roused. Since the scurrilous criticism of his pictures, he had never had much sympathy with the point of view maintained by the editor of the *Telegram*, but he congratulated himself on being broad-minded enough not to let either his personal grievance or his personal friendship influence his judgment. The fact that the *Telegram* had once been unjustly abusive of him could not invalidate to his impartial mind the justice with which it censured Floyd. And such championship as Floyd had received that evening from his fellow manufacturers only made his offense the more glaring. Stewart confessed that he was at last beginning to perceive and appreciate the underlying traits in his friend's character. The qualities and motives which Floyd was displaying in these relations with his men were, as Stewart now saw with entire clearness, precisely those which had governed his actions as trustee for the Rebecca Halket Hospitals. There was in Floyd a ruthless, unscrupulous hardness of character, an insensitiveness of disposition, a view of other men, even friends and dependents, as merely impersonal agents to be used and cast aside, a disregard of all the claims to which a man of sympathy and kindness would be most responsive. The men of New Rome were suffering now at Floyd's hands as Stewart himself had suffered — locked out, deprived of their rights, hampered and cramped in their effort, denied the recognition for which they had striven and to which, no doubt, they were entitled.

The triumphant clear-headedness of this analysis brought Stewart into sudden contemplation of a course of action. The impulse with which he had painted the pictures of Labor was revived, the sympathy which Floyd so reprehensibly lacked grew once more incandescent in his soul. Here in Avalon, where the sinister influences of pride and avarice and lust of power prevailed in detestable completeness, there was a noble work for a man who had wealth and education and the high purpose of a gentleman, and who dared for the right to demolish the idols of his friends.

In the excitement of the thought Stewart paced up and down his room, and at last threw open the window and, leaning out, looked across his lawn on which shone the soft September moon. The cool night air, instead of chilling his enthusiasm, seemed to give it calmness and confidence, the lights of the city throbbing in the distance were responsive to the throbbing eagerness in his breast. He leaned upon the window-sill and thought quite gloriously. To throw himself into this contest would compel renunciation of old ambitions and friendships. The men who had been his clients would turn from an architect who had gone outside of his profession to fight for freedom. What was chivalrous they would regard as unsafe, unbalanced, possibly even criminal. In the further practice of his profession he would be doomed. He could not even retire from it leaving as his last contribution one magnificent achievement to mark his premature withdrawal as deplorable; for even though his plans should be worthy to win the Hospital Competition, Floyd, whom he would be attacking, could hardly allow him the prize. Floyd would be sure to find out before making the award which drawings Stewart had submitted — with no idea of being prejudiced, of course, but the prejudice would be inevitable. Reflecting upon this, Stewart could not help feeling that, in spite of all his despair, his drawings would, under normal conditions, have a good chance of winning, and that by taking the step that must insure defeat he would be doubly a martyr. The thought did not deter him; it fortified him to remember that without the element of personal sacrifice sympathy is futile. The friends that he had made in Avalon were all men whose selfish interests ran parallel with Floyd's. Stewart realized that he would alienate them all if he espoused the workingmen's cause. Well, these friends, though pleasant, had done little for him; they had been indifferent to his work, his talents, his ambition, and he could deny himself their indolent regard. For the same reason it would not be difficult, with his versatility, to give up his profession. Stewart could work with energy and enthusiasm so long as he was receiving applause for that which he produced, but when the applause ceased, the impulse to produce languished. Applause for his architectural achievement had long since passed. Now there began to glimmer for him the light of a kinder, more adoring, more alluring appreciation, which should burn in the hearts of the humble and inspire him to unselfish labor. How great was the need in Avalon of a champion for the workingman, one who would come down from among capitalists and employers to defend the poor and to assist their inarticulate speech! How warmly would such a champion be welcomed!

He kept his wife and her probable sentiments on this matter out of his thoughts.

His resolve was made irrevocably while he stood at the window. Already he was forecasting for himself a brilliant and useful service; he could act as advocate for the workingmen in the newspapers, he would not even shrink from going upon the platform in their behalf, he would give them the benefit of his experience, education, and counsel. Tustin, whose portrait he had once painted, and who, as Stewart had read in the newspapers, was chairman of the executive committee of the union, would of course gladly furnish him with all the specific data for argument. Stewart's imagination, grasping hastily one possibility after another, carried him far afield. He was conscious of a power to express himself in burning words, whether on paper or in speech; once let him gain the ear of the people, and they would be glad to listen. Dreaded by the benighted satraps with whom he had once consorted, beloved by the common people for whom his sympathy had always been deep and tender, though hitherto undemonstrative, ready speaker, wise thinker, public-spirited man, he might eventually be caught up in popular enthusiasm and raised to high office; the city was some time to be purged of gross corruption; if he fought ably for the people now, he might be chosen mayor to do this greater work. The incubus of despair that had lain upon him for the last two months was lifted.

He wrote and mailed that evening a brief letter to Floyd. "I have followed with unhappiness the course of affairs at New Rome. Our long intimacy and the leaning that I should naturally have to your side in the dispute cannot make me ignore what now appears the fundamental fact — that you are using compulsion to deprive American citizens of the rights of liberty and citizenship. When a man reaches such a conviction as I have now reached, it becomes his imperative duty to support those whose rights are being attacked, even though in so doing he opposes one who has long been his friend and to whom he owes much. It is his duty as an American. I have

A LETTER TO A NEWSPAPER

made up my mind, therefore, to offer my services to the men whom you have locked out of employment. Anything that I can do to create a better understanding of their cause and a more active sympathy with the principles for which they stand, I shall do. It may be unreasonable for me to hope that a decision so impartial as this at which I have arrived may not impair our friendship: nevertheless I entertain that hope."

To this letter, dated the twenty-third of September, Floyd sent an immediate reply:

"Dear Stewart: Your judgment upon my affairs seems to me as prompt as it is impartial. Should you require any knowledge of facts in the campaign upon which you are entering, I shall be glad to assist you to it; and in doing this I trust that I may show an impartiality equal to your own."

Stewart puzzled over this note a good deal. He had never known Floyd to indulge in sarcasm, but he felt uneasily that Floyd was sarcastic now, and in that case he wished of course to hit back. The fact that Floyd ignored the studiously offered olive branch indicated a soreness of spirit with which sarcasm might be allied.

By the time that Floyd's note reached him, however, Stewart had had a conference with Tustin; and he decided that personal vengeance for the slur might as well await the first public opportunity — especially as this was not to be delayed. Tustin had furnished him with facts and arguments and desired him to lose no time in writing letters to the newspapers. The gratitude with which the union leader had welcomed so distinguished an accession to the cause pleased Stewart, and he made ready to throw all his energy into the ennobling, self-sacrificing work.

The holiday which he had granted to his draughtsmen he did not himself devote to pleasure. From his interview with Tustin he returned late in the afternoon to his office, and there he began the composition of the first document in the campaign. It was to be a letter to the *Eagle*, the most influential newspaper in Avalon. Stewart's mind, when its interest in a subject had been awakened, worked quickly; on the trip in to Avalon from New Rome he had systematized the notes which Tustin had given him, and after the first fumbling round for an effective introduction, his pen was scampering across the paper. It was a facile and intemperate pen.

He explained that the situation at New Rome was a matter of public concern and that one not associated with either party to the dispute was therefore justified in discussing it publicly. He exploited his friendship with Floyd in order to make his attitude of opposition the more damaging. As for argument, he declared that it was not now essential to take up the question of closed or open shop, though he would discuss that at some future time. For the present time it was sufficient to inquire into the actual incidents that had led up to this situation and from them to determine if the employer had not been a deliberate aggressor whose acts of injury had finally culminated in this attempt to make his workingmen relinquish a right that had never been in dispute. The appointment of a foreman whose personality was offensive to every workman in the mill was a malicious affront; the closing down of the entire plant because of the resentment expressed over this affront was a measure as tyrannical as it was drastic. If public opinion could in any way liberate workingmen from the harsh coercion of such acts, public opinion should be roused. This was the gist of Stewart's first letter to the *Eagle*.

In the editorial column of the issue in which it appeared, there was printed a sharp reply. "As is well known to many," wrote the editor, " no one has less reason for making an unwarranted attack upon Mr. Floyd Halket than the gentleman whose communication is published on this page. Yet his attack is as unwarranted as it is ungenerous. There is not one of his assertions that may pass unchallenged." The editor took up Stewart's

A LETTER TO A NEWSPAPER

charges in detail and refuted them by demonstrating that so far as there had been any coercion, it had proceeded from the leaders of the union, and that the closing down of the mills was due to a humane desire to prevent the violence that had been threatened. The editor concluded by expressing amazement that one gentleman should see fit to attack another publicly upon a matter that could not possibly be construed as of public concern.

Stewart was embittered by this rough rebuke, particularly by the allusion to the ingratitude of his criticism. The arguments which the editor cited did not disturb him; they were based, he knew, upon an inaccurate statement of facts. Tustin's whole account of the trouble had been logical and conclusive enough, and it supported the editor in not one particular. Stewart felt that he would not have resented a proper statement of a differing view; he would merely have set about correcting it. But that his old obligation to Floyd should be thus publicly commented on to his disadvantage appeared to him an insufferable impertinence. It was with such trivialities and irrelevancies that an unprincipled writer would bolster up a weak cause. He reflected that he must endure unfair treatment from the *Eagle*, which was a bigoted newspaper conducted in the interests of the capitalist class — subsidized, no doubt, by the satraps. Criticise him as it pleased, it should hear from him as long as it would print his letters, and he set to work at once upon a second communication, amplifying and repeating his charges.

At noon he went to the club for luncheon; as he entered the reading-room he saw Floyd there, with his hat on, leaning against the mantel-piece and talking to two men who sat in arm-chairs before him. Floyd glanced at Stewart and then nodded with an easy, careless smile. There was no particular sign of invitation in the recognition, and Stewart hesitated a moment; then he decided that he would show there was no hard feeling and he advanced casually, as he would have done at any time, to join the group. Floyd finished in haste what he was saying, turning his back upon Stewart as he did so; then without a glance at either side he walked swiftly away and out of the door. The two men sitting in the armchairs were the manufacturers with whom Stewart had had the discussion a few nights before; one of them now raised a newspaper and began to read, and the other smoked a cigar, apparently lost in reverie. Stewart stood by the mantel-piece for a few moments, that they might have an opportunity to recognize his presence, but as they did not choose to avail themselves of it he finally turned and strolled away without a word. In another part of the room Bennett was sitting, and as Stewart passed near him he looked up and said with the furtive smile that Stewart disliked, —

"That was quite a strong letter of yours in the paper, Lee. But are n't you pretty reckless, doing a thing like that at just this time?"

"I suppose it is to be a fairly adjudged competition," Stewart replied coldly. "And even if I did not suppose so — it may surprise you to know, Mr. Bennett, that I don't always stop to count the cost."

"Ah," said Bennett, dropping his eyes again to his magazine, "that's a bit of wisdom that you will learn with age."

In the dining-room Stewart sat down alone at a table by the window. Two or three of his acquaintances entered within the next few minutes, but none of them seemed to notice his signal inviting them to join him; they went blundering round to lonely and remote tables. Then Bob Dunbar appeared, and Stewart, who detested a solitary meal, beckoned to him in a manner that could not be ignored. Dunbar came up reluctantly with a solemn face.

"Sit down, Bob," said Stewart.

Dunbar hesitated. "I will — for a moment. No, I won't order lunch." He waved the waiter aside and sat

A LETTER TO A NEWSPAPER 389

in a grave silence. Then he began, choosing his words slowly and looking directly into Stewart's face: "That letter of yours in the *Eagle* this morning shocked me very much. I was in the boat that day — it's a good many years ago now — but I remember it if you do not, Stewart. And every one in this place who knows what Floyd Halket did for you that day thinks, as I do, that that letter of yours was a damned — caddish — performance. And I advise you to apologize and retract."

He thrust his chair back from the table and rose, leaving Stewart transfixed, speechless, flushed to the temples with the hot blood of anger and wounded pride. Dunbar was passing out of the dining-room door when Stewart, trailing a napkin in one hand, overtook him and seized him roughly by the arm.

"If — if you throw that day up in my face again!" he said passionately though in a low voice; his nostrils quivered and he spoke as if he had been running a long way instead of merely walking the length of the dining-room. "I've tried to square accounts — no one knows that better than Floyd. I'll have no criticism — I'll allow no reminder — of that thing. I'm answerable to my own conscience — to no one else. And let me tell you now — I will retract nothing."

Dunbar looked at him and said in an unmoved voice, —

"If you do not retract, the impression will remain — that you are a cad."

"Then," said Stewart hotly, "I am done with those who share that impression — even though they are my wife's cousins."

He turned his back on Dunbar and walked slowly to his table. In his pride and anger he could disguise the fact, but he was hard hit; he had been called a cad, and as a cad he was being avoided now by members of his own club. It was too laughable — that these upstart parvenus should apply that term to him who came of as good blood as there was in America. What a guild of greed it was in this town! Sink the small personal equation in the large interests of humanity, touch reprovingly the pocket that had been unrighteously filled — and how the whole pack was upon one, frightened for its privileges, yelling Cad! Cad! But even with his lofty recognition of the ludicrous behavior of these people, Stewart could not be wholly indifferent to their coldness; he desired always the respect of those whom he despised. In spite of the evidence that he had already had, he could not believe that he was regarded by many persons as the opprobrious creature of Bob Dunbar's definition; and without lingering over his luncheon, he passed slowly through the club, pausing to test each man whom he met. He felt in every case a lack of cordiality. Dunbar had hardly overstated the facts; Stewart's letter was everywhere the topic of discussion; those who had read it had been showing it to those who had not, and there was but one opinion as to the propriety of the performance.

It was not only in the club that Stewart was made aware of the altered sentiment with which those who had been his friends regarded him. He received some letters that seemed to him offensively pragmatical and officious; his manner grew less and less conciliatory. His second letter was published in the *Eagle* — under a sneering title of the editor's own application; Stewart began now to take a grim satisfaction in the odds that were against him. There was nothing nobler than to wage a fight for a principle at the expense of one's personal associations and ambitions; and if Stewart's first devotion of himself to the cause had not included crucifixion for caddishness, he soon was ready to push self-sacrifice even beyond that extreme. For though the wound was sore, the compensation for it was immediate. He had but to go on that first afternoon from the inhospitable club to the headquarters of the executive committee at New Rome to be assured of his true value. There indeed his services were appreciated. Stewart began to see that it is the judgment of the common people that is most to be prized, that is sane, normal, unshaken by the gusts of passion and prejudice. It took him not more than a day to become the most radical of advocates. He placed himself willfully and definitely in opposition to all in which the men who were thinking him a cad believed. And even while doing this he never imagined that a social blight would rest upon him permanently or that he might actually have to turn for his familiar friends to men like Tustin and Caskey. He had no doubt whatever that when he chose and when he had taught his bigoted old associates their lesson he could reassume the place in the community which as a true aristocrat he had occupied. For the time being, however, he was contented to show his independence of friendship and disapprobation by avoiding the club, the principal centre of both.

He had written his wife nothing of his new activity; a letter to her on such a subject would be too stupidly economic, and the explanation might better be delayed until he could see her. Besides he suspected that she would be distressed by the polemical character of the affair, and he wished to spare himself the irritation which he would feel if she indulged in hasty and unwarranted criticism. She had an unbecoming confidence in Floyd.

The reckoning, however, was not to be so easily deferred. Two days after the appearance of Stewart's second communication in the *Eagle*, he received a telegram from Lydia announcing that she was coming home at once and would arrive in Avalon late the next afternoon. Stewart was annoyed. She had taken the precaution to insert in the dispatch the words " All well," and therefore it could not be sudden illness, either of herself or of the baby, that was bringing her back to Avalon a month earlier than she had planned to come. It required no great subtlety of mind to guess the reason. Undoubtedly she had been reading, even in Chester, the Avalon *Eagle*.

Stewart loved his wife, and in spite of the disagreeable presumption that she was hastening home to rebuke him, he could not help viewing complacently the increased comfort and happiness that would be his after he had set her right with a few forbearing words. His enforced isolation had worn upon him, for his social instincts were strong and had been pampered. Consequently he was prepared to reply to Lydia's reproaches in a spirit of moderation, if not concession.

When he met her leaving the train, her behavior filled him with gratified surprise. The sweetness and radiance of the face that he stooped to kiss were unclouded by reproach; her first words, "See, Stewart, see how he's grown," as she caused him to bend over the baby in the nurse's arms, proceeded from a mind that was concerned with nothing outside of her own little family. When he asked her why she had decided to come home so abruptly, she answered, —

"I wanted to see you, Stewart; I thought it was about time you were needing me. Weren't you, really? I shall be disappointed if you say no."

He assured her of course that he was in the most desperate need of her. It was not until late that evening that Lydia touched gently upon the subject about which she had allayed suspicion. She said, —

"You've never written me about the plans — whether you got them done to your satisfaction. Friday's the last day, isn't it?"

"Yes. They've been handed in," Stewart answered. "They're done to my satisfaction — but not, I am sure, to the committee's."

"Ah, that's a pity — but we'll hope for the best anyway. Floyd seems to be having some trouble at his mills; do you suppose that will delay the award?"

"Probably not." Stewart glanced at her sharply. "He's shut his mills down; he ought to have more leisure — for all kinds of amateur dabbling."

A LETTER TO A NEWSPAPER

There was a short interval of silence.

"You — you don't approve of the way Floyd's acting?" Lydia ventured. "I've seen the *Eagle* — but I didn't quite understand —"

"No, I don't approve," Stewart said warmly. "He's trying to coerce his men. What's he done? There was a fellow working there that none of the men would have anything to do with — that kind of a man — his fellow workmen would have nothing to do with him, mind you, — and Floyd, to provoke a row with the union, which he wants to put out of business, insults them by making this fellow a foreman. That seems a small affair, but it's only one of many. And when the men, whose patience was about exhausted, protested and showed signs of fight, Floyd calmly shuts down the works and announces he'll starve them out. What kind of treatment is that for a civilized employer to be giving his men?"

"It doesn't seem like Floyd," Lydia said.

"Seem like him or not, that's what he's done."

"Well, even if it is — I couldn't help being sorry, Stewart, that you felt it necessary to write about him as you did."

"It certainly was not a pleasure to me to write in that way. I wish with all my heart that it had been any one else but Floyd. But when you have followed the course of events and heard of them from men who have actually suffered because he has been infected with the extortionate, intolerant, rapacious greed of power that is epidemic in this town — you have to speak, — if you're a man with a conscience. You've got to open the eyes of the people to the truth, you've got to awaken a sentiment that will prevent abuse of power. I knew what it would mean to me if I attacked Floyd. I counted the cost. It has been an expensive matter — as I expected it to be. I have lost the friendship of a great many men — I fear I have lost that of Floyd himself. If you think it took no courage and no self-sacrifice to face that result —"

"Oh, I'm not questioning your courage, dear, or even your self-sacrifice," Lydia interrupted. "But was — was it necessary for you — couldn't you have left it to some one else — and — and perhaps Floyd has his side, too —"

"It was a matter of common humanity to put the facts before the public and awaken a feeling which should make a repetition of such methods impossible," declared Stewart. "I realized this, I felt the necessity; would you have had me be a coward and shirk so great a duty for personal reasons? As to Floyd having a defense — I did nothing, I wrote nothing without first making investigation. It is not Floyd that I am condemning — it is the spirit of absolutism which is so dangerous in this place and which he exemplifies. As for myself, I did not begin the crusade rashly. It is due to my inheritance, I suppose, that I must take up public responsibility when it is placed before me. My family, as far back as I can trace it, has always been identified with some public cause. The necessity for abandoning ourselves to the occasion when the occasion arises, no matter what the cost, seems to be in our blood — and I confess I am rather proud of it."

"I — smaller things mean more to me," said Lydia, somewhat sadly. "Is this affair of Floyd's a public cause, Stewart?"

"It is a manifestation of a tendency that is publicly dangerous — a tendency against which the people need to be educated. I don't mean to stop the work of education when this one trouble has been settled. I shall keep on — writing and speaking perhaps — advocating in every way I can a freer life, a greater consideration for workingmen, a more rigid check upon employers. The very fact that I am not of the workingmen's class, that I'm identified by all my associations with the employer's class, will give strength to my arguments. A man in my position is needed to lead in such a campaign. The subject is one that I've studied a long time. — You remember how interested I was in painting those pictures to show the

A LETTER TO A NEWSPAPER

misery of Labor? This work is only carrying on the same idea."

"But," said Lydia, bewildered, "architecture — your architecture, Stewart — "

"I shall probably keep on doing what I can. But, whether the buildings are ever built or not, I've done, in the Hospitals, my best work. I've got up to a height that I know, inside me, I can never rise above. Here is a new thing that is more important, that interests me beyond anything else; and I feel that I have a useful message to give; I don't see why the fact that I started in as an architect should prevent my uttering it. I've gone so far now that the people who build houses aren't likely any more to come to me as clients. I counted that in as part of the cost. I'm satisfied with what is ahead of me — satisfied and eager to be at it — and it's a greater work, if once it can be done, than building all the churches and hospitals in Avalon."

Lydia remained bewildered, unable to reply. She had come home prepared to deal with a far less comprehensive and humanitarian programme; this case was beyond her simple treatment. She could not approve, she could not believe, she could not sympathize in what Stewart so vaguely planned to do; but she knew not how to interfere. And as she sat wondering what should be a wife's course, a memory came to her unsummoned out of the distant past — of herself wantonly, gayly reaching out from a boat with an oar and pushing a confused swimmer down.

She remained silent.

XXV

INTERLUDE

THE fifteen mill superintendents of the Halket Company, the general superintendent, and the president of the company had sat two hours in conference; the meeting was nearly at an end, and Floyd was summing up his final instructions.

"The main thing for us to remember," he concluded, "is to stand firm, but not to be aggressive. Let all your foremen know and through them try to spread the information that we don't contemplate bringing in strike-breakers or outsiders to start the mills. Make them see that we mean to look after all our old men and keep their places for them whenever they get ready to return to work. But let them know, too, that we're prepared to remain idle for a year, if need be, and incur any amount of loss rather than yield one of the points on which we've been insisting. You might intimate also that if any man chooses to return to work, he shall have the special protection of the management, and that any attempt to prevent him will only call out special efforts for his protection. I want to carry this matter through without any violence. No doubt the shut-down will be protracted, and very likely I could hurry matters to a crisis and compel an early surrender by bringing in new men. But that I will not do. There has been enough bitterness of feeling roused already, and there must be no step taken that may endanger a single life."

"We're to give it out, Mr. Halket, that we will take back the mischief-makers — Tustin, Caskey, and so on?" asked one of the superintendents reluctantly.

"Yes, even them. But we'll discriminate against them to this extent, it will be understood that they return upon sufferance, and that immediate discharge will be the penalty for any further agitation. Tustin's a man of ability, and if he would take hold the right way instead of the wrong, he could make himself very useful here; I'm willing that he should have another chance."

"Well," said the superintendent who had before spoken, "I look on Tustin as a good deal of a sow's ear myself."

There was a laugh in which Floyd joined. "Even so," he said tolerantly, "maybe we can sometime induce him to suffer a sea-change into something new and strange."

"The only way you can do that," retorted the superintendent, "is by putting him first at the bottom of the sea."

"You wait," said Floyd. "We'll make a leather pocket-book out of him yet."

"All right — so long as we don't fill it with banknotes," answered the superintendent, and the conference broke up in laughter. It had leaked out that the week before a walking delegate who had threatened to call a strike at some steel works in Avalon had been bought off by the manufacturer.

Among the superintendents and heads of departments there had grown up a genuine admiration for Floyd; they liked him and had confidence in him, and after the too indulgent policy that had for so long existed in the mills, they found his firm control invigorating. They were themselves all picked men, loyal and devoted to the company's service, privileged to comment and criticise, accustomed to show a good grace if overruled. Floyd for his part usually came away from the weekly conference with them in a better humor than that in which he had gone to it.

Now, after the others had all left the room, Floyd and Gregg remained.

"There are one or two small matters that I want to arrange with you, Mr. Gregg," Floyd said. "There's the case of Tibbs, for instance. He must be thinking I've done him a poor service to bring him on here from East Liverpool, where he had a good job, and then lock him out of the mills. I want you to see that his wages are continued as long as this trouble lasts. And see that the same is done for Farrell. Neither of those men is likely to participate to any large extent in the strike benefits of the union — and I feel it's the company's duty to take care of them."

"Yes, I'll attend to that," Gregg answered. "They'll have judgment enough, I suppose, not to talk about it."

"The other thing," Floyd said, with a faint smile, "is this. Unless you object very strongly, I'm going to give myself a three days' leave of absence."

"I don't see why not. Things here are quiet enough; there's not likely to be anything urgent very soon."

"That's what I think. And I have a matter up in New Hampshire that I want to attend to. I can leave to-night and get back Friday morning — only three days away. So if you're willing, I'll go."

"Yes, indeed — good thing for you. When you come back, you'll find us standing pat; there won't be anything else to do. Why don't you make it a week, Mr. Halket? You need a vacation, and we'll rub along."

Floyd shook his head. "Three days will be enough, I think. Wish me luck and I'll be back here Thursday morning."

He bade the superintendent good-by; downstairs he paused at the telegraph operator's desk to send a dispatch. He addressed it to Marion Clark at Westlake, New Hampshire. "Shall be in Westlake to-morrow afternoon; hope to see you," he wrote.

Though he was careful to make the visit seem so casual, it was for that alone that he was setting out upon the journey. The resolution had sprung suddenly alive that morning out of restlessness. The day before, some one at the club, talking with him about Stewart's inexplicable

vagaries, had mentioned the fact that Lydia had come
home. It was a fact which Floyd considered afterwards,
rather sadly. The summer had had for him no lighter
side. It had not only been a season of sorrow and of
harassing cares; it had also been one of solitary living.
In the daily performance of his duties, he had hardly
realized his loneliness, his isolation, but now that the
works were shut down and he found his employment
diminished, if not, like that of his men, quite cut off, he
could not keep reflection at bay any longer. It exhibited
his life to him as pale and joyless, and rebuked him for
allowing it to be so. When he had been told of Lydia's
return, his first thought was that he would go to her and
experience the agreeable sensation of being in her presence; nothing could inspirit him quite so much as the
society and charm of a woman whom he liked — the woman
whom he most liked. But other considerations checked
this enthusiastic impulse. In the estrangement existing
between himself and Stewart, it was impossible that he
should remain on an unchanged footing with Stewart's
wife. If she believed the charges that Stewart was making,
her good opinion of Floyd must be tarnished; and Floyd
realized that he must submit to the injustice of this rather
than defend himself to her and so perhaps awaken a distrust of her husband. In short, their intimacy was at an
end. If he went to see Lydia, she would ask why he
should not yield the points on which Stewart was attacking him, why he and her husband should be so deplorably
at loggerheads; and then he must either condemn himself or set forth the groundlessness of Stewart's accusations.
She might, she doubtless would, hear other versions than
that which Stewart would give her; but it was her duty
to believe in her husband as far and as long as possible,
and it would be easier for her to maintain her belief, Floyd
thought, if he himself remained away.

In this moment of renunciation, his mind turned to
Marion Clark, who had once pointed out to him the virtue

of a light touch in women; it was something now that he would have very much appreciated, if there had only been some one at hand who could administer it sympathetically. It occurred to him that Marion herself would have been a good comrade at such a time. Occasionally, when he had leisure to be discontented with his life he had suggested to himself the query — would it be more tolerable at this moment if Marion were sharing it? His answer had been invariably a qualified affirmative; at just these particular moments she would probably be a help, he admitted, — but for the rest of the time — he hardly thought her necessary. The shadow of Lydia had always lurked discouragingly in the background of his thoughts. But on this evening the shadow of Lydia ceased to be a resource and lingered only as a persecution. "If it were n't for having always been in love, I suppose I could fall in love now," he sighed. "And that would be a great thing for me — if the girl was willing." But then he went to bed feeling that he was in a weak and silly mood, and having no doubt that when he awoke in the morning he would be more normal.

Somewhat to his surprise, as he sat at breakfast the idea of Marion and her light touch returned to occupy his brain. It was attractive, it began to grow exciting. In the middle of the morning he decided abruptly that he would at once make a short visit of inspection. "She need n't know what I'm up to, and if I cool right off the moment I see her she need never know," Floyd thought. "And it's about a hundred to one that's what will happen." Then he had the additional thought, "But if I only could! I believe it would be a great thing for me." He wavered between an almost ecstatic recollection of her light touch and an almost utter repugnance for her overconfident, positive point of view. Displeased by his weakness, he commanded himself to drop the subject and await the test of a meeting.

Late the following afternoon he got off the train at the

little country station. He was vaguely considering to which one of the two competing and decrepit carryalls he should intrust himself when he became aware that farther down the platform a young woman in a brown driving-coat was signaling to him from the high seat of her trap. She wore a brown veil, pushed up above her eyes; it was hardly a valid excuse for Floyd's uncertainty and hesitation in recognizing her as the person whom he sought. Then he hastened to her.

"Yes, I know you'd probably be safer behind either of those horses," she said, reaching a hand down to him. "But I hope you'll pretend you are n't afraid and get in here with me. Put your bag in behind."

"This flatters me very much," Floyd said as he obeyed her commands. "Am I to suppose that you've been watching and waiting for me on every train?"

"Of course I *should* have done that," she answered, laughing, "if it had been necessary. But as we have only one afternoon train here from anywhere, it was n't difficult to guess when you'd arrive. I think it's about the best hour of the day, too, for a visitor to come and get his first impression — just when the shadows are growing long. Don't you think it's a pretty country?"

"I do," Floyd assured her. "You know, to a fellow fresh — or stale — from Avalon, there's something uncanny about all this stillness — and peacefulness."

"Dear me," she said mildly, "do you find peacefulness uncanny? What shall I do to reassure you? When we make that turn just ahead, you'll see our mountain and lake — they are n't very tremendous, but we like them as well as if they were."

The road led at the turn out upon an exposed high place commanding a view down the valley — a valley of little hills on which rugged farms alternated with forest. Near at hand, however, rose one great conical peak that dominated all the others; no settler's axe had made an indentation on its majestic slope; here and there masses of early-changing foliage flashed like brilliant orange and red pennons among the climbing hosts of sober green. At the base of the mountain was the narrow line of the lake, sapphire blue in the clear light; a spire, the roofs of four or five houses emerged above the trees and indicated the settlement on the shore.

"Yes," said Floyd. "I should think you would like your mountain and your lake." But though he had been impressed by the beauty which the sudden opening up of the valley had revealed, he was more interested in glancing away from it to his companion's face. He wondered if the arrangement of the brown veil, drawn up above her eyes, contributed in some curious way to an expression softer than any he had hoped for — or whether such a look came upon her face in the presence of something that, like the mountain, she loved. When she spoke her voice seemed gentler; the feeling expanded in him that she was, unreservedly, a very pleasant person to be with.

She turned in at a white pillared gateway and drove up an avenue of maple-trees to a large white colonial house; an old-fashioned garden blooming with asters was laid out in front of it; the low box hedges stretched away across the lawn almost to the edge of the lake.

"You're going to stay with us," Marion said. "When I told the family you were coming, they insisted I should go after you and bring you here."

"Thank you; I'd like to stay — if you did n't go after me unwillingly. Your saying your family *insisted* — "

"Oh," she answered, with a laugh, "a girl can make her family the scapegoat for a great many of her own forward acts. I'll have you shown to your room, and then you must hurry down and have a cup of tea with me."

Floyd, following the butler up the staircase, was decidedly of the opinion that a girl who would always rise at once to one's little joke and carry it on so naturally was a pleasant person to be with.

When he came downstairs, she was standing by a window and looking out at a small catboat that was careening on the farther side of the lake. "Papa and his new toy," she explained. "He's perfectly daft over it; the only way we ever get him ashore is by going out and screaming at him through the megaphone. Mamma's out driving, so you and I will have to drink our tea by ourselves."

He suggested, when this ceremony had been finished, that she show him the garden.

"It's only the tag end of it," she said; "it's hardly worth seeing. It was pretty a month ago."

They walked together along the box-bordered paths; in the centre he paused to read the motto on the sun-dial, "I know none but sunny hours."

Then he said abruptly, —

"Is there a train for New York to-night?"

"Good gracious," she cried, "what a question! What's the matter with your room? Are you mad? either kind of mad — angry or insane — which?"

"I may have to go back to-night," he answered. "Very likely you don't know, but I left things at the works in rather an unsettled state; I don't like to be away. I came on to see you — to talk with you for about an hour, maybe — and then go back."

He looked for a moment in grave silence at her face. It had perhaps a little less color now than when she had left the house, but she showed no sign of emotion, hardly even surprise. As she waited for him to speak, she stood with the clear-eyed look of an interested young boy, erect, motionless, with her hands thrust into the pockets of her long coat.

"It's a pretty intimate unbosoming of myself that I've got to ask you to listen to," Floyd said. "I'm likely to make a mess of it however I begin, so I'll start right off by saying that I've been for a good while dissatisfied with my life, and never so much so as this summer. We'll omit the business situation; that is n't what I mean. But the going home at the end of the day to that big forlorn house of my grandfather's, with a lot of servants imposing on me the ceremony and formality that they and I have been brought up to — all that for myself alone — and I have n't felt as if it would be right to make a change; the poor creatures are dependent on that for their living, they 're trying to be useful, and I can't turn them off — it 's all they can do. But I don't care for such solitary state; it bores me; it bores me to do everything; it bores me to eat. The only thing that gets me through my meals is an interesting habit I 've taken up of counting the number of times I chew each mouthful — and keeping a record in a little book; and that 's not a very intellectual amusement, is it?"

"Not very; but it must be a healthful one. You look extremely well."

"Do I? Then I 'm sorry to hear it, for I 'm really in a very bad way and I want sympathy. I 've come to you for sympathy," Floyd said solemnly. "I hope you 'll give it." He hesitated a moment, then he continued with more genuine seriousness, "Of course the whole trouble is, I 'm not satisfied to be a bachelor. I never have been satisfied, since I was old enough to — to care about a girl. There 's one girl that I 'd have married if I could, but Stewart Lee came in ahead of me. I ought n't to have gone on caring for her, but I did; I suppose I always shall, in some sort of way. At the same time I feel that that need n't prevent me from caring for my wife, if I were lucky enough to have a wife, and if she could overlook the fact of — of this other girl."

"Whom you really love," said Marion.

"Ah, it 's hardly fair — or true — to say that," he answered, and he met her eyes with a gentle smile. "I care for you so very much, Marion; you 're the only girl except Lydia for whom I 've ever cared, and I — I should n't be asking you to be my wife if I did n't very much want you —"

"You're asking me, yet it's Lydia that you really love?"

He quailed a little under the reproach in Marion's voice, under the unfaltering yet not wholly ungentle look in her blue eyes.

"Ah," he pleaded, "truly you must not think that. I suppose it's not a very flattering way to propose marriage to a girl. I wanted to be honest. If you could take me in spite of Lydia, you would make me very happy."

"But what consideration do you offer me?" she said. She looked away towards the lake with speculative eyes; her composure remained undisturbed. "Of course I understand that your house is a large one, and you find it requires a great deal of care, which is annoying to you personally and which you would like to transfer to a woman's shoulders; and you find yourself at times rather lonely, and so you want to marry me! I can see why a wife might appear to you a desirable convenience; but, if you don't love the woman, what, besides your big house and your heavy cares and your name, have you to offer her? Not yourself."

"Yes, myself!" cried Floyd earnestly. He faced her with a sudden ardor. "That is n't much to offer, I know; I'm not witty or clever or especially interesting or handsome; but all there is of me goes to you, if you'll have it. To whom else would it go? Not to Lydia — not the smallest part; you don't think that? Why, when I've been downhearted this summer, is n't it you that I've turned to in my mind? and thought — if you were at hand to brace me up! A man cares a great deal for a girl if he keeps thinking of her when he's in trouble. And I don't feel as if it would only be trouble that I'd be bringing you if you would marry me. I don't think I'm an altogether selfish person. I believe that much as I should like being cheered up by you, it would n't be half so agreeable as feeling that now and then I could cheer you up. It would be a very pleasant thing for me if I knew that when I needed it I might always have your sympathy; but even better, I should like knowing that you would always be glad to have mine and would turn to me for it. If I care for you that way, Marion, have n't I a right to ask you to be my wife?"

"If you care for me that way," — she spoke slowly, looking at the ground, and then she raised her eyes to his, — "why did your conscience find it necessary to say that you loved some one else?"

"That means — you will?"

She smiled and held out both hands. "I care for you so very much — myself."

He took her hands and drew her to him and kissed her, without a word; his speechlessness piqued her a little even in that first warm fluttering moment, but when he let her go and she looked up into his face, she was satisfied with what she saw.

"Ah, Floyd," she said, and her eyes lighted up with a gleam of humor through the mist of emotion and affection, "if you have any other confessions that you think you ought to make to me, — don't make them, — never make them."

He continued to look at her in silence, but there was something in the steadfastness of the look which stirred her heart exultantly.

"You 've made me very, very happy," he said at last firmly. "Happier than I ever thought I 'd be."

"It seems to me a very restrained happiness that you permit yourself," she answered with equal firmness. "But some day you will be really happy — for you are going to love me — and you are going to love *only* me."

He smiled and took her hand, but he wished that she had not said this; it was the first little speech in which had rung the jarring note of aggressive confidence.

XXVI

WIDENING THE BREACH

FLOYD arrived in Avalon at an early hour in the morning; and while he sat at breakfast he read the newspaper account of the mass meeting held the night before by his locked-out workmen. Tustin had presided and had urged steadfastness and fortitude under persecution; the report of his speech was mainly an abstract, but there was this much quoted: "To some it may seem that the only weapon left to us is force, — but it is a weapon that we must not be the first to employ. We welcome the assurance given us that it is not the company's intention to import strike-breakers and non-union men; but we must not deceive ourselves as to the purpose of this assurance. That purpose is plain — to cause weakening and dissension amongst us, to invite treason, and to draw from the support of the cause those who may be afraid. Now there is one way and only one to meet treason from within; nobody is more opposed to violence than I am, but intimidation is the only way to deal with traitors." Floyd inferred that the conciliatory policy which he had ordered was viewed with more alarm by the union leaders than one of aggressive action might have been.

Stewart Lee had also addressed the meeting. His speech was not given in full, but it was apparently in the nature of a dedication of himself to the cause. It may have been due to the reporter's translation of the substance of Stewart's remarks into his own easy vocabulary, but Floyd gathered no more vivid impression than could be conveyed by such phrases as, "The necessity for a campaign of education," "The workingmen's most precious possession is their right to organize," "The awakening of the public conscience and the suppression of individual rapacity." There seemed also to have been an allusion to the reluctance with which the speaker had felt himself impelled to raise this protest against the course of one who had long been his close friend. According to the report, the delivery of the speech had been "impassioned," and the audience had responded with "tremendous applause,"—especially when Stewart had pledged himself to contribute, by speaking, writing, and raising money, all that was in his power to the maintenance of the principles for which the workingmen stood.

Consultations which Floyd held that morning with Gregg and with other officials of the company confirmed him in the opinion that the first attempt on the part of any of the men to return to work would provoke an outbreak. Gregg reported that the constabulary of New Rome were in the hands of the union leaders, and that it would be difficult to supply adequate police protection for those who might indicate a desire to accept the company's terms. The sheriff of the county could not be called on for aid until the local resources had been proved inadequate. "We have information," said Gregg, "that Tustin and others of the leaders, for all they profess to deprecate violence, are passing round the word that the first men who weaken are to be run out of town. Every trolley car that comes in from Avalon is watched and anybody who gets off and can't or won't give an account of himself is sent back across the river. The railroad station is patrolled by a guard. I don't believe that Tustin really thinks we mean to run in an army of non-union men, but by using such tactics he keeps alive a feeling of suspicion and animosity against us — and probably he's got the men to think that the only reason strike-breakers haven't been brought in is that all this picketing and patrolling has made them afraid to come."

"That's all right," Floyd said. "They'll soon weary

of that. They won't hold out indefinitely against a waiting game."

Gregg shook his head. "Things won't go on quietly indefinitely," was his comment.

"Has there been any annoyance of Farrell — or Tibbs?"

"None that I have heard of — yet. Well, they may let the old man alone. But I'll bet they've got it in for Farrell."

"Oh, I think it's talk," Floyd said. "Nothing but talk."

He knew that his radiant confidence was insincere; he comforted himself by reflecting that a newly engaged and entirely happy man ought to put a radiant face on all matters. There was, however, a similar lurking insincerity even in his consciousness of happiness; now that he was away from Marion he found himself remembering the unpleasant little sensation given him by her boast of ultimate control over his emotions. Worst of all, he seemed to remember this quite as vividly as he did the more agreeable feelings with which she had inspired him. One memory seemed to set itself against the other and balance it. He felt as if he were merely wearing the mask of the successful lover. He upbraided himself for letting this trivial thing qualify his delight in winning so nice a girl; it was contemptible. He could of course look upon his successful wooing cheerfully, as a comfortable solution of life; Marion would always be a most satisfactory companion. But he had entered into the engagement with far more enthusiasm than this; he could not understand why it should so soon have faded.

In the course of the morning he telephoned to Lydia and asked if she was to be at home that afternoon; finding that she was, he said that he would come in to see her, as he had something to communicate. When he arrived at her house, he guessed that she had anxiously been awaiting him; for no sooner had he entered the hall than her foot was on the stair, and in another moment she came into view; he saw at once the apprehension in her face, he heard it in her voice as she spoke from the stairs, —

"Oh, Floyd! It's something about Stewart!"

"There's where you're wrong," he laughed. "Not a word about Stewart. Now can you guess?"

But she had been so agitated by all her forebodings that great as was her relief she could not immediately turn to any other subject; so she did not heed his question; she gave him her hand and said, "Oh, I'm so troubled about Stewart, Floyd; I was sure it was about Stewart when you telephoned that you had something to tell me. He is so sincere in all that he's doing — and saying; it's all a conviction — almost a religion with him — and he — he's let go — I'm afraid he's lost his grip on other things —" Her eyes were bright with tears. "And I remember — the day I pushed him down with an oar, Floyd; — and now I don't dare to say anything — lest — he's trying to — to find himself, just as he was that day — and if I interfered, I might only push him down again. And this time — something tells me — it would be fatal; not even you could bring him back to me."

"Stewart has sudden enthusiasms that have to go through him like a fever," Floyd said lightly. "This is a little more violent than most, but you mustn't think it's going to finish him."

"It isn't the enthusiasm that I mind." She seated herself in a low chair and leaned forward, resting her chin on her hands. "It's — it's his opposition to you. — The rest of it — his wanting to improve the condition of workingmen — he's earnest and sincere in that, I know; that's really become with him a great purpose. But — it's his starting in against you — and — and, I'm afraid, getting embittered because at once all his old friends have turned against him — my father, for instance; he's always admired Stewart tremendously, but now he's quite out of patience with him; and I think Stewart's found it so with others. And when he's embittered, he may go farther in some ways than he would really intend to go. Yet he is so sincere about the whole subject of workingmen's rights, so eager to improve their condition, that he may be on the verge of accomplishing something splendid, something worth while — and though it grieves me very much to know that he's attacking you, Floyd, I — I can't discourage him."

"Don't try," Floyd answered. "Why, he's got one idea of how to improve our workmen's condition, and I've got another. The question will settle itself, some day — and then he and I can forget we've ever differed."

"You *can* forget," she said. "It is one of the splendid things about you, Floyd, — that you can forget."

"And so can you," he declared. "I believe you've forgotten now that I came to tell you something very interesting and important."

"I had," she admitted. "I've got so self-centred, worrying about Stewart. What is it, Floyd?"

"I'm engaged to be married," he said. "To a friend of yours — Marion Clark. Now what do you think of me?"

He looked down at her with a gay smile; she rose from the low chair and came towards him holding out both hands. "Oh, Floyd!" — she said, and then as he took her hands, her voice broke, her eyes grew soft with tears. "I'm so glad, so very, very glad! I've hoped you might — this long time! There's no one so fine as Marion — unless it's you!"

Smiling at him through her tears, she was the great peril to his happiness. He tried not to think of her, he tried to think of Marion as he answered, —

"You know her better than any one else does. We wanted you — and Stewart — to hear it first. Just as I was the first to hear about you and Stewart — years ago."

"Thank you, Floyd. Stewart will be so pleased. — Ah, I don't believe you know yet all that Marion is — so clear-sighted, so brave, so true! — If she were here and you were away, I think I should be saying that to her about you, Floyd."

The soft emotion in Lydia's voice, the gentle, affectionate appeal in her gray eyes were strangely alluring to Floyd; she leaned upon the back of a chair and looked up at him, and in that attitude all that was trustful, loving, and dependent in her nature seemed to shine forth; the eager, mobile face, the flexible, relaxed figure, the slender hands, all had a suggestion that awoke in Floyd a tender sympathy; she was a woman who as time went on would cling more and more caressingly about the man she loved, become more and more a cherished and essential part of his life. Marion appeared in his thoughts as a contrast to this, a firm, erect figure, resolute, uncompromising, independent, — clear-sighted, true, and brave. In all these virtues there was not the appeal to the imagination and sympathy that Lydia could make unconsciously by leaning on a chair and having her unselfish interest in her eyes.

Floyd went away challenging angrily in his heart the sentimental spirit that could so drag him from the path of loyalty. He was glad that Marion was soon to return to Avalon; reinforced by her presence, he felt he could more successfully cope with the unregenerate inclinations of his heart.

The morning after he had seen Lydia, his office boy brought him Stewart's card. "Ask him to come in," said Floyd; and when a moment later Stewart entered, he rose from his desk and held out his hand.

"Lydia told me — I came to offer my congratulations," Stewart said, and though he grasped Floyd's hand warmly enough, there was constraint in his voice and a slight evasiveness in his eyes. "She 's a bully girl — and it 's what I 've been urging you to do for years. I 'm awfully glad, Floyd, — and I 'll have to write and tell her you 're not such a bad fellow really — "

"As you 've been telling other people I am?" Floyd could not resist saying, with a good-humored smile.

Stewart flushed, but he would not allow Floyd even a temporary advantage. "Fortunately, relations between man and wife need n't be inferred from those between employer and employee," he retorted. "Anyway, I think I can write to her and find something to say. And I hope you're willing to accept my congratulations and good wishes, Floyd — and to believe them sincere?"

Floyd laughed. "Of course, Stewart. Thank you for coming in to tell me."

"You must acknowledge it was rather magnanimous," replied Stewart, "when you left me to hear of it through Lydia. I really think that I'm the one you should have told. — Especially as you were the person that I took into my confidence when Lydia and I were first engaged."

Floyd was too amazed at this display of sensitiveness to attempt any reply.

"You must n't be too suspicious of your friends," continued Stewart. "Just because a sense of public duty and responsibility sometimes prompts them to come out against you, you should n't think that they 've ceased to be your friends. Of course I'm not jealous of Lydia because you chose to tell her. Only I think I was entitled to hear such a thing from your own lips."

"It did n't occur to me that you'd feel there was any slight," Floyd answered, still at a loss as to how to meet this unexpected reproof. "Oh, hang it all, Stewart, let's get back to the main issue. The point is, you were good enough to come in and congratulate me, and I'm mighty glad to have your congratulations and thank you the best I know how. There — shake hands."

With a laugh and still holding his friend's hand, he helped Stewart to get gracefully out of the room.

The next day was the first of October, and the sealed plans submitted in competition for the Rebecca Halket Hospitals were brought into Floyd's private office. The two other judges arrived, — Dr. Edwards and the New York architect; the plans were opened, and the committee went into session. Day after day they sat, patiently scrutinizing and weighing every detail. For more than a week Floyd was able to give almost uninterrupted attention to this task. No problems arose at New Rome to demand his special care. The daily reports from Gregg showed that the town, though idle, was orderly, and that the incessant patrolling and picketing of the union men was on the whole of a peaceable nature. Stewart seemed to be the most active agent for the enemy, and even he was using somewhat less intemperate language than that in which he had first assailed Floyd. How much this modification was due to the quiet influence of Lydia or to the correction of the more astute union leaders, Floyd could not guess; at any rate in the newspaper reports of the speeches which Stewart was making nightly to men of various trades there was no personal attack; the economic and humanitarian aspects of the struggle were those with which the advocate dealt. Besides putting forth these efforts, Stewart conducted a column in the *Evening Telegram* inviting subscriptions to a fund, under the heading, "For Families of Men Locked Out of Employment." He announced in this column that, although there was no immediate need of aid, winter was approaching, and in the event of a protracted struggle, which now seemed only too probable in view of the obstinacy and relentlessness of the management, suffering was to be expected. He felt that steps to relieve this could not be taken too early, and he called on every one who sympathized with brave fighters for liberty to give even the smallest assistance. He himself headed the list of contributions to the fund with one thousand dollars. In comparison with this amount the other subscriptions that he was able to publish looked ludicrously — or pathetically — small. Stewart had not been successful in enlisting the interest of any of his wealthy friends in his charitable purpose. When he had approached two or three men in whose liberality of view he had had reason to believe, he had been bluntly rebuffed. Stung by this treatment and by the coldness of his fellow members at the club, who indeed made him feel that his presence there was unwelcome, he challenged any one to meet him in public or semi-public debate on the question of the lock-out; no one heeded the challenge. It angered Stewart to feel that because the people whom he most wished to reach perversely declined to listen, his educational work was unproductive. He had hoped that he could create at least an impression and rouse some sentiment among the persons of his acquaintance; instead of that he found that the only persons who would listen to him at all were tradespeople and artisans with whom he had no acquaintance and who were already in sympathy with his opinions. In such circumstances he felt he was not making much headway with the propaganda. Nevertheless his support seemed valued by Tustin and the others; he was admitted to the counsels of the leaders, — or thought that he was, — and he was kept contented and zealous by the belief that he was preparing a future for himself politically.

Floyd, although unaware of Stewart's ultimate aspirations, kept himself informed of his friend's activity and wondered at it, with more sadness than bitterness. A talk that he had with Bob Dunbar gave him some light on the reasons which were determining Stewart's course.

"I think," said Dunbar, "if Stewart had been able to feel that he stood a chance of winning this competition, he'd never have run amuck this way. He worked over that; he really did; it was the thing which was to determine his career as architect. It was make or break with him. And at the last I imagine he felt that he'd worked on the plans to no purpose and did n't really have the stuff in him, so he threw it all over and rushed into this business, partly with an hysterical belief in it and partly with a dramatic impulse to make the ruin more complete."

"I should n't wonder," said Floyd sympathetically.

"It's too bad. Perhaps after this affair is settled we can straighten things out with him and get him started right again. Good heavens, I talk like a prig, saying 'we'! I guess it can be left to Lydia safely enough."

"I don't know." Dunbar shook his head. "Lydia's almost too gentle, too affectionate with him. And he takes the bit in his teeth. If you don't mind my saying so, Floyd,"— he laughed,— "Stewart ought to have somebody like your girl to manage him. Marion would deal with his nonsense. I tell you, Floyd, you're a lucky fellow. If ever there was a girl made to help a man and manage him right and get the best out of him, Marion's the one. The only kick I have to make is that you didn't leave her for somebody who needed her more."

"Don't you think I need to have the nonsense taken out of me?" laughed Floyd.

Dunbar's appreciation of Marion gave him something of a chill. It seemed to emphasize her least attractive qualities as her most characteristic. But it was very soon after this that she returned to Avalon, and that Floyd had an opportunity to discover with shame how unkind and unsympathetic had been his apprehensions. He found her far more lovable than he had been supposing her — even if he did not wholly love her. She was really very sweet and gentle, she took an immediate interest in his problems — an interest which was intelligent and not obnoxious, and which was enlivened with a humorous light. Floyd found her, as he had always hitherto found her, a pleasant, happy companion; yet when he was away from her he was indifferent, sensible mainly of the flaws. He knew that in her calm, serene way she was determined to have his whole love, and the knowledge made him perversely stubborn about yielding it — or rather his earnest volition seemed to be swept backward by a stronger current of antipathy. The desire of his nature was for a woman of a confiding cosiness, not for one of a large and generous spaciousness. He could not rid himself of a whimsical notion that living with Marion would be like living in a house containing only a series of vast, beautiful ball-rooms. For all her interest in his affairs, she made him feel that he was an insignificant and unornamental figure. She seemed to him to have a much larger grasp and outlook than he had attained, and to be quite independent of him; his protective instinct found nothing in her for its encouragement; she was too well able to conduct her own life. He felt vaguely that she dwarfed his spirit, that her character furnished no objective for the display and development of such little virtues as he was modestly aware he possessed — a patient wish to help, a desire to use his uncouth powers in the service of some one whose charm was reinforced by an appealing dependence. He could not think of Marion as "nestling" — he hated the word, but he confessed a fondness for the idea. Yet in the maze of subtlety and obscurity which bewildered his inclinations, it never occurred to him that a return to his unpledged state would make him happier, even if it could be accomplished without any cause for self-reproach. He accepted his engagement as an advance to a more satisfactory life, he would accept his marriage as an advance beyond that, — and yet he knew that the path he was traveling could never lead him to the complete fulfillment of the possibilities that he dimly apprehended in his soul.

His unsuspected sensitiveness was touched in a conversation which he had with Marion on the subject of their wedding. They had decided to be married before Christmas; but when there seemed no prospect of an early settlement at New Rome, Floyd said to her that he feared they might have to postpone the wedding indefinitely — perhaps till spring.

"For, you see, I can't be away for more than a day or two at a time while matters are in this state," he said. "Some of those fellows would like nothing better than to get me off on a honeymoon."

"Oh," she answered, "if it's necessary, Floyd, I can wait."

It occurred to him that here had been an opportunity for her to show an affectionate dependence and devotion; it might have been conveyed in the utterance of those very words. But she spoke them merely as the agents of an obvious, common-sense opinion, one so obvious that there was no necessity of connecting with it reluctance or regret.

The mills had been idle for three weeks when Hugh Farrell called on Floyd with a proposal for reopening them.

"There's enough men ready to break away from the Affiliated and go in with me," he said confidently. "Enough to start a couple of mills anyhow. There's a good many more that would be willing but are scared. I'm reckoning only on those that won't be scared — that will have the nerve to walk in first — right past the pickets. I've been feeling around some."

"I think it would be better for you," said Floyd, "to lie low and do nothing for the present. Isn't your situation — and Letty's — pretty uncomfortable? How are you being treated?"

"Oh," said Hugh, "a good many folks don't give us much chance to forget that we're unpopular. But that's all right. That's because the Affiliated's got every one so terrorized. If once we can break in on them — why, the very fellows that are noisiest against me will be the first to desert. I'm not bothering on my own account. What I want is to get busy."

"Well," said Floyd, "you'd better feel round among the men a little longer. I'll think it over."

He consulted Gregg, who was of the opinion that a number of men would be glad to return to work, but doubted if many of them would dare to be the first. A few days later Farrell came to him again.

"It's all right," Farrell said confidently. "Just say the

word, and any morning I'll march in a gang big enough to start two mills — and maybe more. Just let us have one day of work, and the next day you'll have 'em all coming back."

"I'll try it — on one condition," Floyd replied. "That is this: if when you go down to the works you find yourselves forcibly opposed — your entrance, I mean — you give it up, without a fight. I'd rather have this deadlock go on indefinitely than have it end in violence."

Farrell gave his promise and named the day on which he and his men would be ready to enter the mills.

"Very well; the gates will be opened for you at six o'clock in the morning," Floyd replied.

"But don't give it out," Farrell cautioned him. "We've got to work this on the quiet. Only the right fellows are to know — the fellows that can be trusted."

"Yes, of course. And remember — if there's the least sign of trouble, you're to draw out; I want that understood."

Farrell gave his promise.

Two days before the attempt to reopen the works was to be made, the committee on the Rebecca Halket Hospital competition announced the award. Bennett & Durant of Avalon had won the prize. The newspapers all published elaborate descriptions and reproductions of the successful plans. Stewart read the announcement at breakfast and broke out into a furious invective that appalled Lydia.

"Stewart!" she exclaimed entreatingly. "I'm sorry for your disappointment, dear, but — Stewart!"

He continued without heeding her. Then suddenly she spoke to him in a tone that he had never before heard her use. "Stewart! You say such things to me about Floyd!"

But he was so carried away by wrath and mortification that he ignored the unfamiliar warning in her voice.

"That and more too!" he cried. "Ignorance — chicanery — fair competition, indeed! Bennett & Durant!

And that — that" — he struck the picture in the newspaper furiously with his hand — "that wins! See the plans — read the description! No architect, no intelligent, unbiased layman could pass that! The architect on that committee stood alone — the others! God knows what prompted the others!"

"Stewart!" His wife's voice rang sharply on his ears. She rose from her place and stood with angry spots flushing her cheeks, with eyes darting an unaccustomed, scathing light. "I will not hear such things from you. I will not stay in the room where they are said."

As she went out of the door he said viciously, —

"Yes, it needs only you to turn against me."

Then she stopped in the doorway and looked at him in silent scorn. The look did him no good; and he did not follow her up the stairs. Instead, he went downtown, possessed by a furious impulse to visit his office and rend and burn all the notes, drawings, and books which related in any way to the work he had done for the competition. He was rushing past the Halket Building when he came face to face with Floyd, who was about to enter.

The meeting turned Stewart from his purpose.

"I should like to have a few words with you," he said.

"Come up," Floyd answered.

When they entered the outer office of the Halket Company, Floyd signed to the clerk who was sitting there to withdraw. Then he offered Stewart a chair; but Stewart ignored it and stood some distance away from Floyd in the middle of the room.

"I see you have announced your award," he observed.

"Yes. I'm sorry the plans we chose turned out not to be yours."

"You wished to give the buildings to an Avalon architect — and you did not wish to give them to me. With those two conditions, it was easy to pick the winner."

"Stewart, if you mean to insinuate —"

"Insinuate!" Stewart laughed mirthlessly. "It is needless subtlety to insinuate when a fact is so palpable. With architects of the standing and ability of those from New York and Philadelphia and Boston to choose from, how else is the selection of Bennett & Durant — and on such plans! — to be explained?"

"I am under no necessity of explaining it," Floyd said, and though he spoke quietly, an unpleasant sternness had settled on his face. "Better drop the subject, Stewart — or, as has happened before, we may both of us say things that we shall regret."

"When you refer to such past experiences of regret," Stewart replied, "your conscience has the advantage of mine." The two men had stood, since the beginning of their colloquy, several feet apart, uncompromising, motionless, neither of them making any step which might be interpreted as a plea for a more confidential relation. Now, however, Stewart walked slowly up to Floyd and stretching out his arm, pointed his long forefinger threateningly in Floyd's face. "Shall I reconstruct your mental processes for you so that you can view them in all their nakedness with an impartial eye?" he asked; and Floyd folded his arms and gazed impassively beyond the menacing forefinger at Stewart's collar, as if nothing else interested him. "To begin with; you refused to look at my plans; why? Because you wished to appear to the world too lofty and incorruptible to be reached by personal influence and friendship, and because you were of too small a mind to risk this reputation by giving recognition to the best work when it was done by a friend. And also it was perhaps pleasanter for you to keep me from ever working out the penalty for the mistakes I made in the one building which you once permitted me. Perhaps you recall these motives?"

He paused for a reply, but no expression crossed Floyd's impassive face. Stewart dropped his accusing finger and drew a step nearer.

"Next, to demonstrate your chaste and incorruptible spirit, you announced that there would be a competition, open only to the best — the best and Bennett! The committee of judges was of your appointing. You probably knew that you could on any question control a two-thirds vote in the committee. Your placing yourself on that committee was a subtle indication of the purpose that appealed to your love of power, — a purpose not to let go, to keep a supervision of the work in your own hands, even up to the end. With that purpose in mind, you felt it essential that the work should be given to a local man, — not to one of the celebrated outsiders, whom you knew you could not handle. Do I read your mental processes correctly?"

Floyd made no motion and no answer.

"There were two local men entered in this competition — Bennett and myself. You may at one time have entertained a generous impulse to grant your old friend the award, if his drawings seemed to merit it. You may have been the more inclined toward this since it would have enabled you again to show me your power — your power, first to bestow, and afterwards perhaps to interfere. For you knew that I was always sensible of my one great obligation, and it always pleased you to see that I kept it in mind. But something happened which destroyed your benevolent, friendly impulse. It was this: I had the presumption to follow duty rather than discretion; when your treatment of your workingmen became a public scandal, I had to be a witness for the truth; and I knew then that I was sacrificing my own interests. You after that eliminated me from consideration. Bennett alone remained. You gave him the prize. The same impartial, disinterested spirit which had conceived the competition dominated it."

Stewart's tone had grown more venomous as he proceeded; and he delivered the last sentences of his tirade with an insulting, sneering emphasis. When it became quite clear that he had finished, Floyd raised his eyes and let them rest on Stewart's face. There was an inexorable, unpitying gravity in his gaze, and his voice was stern as he said, —

"Your hypothesis presupposes that before the committee made the award I had resorted to the improper act of secretly identifying each set of plans."

"The result presupposes that," Stewart answered jauntily. "The selection of the one utterly incompetent architect among all the competitors."

"You assume," continued Floyd, "that in making the award I was guilty not only of impropriety, but also of dishonesty."

"I assume nothing in dispute of the facts," Stewart replied.

The outer door of the office opened suddenly; the two men turned their heads and saw Hugh Farrell.

"Please go into that room, Mr. Farrell." Floyd pointed to a door. "I will see you in a few moments." He waited until Farrell had disappeared. "And now, sir, this door for you." He walked abruptly to that by which Farrell had entered and flung it open. "I will do you the courtesy to hold it for you myself, instead of calling the office boy."

"And not one word in denial!" cried Stewart triumphantly as he passed out.

Going down in the elevator he was still quivering with the excitement of the meeting. But he was joyous, exultant; he felt that he had issued triumphant from the field. The dignified yet scathing irony, the unassailable logic of his denunciation gave him in the retrospect a gradually increasing satisfaction. As he thought of the silence and impotence of his ungifted victim, he began to feel an easy, almost a forgiving contempt. Then as he was walking up the street he recalled Hugh Farrell's entrance, and began to speculate on its significance. Whatever the purpose of Farrell's visit, it was undoubtedly not undertaken in the interests of the union. Stewart determined to go at once to New Rome and inform Tustin of this suspicious conference; the executive committee of the Affiliated should be kept on its guard.

He found Tustin, Caskey, Ryan, and McGraw in the room over a shoe-store which was the headquarters of the committee. They were all smoking pipes and sitting round a table on which were spread sheets of type-written names. They gave him a friendly welcome; Tustin reached out one foot and jerked a chair toward him as an invitation to sit down.

"I have a bit of news for you, which may or may not be of some account," said Stewart; and he told what he had seen.

Tustin exhibited his faint, confident smile.

"Can you guess what that visit might be about?" he asked, turning to the others; and they all laughed, to Stewart's bewilderment.

"We've been keeping tabs on Farrell," Tustin explained. "If you hadn't told us this, we'd mighty soon have heard. Well, there will be something doing before long — when it comes to an employer picking out one of his men and putting up a plot on the rest of us." He paused for a moment, and then he asked, "Say, did it ever occur to you, Mr. Lee, to inquire into the cause of this special favoring of Farrell?"

"I suppose it's been because he has always tried to make trouble for the union," Stewart answered.

"No, it's more than that. Did it ever occur to you why Mr. Halket should once have interested himself to get you to build Farrell a house?"

"No. I never thought about it particularly."

"And then never lifted a finger to get you to do the same by me and half a dozen others? You never thought of that? Well, now, I'll tell you; it may amuse you to hear. It was because Mrs. Farrell before she was married — I will say I've heard nothing against her since — was Mr. Halket's girl."

"His girl!" Stewart exclaimed.

WIDENING THE BREACH

"Yes. You know." Tustin laughed. "He used to board at her house when he was in the mills. Any of the fellows can tell you,—except Shelton; he always said there was nothing in it, but he has a soft spot anyhow. I lived next door; and my wife always had her suspicions. He and Farrell had some kind of understanding about it, so that they did n't interfere. My wife told me how they managed, but I've forgotten the particulars. When it came time for Mr. Halket to leave the works, then it was arranged for Farrell and the girl to get married. Mr. Halket of course has been interested ever since and done things for 'em; that was part of the trade. He got you to fix 'em up a better house than the rest of us could have; he pretty near furnished the house for 'em; this trying to shove Farrell ahead that we've split on is only another part of it."

"Good Lord!" Stewart exclaimed, and there was sincere regret as well as stupefaction in his voice. With all his readiness to think evil of Floyd, he had never suspected him of this particular depravity, he had always thought him to be what he had been in college — the man of the purest and most blameless life. Stewart was cynical enough about the virtue of most men; yet even now, when his friendship for Floyd had ceased, there remained a sensitiveness that was touched painfully by Tustin's recital. The type of stainless boyhood, for which in his heart Stewart had always had a yearning admiration, the type which had always seemed to him summed up in Floyd, was smirched; that which he had heard seemed to reach back and defile even the innocent years. The regret in his voice had been not for Floyd's fall, but for the loss of an ideal with which in spite of enmity and distrust he had till now associated Floyd unconsciously.

"It seems as if it could hardly be true," Stewart said, after a long pause.

Caskey hammered his pipe against the edge of the table. "It's true, all right," he remarked.

"My wife told me enough," observed Tustin. " Living next door — and knowing 'em all; she gets things straight."

"My God!" cried Stewart, with a sudden passion. "My God!" He struck the table violently with his fist and rose from his chair, and the others looked at him, amazed by the outburst.

He had forgotten the loss of an ideal; he was remembering that with such a motive Floyd had prevailed on him to build the house for Farrell and then had suffered him to pay the excess.

XXVII

NEW ROME AND AVALON

UPSTAIRS, Mrs. Bell and the children were still asleep; in the dining-room, Hugh Farrell and Letty were breakfasting by lamp-light. It was half-past five o'clock; a thick November fog was smothering the dawn.

"It's as well it's a dark morning," Letty said; she tried to speak cheerfully. "You won't be likely to be seen."

Hugh made no answer; he was eating with leisurely enjoyment. But after a moment he glanced up and saw his wife leaning back in her chair and watching him sadly.

"Let! You're not worrying!"

"No, of course not," she answered, with a sudden show of indignation, that he should suspect her of such weakness. "What would I be worrying about?"

"I thought you couldn't be. You're too red-headed. Red heads don't worry; they get mad."

He dodged below the table in affected alarm, and after a moment looked above the edge of it timidly.

"You're the silly," she said; and he reappeared and resumed his breakfast, satisfied at having driven the sadness from her face. After a moment she went to a window to straighten a shade; she stood there, looking out into the weltering fog.

"If you see anything interesting, you might let me know," her husband said; but she did not respond to his teasing; she stood looking out into the blankness. Suddenly she turned and said earnestly,—

"Hugh, you will be careful, won't you?—not to get into any fight."

"Oh," he answered, "you never can tell what I may do when I get my Irish up."

"It's mean to tease me now, Hugh," she said. "You'll promise, won't you?"

"Well," he answered, and he laughed at her affectionately, "I've promised Mr. Halket, and I guess I can do as much for you as for him."

She came over to him quickly and kissed him.

"But," he said, holding her round the waist and looking up at her, "I wouldn't dare to promise if I was red-headed."

"Ah now, Hugh — I don't often get mad — with you. Now, do I?" She spoke quite pleadingly.

"I'd hate to have you get mad any oftener." He rose from the table. "Well, I suppose I'd better be starting out to look for a white horse — "

"What's that?" She interrupted his well-worn joke with the startled exclamation. Not far away a bell had begun to toll, and now as it gathered momentum its peals rang out, hurried and clamorous, tumbling together in crazy, clanging excitement. Hugh listened and stared at his wife.

"It's to warn them you're coming — to start the works!" she cried.

"You're right! You're right!" He ran out into the hall and caught up his overcoat and hat. "I'd better be getting down there."

He was about to open the door when his wife caught his arm. "Hugh!" He looked down at her and saw what she wanted; he kissed her. "You've promised," she cried; and with that reminder to speed him he was gone.

The school-house bell was still clanging, — a danger signal in the dense fog. Hugh, hurrying along the hilltop, was moving in the direction of the sound. He came to the first of the outlying streets and crossed it; he began to see dimly ahead of him the forms of men running as

NEW ROME AND AVALON 429

he was running. He overtook one of them, hoping to find a friend, but the man was Caskey.

"What's the row?" Hugh asked.

"It ain't begun yet," Caskey answered with a grin, and he followed close behind Hugh, down the street leading to the mill entrance. There was assembled a great crowd, indistinct in the fog, motionless and quiet except for an occasional shout. Scattered along the street above were groups of men, hesitating and uncertain, and Hugh began to recognize faces of his allies. Passing in among them, he succeeded in leaving Caskey behind; he caught two men by the arms and said to them so that others might hear, —

"Just work your way through quietly; they won't stop you; it's just a bluff."

He spoke with a commanding reassurance that had its effect; as he walked on, some of the men followed, — but not all; and of those who started, some dropped out after they had gone a little way. Indeed, to pass through the mob that swarmed across the street from the company's offices on one side to the hotel on the other and was packed solidly against the gates of the mill inclosure, seemed impossible.

"The gates ain't open anyhow," murmured one of the men to Hugh.

"They will be at six; I've got Mr. Halket's word for it. — There; there's the gate-keeper on the bridge."

He pointed; the fog had lifted a little, and looking over the crowd they could see a man walking to and fro on the bridge behind the gate.

"Just mix in and work your way through easy," Hugh warned them.

They came straggling along, on both sides of him and behind. They drew near the outer fringe of the crowd, and then suddenly Caskey ran past them, shouting, —

"Look out for them! Here they come!"

There was a moment of silence. "Never mind," Hugh

said, turning to his comrades. "Come along." Then there broke from the crowd a confused outcry; the words, "Back! Get back!" were distinguishable, and at the menace in the shout Hugh, without looking round, was conscious that his followers wavered and fell away. But he walked on proudly himself, determined to vindicate the leadership he had assumed; he walked into the hostile mob. Those on the outside let him enter, jostling him roughly; he tried to worm his way through, but the crowd closed up and imprisoned him; the men round about him wedged tight and laughed. Hugh struggled for more room and turned his head back in the direction from which he had come. None of his friends had followed him. He cried out at the top of his voice, —

"Stand aside, please! We're going to work to-day!"

A burst of laughter rose from the crowd, followed by derisive shouts. "Stop his mouth!" cried some one. Another repeated the appeal, strengthening the colorless possessive. Those around Hugh pressed him more roughly. He was driven against a gigantic, red-bearded man, who towered above every one else; and this man got one arm up and with a silent grin jammed his elbow hard against Hugh's nose and mouth. "I'll stop his mouth," he said, thrusting hard again with his arm. Maddened by the sudden pain, Hugh used all his strength, made the others give back a little, and launched a furious short-arm blow into the giant's stomach. The man cried out in pain. "Fight!" screamed some one. "Kill the scab!" shouted another, and the men nearest Hugh surged in upon him, and those who could get their arms up began beating his head and face. Those farther away jammed together, trying to come close; each man in the crowd was inspired with the wish to deal his blow at the traitor's head. Hugh's arms were pinioned against his sides; defenseless he shut his eyes and lowering his head thrust with it savagely, blindly. The excitement was communicated to the outermost edges of the crowd, where it was the opinion

that not one man but a gang were fighting their way
through, and at the thought those on the outside began to
heave and push and make the pressure in the centre more
intense. In this desperate jam cries of fear and distress
arose. Hugh at the very centre had succumbed, battered
and squeezed into insensibility; but because of his drooping head and closed eyes no one near him realized it, and
whoever could get a fist free pounded him with hearty
hatred.

From the steps of the company's building where he
overlooked the mob, Gregg was shouting that the mills
were not to be started, that no one was going to work;
but his protests were unheard and unheeded. He came
down from the steps and got into the crowd, shouting and
appealing, but quite without avail. Only when the pressure had grown violent beyond endurance and agonized
cries rose from all quarters was there a gradual yielding;
in this slow loosening of the crowd Gregg was unaware
that three men had sunk lifeless to the ground. Two of
them were small and weak old men who had fainted under
the crushing; their friends carried them away to their
homes while the superintendent was haranguing the crowd
on its folly.

During this time a group stood close round Farrell,
concealing him from Gregg's view. He was not dead, and
they were uncertain what to do with him; they were none
of them disposed to take him home and face his wife. But
when the superintendent had finished, they lifted Farrell
and under cover of the dispersing crowd bore him down the
street a little way; a milk-wagon had stopped by the curb,
and they laid him in this and told the driver, a boy, that
he had been hurt in the jam, that they did not know who
he was, and that he ought to be taken to the hospital.
The boy, eager to be of use, drove off at once and delivered the patient. By the time he had done this, the mob
at the mill gates — all except the usual force of pickets —
had dispersed.

The officials of the company received their first intimation of the serious result of the riot when a message was brought from the hospital, asking some one to come and identify the wounded man who had been left there. The two subordinates whom Gregg sent returned with the news that the man was Farrell, that he had not recovered consciousness, and that it was thought his brain had been injured. The superintendent dispatched a message to Farrell's wife and later in the morning telephoned to Floyd, who replied that he would come out to New Rome immediately.

As it happened, he came in the same car with Stewart Lee, who likewise was responding to a telephone summons. Floyd had entered and taken his seat without noticing who was opposite; then he glanced up and saw Stewart looking at him. Stewart nodded, without cordiality; Floyd did not reply, but gazed impassively out of the window. Stewart stared at him for a while and then shook out a newspaper with a contemptuous crackle.

Floyd was the first to leave the car; and after stopping to get the report of the morning's occurrences from Gregg, he hurried up the hill to the hospital. Hugh's condition was more favorable; he had regained consciousness, and it was thought now that, in spite of the fearful beating, he would recover. The doctor described the wounds in a way that made Floyd mutter savagely: "If I can find the brutes who did it!—" He asked if Farrell's wife had been informed; the doctor replied that she had just gone; they had sent her away greatly relieved in mind, but with no assurance as to when she might be able to see her husband.

Floyd returned to the company's offices to consult with Gregg. The superintendent was not sanguine of ever getting information that would lead to the punishment of Farrell's assailants.

"Nobody did anything," he said. "It was just a mob. I saw it pretty much all — and yet I saw nothing."

"Have you got that list — Farrell's list of the men who were with him?"

"Yes."

"Have each one of them examined; maybe you can get something out of them. Hunt up the driver of that milk-wagon and get his description of the fellows that turned Farrell over to him. There's evidence enough somewhere. I foresee, Mr. Gregg, that we shall have to take independent steps to protect our men from violence; there's no police protection for them here."

"None," said Gregg.

"They shall be given protection," Floyd declared emphatically. "Within a week I shall open the mills, and any man that wants to shall walk in to work without fear of being mobbed at the gate."

"Maybe you can manage that. But then they're liable to get mobbed when they go home."

"I'll fix all that if it's necessary. I'll find them places where they can sleep and eat inside the works — under the company's protection. I'll fit up a lot of barges and moor them along the bank; from now on, if a man's willing to work, I mean to take care of him."

"I believe you do — I believe you will," said the superintendent, stirred by the young man's determined speech. "How do you propose to go about it?"

"I'll be able to give you details to-morrow. This afternoon when I get back to Avalon I'll see what arrangements can be made. It was a blunder — thinking we could start things up in this casual, easy-going, good-natured way; and it won't be repeated."

"You're right," cried Gregg, with one of the sudden outbursts of vigor which he showed sometimes and which Floyd loved. "After this you can't sit down and wait any longer. You've got to drive 'em — drive 'em — drive 'em right into the river."

Meanwhile, hardly two blocks away, in their bleak headquarters over the shoe-store, the executive committee of the Affiliated were in session with their literary adviser. Tustin had himself been one of those who had placed Farrell in the milk-wagon, and he was anxious that a fair account of the trouble should be given to the newspapers.

"We had a little fracas here this morning, Mr. Lee," he had begun when Stewart arrived, "and I made bold to telephone and ask if you would n't come out and maybe help us. It's the first violence that's occurred during the lockout — in spite of all the provocation the men have had. Now we've got to expect that the management will hold this up against us — though it was all of their own making. I thought if you would come out and look into the matter and get at the truth of it, you could write it up in an article that would offset the kind of statements the management will send out. Of course we'll give our side of it to the reporters anyway; but it would help a good bit to have something additional — a kind of independent investigation made by some one on the outside — like yourself."

"What are the facts of the case?" asked Stewart.

"Well, I can only give them to you as I know them and saw them, and I'd rather you would n't go too much by my word, I'd rather you'd ask a lot of others about it — though I guess the stories won't differ very much. I told you we'd been keeping tabs on Farrell, and we knew what to expect. We knew that he'd been treacherous enough to agree with Mr. Halket that he'd try to get a gang of men — soreheads and traitors like himself — to sneak in and start up some of the mills; then they expected the rest of us would weaken and come in. That was the underhanded, tricky game, Mr. Lee, that an employer of labor condescended to conspire with one of his employees — and him the one whose wife — But I mentioned that to you before. Well, we got wind of the plot; you were not the only one that helped to put us next to it — "

"I suspected something of the sort," Stewart interrupted. "Go on."

"We passed the word round among a few we could trust to be on hand at half-past five this morning. Then at twenty minutes to six, we set a fellow to ringing the school-house bell — and that brought out the rest. I told the crowd what to expect; I let 'em know there was to be no violence; I said to 'em, 'You're not to be the aggressors; you're just to mass yourselves thick in front of the gate and not budge for anything or anybody.' No violence in that, was there? I was counting that when the scum came thinking to sneak into the works and saw that crowd waiting for 'em, they'd just slink off instead. And so some of 'em did. But there was quite a gang, headed by Farrell, that rushed blustering in, hitting out at everybody, and in self-defense pretty soon we had to close in on 'em and handle 'em. Farrell was the only one of these fellows that got the least hurt in the row — and anybody will tell you he was from the start the hardest fighter; he came into the crowd with blood in his eye. Two of our men at least had to be carried away unconscious, and there's no means of knowing how many others were badly hurt. But that's the episode that will figure in the papers as riot, violence, and outrage by the Affiliated, and all that kind of thing; you see if it don't — and we'd be all the more glad if you could give your time to making an impartial investigation and writing up the truth — getting it all in for this evening's papers."

"Yes, I'll investigate," Stewart answered. He laughed. "I might as well begin right here. What's your account of the matter, Mr. Caskey?"

"It's all as Mr. Tustin's been giving it. I was just behind Farrell when he came rushing down the hill, drawing a gang of his roughs with him; and they went into the crowd like they was going to cut a swath clean through to the gate. I was right behind and I saw it all."

The other members of the executive committee gave

corroborative testimony; Tustin took Stewart out to introduce him to other men who might tell their unbiased stories. Most of them were vague as to just what had happened, but there was no doubt that they all considered Farrell and his "gang" the aggressors. Stewart felt that with the evidence so unanimous and so truthful it was unnecessary to prolong the investigation. The more that he learned, the more indignant did he begin to feel at Floyd's unworthy attempt to make use of a band of lawless, treacherous villains. It occurred to him that this conspiracy was characteristic of the scheming, devious mind which had pursued so crooked a course in the management of the hospital competition.

Wishing, however, to be absolutely impartial, Stewart called at the company's offices; there he was refused all information. The superintendents, acting under instructions from Floyd, were not talking for newspapers. The company was not prepared to rush into print about the affair. This unwillingness on the part of the officials to put in any defense established the conviction which Stewart had already formed; and he made effective use of it in the article which he composed on his return at noon to Avalon. His imagination helped him; he gave a graphic description of the embarrassment, the evasiveness, the evident consciousness of guilt with which the officials received his questions, and contrasted it with the candor of the workingmen. The proportion of two to one in injured, which the Affiliated had sustained as compared with the "strike-breakers," indicated clearly, as he pointed out, that the strike-breakers were the assailants. He made an eloquent plea, asking the public not to jump hastily to the conclusion that men who were sacrificing themselves for a principle and who had conducted themselves throughout with an extraordinary and heroic forbearance had at last resorted to violence; — though if this had been true, it would in the circumstances have been easily understandable. But to the everlasting glory of the men of

New Rome and especially of their leaders, they needed no extenuation; they had stayed their hands; and not until two of their harmless number had been felled unconscious and others were threatened did they in self-defense lay low the leader of this murderous assault. Even then they were magnanimous; not one of the ruffians who had joined in the attack had been injured; all of them had been allowed to depart in peace. For the leader, who had not been dangerously hurt, it was difficult to feel any sympathy; he was a mercenary, hired by the president of the company to collect a ruffianly band and betray those who had been his fellow workmen.

For a document professing to embody the impartial conclusions of a judicially minded investigator, Stewart's article was rather militant in tone. He signed his name to it; the *Telegram* published it; and Lydia had read it by the time he reached home that evening. She did not comment on it until after they had finished dinner and had gone into the library. Stewart had lighted his cigar and was turning over the pages of a magazine when she said, —

"Stewart, I want to have a talk with you."

"That means you are going to be disagreeable," he answered, with a certain sincerity underlying the lightness of his tone.

"I am afraid you will think so. I want to talk with you about the way you are attacking Floyd — and allying yourself with the men who are attacking him."

"Very well." He paused a moment and then said ungraciously, "What do you find to object to in it?"

"The — the spirit of it, Stewart." He tossed his magazine on the table with an air of irritation. "You might champion the workingmen — when you believe in their cause — but — surely it isn't necessary to do it with such a — such an animus against Floyd. The *Telegram* this evening — it isn't fair, Stewart; it isn't fair. I don't see how you can have such animus."

"Why should I not have it?" he asked her bitterly. "Day before yesterday he ordered me out of his office — held the door for me, while I walked out! To-day he cut me as I sat opposite him in a street-car. Who talks of animus!"

She looked dazed. "But why — what had you done, Stewart?"

"Yes, that's the way." He took his cigar from his mouth and indulged in an unpleasant laugh. "'What had I done?' I'd given provocation, of course; it was all my fault, of course; Floyd could never do anything unjust or wrong, of course, — without being driven to it. Well, if you want to know — I'd dropped into his office to pass some entirely proper comments on the hospital award."

"Stewart! You had no more dignity than that!"

"How quick you are to think the worst! Allow me to reassure you, my dear; I behaved with the utmost dignity. Floyd, to be sure, lost both his head and his temper — with the unseemly result which I have stated. And apparently, judging by his performance to-day in the street-car, he has not yet recovered them."

"Even if that is so —"

"You could express more incredulity, my dear, by saying 'Even if that were so,'" he observed sarcastically.

Tears came into Lydia's eyes, and she was silent a few moments; at last she said in a subdued voice, —

"I was only going to ask you, Stewart, if you could not forgive something to Floyd."

"I have been trying to forgive him all my life."

"For saving your life?"

"For making me forever conscious of that obligation. I have made a greater effort to conquer a great natural disinclination toward him than I ever made for any man. I did everything in my power for him when we were in college together; I have tried to do everything that a friend could do since. But it does n't work out; it does n't work out. And now, so far as I am concerned, he has put himself beyond the pale."

"By choosing to manage his own business in his own way!" She felt goaded into an argument sustaining Floyd's cause against that which Stewart had so passionately adopted. But she stopped at once, repressed by the almost superstitious warning; if he was honestly struggling, groping, she must not interfere, she must not thrust him down. "Of course," she continued mildly, "I'm not criticising you, Stewart, for supporting the side that you think is in the right — and when it means a sacrifice to give such support, I think it's a fine thing for a man to stand by his belief. But it seems to me you could do that and not assail Floyd personally; that is all I mean."

"There you show that you do not understand the situation," Stewart replied. "Floyd is himself the source of all the trouble. He precipitated it, and since the first fell, he has plotted other troubles to follow. You cannot carry on a fight against evil without assailing the evil-doer. And when he is prompted to his work by the basest motives — motives lower than those of mere avarice and greed —"

"Stewart!" cried Lydia. "What do you mean?"

"I have said enough — more than I meant," he answered darkly.

"Floyd never had a base motive in his life!"

"Have you so intimate a knowledge of him?"

"Yes."

"Is it so much more intimate than mine?"

"If you suspect him — yes."

"I do not suspect him. I know. You think, my dear, that you know Floyd intimately. I thought a month ago that I did. But no one ever knows intimately another man. Something is always hidden — something that one may stumble upon some time by chance — or that may perhaps never be revealed. I have learned a thing about Floyd recently which, well as I knew him, I should never have suspected; a thing which explains his treatment of his men as it could not otherwise be explained and which makes it all the more abominable. Now I have said to you on this subject all that I propose to say. If you can retain your old belief in Floyd, do it, by all means. Only do not insist upon my sharing it; for that, in view of what I know, is impossible." He reached out and took up his magazine.

Lydia sat looking at her husband with startled eyes.

"Stewart!" she said at last, "Stewart!"

He lowered his magazine reluctantly.

"You say you know — you cast a blight on Floyd's good name. You make it all a mystery, you do not say what you know or how you know it — and I, being a woman, will not ask what this dreadful thing is." She spoke with a swift earnestness in her low voice. "But one thing I have a right to demand — and that is *how* you know. Who gave you your knowledge? What is your proof?"

"The matter has been common talk among the people of New Rome for years," he replied indifferently.

"And you accept the vile slander of men with a grievance — men who hate him — you let them poison your mind! 'Common talk of the people of New Rome!' You listen to some vile gossip — I don't know what — and then come to me and say you know! Oh, Stewart, Stewart! What has made you so cruel, so vindictive! What has warped your mind!"

"It isn't only common talk that makes me know," he answered, so stung by her rebuke that he was hardly conscious of uttering a lie. "I can't go into details — I can't tell you anything about the affair. I will admit that I should n't have spoken of it to you; the words slipped out unintentionally. After all, to condemn Floyd, one need n't go back further than the occurrence of this morning."

"What do you mean by that?"

"I mean that the whole affair was deliberately planned to provoke violence. Floyd hired this gang of turbulent, lawless dare-devils, — the very fellows that all along had been in disrepute among the men; he hired them to make a bluff at going in and starting to work — knowing perfectly well that they would do it in such a way as to mean violence. And violence was what he wanted, the one thing he desired to precipitate; for it's always the case, with the first exhibition of violence the public sympathy swings away from the union, turns to the employer. It was a perfectly obvious play on Floyd's part; in other words, to attain his own personal ends he is willing to stir up riot and strife, willing to provoke men to bloodshed, perhaps even to murder."

Lydia rose from her chair.

"I cannot sit any longer with you to-night, Stewart," she said, speaking slowly, while she looked down at him with steady eyes. "You are imputing to Floyd motives and thoughts that he never had, — motives and thoughts that stain your own soul."

"If you mean that *I* am animated by such motives—" he began hotly, flinging the magazine upon the table.

"I mean that when you impute them to Floyd, it is a reproach to yourself," she answered in an inexorable voice.

She turned and moved away from him with the soft rustle of her trailing skirt — the pleasant sound that he had many times heard joyously when he had been sitting long alone, the pleasant sound that intimated to him from afar his Lydia's gentle grace. He listened to it now as it grew faint and fainter on the stairs; he listened to it with a wild wish that it were coming toward him instead of going away. But he was too proud to follow it, and too angry; he was only regretful because he had said so much; he was not penitent. He picked up again the magazine which he had twice put down.

"Ah, well," he thought, with an indulgence which was as much for himself as for Lydia, " by to-morrow morning she will be all right."

But Lydia had gone into the room where her baby lay

asleep. She had crept toward the little bed in the darkness and now knelt beside it, straining with tear-filled eyes to see the small face on its pillow, listening with eager ears to the soft, the all but noiseless breathing.

"Little Floyd," she murmured after a while, "you are all that is left to me out of my marriage. God keep you! God help me to guide you right!"

XXVIII

IN LOYALTY AND LOVE

WHETHER, when one could have the pleasure and fun there was in being engaged, it was not tempting Providence to take the step farther and get married was the whimsical question that occurred to Floyd in his growing contentment with his situation, his increasing certainty that he had done the right thing. That he could invite Marion to speculate with him on this point, and that they could sit together elaborating humorous theories and arguments with impersonal seriousness, was, even though he might not perceive it, a sign of progress. Indeed, since Marion's return to Avalon, there had been a rapid development of their intimacy, a rapid growth of confidence. In the beginning a laborious sense that this was one of the duties of his position had compelled Floyd to go to her and share with her his problems and perplexities; never before having made any one the partner of his closest thoughts, he yielded with reluctance to this violation of his sanctuary. But gradually he was won by Marion's responsiveness; to make his disclosures ceased to be a duty, became more and more a pleasure. He was sometimes conscious of how much he had missed hitherto through not having at moments some one in whom to confide — some woman. He had had his impulses to confess to Lydia and ask her help, but he had always proudly withheld himself from this; nothing, he felt, could be more unmanly than to pour out to another man's wife one's innermost experiences. But he was finding now that there was nothing unmanly in discussing with Marion problems of a kind which he had always before locked up in his breast and struggled with unaided.

In this growing intimacy Floyd became less sensitive to Marion's positive, dogmatic manner. Occasionally it would be so exhibited as to cause him an inward sigh and a feeling of wonder that a girl so attractive should not realize the value of deference and hesitation. But he grew more indulgent to her failings when he understood that they proceeded from an excess of frankness rather than from conceit, which he had at one time suspected to be her unlovely fault. She was not conceited; she was kind and sympathetic and thoughtful, as conceited persons never are. He decided that she merely had a sense of being adequate to any emergency which might confront her own life; she did not profess adequacy for the emergencies of other people's lives. That, after all, constituted the difference between a worthy self-confidence and a disagreeable conceit.

And yet, though he was growing more and more fond of her all the time, he could not quite abandon the wish that she were somewhat less adequate even to her own emergencies. She would be so much more appealing if she would only once in a while make an appeal! — show, even tentatively, some fluttering little signal of distress!

That which succeeded best in filling this deficiency and winning him to a gentler and more forbearing regard was her enthusiasm for him. She admired him and applauded his course. When he told her that through an agency he had engaged two hundred armed watchmen, who were to be sent up the river by boat to occupy the works and defend returning workmen from assault, she approved the independent act.

"We can get no protection from the New Rome police," he said to her. "They're few in number and they're in sympathy with the Affiliated. We can get no help from the sheriff of the county. He says — properly enough — that he can't go up there with a posse and wait for trouble. So this seems to be the only course left to us.

IN LOYALTY AND LOVE 445

If it's properly managed — and I'm taking every precaution that it shall be — we'll succeed in overawing the riotously disposed."

He told her the details of his plan; she listened with an absorbed interest. He had never felt it necessary to caution her against repeating information which he gave her about his affairs, and he did not caution her now. Indeed she would have felt hurt by the lack of confidence that such a warning might have seemed to imply.

Two days later she went to see Lydia, for whom she had a compassionate sympathy on account of Stewart's rattle-pated course. In the frequent visits which Lydia and she had exchanged since her return to Avalon there had been no reference to the hostile relations existing between Floyd and Stewart. Marion had guessed the proud loyalty to Stewart which was keeping Lydia silent — a sad, proud loyalty which could only shun a discussion, not attempt a vindication. It had been in Marion's mind, from the time when she had learned of the estrangement, to act as peacemaker, but it was a mission on which she did not embark with any of the confidence which Floyd ascribed to her. Indeed she had delayed and delayed, waiting for the favorable moment; and if Floyd had given her a more complete account of the trouble with Stewart, she would probably have continued to hesitate; at least she might have approached the matter differently. But Floyd had glossed over much of the disagreeable history, wishing to spare himself a recital of Stewart's humiliation, wishing, too, not to lower Stewart in the opinion of another. He had given Marion the idea that the whole trouble was due to Stewart's crazy, radical enthusiasm for labor unions and hatred for capitalists; he had left her in ignorance of the successive grievances which Stewart had been accumulating in the practice of his profession.

And now, Marion thought, the time had come for the two to be reconciled. It was a matter for the women to arrange; she went forth hoping that in the course of the interview she might have an opportunity to seek Lydia's coöperation. But though she lay in wait anxiously, the opportunity seemed not to come. The baby, the theatre, her approaching marriage, with the question as to who would be the bridesmaids, were the disconnected subjects which they reviewed, with never an allusion by Lydia to Floyd or Stewart. Marion was watching her observantly; and though she wore a gay red dress from which at first glance her dark beauty seemed to glow with a happy radiance, there was apparent at intervals to Marion's keen eyes the shadow that would drift down over Lydia's face and to Marion's keen ears the note that would dull Lydia's animated voice. Growing more and more aware of this spirit of sadness, Marion was touched with pity; and at last she cried impulsively, —

"Lydia! Why don't we do something about it?"

"About what?"

"Ah, Lydia, you know. The thing that's making you so sad — the thing that's a cloud on all of us. I'm sure Floyd does n't feel harshly toward Stewart; why can't we bring them together again? If you could only persuade Stewart to cease from his attacks — "

"You ask me to assume that it's Stewart who is to blame," Lydia said, with a quick flush.

Marion humored her in her defensive loyalty to her husband.

"It is n't a matter so much of who's to blame; it's the situation. That can't be improved, can it, so long as Stewart is actively hostile to Floyd — printing such things about him as that letter in the newspaper the other night, giving help to the men who are opposing Floyd. If you could only persuade Stewart to stop; then we could come together and try to adjust things between them. But as long as Stewart goes on, there's no hope of adjustment."

"Stewart's acting according to his own convictions and beliefs."

"Perhaps" — Marion spoke with hesitation — "perhaps you might sway him from those."

"Do you believe that a wife — even for her own happiness — ought to turn her husband from his convictions?"

"If she is sure they are mistaken, she might demonstrate that to him. I didn't mean, Lydia, that you should ask him to yield his convictions in deference to your wish."

"So far as his sympathy with the labor union is concerned, and his conviction that it should not be exterminated as Floyd is trying to exterminate it, I don't know that Stewart is mistaken. I can't argue with him about that; I don't know enough; and when he talks to me on the subject I can't see any flaw in his reasoning. He is entirely conscientious in supporting the union — and, in that way, in antagonizing Floyd."

"It isn't his supporting those principles that makes the trouble," Marion insisted. "I'm sure Floyd is liberal enough to grant him that freedom and still look upon him as a friend. But Floyd can't look on him as a friend after such personal attacks as Stewart has made; it's the personal thing that maybe you could smooth out, Lydia; if you could persuade Stewart that Floyd hasn't any such motives as Stewart has been — "

Lydia held out her hand with a look of distress.

"I've tried — I've tried my best. But Stewart when he has an idea can see only that, he sees straight ahead to that, and everything must conform to it. Floyd's cause is a bad one and every action that Floyd takes in the cause is — is a bad action. I can't convince Stewart that it isn't. He's fortified with evidence — evidence — I don't know! Here now — here is the way his mind works; he tells me that the riot the other morning was deliberately provoked by Floyd — that Floyd hired a band of desperate men to make a pretense of going to work, knowing that there would be trouble, hoping there would be — because, after the first violence, public sympathy would cease to be with the workingmen and would turn to him. Stewart has got himself into a frame of mind where he seriously believes that; how, tell me, please, am I to meet such an argument as that? — how, how am I to persuade him?"

Her voice had gathered a passionate swiftness and feeling as she spoke; now she waited, looking at Marion with despairing yet eager eyes.

"Ah, how can he believe that!" Marion exclaimed. "Floyd trying to provoke violence — when his whole purpose from the beginning has been to prevent it! Why else did he shut down the works? You might ask Stewart that. The very thing that Stewart takes as proof — why, Floyd tried to send those men in quietly and secretly, so that there would n't be any trouble. And now — this very night, at eleven o'clock — expressly to prevent violence he's going to land two hundred guards; he's sending them up the river — sending them by night, by boat — by coal-barges even, so that nobody shall see them or suspect and cause a riot; he's sending them just to protect the works and the men who want to work, and to prevent any more violence. His one thought now is to guard the safety of all his men — those opposed to him as well as those who are friendly. If you were to tell Stewart all these things, I don't see how he could any longer believe that Floyd is capable of such — such awful thoughts."

Lydia shook her head. "I feel that Stewart holds things in reserve," she answered. "I appeal to him in one way; he finds a reply in another. — Oh, I can't explain it to you, Marion," she broke off abruptly, "but I 'm afraid it 's hopeless, hopeless. I daresay I ought n't to give up trying; I 've grown discouraged. I 'll do what I can; I 'll do what I can — to make Stewart feel more justly toward Floyd; but I 'll do nothing to turn him from a work in which he believes."

Marion recognized the declaration as the pathetic effort to display faith and loyalty when they could no longer be

IN LOYALTY AND LOVE 449

spontaneously rendered. She took Lydia's hand and kissed her.

"We'll come out of it all right, dear," she said. "All of us. You and Stewart and Floyd and I. Next year you'll be eating your Thanksgiving dinner with us, and we'll be eating our Christmas dinner with you. See if we aren't."

Lydia followed her to the door, reluctant to have this spirit of courage and cheerful confidence depart. It occurred to her that perhaps she had timorously made too little of an effort, and that perhaps in her dread of pushing Stewart down she might neglect the obvious duty of keeping him afloat. She would try if she might not touch him gently without sending him to the bottom.

Floyd dined that evening with Marion and her family, and afterwards started with her in his carriage to the theatre. As they drove, she questioned him about the expedition that was to go up the river that evening. It was all in readiness, he informed her; the steamboat and two barges were in fact leaving at about that time and would reach the works a little after ten o'clock. Marion asked where the watchmen were to sleep and how they were to live, and he explained that the barges had been roofed over and fitted up inside with bunks and that mattresses and bedding were also being transported for use in one of the buildings; arrangements could be made to quarter the men there very comfortably. Then he laughed.

"I don't expect they'll have to endure a siege," he said. "My opinion is that within a few days our men will come flocking in to work. — You're the only person — except Gregg and the agent — that I've told a word of all this to; not even the other superintendents know anything definite about it yet. I don't know, of course, what leakage there may be through the watchmen themselves, but I hope not much; they were all of them cautioned about the necessity of strict silence — and I guess in their business they understand it."

For a moment he was unaware of the consternation which with this speech had fallen on the girl; then, to his amazement, she exclaimed in a low, frightened voice, —

"Oh, Floyd! I — I told!"

"This?" He turned towards her. "You told — this?"

"Yes. Oh, Floyd! — " her words came in quick, fluttering breaths; she seemed on the brink of tears. "I told Lydia — to-day — this afternoon. I never thought — I wanted her to show Stewart how you're doing everything to prevent trouble; she was telling me what Stewart believes, and I wanted her to be able to show him — I told her about this. Oh, Floyd! — let's turn round and go back — let me go home and telephone to Lydia — not to say anything about it; — tell him to turn round, Floyd; she hasn't said anything yet, I'm sure; quick, Floyd, quick!"

While she was pouring out her distressed confession in the voice that he hardly knew as hers, so frightened, so appealing, he looked at her curiously; elation was mounting in his heart. He looked at her, but he could see little of her face in the darkness, nothing of its expression — and he wished with a sudden passionate longing that at this very moment he could see as well as hear! She made him aware that, all unconsciously in her humility and her beseeching, she had crept closer to him; and a tenderness for her that he had never before felt thrilled him and choked his throat. He put his arm round her and drew her closer still.

"Never mind, dear; never mind," he murmured, in an unsteady voice. Though his voice was low, within him his soul was stirred and shouting in joy because she had confessed herself recreant to a trust. What though Stewart, what though all the world knew his plans! this moment *he* knew that he loved the girl in his arms.

"Floyd, you're — you're too gentle with me!" She broke for an instant into a pathetic little sob of relief and

IN LOYALTY AND LOVE

shame. "Had n't we — had n't we better turn back, Floyd? — so that I can telephone to Lydia?"

"Oh, no, we don't need to do that. — Perhaps it would be just as well, when we get downtown, if I stop at a hotel and send her a message. — But don't worry about it any more, Marion; it's all right, really."

"Thank you, Floyd, for — for taking it so. — But I don't see how you can ever trust me with anything again."

He laughed. "Put that with the things that you can't see for yourself — till I show you. I guess there are n't many — but we'll call that one."

He felt her hand groping round, he felt it find his and press it gently.

It was a long drive to the region of theatres and hotels, and happy as he was Floyd could not help considering after a while what might be the consequences of Marion's indiscretion. He could not believe that they might be serious; to imagine them so would be to imagine both an unexampled fierceness and an improbable swiftness of action on Stewart's part. He said after a while with some reluctance, —

"I guess I can't very well telephone to Lydia about this thing, Marion. Would you mind doing it? I think you could put it so that it would be less awkward for her."

"I'd be glad if you'd let me," Marion answered.

The carriage stopped in front of a hotel which was next door to their theatre; as they were going in, Marion asked, in a deprecating voice, "Do my eyes look very red, Floyd?" and he replied, "They look very nice and shiny."

"Ah," she said, with a grateful gleam of humor, "you *are* nice, Floyd, — not to mind even red eyes!"

He waited for her outside the booth while she telephoned; it took longer than he had supposed it would do. When at last she emerged, he knew at once by her white, frightened face that she had something unsuspected and ominous to report.

"I was too late," she said, as they stood withdrawn into

a deep window recess. "Lydia told him at dinner — it was all my fault — I'd advised her — and she was so anxious to show him he was misjudging you — she told him everything — to make it clear what your motives were. And when she was all through, he got up and left the house; he went to New Rome. She feels terribly — so guilty — but she isn't to blame, Floyd, — it was my fault entirely. I didn't tell it to her as a confidence; she called up your house and then mine, trying to reach you and warn you — but we'd gone; and she was in despair."

Floyd was silent a moment. "I guess I'll telephone to Gregg; I'll have to ask you to wait this time," he said. "Sit down here — and don't take it so hard, Marion; there's nothing to feel agitated about," he added kindly. "I'll be with you as soon as I can — too bad that we'll have to miss so much of the first act."

She waited ten minutes for him; then he came to her briskly.

"All right now," he said. "Everything fixed. Pick up your skirts and run."

He hurried her gayly into the theatre; before they went to their seats he called the usher aside for a moment. The first act was nearly over, but the play was a rather obvious kind of farce, and it did not take long to gather up the threads of the plot. Floyd settled down immediately to the enjoyment of the performance; he was especially delighted by a fat woman with a monstrous voice and an involuntary talent for breaking furniture. Marion did not pay very close attention to the play, and would probably not have been much diverted if she had followed it; she was constantly stealing anxious glances at Floyd, trying to decide if his amusement was genuine, if he had really put aside all care, if he had perhaps, in some instant, remarkable way, done something to prevent all possibility of a clash. With a thankful heart she could at least assure herself that his good spirits were not in any degree assumed.

IN LOYALTY AND LOVE

In the middle of the last act the usher came down the aisle and gave Floyd a telegram. Floyd read it and said quietly, —

"I'm sorry, Marion; it's from Gregg, and we'll have to go."

She drew her wraps about her without a question and followed him up the aisle in the dim half-light of the theatre.

XXIX

STEWART TAKES THE FIELD

It irritated Stewart to find, on arriving at his house, that his father-in-law was there. The fact that Mr. Dunbar had been for so long Stewart's most ardent and partisan admirer had made his defection in this crisis the more galling; and when they met, Stewart was always aware of tentative, foolish efforts on the part of the little man for his redemption. These he was accustomed to suppress with inexorable promptness; but on this afternoon he was in no mood to submit to even the most glancing suggestion that he was pursuing a mistaken course. He had been in conference nearly all day with various union leaders, seeking to influence them into taking some positive step in behalf of their brethren at New Rome; but they had been unwilling or stupid or incompetent, and his endeavors had in the end all been profitless. For this reason he was now the less disposed to endure any criticism which hinted of the waste he was making of his time and abilities.

Mr. Dunbar was in the hall with Lydia, on the point of leaving when Stewart entered.

"Hello, Stewart!" he said; and he added with a tactless cordiality that seemed bent on ignoring facts, "How's architecture?"

Stewart hung up his coat with some deliberation before replying. "I guess you'll have to ask Bennett & Durant about that," he said at last as he came forward. He shook hands with his father-in-law and kissed Lydia, but in neither act was there any particular demonstrativeness. Mr. Dunbar's question had completed the work of irritation which his presence had begun.

"Oh, well, I guess you can afford not to begrudge those fellows a little temporary success," Mr. Dunbar continued. "When you get back into harness again, you'll make their fur fly. — And, by the way, Stewart; about this New Rome matter that you're interesting yourself in; you know your taking such a public and radical stand in it is beginning to come back at me. My men are getting stirred up; they know you're my son-in-law, and they think I'm bound to share your sentiments. I don't believe you want to make trouble for me. Of course, in this affair — I daresay Floyd hasn't been entirely wise in all his acts; I've had occasion to differ with his views, as you know; — but still on the general principle his stand is the only one according to which we manufacturers can do business and live — and I hope — "

"Father," broke in Lydia, who in an anxious glance had detected the storm gathering on her husband's face, "you mustn't bother Stewart with such questions now; he's tired; you mustn't bother him. Come, Stewart, and have a cup of tea — or will you lie down for a while and let me read to you?"

"Oh, all right," said Mr. Dunbar good-naturedly. "I didn't realize — Good-night, Stewart; by-by, Lydia."

He went out, and Stewart turned to his wife with an expression of gratitude for the way in which she had shielded him. "Thank you, Lydia," he said. "If you don't mind, you might make me some tea."

The tea and Lydia's gentle eagerness to entertain him developed in him a spirit of contentment; for her part she became tremulous with excitement when he put his cup down and announced that he felt a good deal better. If she could only get him into just the right mood! — and if she could only put things before him in just the right way! She hoped she might find the courage and the words. She would not try to hurry the moment; she would wait patiently. But meanwhile she had to conceal her agitation, and in the effort to do this as well as to prepare his mood, she showed him shy little attentions, a solicitude that amused and pleased him; she "made conversation" with him as eagerly as if he were an unfamiliar visitor to whom she wished to be especially polite. She went to the piano and sang him a new song that she had been practicing that day; he was touched again in a youthful spot by her charm. It was a great comfort to him to find that she was disposed to be his wife again and not his censor — that she was so sweetly trying to atone to him for her injustice. A kindness toward her permeated him; he remembered that it had been a long time since he had shown her a token of this feeling, and he determined that the next day he would look about in the shops downtown until he found something that would be a present worthy of his love.

They went upstairs to dress for dinner; she heard Stewart moving about in his dressing-room, whistling gayly, and that meant, she knew, that he was in a good humor. His whistle slid irrelevantly from aria into ragtime, from rag-time into stately march; and then she heard it swing off into the little song that she had just sung — and that pleased her. He came into her room all dressed before she was quite ready to go down and cried with a boyish glee, "Aha! beat you again, old lady!" She had a happy, fluttering premonition that she would win back her old Stewart this night.

It was not till dinner was half over that she made her attempt. Then she said, —

"I had a call from Marion this afternoon, Stewart."

"And how's Marion?" he asked.

"Nice, as usual. I had to stand up for you, though, against her. Now you'll thank me for that, won't you?" She laughed at him with at the same time a genuine appeal in her eyes for an expression of his pleasure. He did not deny her this.

"You took my part; good for you. Marion was pretty rough on me, was she?"

"Oh, no, she really wasn't, Stewart; she only thought

you were n't being quite fair to Floyd. I told her that
you had been acting all along as you believed — and that
you thought Floyd had been to blame — and especially
for deliberately trying to provoke violence. And then she
gave me her side — Floyd's side — and asked me if I
would n't put it before you; she did it in really the nicest
spirit, Stewart — and I thought you might like to hear."

He did not answer at once; he did not even respond
with his eyes to her anxious glance; and the sanguine
confidence went from her heart. While she waited for
him to speak, she became aware of the coldness that had
settled on her hands; she clasped them together, waiting.

"Well, what did Marion say?" he asked. The enthusiasm which had rung in his voice and which had led her
on so hopefully had all at once failed; she recognized the
unrelenting quality that she had come to dread.

"Why, about the riot the other morning," she began;
and then she hurried the story, as if afraid that he might
cut her short before she had reached her strongest plea.
"Floyd meant to send the men in so quietly — he did n't
think any one would know — he did n't expect there would
be any trouble — and he 'd especially warned them not to
get into trouble, Marion says. She says that he 's been
trying his best to get through without any one's being
hurt on either side. To show me how thorough and careful and anxious he is to take every precaution for this,
she told me what he 's doing to-night."

"What 's that?" asked Stewart; and because he betrayed more interest, Lydia's hope rose again and she
said eagerly, —

"He wants to keep everybody protected; there are n't
police enough in New Rome to do it when the people are
excited as they are now; and he 's sending up two hundred
watchmen, all armed, so that men won't dare to get into
riots around the mills any more."

"That 's interesting," said Stewart, in a tone that convinced Lydia she was making headway. "They 're going up to-night — these watchmen?"

"Yes. And, oh, Stewart, this is the part that shows how careful Floyd is, how anxious to guard against violence, — more even than his thought of sending these men. They 're going up very quietly — by boat — in a way that would never be suspected; because if they went out in the usual way by train or trolley car and tried to get in at the gate, Floyd thought there might be some trouble — some of the men might n't understand why they 'd been sent and might try to keep them out; especially seeing they had guns, the workmen might think it was sort of ominous, I suppose, not understanding the motive. So Floyd arranged to have them go up the river very secretly at night by boat and get into the works from the river side; oh yes, — and so that nobody watching along the shore should suspect the boat and give an alarm about armed men coming, he 's arranged to have them go up in coal-barges, towed by a little tug — coal-barges roofed over, that no one would ever suspect. Of course the only place where riots and violence would be liable to occur is right round the mill gates; and if these watchmen can only be landed quietly in the mills, they can prevent any trouble that may threaten. Don't you think really, Stewart, that this puts Floyd's motives in a better light?"

"Did Marion say what time these watchmen would start — what time they 'd arrive?"

"They were to reach the works at about eleven o'clock."

She waited anxiously for Stewart to pronounce an opinion, to make some slight admission of leniency, even the most grudging. If he would do this, she could have faith; but if he should fail to render justice now —

"You regard this measure as an indication that Floyd has forsworn violence?" Stewart asked the question mildly, looking at his wife with a smile.

"Why, yes, Stewart, of course. What else could it mean?"

"It might be interpreted, perhaps, as a determination to fortify himself by means of violence. However, we differ so radically — we must differ so radically — on the subject of Floyd's motives that there is no use in our discussing such a matter as this."

She had failed; she leaned back in her chair despondently. Stewart was meditating and did not observe the dejected expression on her face. Finally he said, —

"Lydia, will you excuse me for a few moments? I have to telephone."

She sat waiting for him idly, indifferently. At last he returned with a brisk step and an excitement in his manner which she at once noticed.

"Sorry; I'll have to have my coffee and run," he announced. "I thought I could stay at home this evening, but it turns out I can't. A matter of business — "

He swallowed his coffee, and rose. Lydia had been watching him; his nervous eagerness to escape confirmed her suspicion. She accompanied him out into the hall where the servants should not hear, and while he was putting on his overcoat she stood before him, in front of the outer door.

"Stewart," she said, "are you going to New Rome?"

He put on his hat and dropped his hands into his overcoat pockets. There was a hint of defiance in the movement and in his voice as he answered, —

"Yes."

"To make use of the information I have given you?"

"It's a matter of life and death to those men at New Rome."

"You are willing to make use of me — to put me in the position of betraying Floyd's secrets to his enemies?"

"If you choose to look upon it in that way — if you happen to be in possession of Floyd's secrets — I must make even that sacrifice — I must ask you to make it."

"Stewart!" With one arm behind her she leaned

back against the door; her face was white. "If you do this — I can never look upon you as an honorable man again."

He bit his lip angrily and then spoke with repressed anger, —

"Then I must make even that sacrifice. If I did not go to warn those men of this crime against them that is being secretly prepared — where would my honor be? — the men in whose cause I believe, whose counsels I have shared! The one dishonorable thing that I could do to-night, Lydia, would be to stay at home with you."

"Stewart," she said inflexibly, "if you go, I shall despise you all my life."

"Better so than that I should despise myself," he answered hotly. "Assassins on the way — and I not warn the victims! Lydia! you certainly do not mean to hold the door against me!"

She stood a moment, while with his hands in his pockets he waited, looking at her.

"No, Stewart; no," she said; she stepped aside and opened the door. "I'll hold it open for you — and the Stewart that I knew and loved goes out — never to return."

"Ah," he answered, as he passed out, "you are melodramatic to-night."

He was too stirred by the importance of that which he was about to do to feel much discomfort over this parting from his wife. He strode away wishing that she had not made such an unpleasant scene, but he did not tingle long with the memory. His mind turned eagerly to the preparation of the speech that was to awaken the men of New Rome. The dramatic opportunity to put before them this most important, unsuspected news elated him, thrilled him with a sense of power; this night it was his part to be these people's guide, and he would rouse them to such a pitch of righteous wrath as would sweep away forever the vile oppression under which they had suffered. At last he had Floyd in his power! These two thoughts, these two inspirations mingled, and stimulated his brain. As he waited upon the street corner for a car, he ran swiftly over the specific details on which Lydia had so pathetically enlarged, assigned to each its dramatic value, sought with a swift imagination the fiery suggestion that their presentment might contain. Sentences sprang to life whose energy shook him even as he stood. It was a fine mild November night, with the stars shining, the half-moon gleaming among the denuded trees, with no sound except that of a wagon rattling in the distance; then the car that he was to take swung round the curve, and as he stepped out into the street, he flung one hand up and cried hilariously, —

"David and Uriah! David and Uriah!"

When he entered the car, the two girls who were the only other passengers ascribed to their own charms the radiance of his handsome face. They directed at him provocative smiles, but he sat in a corner quite unconscious of their presence and fitted together the speech which was to emancipate New Rome.

It was not yet nine o'clock when he entered the headquarters of the executive committee. Tustin, Gaskey, and McGraw were there awaiting him.

"What's happened?" McGraw asked excitedly. "What's up?"

Stewart had no intention of making any premature disclosures. "Have you called a meeting?" he asked. "Have you got the men together?"

"There's quite a crowd at the hall now," Tustin answered. "There's others coming. When I got your telephone, I sent out at once and began rounding 'em up. We've got Pulaski down there to hold 'em — all he's got to tell 'em is that important news is coming to 'em from Avalon."

"Then we'll go right down there," said Stewart.

"Hold on. It may be all right — but we'd like to hear

about it first and consider it as a committee. The men will wait. You said you could n't tell it by telephone; you can tell it now."

"There's no time to waste about it," Stewart replied decisively. "It's something for all the people to know and at once. I'll tell you when I tell them — right away. Come on, Mr. Tustin."

The union leader was not well pleased by this evasion of his authority.

"I've trusted you, Mr. Lee," he said. "If you've got nothing worth while to tell us — or if it should be something that turned out to be a fake, you'd better just let the committee have it; we've called a mass meeting on your say-so, but we don't want to go before it if it ain't worth while."

"You'll have to trust me as to that," Stewart replied haughtily. "I don't come out here at this time of night on errands that are not worth while."

Tustin opened the door. "Come along, then," he said bluntly.

The hall was the one where the Saturday night dances took place. Pulaski and another man stood at the bottom of the stairs to prevent the admittance of any one about whose loyalty there might be suspicion.

"All right," he said, when Stewart and the members of the executive committee entered. "It's pretty full now." He closed the street door and followed the others up the stairs into the crowded, clamorous hall. Men had climbed up on the few benches placed against the walls and stood lined there, shoulder to shoulder, shouting vociferously to friends whom they recognized in the dense mass oscillating below. On the platform a young man with his slouch hat pulled down over his eyes was playing the piano; the feeble notes of "Home, Sweet Home" were lost in the echoing din.

Tustin and Stewart elbowed their way through the crowd and mounted the platform; the musician descended

STEWART TAKES THE FIELD

into the audience. Stewart took off his overcoat and laid it on the piano; it was perhaps his revelation of himself then in evening clothes as much as anything else which caused an outbreak of applause. There were no chairs on the platform; Tustin stood beside Stewart and held up his hand.

"Most of you know Mr. Stewart Lee," he said. "He is a good friend of ours and he has come here to-night to give us a message of importance."

Then Tustin walked over and sat down on the piano stool. The audience, after a brief applause, stood in an expectant stillness.

"Gentlemen," said Stewart, speaking slowly and with an impressive gravity, "at eight o'clock to-night I learned — it matters not how or from whom — but I learned beyond the possibility of doubt" — he drew and held up his watch — "that within two hours from this time a crushing blow would fall upon your heads. I have come to tell you what you may expect."

He paused; the silence was breathless.

"No doubt you guess the source. The same hand which struck you that foul blow one morning last week before the sun had risen is lifted now with dagger drawn in the dark; it hovers over you now while you stand here, it hovers over your homes where your wives and children await your return — I will give you time to return — to return and arm yourselves!" — Stewart flung the words with a shout — "but let me show you first some of the machinations of that unseen, hovering, grasping, and death-dealing hand.

"You know the story of David and Uriah — how David looked from the housetop and saw Uriah's wife — and Uriah was put in the forefront of the battle, where he fell. You all know the story. But has it occurred to you that here, in New Rome within a few days, this old, old story has been reënacted, with a few modern alterations, yet substantially the same? What matters it that the Uriah whom we know, instead of being an honorable patriot, is a traitorous hireling — or that instead of being slain he is recuperating in a hospital? What matters it, I say? — for the curse on David remains the same. Do you men know who David is?"

He paused for answer, and it came — "Yes — yes!" — an angry shout. Already he had the passion of the men aroused; the intensity of their interest made him desire to prolong his sensation of power.

" Why do I recall to you this thing? It is that you may see how the mind that could conceive that small and double perfidy is the same that plots the greater and more treacherous attack to-night. My friends, you have been cozened into a careless comfort because you have been told that no strike-breakers, no scabs would be introduced into the mills. That is true, my friends; no strike-breakers, no scabs will be introduced into the mills. But there are men worse than strike-breakers, men worse than scabs — and two hundred of these men, armed and ready, are creeping stealthily upon you at this moment through the dark. They do not come by day along the ordinary channels; they move secretly at night, for theirs is a dark and wicked trade. To the American who loves liberty there is no uglier word than that which describes these men — the word 'mercenaries;' and there is no uglier thing. Mercenaries, armed and shipped for a purpose — what purpose? Can you guess? What should you think were you to wake to-morrow and find the mills a fortress — rifles leveled at you if you paused before the gate — each knot-hole in the fence become a port-hole for a gun — and every shed a cover for sharp-shooters to roost? Unless you act to-night, that is what to-morrow you will see."

"Where are they?" shouted a man in the back of the hall, and the question was taken up inarticulately by the crowd. Tustin rose from the piano stool and held up a hand invoking silence.

"You have two hours," cried Stewart, "and I shall not

detain you long. A steamboat is pushing two coal-barges up the Yolin River — coal-barges roofed over, empty of coal, but not empty of men. These barges will be pushed ashore at the mill landing at eleven o'clock to-night. The steamboat will leave them and go back down the river. — And then — single file, two hundred mercenaries armed with rifles will march up the path from the landing, and occupy the mills. And once that occupation is achieved, what next? How many more, if need be, could be poured into the fortress — marching boldly in through the streets? Do you think that mercenaries like these, who live by the sword, will be careful of human life? They are sent that the works may be opened by force of arms — and that means slaughter. Why, the most innocent demonstration that any two or three of you may make, one irresponsible outcry by some one in a crowd, may be the signal for a rifle volley. Once the first shot is fired, who may forecast the bloodshed and murder that will follow? And when by force of arms you are crushed, out comes Uriah from the hospital, marches boldly into the works with his gang, and claims his reward. For nowadays, it is not necessary for David to kill Uriah — only to bargain with him. And you men are forever crushed if these two hundred hired assassins land to-night."

"They shall not land!" cried Tustin, raising his clenched fist before the audience could respond. "Spread the alarm — bring your guns — batter down the gate — we'll meet them, men, — we'll meet them!"

With wild cheering the crowd rushed and jammed at the stairs; Tustin and Stewart remained standing on the platform, Tustin gesticulating with both arms, shouting to keep alive the tumult — "No surrender! — Never let them land!" — any words that could be pitched as fuel to the flame. At last the hall was emptied, the shouting thinned away along the streets, Stewart put on his hat and overcoat and went down the stairs with Tustin. The mill entrance was only a block away, and already a crowd was collected in front of it; Stewart and Tustin started for it running. By the time they came up, two men with axes were smashing down the gates while the others shouted encouragement and jeered at the company's watchman who stood inside, feebly protesting. In a few moments the breach had been made and the mob swarmed in across the bridge and ran to the bank above the landing. This bank was a steep slope of twenty feet or more; at the bottom was the level jutting beach, from which a narrow path slanted up the slag-covered face of the slope. Close along the edge of the bank ran the tracks; Tustin sent men skirmishing to bring in cars and form with them a barricade. From both directions cars of all descriptions — low trucks, flat-cars, high-sided freight cars — were rushed up and strung together — with little intervals between. Stewart walked about, fascinated by the excitement, the shouting, the constant pouring in of men carrying guns, flourishing revolvers, swinging lanterns; the mills which Stewart had seen on other nights wreathed and seamed with fire loomed now sinister dark shapes; about them the lanterns danced fantastically, went writhing up the long black vistas, or shot, comet-like, out of darkness into darkness.

Tustin neglected nothing. From the sloping town a school-house bell began to ring, in hurrying, unmeasured peals.

XXX

THE NIGHT ATTACK

THERE was a blockade of trolley cars in front of the Halket Company's works. Floyd stepped down from the rear platform on which he had been impatiently standing and hurried along the sidewalk. He had expected to find himself at once in the midst of a tumult; but although people were running through the streets and fire-engines and hook-and-ladder wagons were at the mill entrance obstructing all traffic, there was a singular absence of noise. Those whom he passed were mostly women, and they seemed to be scurrying along in a subdued, voiceless panic. From beyond the high board fence in the direction of the river there rose a few remote, unimpressive cries; Floyd was beginning to think that in spite of all the evidence of agitation given by the presence of women and children and fire-engines in the street, there was nothing serious taking place. Then he heard from the direction of the river the sound of shots — three, fired in rapid succession.

The fire-engines, the hook-and-ladder wagons, were deserted by all except their drivers, and were wedged together in possession of the street; a few firemen were dragging a length of hose out of the mill-yards across the bridge. Floyd passed between the wagons and ran up the steps of the company's offices. Gregg and three of his subordinates were standing at the windows of the general superintendent's room when Floyd entered.

"Well, Mr. Gregg?" he asked as he came across the room.

The superintendent turned with a start, as did the others.

"Hell's broke loose down there, Mr. Halket," he said.
"Come — take a look."

He drew Floyd up to the window, which commanded a view of the roadway leading from the bridge to the riverbank. Lights were swinging and darting back and forth and across — lights green and red as well as yellow, for the trainmen's lanterns had been seized — and in the erratic illumination from all these it seemed to Floyd as if the whole population of New Rome must be massed down among the mills. He could see the motion, the agitation in the crowd — people running far off to the left and right, solitary lantern-bearers making their way in the distance toward the river to be suddenly blotted out by some shed; and through the open window he could hear more distinctly than in the street the undertone of sound, the intermittent cries, the desultory rifle shots, once the staccato of a revolver.

"What's happened?" Floyd said, turning sharply away.

"They poured into the works all of a sudden at about half-past nine," Gregg answered. "I sent word down to the ferry below the bridge to intercept the *Emerald Isle* and the barges. But she was ahead of her schedule; and by the time my message reached the ferry, she'd passed under the bridge. There was no way of sending word out to her; the men had the bank all patrolled, and nobody could get out in a boat — or even yell an alarm. They let the *Emerald Isle* push the barges aground at the landing and cut loose; and then they began shooting when the watchmen showed their heads. The *Emerald Isle* tried to tow them off again when she saw what trouble they were in; and then the fire was turned on her; from what I hear, the pilot was wounded if not killed; anyhow, the *Emerald Isle* gave up trying to rescue anybody but herself, and got away as fast as she could. And ever since, those poor devils have been cooped up between decks of the barges, potted at by anybody in town that has a gun. I've got the police and the firemen; — the police could n't do anything — well, there are a couple of thousand people in there now — and the firemen could n't; I thought they might turn the hose on the crowd, but there's no water near enough, and it would be like squirting at a fire with a syringe. The sheriff came and read the riot act, and nobody listened; then he went away to telephone the governor to call out the militia. I don't see as there's anything we can do to help those poor devils, — but just pray for the governor to act."

"I can make an effort," said Floyd. "While I'm gone, telephone the Berwick Coal-Boat Company — no, the office will be closed; call up James D. Berwick at his house; tell him he's got to send a boat up here to take off these barges. Tell him you'll pay any price to the captain and the men who'll do the job — tell him to send 'em ready to fight — and for God's sake at once. Berwick will do it; he'll find the men. — I'll see you later; call him up *at once*, Mr. Gregg."

"But, Mr. Halket — you can't go into that mob — you can't handle it — and — you'll be just the man they're looking for!"

"Please call up Berwick."

"But, Mr. Halket!" Gregg clutched his arm imploringly, and with the other hand pointed to the opera-hat in which Floyd had come straight from the theatre. "That hat anyway! It'll make you a marked man. — Take mine."

"I want to get their notice," Floyd answered. He drew his arm away and went out of the room.

Some women and girls were standing huddled together on the bridge, as if they were afraid to go farther; and when he passed them, they began to hiss. Others a little distance away recognized him and joined in the demonstration. He walked on as if he did not hear, although the sound not only followed him but even went rippling before him; his cheeks were hot; he had not been prepared for this, he felt that nothing could have hurt him so much as this from wives and daughters of his men.

The crowd, swarming off along the lanes between the mills, was less dense than it had appeared; and in order to gain a general view of the situation, Floyd turned and went up one of these by-ways. He escaped the hissing, and in the greater darkness here he was apparently not recognized; the opera-hat, at the same time that it was a distinction, was also something of a disguise. As he walked, he caught fragments of talk — "They say there's two dead bodies lying on the barge." — "How many of our men have been killed?" — "They're goin' to pour oil on the river and set fire to it; that 'll smoke 'em out." — "Why the hell don't somebody bring some dynamite and blow 'em out o' the water?" Floyd soon derived an idea of the temper of the men.

At last he worked his way into the throng on the edge of the bank a hundred yards up the river; and from this position he could dimly see the two barges lying side by side inshore. At intervals, from under or between the freight cars which were lined up below him, darted a flash of light in a downward stab — and the shot would be followed by cheers. Three times from one of the barges there was an answering flash.

It was clear that for the watchmen the only hope was in the coming of a tug to the rescue, or in the yielding of the mob to some impulse of mercy. They could not land, they could not scale the bank and then the barricade of cars; the attempt would mean massacre.

Floyd walked down beside the freight cars through the mob in the direction of the rifle flashes. It was so dark, and men were jostling so eagerly, so blindly to reach some point from which they could see what was happening, that he went on unnoticed. He came to a place where the crowd had given back a few feet from one of the cars; the men in front were stooping, looking under the trucks; and among these men Floyd saw Stewart, peering with the rest.

THE NIGHT ATTACK 471

He turned; there, from under the car, protruded a pair of legs; and at that moment the man to whom the legs belonged discharged a rifle. Anger overwhelmed Floyd — anger that this dastardly creature should lie there in ambush, trying to maim or murder if ever a hand or a head was raised; he stooped and with a sudden passionate strength gripping the man by the ankles, he dragged and flung him with one motion out from under the car. In the next instant, he had wrenched away his rifle; he sprang with it through the narrow gap that separated this car from the next, and hurled it down the slope into the river.

A furious shout went up from the men who had seen and stood astounded. But Floyd turned at once, and seizing the low side of the flat-car, sprang up. A clinker of slag struck him in the chest as he was getting to his feet, but he stumbled to the middle of the car and took off his hat and held it aloft.

"Men!" he cried, but they drowned him with a shout of wrath, — "Halket!" "Shoot him!" "Kill him!" Missiles began to fly.

Floyd shielded his eyes with one arm, holding up his hat. — "Shoot him!" "Kill Halket!"

"Ah, don't! Don't!" came the wild imploring cry from just below — and Stewart leaped forward and began scrambling up on the car. A man rushed out to pull him back; Floyd, shielding his eyes and glancing down, saw that it was Tustin. But Stewart at the man's clutch kicked out frantically even while he climbed and with all his force drove his boot-heel into Tustin's face. Tustin sank upon the ground with a broken jaw, and Stewart sprang up to Floyd, who was shouting at the top of his voice, "Hear me, please! Just a few words! *Just* a few words!"

But Stewart's act had maddened the mob beyond all power of words to control; down close in front of the car men were stooping, digging up clinkers of slag with both hands, cursing and yelling as they stooped to the ground; a man rushed in and flung his lantern at Floyd, but it went to one side, whirling down into the river. Stewart sprang in front of Floyd, faced him, and with his back to the crowd flung both arms wide to protect him. "Lie down, Floyd; lie down!" he besought him; struck heavily in the back by a stone, he lurched forward against Floyd, still crying, "Lie down!"

Floyd tried to pull him to one side and shelter him from the storm of iron and stone and slag; but Stewart flung both arms about Floyd's neck and stood between him and the tempest. Floyd, struggling in the embrace, felt the shock of the missiles battering Stewart's back and shoulders. Down his own head the blood was pouring into both eyes, blinding him. "Please lie down, Floyd, please!" Stewart continued to urge; and Floyd muttered, "All right, old man, — if you'll let me, — you lie down, too."

Floyd heard a shot near by; Stewart groaned a little in his arms. "Lie down, Floyd," Stewart murmured; and then he collapsed at Floyd's feet. Without the thought of it in his heart Stewart had at last paid his debt.

Floyd hurled down into the crowd the useless hat that he had been holding and shook both fists aloft and shouted, "You've killed him, God damn you! You've killed him!" And while he stood shrieking this, which they in their own insane shouting did not hear, while he stood over Stewart blinded by blood, defying them helplessly with his clenched fists, they battered him; and at last he also fell.

XXXI

THE TWO WOMEN

PERHAPS to Joe Shelton, almost as much as to Stewart, Floyd owed his life; for if he had been left to lie in the car indefinitely — as was urged by some of the mob — he must surely have died. But Shelton, though he was unable to restrain the murderous fury, had afterwards found a few comrades who were not relentless, and with these had been allowed to carry off the two bodies.

After three weeks at the hospital, Floyd was convalescent. Three of his teeth had been knocked out, his nose had been smashed, he had a dent in his forehead near the temple an inch long and a quarter of an inch deep to mark the excision of splintered bone; and his face would always be scarred. Except, however, for the stiffness of his left wrist, he would suffer no disability. His broken ribs were mending, and he was assured by Dr. Edwards that he would leave the hospital perfectly sound.

With a languid interest he read in the newspapers more than a week old of the military occupation of New Rome three hours after the crew of the *Lorelei* had rescued the unfortunate watchmen — of whom one had been killed and seven wounded. The arrival of the militia had been Gregg's opportunity; moreover, under universal condemnation and deprived of the leadership of Tustin — whose injury had been severe and would probably prevent him from ever speaking with any distinctness again — the resistance of the Affiliated crumbled. The works were running non-union before Floyd left the hospital; Farrell was already acting as foreman of the rod-mill over a subdued force; Tustin, Caskey, McGraw, and half a dozen others were held for the grand jury on various counts, from murder to inciting riot; and many more were anxiously wondering if they were on the black list which, Gregg had announced, would be dealt with when Mr. Halket was able to resume his duties.

In one of Marion's visits, Floyd had said to her jocularly — yet with a touch of seriousness, too, —

"Maybe you won't feel like marrying a fellow with a Hottentot nose and a dimple in his forehead? I was quite shocked when I first saw myself in the glass — and if you feel you really could n't live in the same house with such a face, — why, you must feel free to say so, my dear."

"Ah, Floyd! You don't think such a thing as that could make any difference!"

"Well, I don't know. Small things make all the difference sometimes, don't they? — in love."

She looked, he did not know why, a little alarmed and she answered, rather sadly, "Not with me, Floyd."

He could not understand her sadness; he supposed he had hurt her by the suggestion — even the humorous one — that she could be so easily inconstant.

"Oh, I did n't suppose you would turn away from me," he said penitently. "But I 've decided I don't know so very much about girls — and I just wanted you to know that — if you had a horrid antipathy or anything — you should feel quite free."

But even this explanation did not seem to clear away the cloud from her face.

She talked with him in these visits a good deal about Lydia; she told him with what fortitude Lydia had accepted her widowhood.

"I suppose it 's that Stewart died in such a way," she suggested.

"Yes," Floyd said; he added musingly, "It was the real Stewart at the end."

Lydia came to see him, when he was able to sit up; she stayed an hour, talking with him about Stewart. Floyd told her how Stewart had died with the unselfish whisper on his lips; it was a detail that she had not known before, and only when Floyd's voice broke in describing it did the tears come into her eyes.

"Ah," she said, "that was my Stewart!"

Floyd understood the triumphant vindication in her repressed cry.

"I was misjudging him," he confessed. "I must always reproach myself, Lydia — I don't know whether he ever told you, but I got so bitter against Stewart that sitting opposite him in a car one day I wouldn't speak. I thought he'd deliberately turned demagogue and was trying to wreck everything — in spite and revenge. I thought so all the more when I learned he'd gone out to give the alarm about the watchmen. But that night, the moment I saw him in the crowd, looking at that fellow under the freight car, I knew I'd misjudged him. It was in his face — awe-struck, sort of frightened; there was nothing cruel in Stewart; I ought to have remembered that. It was just that he had this theoretical interest in causes and people that he knew nothing about — and he took up with them with a child's enthusiasm — and played their game for them as hard as he could, making every point count — but always as a game, never thinking where or how it might end — and then, that night, when he stood in the presence of the fact, when he saw the testing of his theories, he looked stricken, Lydia, stricken — for there was never any cruelty in Stewart. And that cry of his when they began to stone me, 'Ah, don't!' — it rings in my ears — it was so heart-broken — such a prayer! I didn't do justice to Stewart."

"If he could only have lived long enough for me to get to his side and unsay the last words I spoke to him!" Lydia murmured. "His wife did not do justice to him either, Floyd. But his little boy — who never can remember him — shall be brought up to do justice to his memory."

The tender light in her eyes, the sacred feeling in her voice as she said this, revealed to Floyd the source of her serenity. The manner of her husband's death had given her an ideal which she must impress upon her son as his by inheritance, to be guarded proudly as an inheritance, to be kept untarnished in his soul; and she could never have made this ideal so personal to her boy if her husband had not died. She revealed her thought even more clearly to Floyd when she said, with tears shadowing her smile, —

"Hero for godfather, hero for father! Ah, I must teach my little Floyd to live!"

The time came when Floyd was discharged from the hospital. He had asked Marion to drive away with him; he gave orders to the coachman not to take them straight home, but to go through the park. And while their carriage rolled along the snow-covered, lonely roads, arched over by the garlanded trees, Floyd said, —

"You've always put me off and refused to talk business because I wasn't well enough and would get excited. Now I'm well and I won't be put off any longer. When are we going to be married?"

She answered in a low voice, —

"Floyd, I want you to marry Lydia."

"What!" He looked at her dazed; she did not meet his eyes, but she put his arm gently down from her waist.

"Yes. Oh, Floyd, I told you I was going to *make* you love me. I spoke so positively because I was trying so hard to make myself believe it! And I thought as long as Lydia was married — But I haven't Lydia's charm, I haven't her attractiveness, I haven't anything — and now she — she's so forlorn — and she'd love you, Floyd — just as much as you love her! And when you love her, you ought to marry her — it would be wrong for you not to — wrong for you to marry me — and besides, I wouldn't — I won't — I can't!"

She declared it all in gentle, broken exclamations, in a trembling voice, sitting up straight, looking steadfastly away from him.

He smiled at her; the happiness of tears was in his eyes.

"Ah, Marion!" He paused; he drew her toward him with a firmness that would not be denied. "You did n't know — but you 've made me love you — and only you!"

The Riverside Press
Electrotyped and printed by H. O. Houghton & Co.
Cambridge, Mass., U. S. A.

www.ingramcontent.com/pod-product-compliance
Lightning Source LLC
Chambersburg PA
CBHW020345170426
43200CB00005B/49